American Religion
and Philosophy

AMERICAN STUDIES INFORMATION GUIDE SERIES

Series Editor: Donald Koster, Professor of English, Adelphi University, Garden City, New York

Also in this series:

AFRO-AMERICAN LITERATURE AND CULTURE SINCE WORLD WAR II—*Edited by Charles D. Peavy**

AMERICAN ARCHITECTURE AND ART—*Edited by David M. Sokol*

AMERICAN FOLKLORE—*Edited by Richard M. Dorson**

AMERICAN HUMOR AND HUMORISTS—*Edited by M. Thomas Inge**

AMERICAN LANGUAGE AND LITERATURE—*Edited by Henry Wasser**

AMERICAN POPULAR CULTURE—*Edited by Marshall W. Fishwick and Larry Landrum**

THE AMERICAN PRESIDENCY—*Edited by Kenneth E. Davison**

AMERICAN STUDIES—*Edited by David W. Marcell**

ANTHROPOLOGY OF THE AMERICAS—*Edited by Thomas C. Greaves**

EDUCATION IN AMERICA—*Edited by Richard G. Durnin**

HISTORY OF THE UNITED STATES OF AMERICA—*Edited by Ernest Cassara*

NORTH AMERICAN JEWISH LITERATURE—*Edited by Ira Bruce Nadel**

SOCIOLOGY OF AMERICA—*Edited by Charles Mark*

TECHNOLOGY AND HUMAN VALUES IN AMERICAN CIVILIZATION—*Edited by Stephen Cutliff, Judith A. Mistichelli, and Christine M. Roysdon**

THE RELATIONSHIP OF PAINTING AND LITERATURE—*Edited by Eugene L. Huddleston and Douglas A. Noverr*

WOMAN IN AMERICA—*Edited by Virginia R. Terris**

*in preparation

The above series is part of the

GALE INFORMATION GUIDE LIBRARY

The Library consists of a number of separate series of guides covering major areas in the social sciences, humanities, and current affairs.

General Editor: Paul Wasserman, Professor and former Dean, School of Library and Information Services, University of Maryland

Managing Editor: Denise Allard Adzigian, Gale Research Company

American Religion and Philosophy

A GUIDE TO INFORMATION SOURCES

Volume 5 in the American Studies Information Guide Series

Ernest R. Sandeen

James Wallace Professor of History
Macalester College
St. Paul, Minnesota

Frederick Hale

Gale Research Company
Book Tower, Detroit, Michigan 48226

Library of Congress Cataloging in Publication Data

Sandeen, Ernest Robert, 1931—
   American religion and philosophy.

   (American studies information guide series ; v. 5)
   Includes indexes.
   1. Christianity--United States--Bibliography. 2. United States--
Religion--Bibliography. 3. Philosophy, American--Bibliography. I. Hale,
Frederick, joint author. II. Title.
Z7757.U5S25   [BR515]   016.2'00973   73-17562
ISBN 0-8103-1262-X

VITAE

Ernest R. Sandeen is the James Wallace Professor of History at Macalester
College, St. Paul, Minnesota, where he has taught since 1963. Since re-
ceiving his Ph.D. degree from the University of Chicago in 1959, he has
published extensively in the field of American religious studies. He has also
published a number of articles and a book on architectural history. He is a
member of the American Society of Church History, the Society of Architectural Historians, and the American Studies Association.

Frederick Hale is presently living in Norway while engaged in postdoctoral
study and research in immigration and ecclesiastical history at the University
of Oslo. He studied American history under Ernest R. Sandeen in the 1960s.
He received an M.A. degree from Harvard University, University of Minnesota,
and the Johns Hopkins University. He received his Ph.D. from Johns Hopkins
University in 1976. Hale has been a fellow of the German Academic Exchange
at the Universities of Hamburg and Gottingen as well as a Marshall Fellow at
the University of Copenhagen. He is currently completing the translation and
editing of a collection of "America letters" from Danish immigrants and a
manuscript on religious pluralism among Norwegians both in Norway and the
United States.

CONTENTS

Contents

Contents

Contents

Contents

Contents

FOREWORD

Ernest R. Sandeen and Frederick Hale have performed an extraordinary feat in compiling AMERICAN RELIGION AND PHILOSOPHY. Not only have they succeeded in bringing into sharp focus a remarkably large number of works dealing with these subjects, but they also have managed to construct a bibliography that is often fascinating reading because of the quality of their annotations. Too often bibliographical annotations are simply and barely descriptive. Theirs are descriptive and frequently critical in the best sense of the word.

The scholar at virtually any level will find this book useful in leading him to a rich variety of sources on almost every facet of the American experience in religion and philosophy. Beginning with a sound list of general and reference works, the authors move to quite extensive treatment of particular subject areas, such as the religion of North American Indians, New England Puritanism, Transcendentalism, utopian and communitarian groups, black religion, the Social Gospel, and twentieth-century religious movements.

What should make their book particularly attractive and useful to students and teachers in American Studies is the fact that Sandeen and Hale have kept in mind the interdisciplinary aspect of their endeavor. They have not overlooked the important contributions of such disciplines as history, literature, sociology, economics, and even political studies to their basic fields of religion and philosophy. In consequence, their work will be an unparalleled resource for years to come.

Donald N. Koster
Series Editor

PREFACE

This bibliography is intended to provide students and scholars of religion and philosophy in the United States with a general introduction to recent secondary literature and key primary documents. It appears in a series of guides to American Studies because religion and philosophy are treated with special attention to their relationships with the rest of American culture. Rather than concentrating upon these subjects as disciplines with special methodological problems, they are here treated as a part of a broad cultural pattern.

Religion and philosophy fit together nicely in such a bibliography since they grew up as Siamese twins until separated in the late nineteenth century. In some schools the two remain joined to this day. In every academic circle some names from one field remain of great interest in the other; one thinks immediately of Alfred North Whitehead, Reinhold Niebuhr, or Paul Tillich. Since World War II, philosophy has become much more specialized and, as a result, less accessible to the general student of American culture. Furthermore, no such thing as American philosophy can any longer be said to exist; there are only philosophers who happen to be American. Distinctively American expressions of religion, however, continue to flourish.

The study of American religion was greatly aided by the publication of Nelson Burr's CRITICAL BIBLIOGRAPHY OF RELIGION IN AMERICA (1). Our bibliography does not attempt to replace that monumental reference work, but was designed especially to survey the literature which has appeared since that work was published in 1961. Our bibliography, in addition, is organized to fit the categories with which most scholars in these fields work, rather than the confusing division of Burr's work. We hope that our organization, combined with the thorough set of indexes, will make this a useful first work of reference.

Denominational histories are not emphasized in this bibliography. In the case of smaller denominations, the general works and more specialized studies appear in the chronological table of contents at the point at which the denomination first becomes prominent. For example, all material relating to Quakers is found in the eighteenth century section where they are first treated. For students seeking information about larger groups, such as the Baptists, Presbyterians, or Methodists, the subject index will provide the handiest way of retrieving information, since works referring to such groups are scattered throughout the bibliography.

In organizing this work it has become clear that a denomination's integration into the mainstream of American culture can be directly correlated to its dispersion among bibliographic entries. Judaism is not only treated in a separate section but in a separate chapter because so few of the works devoted to the history of Judaism (save in the case of the history of anti-Semitism) seem to be written with any awareness of other religious history. This was once true of the history of American Roman catholicism, but it is fast losing this distinctiveness. The history of Congregationalism in New England cannot any longer be said to exist as denominational history but is completely integrated into the study of colonial America. Denominational histories of Congregationalism are no longer written, and no one is at all interested to inquire whether students of colonial Congregationalism are themselves members of the United Church of Christ. On the other hand, it is unusual for any historian of the Mennonites not to be himself a Mennonite.

Scholarship in the fields of American religion and philosophy has flourished since 1960. In some cases this interest was directed toward what now appear to have been historiographical fads, such as the burst of renewed interest in utopian and communitarian movements in the 1960s. No matter how contemporary society changes, however, nothing seems to affect scholarly fascination for colonial America. Recent scholarship devoted to the seventeenth and eighteenth centuries is uniformly excellent, but does cause some misgivings when compared with the relative paucity of work appearing on twentieth-century subjects. Of course religion was central to understanding colonial culture and is only peripheral to the structure of contemporary America. But how can one explain the virtually complete dearth of new work relating, for example, to nineteenth-century foreign missions, when this is recognized as an area in which religious professions fundamentally influenced the course of American history.

This bibliography would have been a great deal poorer without the assistance of a number of scholars who have suggested valuable additions and corrections to our entries. Our thanks to Sydney E. Ahlstrom, Henry W. Bowden, Charles Chatfield, Philip Gleason, David D. Hall, David Hopper, William R. Hutchison, James B. Stewart, and Conrad Wright. In addition we would like to thank the librarians of Macalester College and the Newberry Library for their special assistance. Donald N. Koster, general editor of this series, and Denise Allard Adzigian, the editor for Gale Research, have helped us a great deal, not least by being patient.

Chapter 1
GENERAL AND REFERENCE WORKS

BIBLIOGRAPHIES AND REFERENCE WORKS

1   Burr, Nelson R., ed. A CRITICAL BIBLIOGRAPHY OF RELIGION IN AMERICA. 2 vols. Princeton, N.J.: Princeton University Press, 1961.

    A comprehensive and indispensable annotated bibliography of most American religious traditions, although in many respects reflecting interpretations that have undergone revision since 1961.

2   _____. RELIGION IN AMERICAN LIFE. New York: Appleton-Century-Crofts, 1971. 190 p.

    An abridged and updated version of Burr (1) organized under the same heading. Brief annotations.

3   Gaustad, Edwin Scott. HISTORICAL ATLAS OF RELIGION IN AMERICA. Rev. ed. New York: Harper and Row, 1976. 208 p. 71 maps, 59 charts and graphs.

    Main currents of denominational history traced through maps, charts and graphs, and accompanying text. Valuable for understanding the settlement patterns of Roman Catholics, Jews, Mormons, and adherents of the larger Protestant denominations.

4   Hardon, John A. THE PROTESTANT CHURCHES OF AMERICA. Rev. ed. Garden City, N.Y.: Doubleday and Co., 1969. 439 p.

    A comprehensive survey of the history and beliefs of the Protestant denominations in the United States, written from a Roman Catholic viewpoint but without hostility. Table of church membership and other statistics.

5   Mead, Frank S. HANDBOOK OF DENOMINATIONS IN THE UNITED STATES. 6th ed. Nashville: Abingdon Press, 1975. 320 p. Bibliog.

A helpful reference book usually updated annually. Identifies more than two hundred Christian, Jewish, and other religious bodies in the United States. Complete with a denominational bibliography and a list of addresses of denominational headquarters.

6   Mode, Peter G., ed. SOURCE BOOK AND BIBLIOGRAPHICAL GUIDE FOR AMERICAN CHURCH HISTORY. Menasha, Wis.: George Banta Publishing Co., 1921. xxiv, 735 p.

An extensive bibliography and collection of documents pertaining to the history of Christianity and, to a much lesser extent, Judaism in colonial America and the United States from the seventeenth through the nineteenth centuries. Focusing on "main-line" Protestant denominations, is less helpful for research in American religion.

7   Suelflow, August R., ed. A PRELIMINARY GUIDE TO CHURCH RECORDS REPOSITORIES. Atlanta: Church Archives Committee, Society of American Archivists, 1969. 108 p.

Lists over five hundred repositories (mostly denominational) and provides information for many of them regarding their addresses, personnel, services, and access policies. Also describes several Jewish archives, but neglects those of many Christian denominations as well as the innumerable collections of church records held by secular libraries and historical societies.

8   Whalen, William J. SEPARATED BRETHREN: A SURVEY OF NON-CATHOLIC CHRISTIAN DENOMINATIONS. Rev. ed. Milwaukee, Wis.: Bruce Publishing Co., 1966. 288 p. Tables, bibliog.

A Catholic effort to describe the various Protestant, Mormon, Eastern Orthodox, and other non-Roman Catholic denominations in the United States. Tables of church membership statistics.

GENERAL WORKS DEVOTED TO RELIGION IN AMERICA

9   Ahlstrom, Sydney E. A RELIGIOUS HISTORY OF THE AMERICAN PEOPLE. New Haven, Conn.: Yale University Press, 1972. xvi, 1,158 p.

A massive, comprehensive study following a traditional line of development from Puritanism to the present. Also explores such dimensions as European backgrounds, oriental religions in the United States, Judaism, and Roman Catholicism, without neglecting relationships between religion and secular culture.

10   Clebsch, William A. AMERICAN RELIGIOUS THOUGHT: A HISTORY.
      Chicago History of American Religion, edited by Martin E. Marty.
      Chicago: University of Chicago Press, 1973. 212 p.

           Extended essays on Jonathan Edwards, Ralph Waldo Emerson,
           and William James connected by brief transitional chapters.

11   Gaustad, Edwin Scott. A RELIGIOUS HISTORY OF AMERICA. New
      York: Harper and Row, 1966. xxiii, 421 p. Illus., bibliog.

           A general history stressing the interplay of religion and secu-
           lar life, paying scant attention to the details of denomina-
           tional history. Extensive use of quotations. Contains a
           chronology of events in American religious history.

12   Greeley, Andrew M. THE DENOMINATIONAL SOCIETY: A SOCIO-
      LOGICAL APPROACH TO RELIGION IN AMERICA. Glenview, Ill.:
      Scott, Foresman, 1972. 266 p.

           Early chapters on the nature, origin, function, and institu-
           tional structure of religion might make this a good first book
           to include in a course of study on the history of American
           religion. Also is a useful summary of many of the author's
           other works.

13   Hudson, Winthrop S. RELIGION IN AMERICA. Rev. ed. New York:
      Charles Scribner's Sons, 1973. xiii, 463 p.

           Reliable history of Christianity and, to some extent, Judaism
           in the United States, paying more attention to Roman Ca-
           tholicism and colonial history than many other surveys, but
           reflecting the tradition of Puritan dominance in American
           Christianity. Bibliographic essay.

14   McNamara, Patrick H., ed. RELIGION AMERICAN STYLE. New
      York: Harper and Row, 1974. 422 p.

           An interesting anthology containing scholarly articles (mostly
           sociologically oriented) and primary materials. Work or-
           ganized around four themes—the relationship of religion and
           society (method), descriptions of various religious communi-
           ties, current areas of religious-social conflict, and public
           reaction to contemporary change.

15   Marty, Martin E. RIGHTEOUS EMPIRE, THE PROTESTANT EXPERIENCE
      IN AMERICA. New York: Dial Press, 1970. 295 p.

           A good up-to-date text, giving extensive treatment to re-
           ligion among blacks and native Americans, and interpreting
           the rise and decline of Protestant hegemony in American
           culture.

16   Mead, Sidney E. THE LIVELY EXPERIMENT: THE SHAPING OF CHRIS-
      TIANITY IN AMERICA. New York: Harper and Row, 1963. xiii,
      220 p.

      A collection of provocative essays, especially illuminating
      the author's views on the interplay of religious liberty, the
      Enlightenment, the frontier, and voluntarism in the develop-
      ment of American Protestantism. See Sandeen (46) for critique.

ANTHOLOGIES DEVOTED TO RELIGION IN AMERICA

17   Ahlstrom, Sydney E., ed. THEOLOGY IN AMERICA: THE MAJOR
      PROTESTANT VOICES FROM PURITANISM TO NEO-ORTHODOXY.
      Indianapolis: Bobbs-Merrill Co., 1967. 630 p.

      Lengthy excerpts from the most important works of Thomas
      Hooker, Jonathan Edwards, William Ellery Channing, Na-
      thaniel William Taylor, Charles Hodge, Ralph Waldo Emerson,
      Horace Bushnell, John Williamson Nevin, Charles Porterfield
      Krauth, Josiah Royce, William James, Walter Rauschenbusch,
      and H. Richard Niebuhr. Also includes a long introductory
      essay on the history of Protestant theology in America.

18   Ferm, Robert L., ed. ISSUES IN AMERICAN PROTESTANTISM. Gar-
      den City, N.Y.: Doubleday and Co., 1969. xxii, 418 p.

      A well-edited collection of documents illustrating the history
      of American Protestantism from the 1630s until the 1960s.
      Emphasis on major English-speaking figures in the larger de-
      nominations.

19   Gaustad, Edwin Scott, ed. RELIGIOUS ISSUES IN AMERICAN HIS-
      TORY. New York: Harper and Row, 1968. xxii, 294 p.

      A well-edited but brief collection of excerpts from docu-
      ments presenting opposing views on such controversial issues
      as the Great Awakening, Darwinism, slavery, and revivalism.
      Selection of topics and documents weighted heavily in favor
      of major Protestant denominations.

20   Handy, Robert T., ed. RELIGION AND THE AMERICAN EXPERIENCE:
      THE PLURALISTIC STYLE. Documentary History of the United States
      Series, edited by Richard B. Morris. New York: Harper Torchbooks,
      1972. 246 p.

      Readings presented under four topical headings: the trans-
      planted European traditions, tensions within Protestantism,
      indigenous patterns of religion, and the search for unity.

21   Hudson, Winthrop S., ed. NATIONALISM AND RELIGION IN AMERI-
      CA: CONCEPTS OF AMERICAN IDENTITY AND MISSION. New
      York: Harper and Row, 1970. xxxiii, 211 p.

         A skillfully compiled anthology of about fifty religious
         leaders, half of whom wrote in the colonial period. Heavily
         Protestant and Anglo-Saxon oriented, but contains a few
         statements by Catholics and Jews.

22   Smith, Hilrie Shelton; Handy, Robert T.; and Loetscher, Lefferts A.,
      eds. AMERICAN CHRISTIANITY: AN HISTORICAL INTERPRETATION
      WITH REPRESENTATIVE DOCUMENTS. 2 vols. New York: Charles
      Scribner's Sons, 1960-63.

         An annotated collection of documents designed for seminary
         history classes, the most comprehensive work of its kind.
         Contains long excerpts pertaining to Protestant, Catholic,
         and other Christian traditions in the United States, and is a
         valuable aid for research in many aspects of American re-
         ligious history. Selections from the sources prefaced by
         interpretive essays and followed by bibliographic suggestions.

THEMATIC INTERPRETATIONS OF RELIGION IN AMERICA

23   Benne, Robert, and Hefner, Philip. DEFINING AMERICA: A CHRIS-
      TIAN CRITIQUE OF THE AMERICAN DREAM. Philadelphia: Fortress
      Press, 1974. 150 p.

         A provocative attack on the enduring myth that the United
         States is a nation ordained by God and that the American
         is the "new Adam."

24   Clebsch, William A. FROM SACRED TO PROFANE AMERICA: THE
      ROLE OF RELIGION IN AMERICAN HISTORY. New York: Harper
      and Row, 1968. 242 p.

         Argues that religion has served to sanctify but lost control
         of six common areas of American life: a sense of special
         mission, the voluntary principle, education, morality, nation-
         ality, and pluralism.

25   Gaustad, Edwin Scott. DISSENT IN AMERICAN RELIGION. Chicago
      History of American Religion, edited by Martin E. Marty. Chicago:
      University of Chicago Press, 1973. 184 p.

         A general essay about the character of dissent and dissenters
         and the problems created when society attempts to deal with
         them. Deals with schismatics, heretics, and misfits in sepa-
         rate chapters.

26   Holland, DeWitte T., ed. PREACHING IN AMERICAN HISTORY;
      SELECTED ISSUES IN THE AMERICAN PULPIT, 1630-1967. Nashville:
      Abingdon Press, 1969. 436 p.

      A collection of essays of uneven quality which may be use-
      ful in discussing the relation of preaching to a specific theo-
      logical or social problem. A better overall analysis of Ameri-
      can preaching in Niebuhr (29) or Thompson (1199).

27   Marty, Martin E., ed. THE RELIGIOUS PRESS IN AMERICA. New
      York: Holt, Rinehart and Winston, 1963. 184 p.

      Four essays placing the Protestant, Roman Catholic, and
      Jewish press in historical perspective and analyzing their
      contemporary roles.

28   Niebuhr, H. Richard. THE KINGDOM OF GOD IN AMERICA. 1935.
      Reprint. Hamden, Conn.: Shoe String Press, 1956. xvii, 215 p.

      A provocative but dated survey of Protestant efforts to create
      a Christian society in North America, a theme author re-
      garded as the most persistent in the history of American
      Christianity.

29   Niebuhr, H. Richard, and Williams, Daniel D., eds. THE MINISTRY
      IN HISTORICAL PERSPECTIVES. New York: Harper and Brothers,
      1956. 331 p.

      Nine essays analyzing the Christian ministry from apostolic
      times until the 1950s. Two deal with American Protestantism:
      "The Rise of the Evangelical Conception of the Ministry in
      America: 1607-1850," by Sidney E. Mead, and "The Protes-
      tant Ministry in America: 1850 to the Present," by Robert
      A. Michaelsen.

30   Rosenberg, Bruce A. THE ART OF THE AMERICAN FOLK PREACHER.
      New York: Oxford University Press, 1970. 265 p.

      A fascinating account of the methods and content of preachers
      and sermons, which derived from pre-literate traditions (such
      as the Homeric bards) but still survive in contemporary so-
      ciety, in the cities, and among whites as well as blacks.
      Examples of the sermons, reduced to written form, provided in
      the last section of the book.

31   Smith, James Ward, and Jamison, A. Leland, eds. RELIGIOUS PER-
      SPECTIVES IN AMERICAN CULTURE. Princeton, N.J.: Princeton
      University Press, 1961. 427 p.

      A group of essays on "Religion and Education," by Will Her-
      berg; "Religion and Law," by Wilber G. Katz; "American

Religion and American Political Attitudes," by William L. Miller; "The Church and Techniques of Political Action," by R. Morton Darrow; "The State, the Church and the Lobby," by Dayton D. McKean; "Religious Music in America," by Leonard Ellingwood; "Religious Expression in American Architecture," by Donald D. Egbert; "The Religious Novel as Best-Seller in America," by Willard Thorp; "The Place of the Bible in American Fiction," by Carlos Baker; and "Religious Poetry in the United States," by R.P. Blackmur.

32 _____. THE SHAPING OF AMERICAN RELIGION. Princeton, N.J.: Princeton University Press, 1961. 514 p.

Essays on "The Protestant Movement and Democracy in the United States," by H. Richard Niebuhr; "Catholicism in the United States," by Henry J. Browne; "Judaism in the United States," by Oscar Handlin; "Religions on the Christian Perimeter," by A. Leland Jamison; "Theology in America: A Historical Survey," by Sydney E. Ahlstrom; "From the Covenant to the Revival," by Perry Miller; "Religion and Modernity, 1865-1914," by Stow Persons; "Religion and Science in American Philosophy," by James Ward Smith; and "Tradition and Experience in American Theology," by Daniel D. Williams.

33 Strout, Cushing. THE NEW HEAVENS AND NEW EARTH: POLITICAL RELIGION IN AMERICA. New York: Harper and Row, 1974. xv, 400 p.

A broad study of the interaction of religious movements with political issues from the Puritans through the twentieth century. Unfortunately, survey neither systematic enough to serve as a text nor sufficiently detailed on any one topic to serve as a reference work.

34 Tuveson, Ernest Lee. REDEEMER NATION: THE IDEA OF AMERICA'S MILLENNIAL ROLE. Chicago: University of Chicago Press, 1968. 238 p.

A brief but provocative interpretation of the belief that the United States is fulfilling God's plan in history, a recurrent theme in American religious thought.

THE HISTORIOGRAPHY OF RELIGION IN AMERICA

See also the comments concerning Perry Miller in chapter 4.

35   Ahlstrom, Sydney E.   "The Problem of the History of Religion in America."
        CHURCH HISTORY 39 (1970): 224-35.

        A critique of the tendency of American Protestant historians
        to oversimplify American religious history by focusing too
        narrowly on mainstream Protestantism while failing to treat
        adequately groups and movements which do not fit the melt-
        ing pot synthesis.

36   Berkhofer, Robert F., Jr.   A BEHAVIORAL APPROACH TO HISTORICAL
        ANALYSIS.   New York: Free Press, 1969.   339 p.

        A study of the necessity and the difficulty of using this
        methodology of social science in historical scholarship.   Call
        to apply social science theories, concepts, and techniques
        opens horizons for new approaches to the field of religious
        history.

37   Bowden, Henry W[arner].   "John Gilmary Shea: A Study of Methods
        and Goals in Historiography."   CATHOLIC HISTORICAL REVIEW 54
        (1968): 235-60.

        Excellent analysis of the method of the first and greatest
        American Catholic Church historian.

38   _____.   "Science and the Idea of Church History, An American De-
        bate."   CHURCH HISTORY 36 (1967): 308-26.

        Analyzes the work of Philip Schaff and Ephraim Emerton as
        examples of the way in which historians of the church worked
        out the implications of the new "scientific" historiography
        of the late nineteenth century.   See also Bowden's longer
        study (1147).

39   Brauer, Jerald C., ed.   REINTERPRETATION IN AMERICAN CHURCH
        HISTORY.   Chicago: University of Chicago Press, 1968.   227 p.

        Includes essays on "Changing Perspectives on Religion in
        America," by Jerald C. Brauer; "The Genius of Jonathan
        Edwards," by William S. Morris; "Horace Bushnell: Cells
        or Crustacea?" by Frederick Kirschenmann; "Negro Chris-
        tianity and American Church Historiography," by Robert T.
        Handy; "Missionary Motivation through Three Centuries," by
        R. Pierce Beaver; "How American Is Religion in America?"
        by Winthrop S. Hudson; "Reinterpretation in American Church
        History," by Sidney E. Mead; and "Reinterpreting American
        Religious History in Context," by Martin E. Marty.

40   Bucher, Glenn R.   "Options for American Religious History."   THEOL-
        OGY TODAY 33 (1976): 178-86.

An analysis of the significance of the works of Sydney Ahl-strom, Edwin Gaustad, Martin Marty, and Robert Handy, and a call for greater emphasis on ethnicity and radical sects to correct traditional focus on "mainline Protestantism."

41   Carter, Paul. "Recent Historiography of the Protestant Churches in America." CHURCH HISTORY 37 (1968): 95-107.

Discusses the broadening of historiography in recent times to include ethnic and religious groups not in the supposed "main-stream" of Protestantism in the United States.

42   Herbst, Jurgen. THE GERMAN HISTORICAL SCHOOL IN AMERICAN SCHOLARSHIP. Ithaca, N.Y.: Cornell University Press, 1965. xvii, 262 p.

A study of the efforts of Herbert Baxter Adams, John W. Burgess, Robert T. Ely, Francis Peabody, and Albion Small to organize American universities on the nineteenth-century German model, and their failure to introduce the methodol-ogy of German social sciences to American academia. Bib-liographical essay.

43   Marty, Martin E. "Ethnicity: The Skeleton of Religion in America." CHURCH HISTORY 41 (1972): 5-21.

Describes the manner in which interpretations of American religion have emphasized sameness rather than particularity and how that interpretation is being replaced by increasing recognition by historians of ethnicity.

44   May, Henry F. "The Recovery of American Religious History." AMERI-CAN HISTORICAL REVIEW 70 (1964): 79-92.

Analyzes the significance and the varieties of American re-ligious historiography since the 1930s, stressing efforts to bridge the gap between traditional denominational historiog-raphy and secular historiography.

45   Mead, Sidney E. "Prof. Sweet's RELIGION AND CULTURE IN AMERI-CA: A Review Article." CHURCH HISTORY 22 (1953): 33-49.

An analysis of the historiography of William Warren Sweet, often called "the father of American church history," fo-cusing on the strengths and weaknesses of Sweet's attempts to combine objective, "scientific" history with the frontier thesis of Frederick Jackson Turner.

46   Sandeen, Ernest R. "THE LIVELY EXPERIMENT: A Review Article." JOURNAL OF RELIGION 44 (1964): 328-34.

Analysis of the contributions of Sidney E. Mead to American religious historiography on the occasion of the publication of his first book of essays (16). Describes Mead as being equally concerned with the problem of religious liberty and the development of American denominationalism. Questions whether historians of American religion have not been too preoccupied with North America and neglected possible influences from Europe.

GENERAL WORKS DEVOTED TO INTELLECTUAL HISTORY

47   Barker, Charles A. AMERICAN CONVICTIONS: CYCLES OF PUBLIC THOUGHT, 1600-1850. Philadelphia: J.B. Lippincott Co., 1970. xix, 632 p.

A broad survey of American intellectual history until 1850, including treatment of several Protestant themes and, to a lesser degree, Roman Catholicism. Attention also given to British and German roots of American secular and religious thought.

48   Curti, Merle E. THE GROWTH OF AMERICAN THOUGHT. 3d ed. New York: Harper and Row, 1964. xx, 939 p.

A comprehensive history of the American mind in its social context by a renowned progressive historian. Remains a standard work, although others have subsequently challenged many of the tenets of the progressive school.

49   Persons, Stow. AMERICAN MINDS: A HISTORY OF IDEAS. New York: Henry Holt and Co., 1958. xii, 467 p.

A chronological cross-section of American intellectual history, including brief treatments of Protestant thought since the seventeenth century, but generally ignoring other religious groups.

50   Schlesinger, Arthur M., and White, Morton, eds. PATHS OF AMERICAN THOUGHT. Boston: Houghton Mifflin Co., 1963. 614 p.

Twenty-seven bibliographical essays by distinguished authors tracing the course of thought in the United States from the 1770s to the twentieth century, emphasizing the period since the 1870s.

GENERAL WORKS DEVOTED TO THE HISTORY OF PHILOSOPHY

51   Blau, Joseph L. MEN AND MOVEMENTS IN AMERICAN PHILOSOPHY. New York: Prentice-Hall, 1952. 403 p.

A general survey of philosophy in America since the eighteenth century, tracing its course through the ages of Enlightenment, transcendentalism, Darwinism, idealism, pragmatism, realism, and nationalism. Bibliographical essay.

52   Cohen, Morris R. AMERICAN THOUGHT: A CRITICAL SKETCH. Edited by Felix Cohen. Glencoe, III.: Free Press, 1954. 360 p.

A general text for American philosophy but organized topically into chapters devoted to historical, scientific, economic, political, legal, and religious thought, and esthetics. Concludes with a brief sketch of their chronological development, especially in the last century.

53   Marnell, William H. MAN-MADE MORALS: FOUR PHILOSOPHIES THAT SHAPED AMERICA. Garden City, N.Y.: Doubleday and Co., 1966. xiii, 412 p.

A readable study of deism, utilitarianism, social Darwinism, and pragmatism, placing each of these philosophical schools in the context of American history and exploring their ethical implications for American society. Bibliographical essay.

54   Riley, I. Woodbridge. AMERICAN THOUGHT FROM PURITANISM TO PRAGMATISM AND BEYOND. New York: Henry Holt and Co., 1915. 438 p.

Largely a summary of Riley's AMERICAN PHILOSOPHY: THE EARLY SCHOOLS (340) up to 1830, with four more chapters added on transcendentalism, evolutionism, idealism, and pragmatism. In spite of the title, there is little "beyond."

55   Schneider, Herbert W. A HISTORY OF AMERICAN PHILOSOPHY. Rev. ed. New York: Columbia University Press, 1963. xviii, 590 p.

The standard history of philosophy in America, tracing its development from the Puritans to the twentieth century and analyzing its heavy dependence on European thought. Bibliographical essay.

56   Sellars, Roy Wood. REFLECTIONS ON AMERICAN PHILOSOPHY FROM WITHIN. Notre Dame, Ind.: University of Notre Dame Press, 1969. 202 p.

A critique of Western philosophy, especially American and British philosophy, from the author's realist perspective, what he calls "referentially direct realisms."

57   Werkmeister, W.H. A HISTORY OF PHILOSOPHICAL IDEAS IN AMERICA. New York: Ronald Press, 1949. xvi, 599 p.

An older standard history of philosophy in America from Puritanism to John Dewey, emphasizing the pragmatic and realist schools of the late nineteenth century.

58 White, Morton G. SCIENCE AND SENTIMENT IN AMERICA: PHILO-SOPHICAL THOUGHT FROM JONATHAN EDWARDS TO JOHN DEWEY. New York: Oxford University Press, 1973. 358 p.

A general interpretation of the history of philosophy in America, emphasizing the importance of such well-known figures as Ralph Waldo Emerson, William James, and Josiah Royce.

59 Winn, Ralph B., ed. AMERICAN PHILOSOPHY. New York: Philosophical Library, 1955. xviii, 318 p.

An encyclopedic reference work for beginning students that is constructed from a great variety of short contributions. Articles on philosophy fields (semantics, ethics, logic, for example), schools (personalism, realism, naturalism), and very brief biographical sketches.

ANTHOLOGIES DEVOTED TO THE HISTORY OF PHILOSOPHY

60 Blau, Joseph L., ed. AMERICAN PHILOSOPHIC ADDRESSES, 1700-1900. New York: Columbia University Press, 1946. xii, 762 p.

Twenty-seven addresses chosen from an unpredictable miscellany of authors. Collection as a whole seems idiosyncratic but some things reprinted difficult to find elsewhere. Includes Charles Ingersoll, Edward Everett, Gulian Verplanck, Cadwallader Colden, Noah Porter, Ezra Stiles Ely, Edwards Amasa Park, and Theodore Unger.

61 Kurtz, Paul, ed. AMERICAN THOUGHT BEFORE 1900: A SOURCE-BOOK FROM PURITANISM TO DARWINISM. New York: Macmillan Co., 1966. 448 p.

Includes the usual philosophical thinkers and a large group of selections from political thinkers as well (Paine, Jefferson, Calhoun). Post-1900 selections in author's companion volume (1336).

62 Muelder, Walter G., and Sears, Laurence, eds. THE DEVELOPMENT OF AMERICAN PHILOSOPHY. Boston: Houghton Mifflin Co., 1940. 533 p.

Chronologically and thematically arranged selections from the works of American thinkers from the eighteenth to the twentieth centuries. Focuses on such well-known figures as

Jefferson, James, Peirce, and Dewey, with excerpts from the works of less renowned persons.

63   Myers, Gerald, ed. THE SPIRIT OF AMERICAN PHILOSOPHY. New York: G.P. Putnam's Sons, 1970. 350 p. Bibliog.

An anthology of excerpts from the works of American thinkers from the colonial period to the twentieth century on six topics: religion, government, morality, reason, metaphysics, and pluralism.

64   White, Morton G., ed. DOCUMENTS IN THE HISTORY OF AMERICAN PHILOSOPHY: FROM JONATHAN EDWARDS TO JOHN DEWEY. New York: Oxford University Press, 1972. xiii, 479 p.

Designed as a companion volume to White (58).

PERIODICALS

65   AMERICAN JEWISH ARCHIVES. Cincinnati, Ohio: Hebrew Union College, Jewish Institute of Religion, 1948-- . Semiannual.

A journal devoted to the preservation of Jewish historical records in the United States.

66   AMERICAN JEWISH HISTORICAL QUARTERLY. Waltham, Mass.: American Jewish Historical Society, 1893-- .

A standard journal devoted to various aspects of Jewish history in the United States.

67   AMERICAN PHILOSOPHICAL QUARTERLY. Oxford, Engl.: Basil Blackwell, 1964-- .

A general philosophical journal, international in authorship and scope of its articles.

68   AMERICAN QUARTERLY. Philadelphia: American Studies Association, University of Pennsylvania, 1949-- .

The journal of the American Studies Association, covering several areas of that composite field. Includes occasional articles dealing with philosophical and religious subjects.

69   CATHOLIC HISTORICAL REVIEW. Washington, D.C.: American Catholic Historical Association, Catholic University of America Press, 1915-- . Quarterly.

Articles by Catholics and others on the history of the Roman

Catholic Church in the United States and abroad.

70   CHURCH HISTORY. Wallingford, Pa.: American Society of Church History, 1932-- . Quarterly.

Nearly half of each issue devoted to a broad range of topics in the field of American Christianity.

71   DIALOGUE, A JOURNAL OF MORMON THOUGHT. Arlington, Va.: Dialogue Foundation, 1965-- . Quarterly.

A fairly new journal devoted to recent Mormon thought, including unorthodox trends.

72   FOUNDATIONS. Rochester, N.Y.: American Baptist Historical Society, 1958-- . Quarterly.

Focuses on Baptist history and theology in the United States.

73   HISTORICAL MAGAZINE OF THE PROTESTANT EPISCOPAL CHURCH. Austin, Tex.: Episcopal Church, Historical Society, 1932-- . Quarterly.

Devoted primarily to the history of the Episcopal Church in the United States, but also carries articles illuminating British-American relations in the field of ecclesiastical history.

74   JOURNAL OF AMERICAN STUDIES. Cambridge: At the University Press, British Association for American Studies, 1967-- . 3/year.

A young, interdisciplinary British journal which to date has carried few articles pertaining to religious or philosophical topics.

75   JOURNAL OF CHURCH AND STATE. Waco, Tex.: Baylor University, 1959-- . 3/year.

Devoted primarily to various aspects of relations between American churches and law and politics, but also publishes articles on church-state relations abroad.

76   JOURNAL OF ECUMENICAL STUDIES. Philadelphia: Temple University, 1964-- . Quarterly.

Devoted to inter-denominational and interfaith relations; not limited to American religion.

77   JOURNAL OF MORMON HISTORY. Ogden, Utah: Mormon History Association, 1974-- . Annual.

Although appearing only once a year, this young journal one of the key vehicles of contemporary Mormon historiography.

78   JOURNAL OF PHILOSOPHY. New York: Columbia University, 1904-- .
      Monthly.

      Highly regarded general philosophical journal, not specifically
      American in its emphases.

79   JOURNAL OF PRESBYTERIAN HISTORY. Philadelphia: United Presby-
      terian Church in the U.S.A., Presbyterian Historical Society, 1901-- .
      Quarterly.

      Devoted to the history of various American denominations in
      this tradition from the colonial period to the twentieth cen-
      tury.

80   LUTHERAN QUARTERLY. Berkeley, Calif.: Pacific Lutheran Theologi-
      cal Seminary, 1949-- .

      Although journal and its antecedents neither specifically
      American nor specifically historical, have contained many
      articles pertaining to various aspects of the Lutheran tradition.

81   MENNONITE QUARTERLY REVIEW. Goshen, Ind.: Mennonite Histori-
      cal Society, Goshen College, 1927-- .

      Contains many historical and theological articles pertaining
      to the various North American denominations in the Anabap-
      tist tradition, although not limited to the Western Hemisphere.

82   METHODIST HISTORY. Lake Junaluska, N.C.: Commission on Archives
      and History of the United Methodist Church, 1962-- . Quarterly.

      Publishes articles on the various Methodist denominations in
      the United States and related topics.

83   NEW ENGLAND QUARTERLY: AN HISTORICAL REVIEW OF NEW
      ENGLAND LIFE AND LETTERS. Brunswick, Maine: Colonial Society
      of Massachusetts, 1928-- .

      A highly-regarded journal carrying frequent articles on the
      ecclesiastical history of New England, especially during the
      colonial period.

84   THE PHILOSOPHICAL REVIEW. Ithaca, N.Y.: Cornell University,
      1892-- . Quarterly.

      Cornell journal general in scope and international in author-
      ship. Contains relatively little specifically American.

85   QUAKER HISTORY. Haverford, Pa.: Friends Historical Association,
      Haverford College Library, 1902-- . Semiannual.

A journal devoted to the history of the Society of Friends, including many articles on Quakers in North America since the colonial period.

86 UTAH HISTORICAL QUARTERLY. Salt Lake City: Utah State Historical Society, 1928-- .

Has carried many articles on the history of Mormons and their relations with other Christians in Utah.

87 WILLIAM AND MARY QUARTERLY. Williamsburg, Va.: Institute of Early American History and Culture, 1892-- .

A highly-regarded journal and valuable tool for studying religion in colonial America.

Chapter 2
NORTH AMERICAN INDIANS

GENERAL WORKS

88   Driver, Harold E. INDIANS OF NORTH AMERICA. 2d ed., rev.
Chicago: University of Chicago Press, 1969. xviii, 632 p. 25 illus.,
45 maps, bibliog.

Anthropologically-based extensive introduction to American
Indian culture. Includes a chapter on religion, magic, and
medicine.

89   Hodge, William H., ed. A BIBLIOGRAPHY OF CONTEMPORARY
NORTH AMERICAN INDIANS. New York: Interland Publishing, 1975.
320 p. Bibliog.

Contains over 2,600 entries, including among its categories
music, dance, and religion.

90   Prucha, Francis Paul, ed. A BIBLIOGRAPHICAL GUIDE TO THE HIS-
TORY OF INDIAN-WHITE RELATIONS IN THE UNITED STATES. Chicago: University of Chicago Press, 1977. 454 p.

Contains over 9,000 entries organized under headings such as
missions and missionaries, federal Indian policy, reform movements, and images of the Indian among whites.

91   _____. THE INDIAN IN AMERICAN HISTORY. Hinsdale, Ill.: Dryden Press, 1971. 126 p. Bibliog.

A collection of excerpts and articles from some of the best
old and new material. Selections from Pearce, Vaughan,
Prucha, Berkhofer, Spicer, and Deloria.

92   Washburn, Wilcomb E. THE INDIAN IN AMERICA. New York: Harper and Row, 1975. xix, 296 p. Bibliog.

The best one-volume introduction to Indian history also contains a chapter on Indian response to religious persuasion.

INDIAN RELIGION

93   Capps, Walter H., ed.   SEEING WITH A NATIVE EYE: CONTRIBUTIONS TO THE STUDY OF NATIVE AMERICAN RELIGION.   New York: Harper and Row, 1976.   160 p.

Contents include "How Many Sheep Will It Hold," by Barre Toelken; "The Roots of Renewal," by Joseph Epes Brown; "Hopi Indian Ceremonies," by Emory Sekaquaptewa; "The Shadow of a Vision Yonder," by Sam D. Gill; "On Seeing With the Eye of the Native European," by W. Richard Comstock; "Native American Attitudes to the Environment," by N. Scott Momaday; "The Contributions of the Study of North American Indian Religions to the History of Religions," by Ake Hultkrantz; and "On Approaching Native American Religion," by Walter H. Capps.

94   Jorgensen, Joseph G.   THE SUN DANCE RELIGION: POWER FOR THE POWERLESS.   Chicago: University of Chicago Press, 1972.   448 p.

Traces the history of the sun dance as a response to the deprivation suffered by Indians at the hands of whites, and describes the manner in which the religion has survived.

95   La Barre, Weston.   THE GHOST DANCE: THE ORIGINS OF RELIGION. New York: Dell Publishing Co., 1970.   xvi, 677 p.

Analysis of the Plains Indians' ghost dance is really only a convenient jumping-off place for the author's analysis of all religion.   Reviewers not agreed on whether this is a work of genius or of folly.

96   Mooney, James.   THE GHOST-DANCE RELIGION AND THE SIOUX OUTBREAK OF 1890.   Abridged and with an introduction by Anthony F.C. Wallace.   1896.   Reprint.   Chicago: University of Chicago Press, 1965.   xxiii, 359 p.   67 illus.

The best source for studying the ghost-dance religion.   Includes a sketch of author's life and texts of more than one hundred ghost-dance chants.

97   Neihardt, John G.   BLACK ELK SPEAKS: BEING THE LIFE STORY OF A HOLY MAN OF THE OGLALA SIOUX.   Illustrated by Standing Bear.   Lincoln: University of Nebraska Press, 1961.   xv, 280 p.

Extremely popular first-person account of the life of Black

Elk, supposedly an autobiography. Transmission and translation of the stories actually very complicated and perhaps
influenced by author's own Bahaism.

98   Ortiz, Alfonso. THE TEWA WORLD: SPACE, TIME, BEING AND BE-
COMING IN A PUEBLO SOCIETY. Chicago: University of Chicago
Press, 1969. xviii, 197 p.

Analysis of the cosmological and ritual systems of an eastern
Pueblo tribe.

99   Underhill, Ruth M. RED MAN'S RELIGION: BELIEFS AND PRACTICES
OF THE INDIANS NORTH OF MEXICO. Chicago: University of Chicago Press, 1965. 301 p. 34 illus., 4 maps, bibliog.

The best single volume introduction to the subject.

INDIAN MISSIONS BEFORE 1800

100   Beaver, R. Pierce, ed. PIONEERS IN MISSION: THE EARLY MIS-
SIONARY ORDINATION SERMONS, CHARGES, AND INSTRUCTIONS:
A SOURCE BOOK ON THE RISE OF AMERICAN MISSIONS TO THE
HEATHEN. Grand Rapids, Mich.: William B. Eerdmans Publishing Co.,
1966. 291 p. Bibliog.

A collection of material relating to ordination of missionaries,
largely to the Indians in New England from 1733 through 1812.

101   Bowden, Henry Warner. "Spanish Missions, Cultural Conflict and the
Pueblo Revolt of 1680." CHURCH HISTORY 44 (1975): 217-28.

Story of the 1680 revolt reconstructed using historical and
anthropological methods. Emphasizes the major role of conflict of religion in that struggle and explains why the struggle
seemed so crucial to the Indians.

102   Boyd, Mark F.; Smith, Hale G.; and Griffin, John W., eds. HERE
THEY ONCE STOOD: THE TRAGIC END OF THE APALACHEE MIS-
SIONS. Gainesville: University of Florida Press, 1951. xvii, 189 p.
Illus.

A collection of documents illuminating Franciscan missionary
work among Indians in Florida and conflict with English-
inspired Indians from Carolina.

103   Gray, Elma E., and Gray, Leslie R. WILDERNESS CHRISTIANS: THE
MORAVIAN MISSION TO THE DELAWARE INDIANS. Ithaca, N.Y.:
Cornell University Press, 1956. xi, 354 p.

Provides description of missionary work and a sociological analysis of the life of the Indians using little-known documentary source materials.

104   Jaenen, Cornelius J. FRIEND AND FOE: ASPECTS OF FRENCH-AMERINDIAN CULTURAL CONTACT IN THE SIXTEENTH AND SEVENTEENTH CENTURIES. New York: Columbia University Press, 1976. 207 p. Bibliog.

Prize-winning analysis of acculturation in New France using anthropological concepts of Wallace, Driver, and revisionist scholars. One long chapter describes efforts at evangelization.

105   Jennings, Francis. THE INVASION OF AMERICA: INDIANS, COLONIALISM, AND THE CANT OF CONQUEST. Chapel Hill: University of North Carolina Press for the Institute of Early American History and Culture, 1975. xviii, 369 p. 7 illus., 4 maps.

First half of the book summarizes what is known about Atlantic Coast Indians. Second half concentrates upon Indians in New England, illustrating author's argument that the Puritans acted merely in self-interest in relation to the aboriginal population.

106   _____. "Virgin Land and Savage People." AMERICAN QUARTERLY 23 (1971): 519-41.

An attack upon Vaughan's position (114).

107   Kellaway, William. THE NEW ENGLAND COMPANY, 1649-1776: MISSIONARY SOCIETY TO THE AMERICAN INDIANS. New York: Barnes and Noble, 1962. 303 p.

A scholarly study of the history of the company which from 1649 through the American Revolution was responsible for providing financial support for Christian missionary work among the Indians of New England.

108   Kennedy, John Hopkins. JESUIT AND SAVAGE IN NEW FRANCE. New Haven, Conn.: Yale University Press, 1950. Reprint. Hamden, Conn.: Archon Books, 1971. 206 p. Bibliog.

A brief Yale dissertation revising and supplementing Parkman's earlier study (155) of the Jesuits in seventeenth-century New France. Well-documented.

109   Ronda, James P. "'We Are Well As We Are': An Indian Critique of Seventeenth-Century Christian Missions." WILLIAM AND MARY QUARTERLY 34 (1977): 66-82.

A surprisingly successful reconstruction of Indian responses to Christian missionaries, showing that the native peoples had a consistent point of view and offered serious criticisms of Christianity.

110   Rooy, Sidney H. THE THEOLOGY OF MISSIONS IN THE PURITAN TRADITION. Grand Rapids, Mich.: William B. Eerdmans Publishing Co., 1965. 346 p.

Summarizes the thought of Richard Sibbes, Richard Baxter, John Eliot, Cotton Mather, and Jonathan Edwards regarding Christian missions, allowing the writers to speak for themselves rather than analyzing their thought.

111   Salisbury, Neal. "Red Puritans: The 'Praying Indians' of Massachusetts Bay and John Eliot." WILLIAM AND MARY QUARTERLY 31 (1974): 27-54.

In contrast to the favorable judgment of Vaughan (114), finds that the missionary endeavors of John Eliot instituted an Indian policy of cultural warfare and minority management.

112   Sheehan, Bernard W. "Indian-White Relations in Early America: A Review Essay." WILLIAM AND MARY QUARTERLY 26 (1969): 267-86.

A very wide-reaching survey of recent literature on Indian-white relations combined with a penetrating analysis of the problems raised by the old and the new history. Highly recommended.

113   Spicer, Edward H. CYCLES OF CONQUEST: THE IMPACT OF SPAIN, MEXICO AND THE UNITED STATES ON THE INDIANS OF THE SOUTHWEST, 1533-1960. Tucson: University of Arizona Press, 1962. xii, 609 p.

Scholarly analysis of ethnic interaction that combines historical and anthropological methods.

114   Vaughan, Alden T. NEW ENGLAND FRONTIER: PURITANS AND INDIANS, 1620-1675. Boston: Little, Brown, and Co., 1965. 430 p.

A thoroughly-researched monograph arguing that the Puritans did not treat the Indians as an inferior race, gave Indians a fair hearing in their courts and placed them on juries, made and honored an equitable treaty with Indian chief, Massasoit, and were not guilty of dispossessing the Indians from their land.

115   Wallace, Anthony F.C. THE DEATH AND REBIRTH OF THE SENECA. New York: Alfred A. Knopf, 1970. xiii, 384 p.

The best general description of the Seneca nation of the
Iroquois and the religion of Handsome Lake.

116 _____. KING OF THE DELAWARES: TEEDYUSCUNG, 1700-1763.
Philadelphia: University of Pennsylvania Press, 1949. xiii, 305 p.

An excellent biography of the Delaware chief, who was
converted to Christianity by the Moravian missionaries.

INDIAN MISSIONS IN THE NINETEENTH CENTURY

117 Beaver, R. Pierce. CHURCH, STATE, AND THE AMERICAN INDIANS.
St. Louis, Mo.: Concordia Publishing House, 1960. 230 p.

Describes cooperation in Indian missions that existed between
Protestant churches and colonial and federal governments up
to 1890.

118 Berkhofer, Robert F., Jr. SALVATION AND THE SAVAGE: AN
ANALYSIS OF PROTESTANT MISSIONS AND THE AMERICAN INDIAN
RESPONSE, 1787-1862. Lexington: University of Kentucky Press,
1965. 186 p. Bibliog.

Scholarly analysis from both anthropological and historical
perspectives. Not at all sympathetic to the aims or results
of the missionaries.

119 Burns, Robert Ignatius. THE JESUITS AND THE INDIAN WARS OF THE
NORTHWEST. New Haven, Conn.: Yale University Press, 1966.
512 p.

Meticulously researched study of the role played by Jesuits
during the Indian wars of 1858-77 in the Pacific Northwest.

120 Drury, Clifford M. MARCUS AND NARCISSA WHITMAN AND THE
OPENING OF OLD OREGON. 2 vols. Glendale, Calif.: A.H.
Clark Co., 1973.

Biography of a missionary family retold, but not substantially
changed, from the author's 1937 account of the same family.

121 Fritz, Henry E. THE MOVEMENT FOR INDIAN ASSIMILATION,
1860-1890. Philadelphia: University of Pennsylvania Press, 1963.
244 p. 9 illus.

A scholarly study of the largely Protestant-inspired policy of
assimilation, often referred to as Grant's "peace policy."
Traces the movement for assimilation (the attempt to trans-
form the Indians into white men) from the Civil War to the

passage of the Dawes Act, the legislative culmination of the movement.

122   Harrod, Howard L. MISSION AMONG THE BLACKFEET. Norman: University of Oklahoma Press, 1971. xxii, 218 p. 16 illus., 3 maps, bibliog.

A fine scholarly treatment of one tribe's interaction with Protestant and Catholic missions over more than a century.

123   Jackson, Helen Hunt. A CENTURY OF DISHONOR: THE EARLY CRU-SADE FOR INDIAN REFORM. Edited by Andrew F. Rolle. New York: Harper Torchbooks, 1965. xxii, 342 p. Illus.

A photographic reproduction of the 1881 edition of this famous book, which awakened the conscience of nineteenth-century Americans.

124   Josephy, Alvin M., Jr. THE NEZ PERCE INDIANS AND THE OPEN-ING OF THE NORTHWEST. New Haven, Conn.: Yale University Press, 1965. xxii, 705 p. 24 illus.

Magnificent narrative treatment of one tribe that had had a particularly tragic encounter with Christianity.

125   McLoughlin, William G. "Indian Slaveholders and Presbyterian Mis-sionaries, 1837-1861." CHURCH HISTORY 42 (1973): 535-51.

Detailed examination of the tangled racial-religious web that was spun when the Old School Presbyterian Board of Foreign Missions took over a mission to some slaveholding Indians in Oklahoma.

126   Prucha, Francis Paul. AMERICAN INDIAN POLICY IN CRISIS: CHRIS-TIAN REFORMERS AND THE INDIAN, 1865-1900. Norman: Univer-sity of Oklahoma Press, 1976. xii, 456 p.

A companion volume to author's earlier work (127). Nar-rates the story of the white humanitarians who believed that only one solution was possible for the Indians--complete Americanization.

127   _____, ed. AMERICANIZING THE AMERICAN INDIANS: WRITINGS BY THE "FRIENDS OF THE INDIAN," 1880-1900. Cambridge, Mass.: Harvard University Press, 1973. 358 p. Bibliog.

A collection of excerpts from Protestant and humanitarian leaders of the movement to "benefit" the Indians by Ameri-canizing them and dispersing them on their own 160 acres. Well-edited.

128   Rahill, Peter J. THE CATHOLIC INDIAN MISSIONS AND GRANT'S
       PEACE POLICY, 1870-1884. Washington, D.C.: Catholic University
       of America Press, 1953. xx, 396 p.

       A scholarly study of missionary activity among Western tribes
       in the United States.

Chapter 3

THE CATHOLIC CHURCH IN AMERICA:
THE COLONIAL PERIOD

GENERAL BIBLIOGRAPHY

129   Cadden, John Paul. THE HISTORIOGRAPHY OF THE AMERICAN
        CATHOLIC CHURCH, 1745-1943. Washington, D.C.: Catholic Uni-
        versity of America Press, 1944. x, 122 p.

            An essay on the development of Catholic historiography in
            the United States until 1943. A valuable aid in the inter-
            pretation of older studies.

130   Ellis, John Tracy, ed. A GUIDE TO AMERICAN CATHOLIC HISTORY.
        Milwaukee, Wis.: Bruce Publishing Co., 1959. viii, 147 p.

            An annotated bibliography of several hundred books and
            other materials pertinent to the history of Catholicism in the
            United States. Also includes a brief guide to manuscript
            depositories.

131   Gleason, Philip. "Coming to Terms with American Catholic History."
        SOCIETAS 3 (1973): 283-312.

            Argues that the terms "Americanization" and "Americanism,"
            which frequently occur in the historiography of Roman Ca-
            tholicism in the United States, were not coined by historians,
            but rather emerged from controversies involving the adapta-
            tion of the Roman Catholic Church to its environment in the
            New World.

132   Kenneally, Finbar, ed. UNITED STATES DOCUMENTS IN THE PROPA-
        GANDA FIDE ARCHIVES: A CALENDAR. 1st series. 6 vols. Wash-
        ington, D.C.: Academy of American Franciscan History, 1966-75.

            Series of calendars containing not only a listing but also a
            short summary of the contents of the documents (mostly let-
            ters), thus allowing the student to form some idea of the
            nature of the document without consulting the original.

133   Vollmar, Edward, ed. THE CATHOLIC CHURCH IN AMERICA, AN
       HISTORICAL BIBLIOGRAPHY. 2d ed. New York: Scarecrow Press,
       1963. 399 p.

       A comprehensive bibliography of Roman Catholicism in the
       United States up to the early 1960s. Includes an essay on
       the development of American Catholic historiography.

134   Weber, Francis J. "American Catholic Historical Societies." CHURCH
       HISTORY 31 (1962): 350-56.

       Lists and describes the founding of the principal Catholic
       societies.

135   Willging, Eugene P., and Hatzfeld, Herta, eds. CATHOLIC SERIALS OF
       THE NINETEENTH CENTURY IN THE UNITED STATES. Washington,
       D.C.: Catholic University of America Press, 1959-- .

       First series in this bibliography appeared, beginning in 1954,
       in the RECORDS OF THE AMERICAN CATHOLIC HISTORI-
       CAL SOCIETY, surveying Catholic periodicals across the
       United States. Appearance of the second series in 1959 in
       separate paperbound volumes consists of a survey of serials
       (including newspapers, magazines, and other specialized
       periodicals in English and more than a half dozen other
       languages) from Minnesota, North and South Dakota, Wis-
       consin, Illinois, and Indiana. An impressive and invaluable
       tool.

GENERAL WORKS

136   Abell, Aaron I., ed. AMERICAN CATHOLIC THOUGHT ON SOCIAL
       QUESTIONS. Indianapolis: Bobbs-Merrill Co., 1968. lv, 571 p.

       A well-edited collection of official and unofficial Roman
       Catholic writings illuminating the diversity of reactions to
       various social problems.

137   Ellis, John Tracy. AMERICAN CATHOLICISM. Rev. ed. Chicago:
       University of Chicago Press, 1969. xviii, 322 p. Bibliog.

       Brief introduction to the history of Catholicism in America
       includes author's candid appraisal of Catholic shortcomings
       in the intellectual and cultural life of the United States.

138   _____, ed. THE CATHOLIC PRIEST IN THE UNITED STATES: HIS-
       TORICAL INVESTIGATIONS. Collegeville, Minn.: St. John's Uni-
       versity Press, 1971. xvii, 488 p.

       Contains five long essays: "The Formation of the American

Priest: An Historical Perspective," by J.T. Ellis; "Bishops
and Their Priests in the United States," by Robert Trisco;
"Before and After Modernism: The Intellectual Isolation of
the American Priest," by Michael V. Gannon; "Diocesan
and Religious Clergy: The History of a Relationship, 1789-
1969," by John P. Marschall; and "The American Priest and
Social Action," by David J. O'Brien.

139 _____. DOCUMENTS OF AMERICAN CATHOLIC HISTORY. 2d ed.
Milwaukee, Wis.: Bruce Publishing Co., 1962. xxii, 667 p.

A well-edited and extensive collection of documents illuminating the course of Catholicism in America from the time of
Spanish conquest until 1961. Many documents included pertaining to the roles played by Catholics in political and
social problems.

140 Gleason, Philip, ed. CATHOLICISM IN AMERICA. New York: Harper and Row, 1970. 159 p.

Essays include "The Formation of the Catholic Minority,"
by T.T. McAvoy; "The Distinctive Tradition of American
Catholicism," by J. Hennesey; "Catholics, Protestants, and
Public Education," by V.P. Lannie; "Irish Catholic Life in
Yankee City," by S. Thernstrom; "German Catholics and the
National Controversy," by C.J. Barry; "Catholicism and
Woman Suffrage," by J.J. Kenneally; "Pro-Germanism and
American Catholicism, 1914-1917," by E. Cuddy; "Catholi-
cism and Americanism in the 1930s," by D.J. O'Brien;
"American Catholics and the Intellectual Life," by J.T.
Ellis; and "The Crisis of Americanization," by P. Gleason.

141 McAvoy, Thomas T. A HISTORY OF THE CATHOLIC CHURCH IN THE
UNITED STATES. Notre Dame, Ind.: University of Notre Dame Press,
1969. 504 p.

A reliable, though not especially readable survey, emphasizing the role of Irish Catholics and the hierarchy and under-
stating the role of minorities and local history.

142 Shields, Currin. DEMOCRACY AND CATHOLICISM IN AMERICA.
New York: McGraw-Hill Book Co., 1958. 310 p. Bibliog.

A political scientist's description and analysis of Catholics'
participation in the democratic process.

THE ENGLISH COLONIES

See also Metzger (530).

143   Agonito, Joseph. "Ecumenical Stirrings: Catholic–Protestant Relations
       during the Episcopacy of John Carroll. " CHURCH HISTORY 45 (1976):
       358–73.

          Survey of relations between Catholics and Protestants, such
          as participation of Protestants in Catholic services and em-
          ployment of Protestant artists to paint pictures in Catholic
          churches.

144   Carroll, John. THE JOHN CARROLL PAPERS. Edited by Thomas
       O'Brien Hanley. 3 vols. Notre Dame, Ind.: University of Notre
       Dame Press, 1976.

          Extremely valuable collection of Carroll's letters and other
          writings. Sheds light on the earliest development of Ameri-
          can Catholicism, 1780–1815.

145   Ellis, John Tracy. CATHOLICS IN COLONIAL AMERICA. Baltimore,
       Md.: Helicon Press, 1965. 486 p.

          An able survey but lacking notes.

146   Gleason, Philip. "The Main Sheet Anchor: John Carroll and Catholic
       Higher Education. " REVIEW OF POLITICS 38 (1976): 576–613.

          Shows the important role of education in Carroll's early epis-
          copate, with the pressing need for priests being the crucial
          factor that stimulated Carroll.

147   Guilday, Peter. THE LIFE AND TIMES OF JOHN CARROLL, ARCH-
       BISHOP OF BALTIMORE, 1735–1815. 1922. Reprint. Westminster,
       Md.: Newman Press, 1954. x, 864 p.

          Well–documented biography.

148   Hennesey, James. "Roman Catholicism, the Maryland Tradition. "
       THOUGHT 51 (1976): 282–95.

          Discussion of religious freedom in Maryland.

149   Melville, Annabelle M. JOHN CARROLL OF BALTIMORE: FOUNDER
       OF THE AMERICAN CATHOLIC HIERARCHY. New York: Charles
       Scribner's Sons, 1955. 338 p. Bibliog.

          A popular, well–documented biography of the important early
          Archbishop of Baltimore, revising work of Peter Guilday (147).

150   Nuesse, Celestine Joseph. THE SOCIAL THOUGHT OF AMERICAN
       CATHOLICS, 1634–1829. Washington, D. C.: Catholic University of
       America Press, 1945. 315 p.

A broad, shallow study of Roman Catholic thought regarding the American Revolution, religious liberty, the western frontier, and the roots of Catholic social reform.

151   Ray, Mary Augustina. AMERICAN OPINION OF ROMAN CATHOLICISM IN THE EIGHTEENTH CENTURY. New York: Columbia University Press, 1936. 456 p. Bibliog.

A comprehensive study of anti-Catholicism in the American colonies during the seventeenth and eighteenth centuries. Helpful for understanding some early roots of Protestant hostility to Catholic immigrants. Well-documented.

THE FRENCH COLONIES

152   Eccles, William J. THE CANADIAN FRONTIER, 1534-1760. New York: Holt, Rinehart and Winston, 1969. xv, 234 p.

A good history of French Canada. Chapter 2 devoted in part to religious history.

153   Jaenen, Cornelius J. THE ROLE OF THE CHURCH IN NEW FRANCE. Toronto: McGraw-Hill Ryerson, 1976. 182 p.

Summary of author's volume FRIEND AND FOE (104) in the first forty pages. Goes on to provide an excellent, thematic analysis of religious life during the eighteenth century.

154   O'Neill, Charles E. CHURCH AND STATE IN FRENCH COLONIAL LOUISIANA: POLICY AND POLITICS TO 1732. New Haven, Conn.: Yale University Press, 1966. xii, 315 p.

Thoroughly researched and rich in insight and documentation.

155   Parkman, Francis. THE JESUITS IN NORTH AMERICA IN THE SEVENTEENTH CENTURY. Boston: Little, Brown, and Co. 1867. lxxxix, 463 p.

An important study by a leading nineteenth-century historian of colonial America, helpful for understanding nineteenth-century attitudes toward European-Indian contacts. However, author recently came under severe attack for his bias and inaccuracies in works by Jaenen (104) and Jennings (105).

156   Thwaites, Reuben Gold, ed. THE JESUIT RELATIONS AND ALLIED DOCUMENTS; TRAVELS AND EXPLORATIONS OF THE JESUIT MISSIONARIES IN NEW FRANCE, 1610-1791; THE ORIGINAL FRENCH, LATIN, AND ITALIAN TEXTS, WITH ENGLISH TRANSLATIONS.

73 vols. Cleveland: Burrow Bros. Co., 1896-1901.

> An index in volumes 72-73. A one-volume selection published under the same title, edited by Edna Kenton (Toronto: McClelland and Stewart, 1901).

157 Wrong, George M. THE RISE AND FALL OF NEW FRANCE. 2 vols. New York: Macmillan Co., 1928. Bibliog.

> A thorough survey of Canadian colonialism in North America from the earliest settlements until 1760. Contains an extensive index, but lacks footnotes. Major treatment of early French-American Catholicism.

THE SPANISH COLONIES

See also Bowden (101) and Spicer (113).

158 Bolton, Herbert Eugene. RIM OF CHRISTENDOM. New York: Macmillan Co., 1936. xiii, 644 p. Illus., maps, photos., bibliog.

> An excellent biography of Eusebio Francisco Kino, the seventeenth-century Italian missionary and explorer of California.

159 _____. THE SPANISH BORDERLANDS: A CHRONICLE OF OLD FLORIDA AND THE SOUTHWEST. New Haven, Conn.: Yale University Press, 1921. xiv, 320 p. Bibliog.

> An antiquated, popular book about Spanish civilization in Florida, Louisiana, Texas, New Mexico, and California. Contains a bilingual bibliography of earlier works.

160 Castaneda, Carlos Eduardo. OUR CATHOLIC HERITAGE IN TEXAS, 1519-1936. 7 vols. Austin, Tex.: Von Boeckman-Jones Co., 1936-58. Bibliog.

> Encyclopedic and highly sympathetic chronicle of Catholicism in Texas from 1519 until 1936. Each volume contains an extensive bibliography and index.

161 Engelhardt, Zephyrin. THE MISSIONS AND MISSIONARIES OF CALIFORNIA. 4 vols. San Francisco: James H. Barry Co., 1908-16. Illus.

> Sympathetic, encyclopedic treatment of Spanish and other Roman Catholic missionaries in California from the earliest settlements through the nineteenth century. Includes book-length index.

162   Gannon, Michael V.   THE CROSS IN THE SAND: THE EARLY CATH-
       OLIC CHURCH IN FLORIDA, 1513-1870. Gainesville: University of
       Florida Press, 1965. xv, 210 p. Bibliog.

       A brief, popular introduction, lacking footnotes.

163   Geiger, Maynard.   THE LIFE AND TIMES OF FRAY-JUNIPERO SERRA,
       O.F.M.   2 vols. Washington, D.C.: Academy of American Franciscan
       History, 1959. Bibliog.

       A thorough and well-documented biography of Junipero Serra
       (1713-84), the Spanish Franciscan and leading figure in early
       California missionary work.

164   Weber, Francis J., ed.   DOCUMENTS OF CALIFORNIA CATHOLIC
       HISTORY (1784-1963).   Los Angeles: Dawson's Book Shop, 1965.   xiv,
       364 p.

       A collection of sixty-five concisely edited documents, some
       of which are excerpts from secondary works, complete with
       a short index. Little introductory material.

Chapter 4

PURITANISM

References in this chapter are limited to New England. Works relating to religious life in the middle and southern colonies during the seventeenth century usually focus upon a specific religious community or denomination, such as the Anglicans, Baptists, or Presbyterians. This literature is covered in chapters 5 and 6.

GENERAL WORKS

165   Bremer, Francis J. THE PURITAN EXPERIMENT: NEW ENGLAND SOCIETY FROM BRADFORD TO EDWARDS. New York: St. Martin's Press, 1976. 255 p.

   A good introduction to seventeenth-century New England that avoids overemphasizing religious life in Massachusetts. Good guide to recent literature.

166   Hall, David D. "Understanding the Puritans." In THE STATE OF AMERICAN HISTORY, edited by Herbert J. Bass, pp. 330-49. Chicago: Quadrangle Books, 1970.

   An excellent discussion of the historiographic problems of Puritanism that begins with a discussion of the work of Perry Miller.

167   _____, ed. PURITANISM IN SEVENTEENTH-CENTURY MASSACHU-SETTS. New York: Holt, Rinehart and Winston, 1968. 122 p.

   Includes essays and selections by Miller, Morison, Simpson, Morgan, Parrington, Bailyn, Schneider, and Rutman.

168   Rutman, Darrett B. AMERICAN PURITANISM: FAITH AND PRACTICE. Philadelphia: J.B. Lippincott Co., 1970. 151 p.

   Discusses the methodological problems of studying the Puritans. Designed for undergraduates.

169   Sweet, William Warren. RELIGION IN COLONIAL AMERICA. New
       York: Charles Scribner's Sons, 1949. xiii, 367 p.

       An old but useful survey, completed in 1942, describing the
       ecclesiastical heterogeneity of colonial America.

170   Vaughan, Alden T., ed. THE PURITAN TRADITION IN AMERICA,
       1620-1730. Documentary History of the United States series. New York:
       Harper Torchbooks, 1972. 366 p.

       Contains a good survey of the historical writing on Puritan-
       ism in introduction.

171   Vaughan, Alden T., and Bremer, Francis J., eds. PURITAN NEW
       ENGLAND: ESSAYS ON RELIGION, SOCIETY, AND CULTURE. New
       York: St. Martin's Press, 1977. 395 p.

       A good anthology of twenty-one scholarly articles dealing
       with New England, 1630-1789, including Walzer, "Puritan-
       ism as a Revolutionary Ideology"; Miller, "The Marrow of
       Puritan Divinity"; Ronald Cohen, "Church and State in
       Seventeenth-Century Massachusetts: Another Look at the
       Antinomian Controversy"; Bercovitch, "The Historiography of
       Johnson's WONDER-WORKING PROVIDENCE"; and Robert
       Pope, "New England Versus the New England Mind: The
       Myth of Declension."

172   Ziff, Larzer. PURITANISM IN AMERICA: NEW CULTURE IN A NEW
       WORLD. New York: Viking Press, 1973. 338 p.

       Eminently readable attempt to synthesize intellectual, re-
       ligious, social, and economic history into a single narrative.

THE WORK OF PERRY MILLER

Miller (1905-1964) was the greatest historian of American Puritanism. Older
views of the Puritans have been revised in the light of his work, and virtually
all contemporary scholarship on Puritanism has begun in dialogue with this
master. His most important works on Puritanism are listed in this section in
chronological order along with a few comments on the scope of his achieve-
ment by other scholars. His other works can be found in other sections of
the bibliography--226, 230, 281, 319, 723, 866, and 867.

173   Miller, Perry. ORTHODOXY IN MASSACHUSETTS, 1630-1650. Cam-
       bridge, Mass.: Harvard University Press, 1933. 353 p.

       Miller's doctoral dissertation and first book. Was so brash
       as to claim that the religion of the Puritans should be exam-
       ined on its own terms. In the process, cleared up much

confusion about the nature of the Congregational churches, especially the agreement in America of separating and non-separating sects. An excellent introduction by David D. Hall in Harper Torchbook reissue.

174 _____. THE NEW ENGLAND MIND: THE SEVENTEENTH CENTURY. New York: Macmillan Co., 1939. 528 p.

Probably Miller's greatest work. A topical analysis of the leading ideas of seventeenth-century New England. First examines the intellectual tradition going back to Augustine, emphasizing the nature of Christian piety. Turns next to Puritan epistemology, discussing the use of reason and the nature of nature, emphasizing the role of Petrus Ramus' logic in Puritan thinking. Examines the Puritan definition of man and the role of conversion in their churches, their style of preaching, and the character of the covenant.

175 _____. THE NEW ENGLAND MIND: FROM COLONY TO PROVINCE. Cambridge, Mass.: Harvard University Press, 1953. 513 p.

Usually thought to be the sequel to THE NEW ENGLAND MIND: THE SEVENTEENTH CENTURY, is actually a continuation of the historical narrative begun in ORTHODOXY IN MASSACHUSETTS. Beginning about 1648, provides a full narrative exposition of his view that the last half of the century was marked by declension and the splintering of society--the part of his work that has come under the most consistent attack in recent years.

176 _____. ERRAND INTO THE WILDERNESS. Cambridge, Mass.: Harvard University Press, 1956. 244 p.

Contains the following Miller essays: "Errand into the Wilderness," "Thomas Hooker and the Democracy of Connecticut," "The Marrow of Puritan Divinity"--one of his most famous short pieces, "Religion and Society in the Early Literature of Virginia," "The Puritan State and Puritan Society," "Jonathan Edwards and the Great Awakening," "The Rhetoric of Sensation"--a small masterpiece in textual analysis of Edwards' sermons, "From Edwards to Emerson," "Nature and the National Ego," and "The End of the World."

177 _____. NATURE'S NATION. Cambridge, Mass.: Belknap Press of Harvard University Press, 1967. xvi, 298 p.

Contains the following of Miller's essays: "The Shaping of the American Character," "Declension in a Bible Commonwealth," "'Preparation for Salvation' in Seventeenth-Century New England," "The Great Awakening from 1740-1750,"

"From Covenant to the Revival," "The Insecurity of Nature,"
"Theodore Parker: Apostasy within Liberalism," "The Location of American Religious Freedom," "Emersonian Genius and
the American Democracy," "Thoreau in the Context of International Romanticism," "Melville and Transcendentalism,"
"The Romantic Dilemma in American Nationalism and the
Concept of Nature," "An American Language," "The Ro-
mance and the Novel," and "Sinners in the Hands of a
Benevolent God."

178   Miller, Perry, and Johnson, Thomas H., eds. THE PURITANS: A
        SOURCEBOOK OF THEIR WRITINGS. Rev. ed. 2 vols. New York:
        Harper and Row, 1963.

        An admirably edited collection of primary source material
        from all aspects of seventeenth-century New England life:
        sermons, diaries, travel accounts, histories. Also contains
        a long introduction by Miller that usefully summarizes his
        work in THE NEW ENGLAND MIND (174-75).

179   Marsden, George M. "Perry Miller's Rehabilitation of the Puritans: A
        Critique." CHURCH HISTORY 39 (1970): 91-105.

        Criticizes Miller's view that the Puritans revised Calvin's
        theology. Argues that Miller underplayed the Christian as-
        pects of Puritan thought.

180   Middlekauff, Robert. "Perry Miller." In PASTMASTERS: SOME ES-
        SAYS ON AMERICAN HISTORIANS, edited by Marcus Cunliffe and
        Robin W. Winks, pp. 167-90. New York: Harper and Row, 1969.

        Able and non-technical, designed as an introduction for be-
        ginning students. Contains a short biographical sketch of
        Miller as well as analysis of his works.

181   Wise, Gene. "Implicit Irony in Perry Miller's NEW ENGLAND MIND."
        JOURNAL OF THE HISTORY OF IDEAS 29 (1968): 379-600.

        A discussion of consensus historiography, usefully comparing
        the approaches of Miller and Thomas J. Wertenbaker.

THE EARLY SEVENTEENTH CENTURY

For works discussing Puritan-Indian relations, see Beaver (100), Jennings (105),
Kellaway (107), Ronda (109), Rooy (110), Salisbury (111), and Vaughan (114).

182   Ames, William. THE MARROW OF THEOLOGY. Edited and translated
        by John Eusden. Boston: Pilgrim Press, 1968. xiii, 353 p.

An important source for Puritan thought. This translation
made from the 3d Latin edition of 1629.

183   Bercovitch, Sacvan. THE PURITAN ORIGINS OF THE AMERICAN
      SELF. New Haven, Conn.: Yale University Press, 1975. 250 p.

      An important but difficult and complex book devoted to an
      analysis of the rhetoric of seventeenth-century writers. Fo-
      cuses particularly on Cotton Mather, whose life of John
      Winthrop (a work almost completely neglected in modern
      times) provides author with the concept of the "American
      Nehemiah." Attempts to account for the sense of pur-
      posiveness and identity with the land that has seemed to
      mark off the Puritans as the first and archetypal Americans.

184   Breen, T.H. THE CHARACTER OF A GOOD RULER: A STUDY OF
      PURITAN POLITICAL IDEAS IN NEW ENGLAND, 1630-1730. New
      Haven, Conn.: Yale University Press, 1970. xx, 301 p.

      Traces the secularization of the ideal of the "good ruler"
      --the movement from dependence upon godliness to the de-
      sire to protect property--and locates the transition point in
      the Glorious Revolution.

185   Burg, B.R. "The Cambridge Platform: A Reassertion of Ecclesiastical
      Authority." CHURCH HISTORY 43 (December 1974): 470-87.

      A careful summary of the events that led up to the meeting
      of the Congregational Synod and an assessment of the re-
      lationship of clergy and secular officials.

186   Hall, David D. THE FAITHFUL SHEPHERD: A HISTORY OF THE NEW
      ENGLAND MINISTRY IN THE SEVENTEENTH CENTURY. Chapel Hill:
      University of North Carolina Press, for the Institute of Early American
      History and Culture, 1972. 303 p.

      A careful delineation of the changing function and status of
      Congregational ministers, an analysis which illuminates some
      of the critical issues relating to the Cambridge Platform and
      the ministerial crisis of legitimacy in the late seventeenth
      century.

187   Holifield, E. Brooks. THE COVENANT SEALED: THE DEVELOPMENT
      OF PURITAN SACRAMENTAL THEOLOGY IN OLD AND NEW ENG-
      LAND, 1570-1720. New Haven, Conn.: Yale University Press, 1974.
      248 p. Bibliog.

      Traces the development of Puritan thought in response to Bap-
      tist and Quaker challenges to the sacraments generally and
      to baptism in particular. Treatment of sacramental theology

in late seventeenth century covers a much-neglected topic. Full scholarly notation.

188   Lucas, Paul R. VALLEY OF DISCORD: CHURCH AND SOCIETY ALONG THE CONNECTICUT RIVER, 1636-1725. Hanover, N.H.: University Press of New England, 1976. xvi, 275 p.

A work of social history of the kind pioneered by Lockridge (242) and Bushman (271). Focuses upon the years antecedent to those covered by Bushman, finding that the valley was characterized not by harmony but by dissension and a search for order from the beginning.

189   McGiffert, Michael. "American Puritan Studies in the 1960s." WILLIAM AND MARY QUARTERLY 27 (1970): 36-67.

A thorough survey of the field in the years since the death of Perry Miller in 1964. Excellent bibliographic treatment.

190   Maclear, James F. "The Heart of New England Rent: The Mystical Element in Early Puritan History." MISSISSIPPI VALLEY HISTORICAL REVIEW 42 (1956): 621-52.

Calls for "a radically different approach," which would begin with a full recognition of the emotional, experiential, and, ultimately, mystical element in the synthesis that stood at the center of Puritan evangelical religion. One of the earliest criticisms of Perry Miller's too-intellectual description of Puritan religion.

191   _____. "New England and the Fifth Monarchy: The Quest for the Millennium in Early American Puritanism." WILLIAM AND MARY QUARTERLY 32 (1975): 223-60.

Excellent treatment of millenarian aspects of seventeenth-century theology, particularly in the works of John Cotton and John Eliot. Compares their work to English millenarians. Reprinted in work by Vaughan and Bremer (171).

192   Middlekauff, Robert. THE MATHERS: THREE GENERATIONS OF PURITAN INTELLECTUALS, 1596-1728. New York: Oxford University Press, 1971. 440 p.

Possibly the most significant and creative contribution to Puritan scholarship since that of Perry Miller. Describes the work of Richard, Increase, and Cotton Mather, culminating in an analysis of the grandson (Cotton). Attempts to reverse the generally unfavorable view of Cotton Mather.

193   Morgan, Edmund S. THE PURITAN DILEMMA: THE STORY OF JOHN
       WINTHROP. Boston: Little, Brown, and Co., 1958. 224 p.

       Possibly the best introduction to Puritan thought now in print.
       A compelling study of the most significant layman among the
       first generation of immigrants to Massachusetts. At the same
       time, provides readers with good insight into general social
       and religious history. An eminently teachable book.

194   _____. VISIBLE SAINTS: THE HISTORY OF A PURITAN IDEA. New
       York: New York University Press, 1963. 159 p.

       Excellent essay on Puritan religious experience, especially
       important in demonstrating how the practice of making a
       public testimony of religious conversion developed among
       Massachusetts Bay churches.

195   Pettit, Norman. THE HEART PREPARED: GRACE AND CONVERSION
       IN PURITAN SPIRITUAL LIFE. New Haven, Conn.: Yale University
       Press, 1966. 252 p.

       Important study of the doctrine of preparation for salvation
       from the Reformation to the eighteenth century. Somewhat
       modifies Perry Miller's description of Covenant theology.
       A different interpretation in Holifield's work (187).

196   Shepard, Thomas. GOD'S PLOT: THE PARADOXES OF PURITAN
       PIETY: BEING THE AUTOBIOGRAPHY AND JOURNAL OF THOMAS
       SHEPARD. Edited by Michael McGiffert. Amherst: University of
       Massachusetts Press, 1972. 252 p.

       Republication (original from seventeenth century) of a vivid
       and compelling personal narrative by a minister (1605-49)
       who lived through the first generation of New England Puri-
       tanism.

197   Simpson, Alan. PURITANISM IN OLD AND NEW ENGLAND. Chi-
       cago: University of Chicago Press, 1955. 125 p.

       Six lectures on the impact of Puritanism on English and
       American institutions. Has stood the test of time.

198   Solberg, Winton U. REDEEM THE TIME: THE PURITAN SABBATH IN
       EARLY AMERICA. Cambridge, Mass.: Harvard University Press, 1977.
       416 p.

       Examines the effect of Puritan observance of the sabbath on
       colonial life and its long-lived impact upon American cul-
       ture.

199   Sprunger, Keith L. THE LEARNED DOCTOR WILLIAM AMES: DUTCH
        BACKGROUNDS OF ENGLISH AND AMERICAN PURITANISM. Urbana:
        University of Illinois Press, 1972. 289 p.

> A comprehensive and reliable biography of an influential
> figure, supplemented with a good description of Dutch Puri-
> tanism. Section of the book containing a theological ana-
> lysis of Ames's work less useful.

200   Tipson, Baird. "Invisible Saints: The 'Judgment of Charity' in the
        Early New England Churches." CHURCH HISTORY 44 (1975): 460-71.

> An interesting and important article. Argues that the minis-
> ters in Massachusetts Bay decisively broke with Christian
> tradition in demanding internal evidence of grace during the
> prospective member's "relation" of his Christian experience.
> Notes that, traditionally, "judgment of charity" implied
> only an expectation of external conformity to Christian
> standards, recognizing that knowledge of the "heart" was
> impossible. Speculates that this development occurred not
> so much in an effort to purify the church as to guarantee
> the individual's salvation.

201   Wall, Robert. MASSACHUSETTS BAY: THE CRUCIAL DECADE, 1640-1650.
        New Haven, Conn.: Yale University Press, 1972. 292 p.

> A narrow monograph useful for its discussion of the case of
> Samuel Gordon, a dissident who appealed his cause to Eng-
> land and created difficulties for Massachusetts authorities.

202   Williams, George H., et al., eds. THOMAS HOOKER: WRITINGS IN
        ENGLAND AND HOLLAND, 1626-1633. Cambridge, Mass.: Harvard
        University Press, 1976. 435 p.

> Contains four essays on Hooker (a sketch of his life by Wil-
> liams, a discussion of the "order of salvation" in Hooker's
> theology by Norman Pettit, and two essays on editorial-
> canonical problems connected with Hooker's writings), ten
> of Hooker's works, and a complete bibliography of Hooker's
> writings.

203   Ziff, Larzer. THE CAREER OF JOHN COTTON: PURITANISM AND
        THE AMERICAN EXPERIENCE. Princeton, N.J.: Princeton University
        Press, 1962. 280 p.

> Provocative and suggestive. Not so much a biography as a
> delineation of the social and intellectual structure of New
> England Puritanism during its first thirty years. Emphasis on
> Cotton's cautious and unhurried quest for theological coher-
> ence goes far to defend him from charges of hypocrisy or
> weakness, especially in connection with the Antinomian con-
> troversy.

THE LATE SEVENTEENTH CENTURY

204   Elliott, Emory. POWER AND THE PULPIT IN PURITAN NEW ENGLAND.
       Princeton, N.J.: Princeton University Press, 1975. xii, 240 p.

       Psychohistorical analysis of the sermonic literature of the
       second and third generation of Puritan ministers. Argues
       that the first generation, seeking to maintain control, used
       sermonic language implying that the second generation must
       remain dependent. Language of the pulpit changed to as-
       surance and not judgment when the next generation gained
       power.

205   Jones, James W. THE SHATTERED SYNTHESIS: NEW ENGLAND PU-
       RITANISM BEFORE THE GREAT AWAKENING. New Haven, Conn.:
       Yale University Press, 1973. 207 p.

       Argues that the evangelical-liberal split of the First Great
       Awakening was only confirmed and not created by that re-
       vival. Uses, as basis, the biographical sketches and theo-
       logical analysis of ten clergymen: John Norton (1606-63),
       Giles Fermin (1614-97), Samuel Willard (1640-1707), Cotton
       Mather (1663-1728), Benjamin Colman (1673-1747), Solomon
       Stoddard (1643-1729), Lemuel Brant (1721-54), Ebenezer Gay
       (1696-1787), Jonathan Mayhew (1720-66), and Charles Chauncy
       (1705-87). Work has been faulted for over-emphasizing the
       monolithic character of Puritanism. Useful biographical
       material, especially for the lesser-known figures.

206   Lowrie, Ernest Benson. THE SHAPE OF THE PURITAN MIND: THE
       THOUGHT OF SAMUEL WILLARD. New Haven, Conn.: Yale Uni-
       versity Press, 1974. 251 p.

       Examination of Willard's COMPLEAT BODY OF DIVINITY
       (1726) an effort to show how one late-seventeenth-century
       theologian integrated natural and revealed religion. A
       technical treatise that will be difficult for the beginning
       student, albeit rewarding.

207   Mather, Cotton. THE DIARY OF COTTON MATHER, D.D., F.R.S.
       FOR THE YEAR 1712. Edited by William R. Manierre II. Charlottes-
       ville: University Press of Virginia, 1964. 143 p.

       An admirable introduction to the mind of Mather for those
       who wish a representative slice of the man.

208   _____. MAGNALIA CHRISTI AMERICANA, OR THE ECCLESIASTICAL
       HISTORY OF NEW ENGLAND, BOOKS I AND II. Edited by Kenneth
       B. Murdock and Elizabeth W. Miller. Cambridge, Mass.: Harvard
       University Press, 1977. 512 p.

First two books of the new scholarly and critical edition of
Mather's 1702 masterpiece. Will certainly focus further attention on Mather, whose work has recently been the object
of increased scholarly interest. The traditional nineteenth-
century edition of MAGNALIA, edited by Thomas Robbins,
recently reprinted (2 vols. New York: Russell and Russell,
1967). Has also been an abridgement edited by Raymond
J. Cunningham (New York: Frederick Ungar Publishing Co.,
1970. 148 p.).

209   Middlekauff, Robert. "Piety and Intellect in Puritanism." WILLIAM
AND MARY QUARTERLY 22 (1965): 457-70.

Discussion of the interplay of ideas and feelings in Puritan
psychology, using materials from the diaries of Cotton Mather
and Samuel Sewall. Argues that there was as much influence
of ideas on feelings as vice versa.

210   Plumstead, A.W. THE WALL AND THE GARDEN: SELECTED MAS-
SACHUSETTS ELECTION SERMONS, 1670-1775. Minneapolis: University of Minnesota Press, 1968. 390 p.

A collection of well-edited sermons, which illustrates the
shift from the theme of "errand" in older Puritanism to the
themes of natural law and reason in eighteenth-century Massachusetts.

211   Pope, Robert G. THE HALF-WAY COVENANT: CHURCH MEMBER-
SHIP IN PURITAN NEW ENGLAND. Princeton, N.J.: Princeton University Press, 1969. 321 p.

A scholarly analysis of the functioning of the Half-Way
Covenant that challenges the assumption that this change in
Puritan church membership procedures can be used as evidence of a decline in religious vitality. Received mixed
reviews. Another article by author, on the problem of declining faith, reprinted in Vaughan and Bremer's work (171).

212   Rutman, Darrett B. "God's Bridge Falling Down: 'Another Approach'
to New England Puritanism Assayed." WILLIAM AND MARY QUAR-
TERLY 19 (1962): 408-21.

Attempts a refutation of the idea that the Half-Way Covenant
may have been a sign of fervor and not decline.

213   Sewall, Samuel. THE DIARY OF SAMUEL SEWALL, 1674-1729. Ed-
ited by M. Halsey Thomas. 2 vols. New York: Farrar, Straus, and
Giroux, 1973. Paperback abridgement also available, edited by Harvey
Wish. New York: Capricorn Books, 1967. 189 p.

Completely reedited version of the Massachusetts Historical Society publication, compared and corrected from the original, is marvellous source for late-seventeenth-century social history. Text of THE SELLING OF JOSEPH reprinted in an appendix.

214 _____. THE SELLING OF JOSEPH. Edited by Sidney Kaplan. Amherst: University of Massachusetts Press, 1969. 66 p.

One of the earliest antislavery tracts in American history. First published in 1700.

215 Smith, Peter H. "Politics and Sainthood: Biography by Cotton Mather." WILLIAM AND MARY QUARTERLY 20 (1963): 186-206.

Illustrates the political function of Mather's biographical penchant, showing how Mather shaped the past to fit his present problems--especially in connection with the Glorious Revolution and the Half-Way Covenant.

216 Van Dyken, Seymour. SAMUEL WILLARD, 1640-1707: PREACHER OF ORTHODOXY IN AN ERA OF CHANGE. Grand Rapids, Mich.: William B. Eerdmans Publishing Co., 1972. 224 p.

This life of Willard, pastor of the Old South Church in Boston from 1676 until his death, concerned primarily with his theology and contains little social history.

217 Winslow, Ola Elizabeth. SAMUEL SEWALL OF BOSTON. New York: Macmillan Co., 1964. 235 p.

A competent biography from a scholar who has specialized in biography, but may not be as useful an introduction to Sewall's life as his own diary (213).

THE ANTINOMIAN CONTROVERSY AND DISCIPLINE
IN THE CHURCHES

218 Battis, Emery. SAINTS AND SECTARIES: ANNE HUTCHINSON AND THE ANTINOMIAN CONTROVERSY IN THE MASSACHUSETTS BAY COLONY. Chapel Hill: University of North Carolina Press for the Institute of Early American History and Culture, 1962. 379 p.

The most detailed retelling of the trial of America's first heretic and the classic confrontation of wills and ideas. Both blamed and praised for its vivid style and psychoanalytic explanations, has been uniformly appluaded for analysis of the social status of the groups involved in the controversy.

219 Erikson, Kai T. WAYWARD PURITANS: A STUDY IN THE SOCIOL-
OGY OF DEVIANCE. New York: John Wiley and Sons, 1966. xv,
228 p.

> Considers three "crime waves" and the impact they had in
> New England--the Antinomian controversy, the Quaker per-
> secutions, and the witchcraft hysteria.

220 Hall, David, ed. THE ANTINOMIAN CONTROVERSY; 1636-1638: A
DOCUMENTARY HISTORY. Middletown, Conn.: Wesleyan University
Press, 1968. 447 p.

> A valuable collection of the most important primary sources.

221 Oberholzer, Emil, Jr. DELINQUENT SAINTS: DISCIPLINARY AC-
TION IN THE EARLY CONGREGATIONAL CHURCHES OF MASSA-
CHUSETTS. New York: Columbia University Press, 1956. 379 p.

> Presents a wealth of data from individual court cases to illus-
> trate behavior patterns.

222 Stoever, William K.B. "Nature, Grace and John Cotton: The Theological Dimension in the New England Antinomian Controversy."
CHURCH HISTORY 44 (1975): 22-33.

> A thorough and quite technical discussion of theological is-
> sues separating Hutchinson and Cotton from the magistrates.
> Concludes that recent judgments in favor of Cotton are un-
> fair to the magistrates who were acting in defense of both
> political and theological legitimacy. Book-length treatment
> of this subject by author forthcoming.

ROGER WILLIAMS

223 Brockunier, Samuel H. THE IRREPRESSIBLE DEMOCRAT, ROGER WIL-
LIAMS. New York: Ronald Press, 1940. xii, 305 p.

> Not so much a first fresh look at Williams during a period
> of scholarly reassessment as it is a restatement of nineteenth-
> century attitudes toward Williams.

224 Covey, Cyclone. THE GENTLE RADICAL: A BIOGRAPHY OF ROGER
WILLIAMS. New York: Macmillan Co., 1966. 273 p.

> Biography gives more information about Williams' friends and
> social context than about the man himself.

225 Garrett, John. ROGER WILLIAMS: WITNESS BEYOND CHRISTEN-
DOM, 1603-1683. New York: Macmillan Co., 1970. 306 p.

A biographical sketch followed by seven topical chapters emphasizing the social forces at work in Williams' world.

226   Miller, Perry. ROGER WILLIAMS: HIS CONTRIBUTION TO THE AMERI-
CAN TRADITION.   Indianapolis: Bobbs-Merrill Co., 1953.   273 p.

A combination of Williams's words, selected and edited from the Narragansett Club edition of his works (230), and author's incisive interpretation.   Compare with Morgan (227).

227   Morgan, Edmund S.   "Miller's Williams."   NEW ENGLAND QUAR-
TERLY 38 (1965): 513-23.

A critique of Perry Miller's interpretation of Roger Williams.

228   _____.   ROGER WILLIAMS: THE CHURCH AND THE STATE.   New
York: Harcourt, Brace, and World, 1967.   170 p.

A largely successful attempt to provide a lucid exposition of the often murky thought of Rhode Island's founder.

229   Reinitz, Richard.   "The Typological Argument for Religious Toleration:
The Separatist Tradition and Roger Williams."   EARLY AMERICAN LIT-
ERATURE 5 (1970): 74-97.

A discussion of Williams' use of typological arguments and the possible sources of that kind of argument rather than a discussion of toleration.

230   Williams, Roger.   THE COMPLETE WRITINGS.   7 vols.   New York:
Russell and Russell, 1963.

First six volumes reprinted from the nineteenth-century Narragansett Club Edition.   Five tracts not included in the earlier edition, plus a short essay on Williams by Perry Miller in volume seven.

231   Winslow, Ola E.   MASTER ROGER WILLIAMS: A BIOGRAPHY.   New
York: Macmillan Co., 1957.

A clear account of the basic details of Williams's life.

SALEM AND WITCHCRAFT

232   Boyer, Paul, and Nissenbaum, Stephen.   SALEM POSSESSED: THE SO-
CIAL ORIGINS OF WITCHCRAFT.   Cambridge, Mass.: Harvard University Press, 1974.   xxi, 231 p.

A masterful and enthusiastically-received social history of

Salem Village at the point of its historic trauma. Account based upon little-utilized evidence. Offers the most convincing explanation of the Salem witchcraft mania now in print.

233 _____, eds. SALEM-VILLAGE WITCHCRAFT: A DOCUMENTARY RECORD OF LOCAL CONFLICT IN COLONIAL NEW ENGLAND. Belmont, Calif.: Wadsworth Publishing Co., 1972. 416 p.

A collection of primary sources designed for undergraduates. Perhaps as useful for the social history of Salem as for the study of witchcraft.

234 Demos, John. "John Godfrey and His Neighbors: Witchcraft and the Social Web in Colonial Massachusetts." WILLIAM AND MARY QUARTERLY 33 (1976): 242-65.

Fascinating narrative of an obscure man who was frequently charged with witchcraft--uncommon among males. Court records assiduously tracked down and psycho-historical insights judiciously employed to present a vigorous portrayal of this vitriolic and greedy man, who, by the way, was never convicted.

235 _____. "Underlying Themes in the Witchcraft of Seventeenth-Century New England." AMERICAN HISTORICAL REVIEW 75 (1970): 1311-26. Reprinted in COLONIAL AMERICA: ESSAYS IN POLITICS AND SOCIAL DEVELOPMENT. Edited by S. N. Katz. Boston: Little, Brown, and Co., 1971.

A provocative article that relates the outbreak of witchcraft to elements in the personality and social structure of Massachusetts. Emphasizes that the basic problems of that society were ones of authority and aggression.

236 Hansen, Chadwick. WITCHCRAFT AT SALEM. New York: George Braziller, 1969. xvii, 252 p.

Argues that we are mistaken not to recognize the presence of demonic forces at work in Salem, in spite of the fact that they might have different names in contemporary society.

237 Miller, Arthur. THE CRUCIBLE, A PLAY IN FOUR ACTS. New York: Viking Press, 1953. 145 p.

A play set in Salem and reflecting an understanding of those events, but the witchcraft that alarmed the author was the McCarthy anti-Communist crusade.

238   Starkey, Marion L. THE DEVIL IN MASSACHUSETTS: A MODERN IN-
        QUIRY INTO THE SALEM WITCH TRIALS. New York: Alfred A.
        Knopf, 1949. xviii, 310 p.

        Perhaps the best introduction to witchcraft in Salem and
        certainly the most dramatic narrative of the events.

239   Upham, Charles W. SALEM WITCHCRAFT: WITH AN ACCOUNT OF
        SALEM VILLAGE. 2 vols. Boston: Wiggin and Lunt, 1867. Reprint.
        New York: Frederick Ungar Publishing Co., 1959.

        A careful, amazingly thorough analysis of the social back-
        ground to the witchcraft controvery. Still remains valuable.

LOCAL STUDIES

240   Jones, Mary Jeanne Anderson. CONGREGATIONAL COMMON-
        WEALTH: CONNECTICUT, 1636-1662. Middletown, Conn.: Wesleyan
        University Press, 1968. xiii, 233 p.

        Analyzes the origin of the colony's first constitution, the
        Fundamental Orders, and evaluates it in relationship to
        Puritanism. A careful but bland study.

241   Langdon, George D., Jr. PILGRIM COLONY: A HISTORY OF NEW
        PLYMOUTH, 1620-91. New Haven, Conn.: Yale University Press,
        1966. 257 p.

        A scholarly study of institutional development.

242   Lockridge, Kenneth A. A NEW ENGLAND TOWN: THE FIRST HUN-
        DRED YEARS: DEDHAM, MASSACHUSETTS, 1636-1736. New York:
        W.W. Norton, 1970. 223 p.

        Begins with the assumption that one can learn more about the
        history of preindustrial America by studying one town in
        detail than by knowing a little something about many places.
        Resultant study widely acclaimed and influential. Most im-
        portant theme the creation and failure of Dedham as a
        utopian, closed, corporate community. Also includes anal-
        ysis and description of Dedham's church and minister.

243   Powell, Sumner C. PURITAN VILLAGE: THE FORMATION OF A NEW
        ENGLAND TOWN. Middletown, Conn.: Wesleyan University Press,
        1963. 218 p.

        A pioneering study of Sudbury, Massachusetts, which shows
        how the various agrarian and social patterns of England
        were transferred to New England and how the families rep-
        resenting these variant traditions worked out their town

government in this formative period of the colony's history.

244   Rutman, Darrett B. WINTHROP'S BOSTON: PORTRAIT OF A PURITAN
TOWN. Chapel Hill: University of North Carolina Press, 1965. 324 p.

A multifaceted treatment, combining religious and intellectual
history with geography and demography. Provides a full and
interesting account of the city and its inhabitants.

245   Worthley, Harold Field. AN INVENTORY OF THE RECORDS OF THE
PARTICULAR (CONGREGATIONAL) CHURCHES OF MASSACHUSETTS
GATHERED, 1620–1805. Harvard Theological Studies, vol. 25. Cam-
bridge, Mass.: Harvard University Press, 1970. 734 p.

Invaluable research tool in a narrowly specialized area: An
attempt to list every Congregational church organized in
Massachusetts before 1806. Includes description of church
records and their location, and lists the past ministers, dea-
cons, and elders.

FAMILY AND SOCIAL HISTORY

246   Dunn, Richard S. PURITANS AND YANKEES: THE WINTHROP DY-
NASTY OF NEW ENGLAND, 1630–1717. Princeton, N.J.: Princeton
University Press, 1962. 379 p.

A study of four members of this most influential Boston family: John the Elder, John Jr., Wait, and Fitz. In the process of describing these men, also recounts a large part of
the history of seventeenth-century Massachusetts.

247   Foster, Stephen. THEIR SOLITARY WAY: THE PURITAN SOCIAL
ETHIC IN THE FIRST CENTURY OF SETTLEMENT IN NEW ENGLAND.
New Haven, Conn.: Yale University Press, 1971. 214 p.

A revised dissertation which presents, in general, a useful
discussion. Not without problems.

248   Greven, Philip J., Jr., ed. CHILD-BEARING CONCEPTS, 1628–1861.
Itasca, Ill.: F.E. Peacock, 1973. 181 p.

Anthology of literature relating to child-rearing, mostly by
American authors. Includes John Locke, Jonathan Edwards,
John Wesley, and John Witherspoon. Designed for under-
graduates.

249   Morgan, Edmund S. THE PURITAN FAMILY: RELIGION AND DO-
MESTIC RELATIONS IN SEVENTEENTH-CENTURY NEW ENGLAND.
New ed., rev. and enlarged. New York: Harper and Row, 1966.
196 p.

Expanded version of Morgan's dissertation first published in
1942. Covers relationships of husbands and wives, parents
and children, masters and servants, and discusses education.

249A   Stannard, David E. THE PURITAN WAY OF DEATH: A STUDY IN RE-
LIGION, CULTURE, AND SOCIAL CHANGE. New York: Oxford
University Press, 1977. xii, 236 p.

Brief treatment of the attitudes toward and rituals surrounding death in Puritan New England, set in the context of a
general discussion of death in American culture.

250   Winslow, Ola E. MEETINGHOUSE HILL, 1630-1783. New York:
Macmillan Co., 1952. 344 p.

An anecdotal narrative history of the building and mainte-
nance of New England meeting houses and of the conduct
among clergy and congregation. Contains some materials
difficult to find elsewhere.

LITERATURE AND THE ARTS

251   Bercovitch, Sacvan, ed. THE AMERICAN PURITAN IMAGINATION:
ESSAYS IN REVALUATION. New York: Cambridge University Press,
1974. 274 p.

A useful collection of eleven essays drawn either from recent books or journals concentrates upon the imagination of
the Puritans and examines their literary work as literature
rather than theology. Excellent introduction by editor.

252   _____. TYPOLOGY AND EARLY AMERICAN LITERATURE. Amherst:
University of Massachusetts Press, 1972. 340 p. Bibliog.

A collection of scholarly essays on typology, a favorite interpretive device of Christian writers that has not received
much discussion in Puritan studies before Brumm (254). Background of typology reviewed and its place in the writings
of Bradford, Williams, Cotton Mather, Taylor, and Edwards
examined.

253   Bradstreet, Anne. THE WORKS OF ANNE BRADSTREET. Edited by
Jeannine Hensley. Foreword by Adrienne Rich. John Harvard Library.
Cambridge, Mass.: Belknap Press of Harvard University, 1967. 321 p.

A good, scholarly edition of the works of this Puritan poet
(1612-72).

254   Brumm, Ursula. AMERICAN THOUGHT AND RELIGIOUS TYPOLOGY.
       Translated by John Hoaglund. New Brunswick, N.J.: Rutgers Univer-
       sity Press, 1970. 267 p.

       Typology, from Cotton Mather to the work of Hawthorne and
       Melville, discussed in this pioneering work. First published
       in German in 1963.

255   Donnelly, Marian Card. THE NEW ENGLAND MEETING HOUSES OF
       THE SEVENTEENTH CENTURY. Middletown, Conn.: Wesleyan Uni-
       versity Press, 1968. 165 p.

       Scholarly study by an architectural historian who traces the
       style of meeting houses back to European sources.

256   Eames, Wilberforce. EARLY NEW ENGLAND CATECHISMS: A BIB-
       LIOGRAPHICAL ACCOUNT OF SOME CATECHISMS PUBLISHED BE-
       FORE THE YEAR 1800, FOR USE IN NEW ENGLAND. 1898. Reprint.
       Detroit: Singing Tree Press, 1969. 111 p.

       Actually an essay as much as a bibliography, covering a sig-
       nificant aspect of New England life.

257   Gay, Peter. A LOSS OF MASTERY: PURITAN HISTORIANS IN
       COLONIAL AMERICA. Berkeley and Los Angeles: University of Cali-
       fornia Press, 1966. 164 p.

       Three essays, originally lectures on William Bradford, Cotton
       Mather, and Jonathan Edwards, the first interesting, the last
       two less successful.

258   Murdock, Kenneth B. LITERATURE AND THEOLOGY IN COLONIAL
       NEW ENGLAND. Cambridge, Mass.: Harvard University Press, 1949.
       235 p.

       A brief account of the relationship between Puritan theology
       and Puritan literary theory and practice. Covers history,
       autobiography, and poetry.

259   Shea, Daniel B., Jr. SPIRITUAL AUTOBIOGRAPHY IN EARLY AMERI-
       CA. Princeton, N.J.: Princeton University Press, 1968. 280 p.

       Detailed study of twenty autobiographies written between
       1650 and 1800 by Quaker and Puritan clergy and laypersons.
       Emphasizes the character of the genre as formal and public.

260   White, Elizabeth W. ANNE BRADSTREET, "THE TENTH MUSE." New
       York: Oxford University Press, 1971. xvi, 410 p.

       Biography of Bradstreet (1612-72), which focuses on the
       gradual development of the poetic craftsman. Critical work
       on individual poems not entirely satisfactory.

261   Ziff, Larzer, ed. JOHN COTTON ON THE CHURCHES OF NEW
       ENGLAND. Reprint. John Harvard Library. Cambridge, Mass.:
       Belknap Press of Harvard University, 1968. 403 p.

           Reprints the text of three significant works by Cotton: "A
           Sermon Delivered at Salem" (1636), "The Keys of the King-
           dom of Heaven" (1644), and "The Way of the Congregational
           Churches Cleared" (1648). Useful introduction.

EDWARD TAYLOR

262   Taylor, Edward. EDWARD TAYLOR'S CHRISTOGRAPHIA. Edited by
       Norman S. Grabo. New Haven, Conn.: Yale University Press, 1962.
       507 p.

           A transcription of fourteen sermons preached between 1701
           and 1703 by the Westfield, Massachusetts, mystic and minis-
           ter (1642?-1729), whose work has recently been receiving a
           great deal of scholarly attention.

263   _____. EDWARD TAYLOR'S TREATISE CONCERNING THE LORD'S
       SUPPER. Edited by Norman S. Grabo. East Lansing: Michigan State
       University Press, 1966. lvi, 263 p.

           Republication of this treatise with a good introduction and
           scholarly apparatus.

264   _____. POEMS. Edited by Donald E. Stanford. New Haven, Conn.:
       Yale University Press, 1960. lxii, 543 p.

           The best edition of Taylor's poetry.

265   Grabo, Norman S. EDWARD TAYLOR. New York: Twayne Publishers,
       1962. 192 p.

           Critical study of life and work of one of America's first
           poets, whose verse had remained unpublished until 1939.
           Relates Taylor's work to British contemporaries.

266   Keller, Karl. THE EXAMPLE OF EDWARD TAYLOR. Amherst: Uni-
       versity of Massachusetts Press, 1975. xiv, 319 p.

           A scholarly analysis of Taylor's life and writings. A sketch
           of the minister and poet's life, with treatment of his second-
           ary works, in first half of book. Last half devoted to anal-
           ysis of PREPARATORY MEDITATIONS. Parallels between
           Taylor's poetry and primitive painting explored in chapter
           10.

267   Scheick, William J.   THE WILL AND THE WORDS: THE POETRY OF
       EDWARD TAYLOR.   Athens: University of Georgia Press, 1974.   xvi,
       181 p.

>   Scholarly analysis of the thought of Taylor attempts to pro-
>   vide the background underlying his theology, so the reader
>   will be able to better understand his poetry.

268   Stanford, Donald E.   "Edward Taylor's Metrical History of Christianity."
       AMERICAN LITERATURE 33 (1961):   279-95.

>   Includes quotations from manuscript poem in the Redwood
>   Library and Athenaeum of Newport, Rhode Island.

Chapter 5

THE FIRST GREAT AWAKENING

GENERAL WORKS DEVOTED TO THE EIGHTEENTH CENTURY

269   Bumsted, J[ohn]. M., and Van de Wetering, John E. WHAT MUST I DO TO
BE SAVED? THE GREAT AWAKENING IN COLONIAL AMERICA.
Berkshire Studies in History. Hinsdale, Ill.: Dryden Press, 1976. 184 p.

> A very useful, brief introduction to the religious revival of
> the eighteenth century. More heavily weighted toward so-
> cial history in contrast to Gaustad (290), where emphasis
> upon the theology of Jonathan Edwards and Charles Chauncy.

270   Bushman, Richard L. FROM PURITAN TO YANKEE: CHARACTER
AND THE SOCIAL ORDER IN CONNECTICUT, 1690-1765. Cambridge,
Mass.: Harvard University Press, 1967. 343 p.

> Ground-breaking study of great value, emphasizing the struc-
> ture of the social order and including significant sections on
> religion.

271   Davidson, James West. THE LOGIC OF MILLENNIAL THOUGHT:
EIGHTEENTH CENTURY NEW ENGLAND. New Haven, Conn.: Yale
University Press, 1977. xii, 308 p.

> Thorough but rambling discussion of the book of Revelation
> and the idea of the millennium in eighteenth-century New
> England thought.

272   Heimert, Alan E. RELIGION AND THE AMERICAN MIND FROM THE
GREAT AWAKENING TO THE REVOLUTION. Cambridge, Mass.:
Harvard University Press, 1966. 668 p.

> An important, influential, and much controverted study that
> attempts to trace a direct line of influence from the left
> wing of the First Great Awakening (the evangelical and
> dissenting Calvinists epitomized by Jonathan Edwards) to the
> American Revolution. In the process, develops a critique of
> the other wing--the liberals--and argues for their lesser

significance in the coming of the war. The best discussion of the issues raised by this book found in C.C. Goen, "The Intellectual History of 18th Century America as Rewritten by Alan Heimert," JOURNAL OF THE LIBERAL MINISTRY 9 (1969): 24-31.

273   McLoughlin, William G. NEW ENGLAND DISSENT, 1630-1833: THE BAPTISTS AND THE SEPARATION OF CHURCH AND STATE. 2 vols. Cambridge, Mass.: Harvard University Press, 1971. 1,324 p.

Monumental and magisterial work. Useful both as denominational history of the Baptists and eighteenth-century Separatists and as a study of the coming of religious liberty. See also long review article by William R. Estep, CHURCH HISTORY 41 (1972): 246-52.

274   May, Henry F. THE ENLIGHTENMENT IN AMERICA. New York: Oxford University Press, 1976. xix, 419 p.

An important book. A general history of the Enlightenment in America that deals very substantially with religion. Deals with the Enlightenment "with Protestantism always in the background as matrix, rival, ally, and enemy. It is not about the Enlightenment and religion, but rather about the Enlightenment as religion."

275   Meyer, Donald H. DEMOCRATIC ENLIGHTENMENT. New York: G.P. Putnam's Sons, 1976. 257 p.

A useful primer on the Enlightenment designed for undergraduate classes. Has a good deal to say about religion and comments extensively on Jonathan Edwards, Benjamin Franklin, John Witherspoon, and William Ellery Channing.

276   Smith, Timothy L. "Congregation, State, and Denomination: The Forming of the American Religious Structure." WILLIAM AND MARY QUARTERLY 25 (1968): 155-76.

Raises the question of whether the congregation instead of the denomination or the state ought not be the focus of study in religious history.

277   Tracy, Joseph. THE GREAT AWAKENING: A HISTORY OF THE REVIVAL OF RELIGION IN THE TIME OF EDWARDS AND WHITEFIELD. Boston: Tappan and Dennet, 1842. Reprint. New York: Arno Press, 1969. 433 p.

The oldest and still the first book cited in later studies of the Awakening. Reprints a great deal of primary source material.

ANTHOLOGIES DEVOTED TO THE FIRST GREAT AWAKENING

278   Bumsted, John M., ed. THE GREAT AWAKENING: THE BEGINNING OF EVANGELICAL PIETISM IN AMERICA. Waltham, Mass.: Ginn-Blaisdell Publishing Co., 1970. 192 p.

    A source book emphasizing the role of pietism. Contains selections from Canadian sources and from Middle Colony Moravians and Brethren as well as the more common sources from New England.

279   Bushman, Richard L., ed. THE GREAT AWAKENING: DOCUMENTS ON THE REVIVAL OF RELIGION, 1740-1745. New York: Atheneum, published for the Institute of Early American History and Culture, 1970. 174 p.

    A source book that concentrates heavily on religious life in New England and the phenomenon of conversion.

280   Lovejoy, David S., ed. RELIGIOUS ENTHUSIASM AND THE GREAT AWAKENING. Englewood Cliffs, N.J.: Prentice-Hall, 1969. 115 p.

    A source book that focuses particularly on the problem of "enthusiasm." Suitable for advanced undergraduates.

281   Miller, Perry, and Heimert, Alan, eds. THE GREAT AWAKENING: DOCUMENTS ILLUSTRATING THE CRISIS AND ITS CONSEQUENCES. Indianapolis: Bobbs-Merrill, 1967. 663 p.

    A source book which closely follows the structure of Heimert (272), containing an introduction of nearly fifty pages which usefully summarizes his views. Difficult-going for undergraduates.

282   Nissenbaum, Stephen, ed. THE GREAT AWAKENING AT YALE COLLEGE. Belmont, Calif.: Wadsworth Publishing Co., 1972. 263 p.

    A collection of primary source materials designed for undergraduates.

283   Rutman, Darrett B., ed. THE GREAT AWAKENING: EVENT AND EXEGESIS. New York: John Wiley and Sons, 1970. 200 p.

    Nine interpretive essays plus a collection of source materials. Suitable for beginning students.

GEORGE WHITEFIELD

284   Belden, Albert D. GEORGE WHITEFIELD: THE GREAT AWAKENER: A MODERN STUDY OF THE EVANGELICAL REVIVAL. Rev. ed. New York: Macmillan Co., 1953. 302 p.

A sympathetic biography of the Anglican priest and Methodist preacher who became leader of the revival in the North American colonies. First published in 1930.

285   Henry, Stuart C. GEORGE WHITEFIELD: WAYFARING WITNESS. New York: Abingdon Press, 1957. 224 p.

First part a biographical sketch and second, "The Message and How It was Received." A well written and researched study.

286   Kenney, William H. III. "Alexander Garden and George Whitefield: The Significance of Revivalism in South Carolina, 1738-1741." SOUTH CAROLINA HISTORICAL MAGAZINE 71 (1970): 1-16.

Narrates details of the controversy between Whitefield and Anglican commissary Garden.

287   _____. "George Whitefield, Dissenter Priest of the Great Awakening, 1739-41." WILLIAM AND MARY QUARTERLY 26 (1969): 75-93.

Recounts how Whitefield, although an Anglican, attacked the Church of England's latitudinarianism, was in turn rebuffed by fellow Anglicans, and won his greatest following among principally dissenting congregations.

288   Stein, Stephen J. "George Whitefield on Slavery: Some New Evidence." CHURCH HISTORY 42 (1973): 243-56.

Discusses Whitefield's ambiguity regarding slavery, especially arguing a case for attributing to him the authorship of an anonymous theological defense of slavery published in 1743.

THE FIRST GREAT AWAKENING IN NEW ENGLAND

289   Cowing, Cedric B. "Sex and Preaching in the Great Awakening." AMERICAN QUARTERLY 20 (1968): 624-44.

Argues that the Awakening changed the sex ratio within the churches, bringing many more adult males into fellowship than had been true in earlier decades. Discounts the view of Charles Francis Adams and others that the revival appealed to the psychologically weak portion of the community or that it encouraged more sexual promiscuity. Based upon considerable demographic data.

290   Gaustad, Edwin Scott. THE GREAT AWAKENING IN NEW ENGLAND. New York: Harper and Row, 1957. 173 p.

Probably the best first book on the Great Awakening for the beginning student. A concise narrative giving special attention to the theology of Jonathan Edwards and Charles Chauncy.

291   Goodwin, Gerald J. "The Myth of 'Arminian-Calvinism' in Eighteenth Century New England." NEW ENGLAND QUARTERLY 41 (1968): 213-37.

   Argues that the gradual Arminianizing of Puritan theology after 1700 is a myth and that New England ministers recognized and opposed Arminianism.

292   Greven, Philip J., Jr. "Youth, Maturity, and Religious Conversion: A Note on the Ages of Conversion in Andover, Massachusetts, 1711-1749." ESSEX INSTITUTE HISTORICAL COLLECTIONS 108 (1972): 119-34.

   A historical study suggesting that the age of religious conversion is directly correlated to the age of maturity, and that a study of conversion ages may be a key to understanding the developmental cycles of individuals.

293   Sklar, Robert. "The Great Awakening and Colonial Politics: Connecticut's Revolution in the Minds of Men." CONNECTICUT HISTORICAL SOCIETY BULLETIN 28 (1963): 81-95.

   Discusses the events of the 1740s, showing how they undermined the stability of the colony's government and led to revolutionary actions. A divergent view in Walsh (295).

294   Van de Wetering, John E. "The 'Christian History' of the Great Awakening." JOURNAL OF PRESBYTERIAN HISTORY 44 (1966): 122-29.

   Analysis of Thomas Prince, Jr.'s "Christian History" (Boston, 1744-45), a basic source of information about the events of the Great Awakening.

295   Walsh, James. "The Great Awakening in the First Congregational Church of Woodbury, Connecticut." WILLIAM AND MARY QUARTERLY 28 (1971): 543-62.

   In contrast to many other studies, demonstrates that the revival could pass through a community without causing strife or disruption.

296   Warch, Richard. SCHOOL OF PROPHETS, YALE COLLEGE, 1701-1740. New Haven, Conn.: Yale University Press, 1973. xii, 339 p.

   An excellent scholarly treatment of intellectual, social, and religious dimensions of Yale.

297   White, Eugene E. PURITAN RHETORIC: THE ISSUE OF EMOTION IN
       RELIGION. Carbondale: Southern Illinois University Press, 1972.
       229 p.

       Begins with concise and provocative survey of Puritan preach-
       ing, tracing the tension between reason and emotion from the
       early seventeenth century through the First Great Awakening.
       Text of five sermons by Jonathan Edwards, Charles Chauncy,
       and John Gay in second part. Structural analysis of Puritan
       rhetoric provided in part three.

298   Youngs, J. William T., Jr. GOD'S MESSENGERS: RELIGIOUS LEADER-
       SHIP IN COLONIAL NEW ENGLAND, 1700-1750. Baltimore, Md.:
       Johns Hopkins Press, 1976. 176 p.

       This Brewer prize essay an example of the new social history.
       Discusses problems of the ministerial profession and questions
       whether the clergy's status did not undermine traditional Cal-
       vinism.

JONATHAN EDWARDS

Works

Edwards (1703-1758) has become the focus of enormous scholarly interest. A
new edition of his works, five volumes of which have now appeared (299-303),
has been in progress at Yale University for over a decade with no completion
date in sight. The publication of Edwards's "Miscellanies," edited by Thomas
A. Schafer, has been eagerly and anxiously awaited for several years and is
expected to add further interest to this field. A number of volumes of Edwards's sermons is also in progress. Two editions of his works appeared in the
nineteenth century, neither of them complete but both of them still useful.
The ten-volume edition edited by Sereno E. Dwight (New York, 1829-30) included the first publication of much manuscript material, including the text
since known as "The Mind."

299   Edwards, Jonathan. FREEDOM OF THE WILL. Edited by Paul Ramsey.
       THE WORKS OF JONATHAN EDWARDS, vol. 1. New Haven, Conn.:
       Yale University Press, 1957. xii, 494 p.

       The text of what is usually considered Edwards's greatest
       work, written from 1753 to 1754 while he was serving as
       minister in the Stockbridge Indian mission. Good editorial
       introduction. A long review and general summary of Ed-
       wards's scholarship in William Morris, "The Reappraisal of
       Edwards," NEW ENGLAND QUARTERLY 30 (1957): 515-25.

300 _____. RELIGIOUS AFFECTIONS. Edited by John E. Smith. THE WORKS OF JONATHAN EDWARDS, vol. 2. New Haven, Conn.: Yale University Press, 1959. 526 p.

> The treatise published in this volume first issued in 1746. Fills a place between Edwards's first account of the revivals in 1735, entitled A FAITHFUL NARRATIVE, THOUGHTS CONCERNING THE REVIVAL (1742), and his most profound work, FREEDOM OF THE WILL (1754). Struggles to defend the role of emotion in religion by giving a series of twelve signs by which true religious affections can be distinguished from false. Good editor's introduction.

301 _____. ORIGINAL SIN. Edited by Clyde A. Holbrook. THE WORKS OF JONATHAN EDWARDS, vol. 3. New Haven, Conn.: Yale University Press, 1970. 448 p.

> Republication of Edwards's 1758 text, defending the doctrine of original sin. Good introduction.

302 _____. THE GREAT AWAKENING. Edited by Clarence C. Goen. THE WORKS OF JONATHAN EDWARDS, vol. 4. New Haven, Conn.: Yale University Press, 1972. 595 p.

> Contains the texts of "A Faithful Narrative," "The Distinguishing Marks," "Some Thoughts Concerning the Revival," "Letters Relating to the Revival," and also the preface to Bellamy's TRUE RELIGION, the earliest of Edwards's descriptions and defenses of the emotionalism expressed during the Great Awakening. Good editor's introduction.

303 _____. APOCALYPTIC WRITINGS. Edited by Stephen J. Stein. THE WORKS OF JONATHAN EDWARDS, vol. 5. New Haven, Conn.: Yale University Press, 1977.

> The first published text of Edwards's private commentary on the book of Revelation.

304 _____. IMAGES OR SHADOWS OF DIVINE THINGS. Edited by Perry Miller. New Haven, Conn.: Yale University Press, 1948. 151 p.

> A typically thorough Miller introduction of 41 pages precedes the text of this notebook of 212 entries intended for a fuller work which Edwards never completed.

305 _____. "THE MIND" OF JONATHAN EDWARDS, A RECONSTRUCTED TEXT. Edited by Leon Howard. Berkeley and Los Angeles: University of California Press, 1963. xii, 151 p.

> Argument by editor that text of this unfinished manuscript needs to be reordered if Edwards's thought is to be compre-

hended. Effort by Howard to accomplish this reordering has not been judged successful by everyone.

306 _____. THE PHILOSOPHY OF JONATHAN EDWARDS FROM HIS PRIVATE NOTEBOOKS. Edited by Harvey G. Townsend. Eugene: University of Oregon, 1955. xxii, 270 p.

This partial transcription the only printed version available until the Yale edition of Edwards's "Miscellanies" appears.

307 _____. REPRESENTATIVE SELECTIONS. Edited by Clarence H. Faust and Thomas H. Johnson. Rev. ed. New York: Hill & Wang, 1962. cxlii, 434 p.

A standard, popular collection of excerpts from Edwards's works. Contains a good deal of material from his psychological writings.

Secondary Works

See also the essays on Edwards in Miller (176).

308 Aldridge, Alfred O. JONATHAN EDWARDS. Great American Thinkers Series. New York: Washington Square Press, 1964. 181 p.

A short sketch of Edwards's life followed by brief analysis of each of his major works.

309 Bushman, Richard L. "Jonathan Edwards and the Puritan Consciousness." JOURNAL FOR THE SCIENTIFIC STUDY OF RELIGION 5 (1966): 383-96.

Using the life of Edwards, attempts to construct a picture of the piety of the eighteenth century. Reprinted in Vaughan and Bremer (171).

310 _____. "Jonathan Edwards as a Great Man: Identity, Conversion and Leadership in the Great Awakening." SOUNDINGS 52 (1969): 15-46.

An attempt to apply Erik Erikson's development model to "young man Edwards." An interesting perspective on the childhood and development of Edwards.

311 Carse, James. JONATHAN EDWARDS AND THE VISIBILITY OF GOD. New York: Charles Scribner's Sons, 1967. 191 p.

Not so much a contribution to Edwards's scholarship as an attempt to use Edwards's ministry as springboard for a general essay on the American past.

312   Cherry, Conrad. THE THEOLOGY OF JONATHAN EDWARDS: A RE-
       APPRAISAL. Garden City, N.Y.: Doubleday and Co., 1966. 270 p.

       Concentrates on Edwards's doctrine of faith, stating that this
       is the key to understanding him as a Calvinist theologian.
       Argues that if the twentieth century is to understand him at
       all, it must make the effort to understand his Calvinism.

313   Davidson, Edward H. JONATHAN EDWARDS: THE NARRATIVE OF
       A PURITAN MIND. Riverside Studies in Literature. Boston: Houghton
       Mifflin Co., 1966. xii, 161 p.

       A good biographical essay that integrates treatments of Ed-
       wards's life and thought, relating his Puritan convictions to
       his understanding of the new empiricism of John Locke.

314   Delattre, Roland Andre. BEAUTY AND SENSIBILITY IN THE THOUGHT
       OF JONATHAN EDWARDS: AN ESSAY IN AESTHETICS AND THEO-
       LOGICAL ETHICS. New Haven, Conn.: Yale University Press, 1968.
       238 p.

       An exhaustive analysis of the place of beauty in Edwards's
       system. An especially penetrating work and one of the
       best books on Edwards.

315   Elwood, Douglas J. THE PHILOSOPHICAL THEOLOGY OF JONA-
       THAN EDWARDS. New York: Columbia University Press, 1960. xii,
       220 p.

       An analysis of Edwards's thought that seeks to show how his
       philosophy and theology are linked by the concept of the
       "immediacy" of man's knowledge of God.

316   Helm, Paul. "John Locke and Jonathan Edwards: A Reconsideration."
       JOURNAL OF THE HISTORY OF PHILOSOPHY 7 (1969): 51-61.

       States that the undoubted influence of Locke on Edwards
       needs to be qualified. Should not classify Edwards as an
       empiricist and so exaggerate Locke's influence as to say
       that Edwards's philosophy was Locke-inspired.

317   Holbrook, Clyde A. THE ETHICS OF JONATHAN EDWARDS: MORAL-
       ITY AND AESTHETICS. Ann Arbor: University of Michigan Press,
       1973. 227 p.

       Considered by scholars as a standard authority on this as-
       pect of Edwards's theology since 1944, when first produced
       as a doctoral dissertation. Appeared as a book in 1973,
       revised, and brought up to date in bibliographical references.
       Does not entirely agree with Delattre (314).

318 _____. "Jonathan Edwards and His Detractors." THEOLOGY TODAY 10 (1963): 384-96.

> A most useful summary of the history of Edwardsean scholarship, concentrating upon those who have not found him congenial.

319 Miller, Perry. JONATHAN EDWARDS. New York: William Sloan Associates, 1949. 348 p.

> Probably the least successful and certainly the most difficult work by Miller. Nevertheless, repays the effort of diligent reading. Unsuccessfully attempts to sandwich chapters of biographical narration between passages of analysis of Edwards's thought. Book described by Conrad Cherry (312) as a "brilliant portrayal of Edwards as an American precursor of modern epistemology and physical theory." Still, complains that Miller ignored Edwards's foremost role as a theologian. Related article by Vincent Tomas, "The Modernity of Jonathan Edwards." NEW ENGLAND QUARTERLY 25 (1952): 60-84.

320 Murphy, Arthur E. "Jonathan Edwards on Free Will and Moral Agency." PHILOSOPHICAL REVIEW 48 (1959): 181-202.

> Essay, provoked by the republication of Edwards's FREEDOM OF THE WILL (299), takes issue with editor Paul Ramsey's interpretation of Edwards.

321 Pierce, David C. "Jonathan Edwards and the 'New Sense of Glory.'" NEW ENGLAND QUARTERLY 41 (1968): 82-95.

> Finds a double vision in Edwards's descriptions of his religious experience: a set of contrasting pieties, one of which suggests the Puritan tradition, the other a newer almost romantic rapprochement between God and nature.

322 Schafer, Thomas A. "Jonathan Edwards and Justification by Faith." CHURCH HISTORY 20 (1951): 55-67.

> Argues that Edwards went beyond the doctrine of justification, which had been inherited from the Reformation, to explore the acts and relations that underlie it. Thereby, pushed American theology during the next century to concentrate on questions of original sin, freedom of the will, and the relation of natural to supernatural conversion.

323 _____. "Jonathan Edwards' Conception of the Church." CHURCH HISTORY 24 (1955): 51-66.

> Argues that Edwards's refusal to separate "the visible and invisible churches, his preference for a polity more repre-

sentative of the larger Church, and the emphasis which he
places upon the Church's 'means of grace'" all contrast with
his reputation as a fiery evangelist and predestinarian.

324   Scheick, William J. THE WRITINGS OF JONATHAN EDWARDS:
THEME, MOTIF, AND STYLE. College Station: Texas A & M University Press, 1975. xiv, 162 p.

Focuses on Edwards's rhetoric rather than his theology, seeking to explain Edwards's thought through literary analysis of
his sermons and tracts. Like many contemporary scholars,
attempts to correct Perry Miller's too exclusive emphasis on
Edwards's Lockean empiricism. Recognizes that Edwards ex-
perimented with sermon form, but emphasizes the autobiographical dimension of even Edwards's public writings.

325   Simonson, Harold P. JONATHAN EDWARDS: THEOLOGIAN OF THE
HEART. Grand Rapids, Mich.: William B. Eerdmans Publishing Co.,
1974. 174 p.

A critique of Miller's discussion of Edwards's epistemology
(319). Attempt to demonstrate that what the author calls
"an epistemology of religious conversion" forms a more
adequate basis for understanding Edwards.

326   Winslow, Ola E. JONATHAN EDWARDS, 1703-1758; A BIOGRAPHY.
New York: Macmillan Co., 1940. 406 p.

Probably the best narrative of the events of Edwards's life.
Shown as a prodigious metaphysical athlete and as a sorely-
tried saint rather than as a cardinal mind of his age. Attempts to humanize the figure of Edwards.

THE NEW ENGLAND THEOLOGY

327   Berk, Stephen E. CALVINISM VERSUS DEMOCRACY: TIMOTHY
DWIGHT AND THE ORIGINS OF AMERICAN EVANGELICAL ORTHO-
DOXY. Hamden, Conn.: Archon Press, 1974. xii, 252 p.

Argues that the Edwardsean tradition was divided between a
Hopkinsian half, which was heavily doctrinal and rigidly
traditional, and a Dwightean other half, which was more
practical and experience-oriented. Suggestive but weak.

328   Cecil, Anthony C., Jr. THE THEOLOGICAL DEVELOPMENT OF ED-
WARDS AMASA PARK: LAST OF THE "CONSISTENT CALVINISTS."
Missoula, Mont.: American Academy of Religion and Scholars Press,
1974. 342 p.

Intellectual biography of the mid-nineteenth century theologian at Andover Seminary and the last in a long line of
teachers of the New England theology.

329   Cunningham, Charles E.   TIMOTHY DWIGHT, 1752-1817; A BIOGRA-
PHY.   New York: Macmillan Co., 1942.   403 p.

A good life story of this theologian and president of Yale,
who has long been famous for stemming the tide of French
Revolution-inspired radicalism in that college and replacing
it with evangelical piety.

330   Ferm, Robert L.   JONATHAN EDWARDS THE YOUNGER, 1745-1801.
Grand Rapids, Mich.: William B. Eerdmans Publishing Co., 1976.
214 p.

Carefully researched biography of the son of the great North-
ampton theologian.   Examines the party structure of the
New England churches.

331   Foster, Frank H.   A GENETIC HISTORY OF THE NEW ENGLAND
THEOLOGY.   Chicago: University of Chicago Press, 1907.   xv,
568 p.

Although very old, remains indispensable for its treatment
of the post-Edwardsean theological development in New
England.   Actually begins in the seventeenth century with
description of Edwards's work, but here, as in his work on
Unitarianism, has been superseded by more recent scholarship.   Still helpful for his treatment of Bellamy, Hopkins,
and Edwards the Younger, along with nineteenth-century
figures like Edwards A. Park.

332   Haroutunian, Joseph.   PIETY VERSUS MORALISM: THE PASSING OF
THE NEW ENGLAND THEOLOGY.   New York: Henry Holt and Co.,
1932.   Reprinted with an introduction by Sydney E. Ahlstrom.   New
York: Harper and Row, 1970.   xxv, 329 p.

Written during the first impact of the 1930s' reassessment of
liberalism and renewed appreciation of the tragic sense of
life.   Covers much the same ground as Foster (331), but with
a more sympathetic feeling for the eighteenth-century Calvinist theologians.   A nice appreciation of author provided
by Ahlstrom in the introduction to the 1970 edition.

333   Mead, Sidney E.   NATHANIEL WILLIAM TAYLOR, 1786-1858: A
CONNECTICUT LIBERAL.   Chicago: University of Chicago Press,
1942.   259 p.

First book by author a revision of his dissertation completed under W.W. Sweet. Not really a biography of Taylor, but is a well-written analysis of the New Haven theological scene during the early nineteenth century with chapters devoted to Timothy Dwight and Lyman Beecher as well as Taylor.

334   Morse, James K. JEDIDIAH MORSE, A CHAMPION OF NEW ENGLAND ORTHODOXY. New York: Columbia University Press, 1939. 179 p.

Sympathetic biography of the violent controversialist Jedidiah Morse, who battled the illuminati, the Unitarians, and anyone who seemed to flag in support of orthodoxy.

335   Silverman, Kenneth. TIMOTHY DWIGHT. New York: Twayne Publishers, 1969. 174 p.

A useful biography.

336   Smith, Hilrie Shelton. CHANGING CONCEPTIONS OF ORIGINAL SIN: A STUDY OF AMERICAN THEOLOGY SINCE 1750. New York: Charles Scribner's Sons, 1955. 242 p.

A concise and lucid study of the decline and revival of this central doctrine among American Protestants, focusing on eighteenth-century liberals, the "New Haven theology" of Nathaniel William Taylor, Horace Bushnell, progressive orthodoxy, and neo-orthodoxy.

PHILOSOPHY IN THE COLONIAL PERIOD

337   Bryson, Gladys. MAN AND SOCIETY; THE SCOTTISH INQUIRY OF THE 18TH CENTURY. Princeton, N.J.: Princeton University Press, 1945. 287 p.

A general treatment of Scottish philosophy, with chapters devoted to man's place in nature, man's past, human nature, society, and institutions.

338   Buranelli, Vincent. "Colonial Philosophy." WILLIAM AND MARY QUARTERLY 16 (1959): 343-62.

Comprehensive summary of writings in the field beginning with a thorough and stimulating discussion of Woodbridge Riley (340).

339   Newlin, Claude M. PHILOSOPHY AND RELIGION IN COLONIAL AMERICA. New York: Philosophical Library, 1962. 212 p.

Actually limited to eighteenth-century New England, contains a very general account of the philosophy of Jonathan Edwards and Samuel Johnson as well as of a few less well-known figures.

340   Riley, I. Woodbridge. AMERICAN PHILOSOPHY: THE EARLY SCHOOLS. New York: Dodd, Mead, and Co., 1907. 595 p.

A general survey of American philosophy in the colonial era and early years of the nineteenth century, describing Puritanism, idealism, deism, materialism, and realism.

341   Schneider, Louis, ed. THE SCOTTISH MORALISTS ON HUMAN NATURE AND SOCIETY. Chicago: University of Chicago Press, 1967. lxxviii, 290 p.

A collection of extracts arranged topically from the writings of philosophers such as Hume, Hutcheson, Stewart, Smith, Ferguson, and Reid. Includes introduction and bibliographical note.

342   Sloan, Douglas. THE SCOTTISH ENLIGHTENMENT AND THE AMERICAN COLLEGE IDEAL. New York: Teachers College Press of Columbia University, 1971. 298 p.

A collection of seven loosely-connected essays useful in their treatment of the Scottish Common Sense philosophy and its connection to Presbyterian education.

SAMUEL JOHNSON

Johnson (1696-1772), a Congregational minister, converted to Anglicanism in 1722 and became a leading advocate of the newer rationalism in theology. Also a friend of the British philosopher, Berkeley, he helped to popularize his work in America. Johnson ended his career in New York as president of King's College, later to become Columbia University.

343   Ellis, Joseph J. THE NEW ENGLAND MIND IN TRANSITION: SAMUEL JOHNSON OF CONNECTICUT, 1696-1772. New Haven, Conn.: Yale University Press, 1973. 292 p.

An excellent biography with attention given to Johnson's work as a philosopher.

344   Fiering, Norman S. "President Samuel Johnson and the Circle of Knowledge." WILLIAM AND MARY QUARTERLY 28 (1971): 199-236.

Traces the shift of moral philosophy to a dominant place in Johnson's thought.

345 Johnson, Samuel. SAMUEL JOHNSON, HIS CAREER AND WRITINGS.
Edited by Herbert W. Schneider and Carol Schneider. 4 vols. New
York: Columbia University Press, 1929.

> The standard edition of his works. Contents in volume 1,
> Johnson's autobiography and some correspondence; volume 2,
> his philosophical writings; volume 3, papers relating to his
> clerical career; and volume 4, papers related to King's Col-
> lege.

THE ANGLICAN CHURCH

General Works

346 Albright, Raymond W. A HISTORY OF THE PROTESTANT EPISCOPAL
CHURCH. New York: Macmillan Co., 1964. 406 p. Bibliog.

> A scholarly, well-written but not very critical narrative his-
> tory of the denomination.

347 Bridenbaugh, Carl. MITRE AND SCEPTRE: TRANSATLANTIC FAITHS,
IDEAS, PERSONALITIES AND POLITICS, 1689-1775. New York: Oxford University Press, 1962. 354 p.

> A history of the Anglican attempt to secure an Episcopal
> establishment in the colonies, particularly during the 1760s
> under the leadership of Archbishop Thomas Secker. Re-
> constructs a clear picture of the personalities involved,
> traces the transatlantic connections of both Anglicans and
> dissenters, and works out the dynamics of the controversy
> and its relationship to the American Revolution. An ex-
> tended critique of this argument offered by William M.
> Hogue, "The Religious Conspiracy Theory of the American
> Revolution," CHURCH HISTORY 45 (1976): 277-92.

348 Calam, John. PARSONS AND PEDAGOGUES: THE S.P.G. ADVEN-
TURE IN AMERICAN EDUCATION. New York: Columbia University
Press, 1971. 249 p.

> Founded in 1701, the Society for the Propagation of the
> Gospel in Foreign Parts (S.P.G.), the Anglican missionary
> society active in providing clergy and schools for the col-
> onies of the British Empire. This study relatively better in
> its treatment of the schools than of the S.P.G. itself.

349 Goodwin, Gerald J. "The Anglican Reaction to the Great Awakening."
HISTORICAL MAGAZINE OF THE PROTESTANT EPISCOPAL CHURCH
35 (1966): 343-71.

Finds the sources of Anglican antagonism to be the Great
Awakening in revivalism, the conflict with dissenters, and
the role of George Whitefield.

350   Manross, William W. A HISTORY OF THE AMERICAN EPISCOPAL
CHURCH. 3d ed., rev. New York: Morehouse-Gorham, 1959.
420 p.

A standard history of the denomination first published in
1935. Brought up to the 1950s in this edition.

New England

351   Steiner, Bruce E. "Anglican Officeholding in Pre-Revolutionary Connecticut: The Parameters of New England Community." WILLIAM AND
MARY QUARTERLY 31 (1974): 369-406.

Demonstrates that Anglican officeholding in the late eighteenth
century was higher than might be supposed. Can be ac-
counted for on the grounds that ties of kinship and neighbor-
hood proved stronger than theological antagonism.

352   _____. "New England Anglicanism: A Genteel Faith?"
WILLIAM AND MARY QUARTERLY 27 (1970): 122-35.

Argues that Anglicanism was in good part a lower class
movement.

353   _____. SAMUEL SEABURY, 1729-1796: A STUDY IN THE HIGH
CHURCH TRADITION. Athens: Ohio University Press, 1972. 508 p.

Valuable for its clear exposition of the High Church tradition
in the eighteenth century.

354   Tucker, Louis L. "The Church of England and Religious Liberty at
Pre-Revolutionary Yale." WILLIAM AND MARY QUARTERLY 17
(1960): 314-28.

Explores the policy of President Thomas Clap, who for a
short time during 1753-54 attempted to force Anglicans to
attend Congregational services.

The Middle Colonies

355   Burr, Nelson R. THE ANGLICAN CHURCH IN NEW JERSEY. Philadelphia: Church Historical Society, 1954. xvi, 768 p.

A good history, demonstrating that the church could function
without being established.

356   Klingberg, Frank J. ANGLICAN HUMANITARIANISM IN COLONIAL
        NEW YORK. Philadelphia: Church Historical Society, 1940. 295 p.
        Bibliog.

> A series of essays, some published previously, concerned
> with the Society for the Propagation of the Gospel (S.P.G.)
> and its relationship with Indians and slaves. Includes the
> text of three S.P.G. sermons from William Fleetwood,
> Thomas Secker, and William Warburton.

357   Rightmeyer, Nelson W. THE ANGLICAN CHURCH IN DELAWARE.
        Philadelphia: Church Historical Society, 1947. 217 p.

> Topical treatment of the church covering parish life, educa-
> tion, missions to Negroes, and effects of the transition from
> colonial to republican government.

358   _____. MARYLAND'S ESTABLISHED CHURCH. Baltimore: Church
        Historical Society for the Diocese of Maryland, 1956. 239 p.

> History of the church through the colonial period, aimed at
> disproving the assertion that the clergy there were disrepu-
> table.

The Southern Colonies

359   Crane, Verner W. "Dr. Thomas Bray and the Charitable Colony Pro-
        ject, 1730." WILLIAM AND MARY QUARTERLY 19 (1962): 49-63.

> Explores the degree of Bray's involvement in the founding of
> Georgia.

360   Ervin, Spencer. "The Anglican Church in North Carolina, 1663-1823."
        HISTORICAL MAGAZINE OF THE PROTESTANT EPISCOPAL CHURCH
        25 (1956): 102-61.

> A description of the difficult history of the Anglican Church
> in North Carolina, where a diverse population frustrated its
> establishment.

361   Isaac, Rhys. "Religion and Authority: Problems of the Anglican Estab-
        lishment in Virginia in the Era of the Great Awakening and the Parsons'
        Cause." WILLIAM AND MARY QUARTERLY 30 (1973): 3-36.

> Detailed treatment of religious turmoil by a skilled historian
> who is doing pioneering work in southern colonial social
> history.

362   Middleton, Arthur P. "The Colonial Virginia Parson." WILLIAM AND
        MARY QUARTERLY 26 (1969): 425-40.

Maintains that most colonial Anglicans were fairly well off, offering sketches of two ministers (Jonathan Boucher and Devereux Jarratt) as evidence.

363   Rouse, Park, Jr. JAMES BLAIR OF VIRGINIA. Chapel Hill: University of North Carolina Press, 1971. 336 p.

A clear, well-documented, but narrowly-conceived life of the eighteenth-century Anglican commissary and founder of the College of William and Mary.

364   Seiler, William H. "The Anglican Parish Vestry in Colonial Virginia." JOURNAL OF SOUTHERN HISTORY 22 (1956): 310-37.

Examines the duties of the parish clergy who, in the absence of bishops, were forced to develop their own forms of local government.

365   Thompson, Henry P. THOMAS BRAY. London: Society for Promoting Christian Knowledge, 1954. 119 p.

Life of Bray (1656-1730), who served for a short time as commissary in Maryland and was instrumental in helping to found the Society for Promoting Christian Knowledge and the Society for the Propagation of the Gospel.

EIGHTEENTH-CENTURY SEPARATISM

See also McLoughlin (273).

366   Backus, Isaac. ISAAC BACKUS ON CHURCH, STATE, AND CALVINISM; PAMPHLETS, 1754-1789. Edited by William G. McLoughlin. John Harvard Library. Cambridge, Mass.: Belknap Press of Harvard University Press, 1968. 526 p.

A reprinting of twelve Backus pamphlets which are especially good in illustrating the kind of difficulties suffered by eighteenth-century Baptists in Massachusetts. A sixty-page introduction by McLoughlin.

367   Bumsted, J[ohn].M. "A Caution to Erring Christians: Ecclesiastical Disorder on Cape Cod, 1717-1738." WILLIAM AND MARY QUARTERLY 28 (1971): 413-38.

A case-study suggesting that revivalism of the First Great Awakening may have been given too much emphasis as a divisive force.

368   _____. "Revivalism and Separatism in New England: The First Society of Norwich, Connecticut, as a Case Study." WILLIAM AND
MARY QUARTERLY 24 (1967): 588-612.

Explains how the First Great Awakening affected the church
of the Reverend Benjamin Lord. The broader movement described by Goen (369) and McLoughlin (273) portrayed here
in microcosm.

369   Goen, Clarence C. REVIVALISM AND SEPARATISM IN NEW ENG-
LAND, 1740-1800: STRICT CONGREGATIONALISTS AND SEPARATE
BAPTISTS IN THE GREAT AWAKENING. New Haven, Conn.: Yale
University Press, 1962. 370 p.

Describes the growth and decline of about one hundred Separate congregations and traces the steps by which a large
proportion were assimilated into the Baptist denomination.
A useful, pioneering study.

370   McLoughlin, William G. ISAAC BACKUS AND THE AMERICAN PIETIST
TRADITION. Boston: Little, Brown, and Co., 1967. 252 p.

Although published before author's NEW ENGLAND DISSENT
(273), usefully summarizes many of the findings for eighteenth-
century Baptists which are discussed in more detail in his
larger work.

THE FIRST GREAT AWAKENING: MIDDLE AND
   SOUTHERN COLONIES

371   Gewehr, Wesley M. THE GREAT AWAKENING IN VIRGINIA, 1740-
1790. Durham, N.C.: Duke University Press, 1930. 292 p.

Treats the Virginia phase of the Great Awakening by denominations, devoting two chapters to the Presbyterians, and
one each to the Baptists and Methodists. Argues in remain-
der of the book that revivalism contributed to the rise of
democracy, improvement of education, and creation of a
social revolution.

372   Maxson, Charles H. THE GREAT AWAKENING IN THE MIDDLE COLO-
NIES. Chicago: University of Chicago Press, 1920. 158 p.

Narrative self-consciously intended to supplement work by
Tracy (277). Concentrates on 1740 as a crucial year in the
Great Awakening and describes the careers of Theodore J.
Frelinghuysen, William and Gilbert Tennent, and George
Whitefield.

Chapter 6

THE FORMATION OF THE DENOMINATIONAL PATTERN

BAPTISTS

Works related to Baptist history will also be found in sections devoted to Roger Williams (223-231), the Eighteenth Century and Separatism (273, 366, 370), the Denominational Pattern (728), the Ante-Bellum South (993, 998), Black Religion (1030), Southern Churches since the Civil War (1067, 1070, 1075), Denominations in the Gilded Age (1103, 1110), and Ecumenism (1317).

373   Baker, Robert A. THE SOUTHERN BAPTIST CONVENTION AND ITS PEOPLE, 1607-1972. Nashville: Broadman Press, 1974. 477 p.

A survey of the life of the convention and its constituency by a life-long historian of the denomination. Considerable attention paid to the statistics of denominational growth.

374   Baxter, Norman A. HISTORY OF THE FREEWILL BAPTISTS: A STUDY IN NEW ENGLAND SEPARATISM. Rochester, N.Y.: American Baptist Historical Society, 1957. 212 p.

Case study of sect's evolution into a denomination using both secondary and primary sources. Originally a doctoral dissertation.

375   Bordin, Ruth B. "The Sect to Denomination Process in America: The Freewill Baptist Experience." CHURCH HISTORY 34 (1965): 77-94.

An interesting, careful examination of the Freewill Baptists during the nineteenth century using the Troeltsch-Niebuhr thesis as the focus.

376   Isaac, Rhys. "Evangelical Revolt: The Nature of the Baptists' Challenge to the Traditional Order in Virginia, 1765-1775." WILLIAM AND MARY QUARTERLY 31 (1974): 345-68.

A beautifully-written and illuminating study of the manner

in which dancing, cockfighting and card playing
were utilized by the Virginia gentry to establish
their own social position. Relates how the lower
classes challenged this gentry by joining the evangelicals and rejecting the older social order.

377   Kendall, W. Fred. A HISTORY OF THE TENNESSEE BAPTIST CON-
VENTION. Brentwood: Tennessee Baptist Convention, 1974. 384 p.

A history of the Southern Baptists in Tennessee.

378   Lumkin, William L. BAPTIST FOUNDATION IN THE SOUTH: TRAC-
ING THROUGH THE SEPARATES THE INFLUENCE OF THE GREAT
AWAKENING, 1754-1787. Nashville: Boardman Press, 1961. 166 p.

A superficial treatment not based upon primary research and
depending upon explanations related to the frontier thesis
or the supposed democratic aspects of the Anabaptist tradition.

379   Maring, Norman H. BAPTISTS IN NEW JERSEY, A STUDY IN TRAN-
SITION. Valley Forge, Pa.: Judson Press, 1964. 379 p.

A narrative history covering the whole extent of the American Baptist experience in one state.

380   Morgan, David T., Jr. "The Great Awakening in North Carolina,
1740-1775: The Baptist Phase." NORTH CAROLINA HISTORICAL
REVIEW 45 (1968): 264-83.

Narrative of eighteenth-century Baptist history in North
Carolina. Attributes the origin of New Light Baptists there
to the influence of Whitefield.

381   Paschal, George W. A HISTORY OF NORTH CAROLINA BAPTISTS.
2 vols. Raleigh: General Board, North Carolina State Baptist Convention, 1930, 1955.

Detailed and thorough treatment devoted mainly to the colonial period.

382   Ryland, Garnett. THE BAPTISTS OF VIRGINIA, 1699-1926. Richmond:
Virginia Baptist Board of Missions and Education, 1955. 372 p.

A scholarly narrative history with notes, sources, and index.

383   Starr, Edward C., ed. A BAPTIST BIBLIOGRAPHY. 25 vols. Rochester, N.Y.: American Baptist Historical Society, 1947-76.

A monumental catalogue of materials. Unannotated, but
giving locations for the materials cited.

384   Torbet, Robert G. A HISTORY OF THE BAPTISTS. Rev. ed. Valley
      Forge, Pa.: Judson Press, 1973. 585 p.

      The standard introduction to Baptist history since its first
      publication in 1950.

385   Townsend, Leah. SOUTH CAROLINA BAPTISTS, 1670-1805. Florence,
      S.C.: Florence Printing Co., 1935. 391 p.

      A scholarly study of this group treating the state section by
      section.

386   Wood, James E., Jr., ed. BAPTISTS AND THE AMERICAN EXPERIENCE.
      Valley Forge, Pa.: Judson Press, 1976.

      Twenty Baptist scholars comment on such topics as the role
      of Baptists in forming the American tradition, religious lib-
      erty, human rights, and pluralism.

METHODISTS

387   Asbury, Francis. JOURNAL AND LETTERS. Edited by Elmer E. Clark,
      J.M. Potts, and J.S. Payton. 3 vols. Nashville: Abingdon Press,
      1958.

      More readable and informative a record of the life of this
      Methodist pioneer bishop than any of the dozen or so later
      biographic attempts. Contents in volume 1, Asbury's de-
      parture from England for America in 1771, and other events
      through 1793; volume 2, continuing the story up to his death
      in 1816; and volume 3, his letters.

388   Baker, Frank. FROM WESLEY TO ASBURY: STUDIES IN EARLY
      AMERICAN METHODISM. Durham, N.C.: Duke University Press,
      1976. xiv, 223 p.

      Eleven scholarly essays written earlier but not previously
      published, devoted to the eighteenth-century origins of
      American Methodism. Begins with John Wesley's own un-
      fortunate Georgia ministry up to the year 1784.

389   Baker, Gordon Pratt, ed. THOSE INCREDIBLE METHODISTS: A HIS-
      TORY OF THE BALTIMORE CONFERENCE OF THE UNITED METHOD-
      IST CHURCH. Baltimore, Md.: Commission on Archives and History
      of the Baltimore Conference, 1972. 597 p.

      An unusually good local history, cooperatively produced.
      Also contains chapter on the Washington Annual Conference
      for Black Methodists and another on women.

390   Barclay, Wade C. EARLY AMERICAN METHODISM, 1769-1844. New
        York: Board of Missions and Church Extension of the Methodist Church,
        1950. 449 p.

        A topical treatment of the growth of American Methodism.
        Extremely detailed but very useful to the serious student.

391   Bucke, Emory S., ed. THE HISTORY OF AMERICAN METHODISM.
        3 vols. New York: Abingdon Press, 1964.

        A vast collaborative history that serves better as a reference
        work than as a book to read straight through, since each
        volume contains about 700 pages. Individual chapters ex-
        cellent sources for information on such subjects as the
        formation of the Methodist Protestant Church, the African
        Methodist Episcopal Church, or Methodism and American
        Society, 1900-1939. Written in most cases by qualified
        scholars.

392   Cameron, Richard M. METHODISM AND SOCIETY IN HISTORICAL
        PERSPECTIVE. Edited by Board of Social and Economic Relations of
        the Methodist Church. New York: Abingdon Press, 1961. 394 p.

        The history of American Methodism to 1908, with emphasis
        upon such issues as slavery, temperance, and the Social
        Gospel.

393   Kilgore, Charles F. THE JAMES O'KELLY SCHISM IN THE METHOD-
        IST EPISCOPAL CHURCH. Mexico City: Casa Unida de Publicaciones,
        1963. 101 p.

        A competent study of the 1792-93 schism, which produced a
        small denomination very similar to the Disciples of Christ.

394   Luccock, Halford E.; Hutchinson, Paul; and Goodloe, Robert W. THE
        STORY OF METHODISM. 1926. Rev. ed. New York: Abingdon-
        Cokesbury Press, 1949. 528 p.

        An extraordinarily readable, popularly-styled denominational
        history.

395   Maser, Frederick E. THE DRAMATIC STORY OF EARLY AMERICAN
        METHODISM. New York: Abingdon Press, 1965. 109 p.

        Slim volume published to celebrate the bicentennial of the
        denomination in America. Covers events up to 1784 in
        straightforward narrative style.

396   Norwood, Frederick A. THE STORY OF AMERICAN METHODISM: A
        HISTORY OF THE UNITED METHODISTS AND THEIR RELATIONS.

Nashville: Abingdon Press, 1974. 448 p.

> The best one-volume introduction to American Methodism.
> A scholarly treatment, but not so interesting a narrative as
> that by Luccock (394).

397   Rudolph, L.C. FRANCIS ASBURY. Nashville: Abingdon Press, 1966.
       240 p.

> Provides a shortcut for those unwilling to read Asbury's
> JOURNALS (387). Done well enough but is, as must be
> all biographies of Asbury, only a synopsis of his words.

398   Sweet, William W. METHODISM IN AMERICAN HISTORY. 1933.
       2d ed. Nashville: Abingdon Press, 1954. 472 p.

> An introduction to Methodism by a famous American histo-
> rian. Does not cover the post-Civil War period adequately.

QUAKERS

General

399   Brinton, Howard H. FRIENDS FOR THREE HUNDRED YEARS: THE
       HISTORY AND BELIEFS OF THE SOCIETY OF FRIENDS SINCE GEORGE
       FOX STARTED THE QUAKER MOVEMENT. New York: Harper and
       Brothers, 1952. 239 p.

> An excellent intellectual history of the Quakers.

400   _____. QUAKER JOURNALS: VARIETIES OF RELIGIOUS EXPERI-
       ENCE AMONG FRIENDS. Wallingford, Pa.: Pendle Hill Publications,
       1972. 144 p.

> Based on a summary of 300 Quaker diaries written through-
> out American history. Provides a picture of the continuities
> of religious life within this denomination, with many lengthy
> quotations from the diaries adding to the value of the work.

401   Brock, Peter. PIONEERS OF THE PEACEABLE KINGDOM: THE
       QUAKER PEACE TESTIMONY FROM THE COLONIAL ERA TO THE
       FIRST WORLD WAR. Princeton, N.J.: Princeton University Press,
       1970. xvi, 382 p.

> A paperbound republication of several chapters from author's
> longer work (1531).

402   Russell, Elbert. THE HISTORY OF QUAKERISM. New York: Macmil-
       lan Co., 1943. 586 p.

A good introduction to the denomination. Devoted to America exclusively after page 183.

403   Trueblood, G. Elton. THE PEOPLE CALLED QUAKERS. New York: Harper and Row, 1966. 298 p.

A successful popular history of the Quakers that would be an appropriate first book for students. Covers both the British and the American experience.

404   West, Jessamyn, ed. THE QUAKER READER. New York: Viking Press, 1962. xviii, 523 p.

A very useful compendium of Quaker sources, about half of which are American.

The Colonial Period

See also James (528).

405   Bauman, Richard. FOR THE REPUTATION OF TRUTH: POLITICS, RE-LIGION, AND CONFLICT AMONG PENNSYLVANIA QUAKERS, 1750-1800. Baltimore, Md.: Johns Hopkins University Press, 1971. xviii, 258 p.

Covers the era in which the Society of Friends lost control of the government of Pennsylvania and, in the process, re-shaped its self-image. A well-written scholarly analysis structured by anthropological insights but clearly compre-hensible to general readers.

406   Beatty, Edward C.O. WILLIAM PENN AS SOCIAL PHILOSOPHER. New York: Columbia University Press, 1939. xiii, 338 p.

Topical analysis of Penn's thought under a dozen headings including his attitudes toward pacifism, wealth, religious toleration, education, and the American Indian.

407   Butler, Jon. "'Gospel Order Improved': The Keithian Schism and the Exercise of Quaker Ministerial Authority in Pennsylvania." WILLIAM AND MARY QUARTERLY 31 (July 1974): 431-52.

Analyzes the main issue in this schism within eighteenth-century Quakerism, showing how Keith attacked the author-ity of the "public friends"—the ministry-equivalent in Penn-sylvania.

408   Drake, Thomas E. QUAKERS AND SLAVERY IN AMERICA. New Haven, Conn.: Yale University Press, 1950. 245 p.

A history of the part played by the Quakers in the abolition of slavery from the time of George Fox down to John
Greenleaf Whittier.

409   Dunn, Mary Maples. WILLIAM PENN: POLITICS AND CONSCIENCE.
      Princeton, N.J.: Princeton University Press, 1967. 206 p.

      A thin and disappointing book describing Penn's career as
      a political thinker and an active politician.

410   Endy, Melvin B., Jr. WILLIAM PENN AND EARLY QUAKERISM.
      Princeton, N.J.: Princeton University Press, 1973. 410 p.

      Attempts to revise historians' judgments about the relation-
      ship of early Quakerism and Puritanism in this scholarly
      study of Penn's religious thought. Thorough analysis of
      Penn shows him to belong theologically to the left wing
      of Puritanism--the radical spiritualists.

411   Frost, J. William. THE QUAKER FAMILY IN COLONIAL AMERICA:
      A PORTRAIT OF THE SOCIETY OF FRIENDS. New York: St. Mar-
      tin's Press, 1973. 248 p.

      Shows how the Quakers evolved into an ingrown, tribalistic
      club of birthright members bound to a regimented ritual.
      Chapters on discipline, childhood, education and school life,
      youth, courtship, and marriage.

412   James, Sydney V. A PEOPLE AMONG PEOPLES: QUAKER BENEV-
      OLENCE IN EIGHTEENTH CENTURY AMERICA. Cambridge, Mass.:
      Harvard University Press, 1963. 405 p.

      A lucid study of Quaker social attitudes. Demonstrates that
      the humanitarianism so typical of twentieth-century Quakers
      was a late development in their history, arising out of an
      eighteenth-century redefinition of their sect.

413   Kirby, Ethyn W. GEORGE KEITH, 1638-1716. New York: D. Apple-
      ton, Century Co., 1942. 177 p. Bibliog.

      A scholarly life of a religious pilgrim who joined the Quakers
      early in life, came to America where he led a schism in
      1690-95, and then returned to England where he became an
      Anglican vicar.

414   Marietta, Jack D. "Wealth, War and Religion: The Perfecting of
      Quaker Asceticism, 1740-1783." CHURCH HISTORY 43 (1974):
      230-41.

      States that the outbreak of several wars in the eighteenth

century, especially the Revolutionary War, forced Quakers
to choose between their property and their beliefs and
greatly sharpened their awareness of the spiritually corro-
sive effect of wealth on their religion.

415   Nash, Gary B. QUAKERS AND POLITICS: PENNSYLVANIA, 1681-
1726. Princeton, N.J.: Princeton University Press, 1968. xii, 362 p.

Excellent scholarly narrative treatment including analysis of
the Keithian crisis which was the schism he led in 1690-95.

416   Peare, Catherine O. JOHN WOOLMAN, CHILD OF LIGHT: THE
STORY OF JOHN WOOLMAN AND THE FRIENDS. New York: Van-
guard Press, 1954. 254 p.

Biography of an early Quaker abolitionist (1720-72). Designed for the general reader.

417   _____. WILLIAM PENN: A BIOGRAPHY. Philadelphia: J.B. Lippincott, 1957. Reprint. Ann Arbor, Mich.: Ann Arbor Paperbacks,
1966. 448 p.

A well-written biography designed for the general reader.

418   Penn, William. THE WITNESS OF WILLIAM PENN. Edited by F.B.
Tolles and E.G. Alderfer. New York: Macmillan Co., 1957. xxx,
205 p.

An anthology of Penn's writing provided with copious head-
notes and annotation.

419   Riewald, J.G. REYNTER JANSEN OF PHILADELPHIA, EARLY AMERI-
CAN PRINTER: A CHAPTER IN SEVENTEENTH-CENTURY NON-
CONFORMITY. Groningen, Netherlands: Wolters-Nordhoof Publishing,
1970. 312 p.

An interesting and well-researched study, which is certainly
too specialized to attract any but those fascinated either
by printing or Quakers.

420   Tolles, Frederick B. JAMES LOGAN AND THE CULTURE OF PRO-
VINCIAL AMERICA. Boston: Little, Brown, and Co., 1957.
228 p.

Biography of a Pennsylvania Quaker leader (1674-1751) who
involved himself heavily in the westward movement as a
trader, speculator, and diplomat.

421   _____. MEETING HOUSE AND COUNTING HOUSE; THE QUAKER
MERCHANTS OF COLONIAL PHILADELPHIA, 1682-1763. Chapel Hill:

University of North Carolina Press, for the Institute of Early American History and Culture, 1948. xiv, 292 p.

> Analyzes the cultural sources of Quaker success and shows how quickly success in the counting house brought a decline of interest in the meeting house.

422 _____. QUAKERS AND THE ATLANTIC CULTURE. New York: Macmillan Co., 1960. 160 p.

> Chapter 6 devoted to the reaction of Philadelphia Friends to the Great Awakening. Discusses the ways in which these Quakers had outgrown such religious "enthusiasm."

423 Woolman, John. THE JOURNAL AND MAJOR ESSAYS OF JOHN WOOLMAN. Edited by P.P. Moulton. Library of Protestant Thought. New York: Oxford University Press, 1971. 354 p.

> The most recent and most scholarly of the three modern editions of the journal of John Woolman, an eighteenth-century Quaker leader and early abolitionist.

424 Zimmerman, John J. "Benjamin Franklin and the Quaker Party, 1755-56." WILLIAM AND MARY QUARTERLY 17 (1960): 291-313.

> Recounts the manner in which Quakers responded to the French and Indian War and how Franklin (a non-Quaker) came to a place of leadership in the Quaker party.

Since the Revolution

425 Bronner, Edwin B., ed. AN ENGLISH VIEW OF AMERICAN QUAKERISM: THE JOURNAL OF WALTER ROBSON IN 1877. Philadelphia: American Philosophical Society, 1970. 162 p.

> A travel journal.

426 Byrd, Robert O. QUAKER WAYS IN FOREIGN POLICY. Toronto: University of Toronto Press, 1960. 230 p.

> Applies discussion of some basic concepts of Quakerism and international relations to a chronological discussion of Quakerism and foreign policy.

427 Doherty, Robert W. THE HICKSITE SEPARATION: A SOCIOLOGICAL ANALYSIS OF RELIGIOUS SCHISM IN EARLY NINETEENTH-CENTURY AMERICA. New Brunswick, N.J.: Rutgers University Press, 1967. 157 p.

> Presents an analysis of the socioeconomic factors that charac-

terized the Hicksite and Orthodox parties in this Quaker dispute—wealth, place of residence, length of residence, and occupation. Contains appendixes and notes.

428 Elliott, Errol T. QUAKERS ON THE AMERICAN FRONTIER. Richmond, Ind.: Friends United Press, 1969. 434 p.

A description of Midwestern and West Coast Friends since the mid-nineteenth century.

429 Forbush, Bliss. ELIAS HICKS, QUAKER LIBERAL. New York: Columbia University Press, 1956. xxii, 355 p. 10 illus.

A detailed, beautifully-written, scholarly biography of Hicks (1748-1830), leader of the 1827 schism. Best study of the schism available, although Doherty (427) suggests that Forbush has exaggerated Hicks's liberalism.

430 Roberts, Arthur O. THE ASSOCIATION OF EVANGELICAL FRIENDS: A STORY OF QUAKER RENEWAL IN THE TWENTIETH CENTURY. Newberg, Oreg.: Barclay Press, 1975. 58 p.

A sketch of the history of the evangelical or Fundamentalist branch of the Quaker denomination from its origin in 1927.

PRESBYTERIANS

General

431 Armstrong, Maurice W.; Loetscher, Lefferts A.; and Anderson, C.A. THE PRESBYTERIAN ENTERPRISE: SOURCES OF AMERICAN PRESBYTERIAN HISTORY. Philadelphia: Westminster Press, 1956. 336 p.

A useful reader of primary sources.

432 Gillette, Gerald W. "A Checklist of Doctoral Dissertations on American Presbyterian and Reformed Subjects, 1912-1965." JOURNAL OF PRESBYTERIAN HISTORY 45 (1967): 203-21.

Entries are categorized by chronological eras, with two special sections devoted to Reinhold Niebuhr and Paul Tillich.

433 Klett, Guy S. PRESBYTERIANS IN COLONIAL PENNSYLVANIA. Philadelphia: University of Pennsylvania Press, 1937. 297 p.

A useful analysis based upon extensive research in primary sources.

434   Slosser, Gaius J., ed. THEY SEEK A COUNTRY: THE AMERICAN
       PRESBYTERIANS, SOME ASPECTS. New York: Macmillan Co., 1955.
       xvi, 330 p.

>   About the only general account of the history of the Presby-
>   terian denomination published in this century. Unfortunately,
>   like many denominational histories, lacks perspective and
>   seems self-serving.

435   Smith, Elwyn A. THE PRESBYTERIAN MINISTRY IN AMERICAN CUL-
       TURE: A STUDY IN CHANGING CONCEPTS, 1700-1900. Philadel-
       phia: Westminster Press, 1962. 269 p.

>   The education of ministers and the role of Princeton Semi-
>   nary especially emphasized in this essay.

436   Thompson, Ernest T. PRESBYTERIANS IN THE OLD SOUTH. 3 vols.
       Richmond, Va.: John Knox Press, 1963-73.

>   The approximate area of the Confederate states treated in
>   this monumental historical work. Volume 1 carries story
>   down to 1861; volume 2, to 1890; and volume 3, to 1972.

The Colonial Period

See also McLoughlin (125)

437   Leyburn, James G. THE SCOTCH-IRISH: A SOCIAL HISTORY. Chap-
       el Hill: University of North Carolina Press, 1962. xix, 377 p. 5
       maps.

>   Traces immigration from Scotland and Ulster to America.
>   Devoted mostly to colonial period with considerable atten-
>   tion to religious situation in Great Britain and the Presby-
>   terian churches established in the United States.

438   Pears, Thomas C., Jr., and Klett, Guy S. "Documentary History of
       William Tennent and the Log College." JOURNAL OF THE PRESBY-
       TERIAN HISTORICAL SOCIETY 28 (1950): 38-62.

>   A useful collection of extracts from primary sources relating
>   to the life of Tennent (1673-1746).

439   Pilcher, George W. SAMUEL DAVIES, APOSTLE OF DISSENT IN
       COLONIAL VIRGINIA. Knoxville: University of Tennessee Press,
       1971. 230 p.

>   A generally careful biography of one of the leading Presby-
>   terians of the eighteenth century, but weak in relating him
>   to the Great Awakening.

440   Schlenther, Boyd S., ed. THE LIFE AND WRITINGS OF FRANCIS
        MAKEMIE. Philadelphia: Presbyterian Historical Society, 1971.
        287 p.

> Hardly more than a brief sketch of Makemie's life, but the
> major portion of the book contains all the extant writings
> of the man (1658-1708), who played a significant role in
> the establishment of Presbyterianism in Virginia, Maryland,
> and North Carolina.

441   Stohlman, Martha L. L. JOHN WITHERSPOON: PARSON, POLITICIAN,
        PATRIOT. Philadelphia: Westminster Press, 1976. 176 p.

> Narrowly-focused life story of Witherspoon (1723-94), who
> was a Presbyterian clergyman, president of College of New
> Jersey (now Princeton University), and a signer of the Dec-
> laration of Independence.

442   Trinterud, Leonard J. THE FORMING OF AN AMERICAN TRADITION:
        A RE-EXAMINATION OF COLONIAL PRESBYTERIANISM. Philadelphia:
        Westminster Press, 1949. 352 p.

> A superb narrative history of Presbyterianism before the Revo-
> lution, written by a great master of this field.

443   _____, ed. A BIBLIOGRAPHY OF AMERICAN PRESBYTERIANISM
        DURING THE COLONIAL PERIOD. Philadelphia: Presbyterian His-
        torical Society, 1968. Unpaged.

> Lists over one thousand printed sources useful in Presbyte-
> rian historiography.

GERMAN PIETISTS

444   Benz, Ernst. "Ecumenical Relations between Boston Puritanism and
        German Pietism: Cotton Mather and August Hermann Francke." HAR-
        VARD THEOLOGICAL REVIEW 45 (1961): 159-93.

> An interesting description written by the German scholar
> most familiar with the Francke archives.

445   Frantz, John B. "The Awakening of Religion among the German Settlers
        in the Middle Colonies." WILLIAM AND MARY QUARTERLY 33
        (1976): 266-88.

> A good survey of the state of religion among eighteenth-
> century Germans. Emphasizes how indifferent or poorly-
> churched they had become and how such varied evangelical
> groups as the Dunkers and the Moravians attempted, with
> good success, to change the situation.

446   Mol, J.J. THE BREAKING OF TRADITIONS: THEOLOGICAL CON-
       VICTIONS IN COLONIAL AMERICA. Berkeley, Calif.: Glendessary
       Press, 1968. 94 p.

              Seeks to prove that evangelical-pietistic ministers in the
              Dutch Reformed and German Lutheran denominations during
              the eighteenth century adjusted to the American scene better
              than did their more orthodox brethren.

447   Rothermund, Dietmar. THE LAYMAN'S PROGRESS: RELIGIOUS AND
       POLITICAL EXPERIENCE IN COLONIAL PENNSYLVANIA, 1740-1770.
       Philadelphia: University of Pennsylvania Press, 1962. 202 p.

              A summary of the process of secularization, especially as it
              affected the German sects.

448   Stoeffler, F. Ernest. THE RISE OF EVANGELICAL PIETISM. Leiden,
       Netherlands: E.J. Brill, 1965. 257 p.

449   _____. GERMAN PIETISM DURING THE EIGHTEENTH CENTURY.
       Leiden, Netherlands: E.J. Brill, 1973. 265 p.

              The best introduction now available to the European back-
              ground of the pietist tradition in these two volumes. This
              aspect often neglected amidst the dozens of volumes that
              concentrate upon the English experience. Concentration
              upon the seventeenth century in the first work; the latter
              covers the life of Francke, the influence of the University of
              Halle, Wurttemberg pietism, Zinzendorf, and the Moravians.

450   _____, ed. CONTINENTAL PIETISM AND EARLY AMERICAN CHRIS-
       TIANITY. Grand Rapids, Mich.: William B. Eerdmans Publishing Co.,
       1976. 276 p.

              A collection of seven scholarly essays pointing out the place
              of pietism in the history of the following colonial religious
              communities: Lutherans, Reformed churches, Mennonites,
              Moravians, "radical pietists," Methodists, and Brethren.

REFORMED-CALVINISTS

451   Corwin, Edward T.; Dubbs, J.H.; and Hamilton, J.T. A HISTORY OF
       THE REFORMED CHURCH, DUTCH, THE REFORMED CHURCH, GERMAN,
       AND THE MORAVIAN CHURCH. American Church History Series.
       New York: Christian Literature Co., 1895. xviii, 525 p.

              Comprised of three separate narratives by the respective
              authors.

452   Harmelink, Herman.   "Another Look at Frelinghuysen and His 'Awaken-
      ing.'" CHURCH HISTORY 37 (1968): 423-38.

      Challenges the traditional view of him as an early leader
      of the First Great Awakening by showing the unreliability
      of the evidence used by his supporters and the unflattering
      picture of the man revealed in the records of the Classis of
      Amsterdam.

453   Horstmann, Julius H.E., and Wernecke, Herbert H. THROUGH FOUR
      CENTURIES; THE STORY OF THE BEGINNINGS OF THE EVANGELI-
      CAL AND REFORMED CHURCH. St. Louis, Mo.: Eden Publishing
      House, 1938. 124 p.

      Denominational history written to celebrate the merger of
      these two groups.

454   Smith, George L. RELIGION AND TRADE IN NEW NETHERLAND;
      DUTCH ORIGINS AND AMERICAN DEVELOPMENT. Ithaca, N.Y.:
      Cornell University Press, 1973. xiii, 266 p.

      Sets out to do for New York what books by Rutman (244)
      did for Boston and Tolles (421) did for Philadelphia--examine
      the interaction of commerce with the religious culture, des-
      cribing how the colony became increasingly secularized with
      the growth of prosperity.

455   Tanis, James. DUTCH CALVINISTIC PIETISM IN THE MIDDLE COLO-
      NIES: A STUDY IN THE LIFE AND THEOLOGY OF THEODORUS
      JACOBUS FRELINGHUYSEN. The Hague, Netherlands: Martinus
      Nijhoff, 1967. 203 p.

      A thorough, scholarly biography of this leader in the First
      Great Awakening. Traces the European influences on his
      theology.

CHURCH OF THE BRETHREN, GERMAN BAPTISTS, AND DUNKERS

456   Durnbaugh, Donald F., ed. THE BRETHREN IN COLONIAL AMERICA:
      A SOURCE BOOK ON THE TRANSPLANTATION AND DEVELOPMENT
      OF THE CHURCH OF THE BRETHREN IN THE EIGHTEENTH CENTURY.
      Elgin, Ill.: Brethren Press, 1967. 659 p.

      A collection of translated documents pertaining to this Ger-
      man pietist sect in the American colonies.

457   _____. THE CHURCH OF THE BRETHREN PAST AND PRESENT. El-
      gin, Ill.: Brethren Press, 1971. 182 p.

A collection of nine essays offering a brief account of the denomination's history and its present concerns.

458 Durnbaugh, Donald F., and Shultz, L.W., eds. A BRETHREN BIBLIOG-RAPHY, 1713-1963: TWO HUNDRED YEARS OF BRETHREN LITERATURE. Elgin, Ill. Brethren Press, 1964. 177 p.

A thorough work with frequent annotations.

459 Sachse, Julius F. THE GERMAN PIETISTS OF PROVINCIAL PENNSYL-VANIA, 1694-1708. Philadelphia: privately printed, 1895. xviii, 504 p.

460 _____. THE GERMAN SECTARIANS OF PENNSYLVANIA, 1708-1800; A CRITICAL AND LEGENDARY HISTORY OF THE EPHRATA CLOISTER AND THE DUNKERS. 2 vols. Philadelphia: privately printed, 1899. Illus.

Rare, interesting, and extremely valuable compendia of information. Lavishly illustrated with old wood cuts.

461 Sappington, Roger E. THE BRETHREN IN VIRGINIA: THE HISTORY OF THE CHURCH OF THE BRETHREN IN VIRGINIA. Harrisonburg, Va.: Committee for Brethren History, 1973. 520 p.

A competent work, but one devoted in large part to the history of individual congregations.

462 _____. BRETHREN SOCIAL POLICY, 1908-1958. Elgin, Ill.: Brethren Press, 1961. 220 p.

Surveys Brethren attitudes toward and participation in such social issues as temperance, racism, and pacifism.

MORAVIANS

See also Gray (103) and Wallace (115).

463 Gollin, Gillian Lindt. MORAVIANS IN TWO WORLDS: A STUDY OF CHANGING COMMUNITIES. New York: Columbia University Press, 1967. 302 p.

Comparative religious, social, and economic study of Moravian communities in Herrnhut, Germany, and Bethlehem, Pennsylvania.

464 Hamilton, John Taylor, and Hamilton, Kenneth G. HISTORY OF THE MORAVIAN CHURCH: THE RENEWED UNITAS FRATRUM, 1722-1957. Bethlehem, Pa.: Interprovincial Board of Education, Moravian Church in America, 1967. 723 p.

Revised edition of the narrative published by Corwin (451); but since that earlier edition included only about one hundred pages devoted to the Moravians, can consider this a virtually new work.

465   Murtagh, William J. MORAVIAN ARCHITECTURE AND TOWN PLAN-NING: BETHLEHEM, PENNSYLVANIA, AND OTHER EIGHTEENTH-CENTURY AMERICAN SETTLEMENTS. Chapel Hill: University of North Carolina Press, 1967. 145 p.

Based on builders' sketches as well as ample other documentation. Emphasizes the Germanic character of the structures.

466   Weinlick, John Rudolf. COUNT ZINZENDORF. New York: Abingdon Press, 1956. 240 p.

Sympathetic narrative biography of the founder of the Moravians, who travelled to North America to supervise their establishment here.

AMISH

467   Bachman, Calvin George. THE OLD ORDER AMISH OF LANCASTER COUNTY. Lancaster: Pennsylvania German Society, 1961. 294 p.

A description of Amish religion and society in Lancaster County, Pennsylvania, based on author's personal observations. Superseded by Hostetler (468).

468   Hostetler, John A. AMISH SOCIETY. Baltimore, Md.: Johns Hopkins Press, 1963. xviii, 347 p. Bibliog.

The best scholarly treatment of the Amish, exploring many aspects of their social life.

469   _____, ed. ANNOTATED BIBLIOGRAPHY ON THE AMISH. Scottsdale, Pa.: Mennonite Publishing House, 1951. xx, 100 p.

A comprehensive but dated bibliography of various kinds of published and unpublished sources relating to the Amish. Works listed in both German and English.

470   Schieder, Elmer, and Schieder, Dorothy. A PECULIAR PEOPLE: IOWA'S OLD ORDER AMISH. Ames: Iowa State University Press, 1975.

Describes their social life, religious services, farming practices, communications with other Amish groups, and views on education.

HUTTERITES

471   Bennett, John W. HUTTERIAN BRETHREN: THE AGRICULTURAL ECON-
OMY AND SOCIAL ORGANIZATION OF A COMMUNAL PEOPLE.
Stanford, Calif.: Stanford University Press, 1967. 298 p.

      Although not intended as a study of Hutterian religious life,
well-researched study of Saskatchewan Hutterites nevertheless throws considerable light on their total existence.

472   Conkin, Paul K. TWO PATHS TO UTOPIA: THE HUTTERITES AND
THE LLANO COLONY. Lincoln: University of Nebraska Press, 1964.
212 p. Bibliog.

      An attempt to contrast the religious and secular urge toward
community by studying an example of each. Sound scholarly
treatment.

473   Gross, Paul S. THE HUTTERITE WAY: THE INSIDE STORY OF THE
LIFE, CUSTOMS, RELIGION, AND TRADITIONS OF THE HUTTERITES.
Saskatoon, Can.: Freeman Publishing Co., 1965. xvii, 219 p.

474   Hostetler, John A. HUTTERITE SOCIETY. Baltimore, Md.: Johns
Hopkins University Press, 1974. xvi, 403 p. Bibliog.

      An excellent study of the community life of Hutterian Breth-
ren in Canada and the United States. Several helpful appendixes and photographs.

475   Hostetler, John A., and Huntington, Gertrude Enders. THE HUTTERITES.
IN NORTH AMERICA. New York: Holt, Rinehart and Winston, 1967.
119 p. Bibliog.

      The best introduction of books on the subject. Contains
several photographs.

476   Riley, Marvin P., ed. THE HUTTERITE BRETHREN: AN ANNOTATED
BIBLIOGRAPHY WITH SPECIAL REFERENCE TO SOUTH DAKOTA HUT-
TERITE COLONIES. Brookings: South Dakota State University, 1965.
188 p.

      Helpful and not as limited geographically as title indicates.

MENNONITES

477   Bender, Harold Stauffer. TWO CENTURIES OF AMERICAN MENNON-
ITE LITERATURE: A BIBLIOGRAPHY OF MENNONITICA AMERICANA,
1727-1928. Goshen, Ind.: Mennonite Historical Society, 1929. xii,
181 p.

Covers all Mennonite groups. Many works cited in German.

478 Brunk, Harry Anthony. HISTORY OF MENNONITES IN VIRGINIA, 1727–1960. 2 vols. Verona, Va.: McClure Printing Co., 1959–72. Bibliog.

Exhaustive history with emphasis on "Old Mennonites."

479 Epp, Frank H. MENNONITES IN CANADA, 1786–1820: THE HISTORY OF A SEPARATE PEOPLE. Toronto: Macmillan of Canada, 1974. 480 p. 16 illus., 20 maps, 46 tables.

A beautifully designed history of all Mennonite-affiliated groups in Canada, sponsored by a joint committee of Mennonite historical societies.

480 Erb, Paul. SOUTH CENTRAL FRONTIERS: A HISTORY OF THE SOUTH CENTRAL MENNONITE CONFERENCE. Scottsdale, Pa.: Herald Press, 1974. 519 p. Bibliog.

A history of the largest American Mennonite denomination's churches in Mississippi, Louisiana, Texas, Arkansas, Oklahoma, Missouri, and Kansas from the 1860s to the present. Many facts but little analysis.

481 Gingerich, Melvin. THE MENNONITES IN IOWA. Iowa City: State Historical Society of Iowa, 1939. 419 p.

A thorough but derivative history of the approximately 4,000 Mennonites in Iowa.

482 Hiebert, Clarence. THE HOLDEMAN PEOPLE: THE CHURCH OF GOD IN CHRIST, MENNONITE, 1859–1969. South Pasadena, Calif.: William Carey Library, 1973. xxii, 663 p. Bibliog.

A well-documented if poorly edited history and description of one tiny sect of American Mennonites. Extensive bibliography of published and unpublished materials in German and English.

483 Horst, Samuel. MENNONITES IN THE CONFEDERACY. Scottsdale, Pa.: Herald Press, 1967. 148 p. Bibliog.

A brief but well-documented study of the pacifism of Southern Mennonites during the Civil War.

484 Juhnke, James C. A PEOPLE OF TWO KINGDOMS: THE POLITICAL ACCULTURATION OF THE KANSAS MENNONITES. Newton, Kans.: Faith and Life Press, 1975. 215 p.

Argues that Kansas Mennonites wish both to remain good
Mennonites and to be accepted as good Americans. In analyzing their political views and voting patterns, finds tension existing between these two goals but a basic pattern
of Republican and right-wing political behavior emerging.

485   MENNONITE ENCYCLOPEDIA. 4 vols. Scottsdale, Pa.: Mennonite
Publishing House, 1955-59.

An indispensable reference tool.

486   Pannabecker, Samuel Floyd. OPEN DOORS: A HISTORY OF THE
GENERAL CONFERENCE MENNONITE CHURCH. Newton, Kans.:
Faith and Life Press, 1975. 416 p.

A scholarly contribution to the history of this denomination
by the former president of the Mennonite Biblical Seminary,
based upon his 1944 dissertation.

487   Redekop, Calvin W. THE OLD COLONY MENNONITES: DILEMMAS
OF ETHNIC MINORITY LIFE. Baltimore, Md.: Johns Hopkins Press,
1969. xiv, 302 p. 22 illus.

Attempts to combine a history of this group in Manitoba
and Mexico with sociological-anthropological analysis.
Based upon several years of field research.

488   Smith, C. Henry. THE STORY OF THE MENNONITES. 4th ed.
Newton, Kans.: Mennonite Publication Office, 1957. 856 p.

A standard, comprehensive history of Mennonites in Europe
and the Americas from the Reformation through World War II.

489   Stoltzfus, Grant M. MENNONITES OF THE OHIO AND EASTERN
CONFERENCE. Scottsdale, Pa.: Herald Press, 1969. 459 p. Bibliog.

A chronicle tracing this conference of the largest Mennonite
denomination (sometimes called "Old Mennonites") and its
antecedents. Lists of congregations and leaders, and chro-
nologies of conference meetings and other events.

490   Wenger, John C. HISTORY OF THE MENNONITES OF THE FRANCO-
NIA CONFERENCE. Telford, Pa.: Franconia Mennonite Historical
Society, 1937. xvi, 523 p. Bibliog.

A detailed chronicle of one Pennsylvania conference of the
largest Mennonite denomination. Several documents and a
bibliography of published and unpublished materials, chiefly
in English.

491 _____. THE MENNONITE CHURCH IN AMERICA. Scottsdale, Pa.: Herald Press, 1966. 384 p.

> Written by a Mennonite historian primarily for Mennonites, can still serve as a useful introduction to the denomination. Lancaster County, Pennsylvania home of the largest single concentration of these "Old Mennonites."

492 _____. THE MENNONITES IN INDIANA AND MICHIGAN. Scottsdale, Pa.: Herald Press, 1961. xv, 470 p. Bibliog.

> A detailed chronicle with thumbnail biographies of several hundred clergymen and historical sketches of local churches.

LUTHERANS IN THE COLONIAL PERIOD

Works relating to the various Lutheran synodical traditions are listed in chapter 15.

493 Eisenberg, William Edward. THE LUTHERAN CHURCH IN VIRGINIA, 1717–1962. Roanoke, Va.: Trustees of the Virginia Synod, Lutheran Church in America, 1967. 731 p. Illus., documents.

> A detailed history complete with lists of pastors and conventions.

494 Muhlenberg, Henry Melchior. THE JOURNALS OF HENRY MELCHIOR MUHLENBERG. Translated by Theodore G. Tappert and John W. Doberstein. 3 vols. Philadelphia: Evangelical Lutheran Ministerium of Pennsylvania and Adjacent States, 1942–58.

> Journals of Muhlenberg (1711–87), the patriarch of Lutheranism in North America who played a significant role in the American Revolution, an excellent source of social history. A one-volume abridgement of the journal published by Tappert and Doberstein, eds., THE NOTEBOOK OF A COLONIAL CLERGYMAN (Philadelphia: Muhlenberg Press, 1959).

495 Qualben, L.P. THE LUTHERAN CHURCH IN COLONIAL AMERICA. New York: Thomas Nelson and Sons, 1940. 320 p. Illus.

> A dated but still useful concise history of Lutheranism in North America prior to 1789, placing Lutherans into the religious heterogeneity of the Middle Colonies, where they were most numerous. Illustrated with several crude maps and diagrams on historical and theological topics.

496 Wallace, Paul A.W. THE MUHLENBERGS OF PENNSYLVANIA. Philadelphia: University of Pennsylvania Press, 1950. 358 p.

A history of the Muhlenberg family from the emigration of Henry Melchior Muhlenberg, often called "the patriarch of Lutheranism in North America," from Germany in 1742 until the early years of the nineteenth century.

Chapter 7

RELIGION IN THE ERA OF THE AMERICAN REVOLUTION

DEISM AND LIBERTY

Many of the "founding fathers" (men such as Franklin, Washington, and Jefferson) were deists. Because of this association, it has often been assumed that
Deism played a special role in supporting the ideology of the American Revolution. Scholars such as Heimert (272) and McLoughlin (273), however, reject
the argument that Deism was more directly responsible for creating a climate
of opinion receptive to revolution than was the evangelicalism generated in
the Great Awakening. Furthermore, not all religious liberals supported political democracy, a point made by Stearns (517) in the case of John Wise. In
the history of philosophy, Deism has played a more significant role than in the
history of religion; see chapter 1 of Wright (852).

497   Akers, Charles W. CALLED UNTO LIBERTY: A LIFE OF JONATHAN
       MAYHEW, 1720-1766. Cambridge, Mass.: Harvard University Press,
       1964. 286 p.

            A good study of the man who led clerical opposition to the
            British and Anglicanism while also serving as a spokesman
            of liberal Arminianism even though he was despised and
            ostracized by most of his Congregational colleagues in Bos-
            ton.

498   Aldridge, Alfred Owen. BENJAMIN FRANKLIN AND NATURE'S GOD.
       Durham, N.C.: Duke University Press, 1967. 279 p.

            Benjamin Franklin's religious beliefs, never systematically
            treated by himself, here given thin anecdotal rather than
            analytical treatment.

499   _____. MAN OF REASON: THE LIFE OF THOMAS PAINE. New
       York: J.B. Lippincott Co., 1959. 348 p.

            A competent scholarly biography by a scholar who has spent
            much of his career studying Paine.

500 Boller, Paul F., Jr. GEORGE WASHINGTON AND RELIGION. Dallas, Tex.: Southern Methodist University Press, 1963. 235 p.

> A sensible and scholarly study that shows Washington to
> have had no twinge of evangelical sympathies, but a strong
> belief in Providence: in short that his faith was fairly
> typical of eighteenth-century Deists. A summary of this
> volume published under the same title in WILLIAM AND
> MARY QUARTERLY 17 (1960): 486-506.

501 Boorstin, Daniel J. THE LOST WORLD OF THOMAS JEFFERSON.
New York: Henry Holt and Co., 1948. 306 p.

> An examination of Jefferson's writings along with those of
> a small group of men who belonged to the American Philosophical Society in Philadelphia.

502 Butterfield, Lyman H. "Elder John Leland, Jeffersonian Itinerant."
PROCEEDINGS OF THE AMERICAN ANTIQUARIAN SOCIETY 62
(1952): 155-242.

> Emphasizes Baptist leader Leland's role in winning religious
> liberty in Virginia.

503 Buxbaum, Melvin H. BENJAMIN FRANKLIN AND THE ZEALOUS
PRESBYTERIANS. University Park, Pa.: Pennsylvania State University
Press, 1975. 265 p.

> Gives an account of Franklin's controversies with Calvinists,
> first with the establishment in Boston, later with largely
> Presbyterian frontiersmen, and eventually with Presbyterian
> members of the Pennsylvania and New Jersey legislatures.
> Attempts to picture Franklin as being more hostile and vicious than in the traditional view of him.

504 Chapman, Clayton H. "Benjamin Colman and Philomena." NEW ENGLAND QUARTERLY 42 (1969): 214-31.

> In discussion of the impact of Elizabeth Singer (pseudonym
> Philomena) upon the young Colman (1652-1725), attributes
> the tempering of his rationalism to her influence.

505 Cook, George A. JOHN WISE, EARLY AMERICAN DEMOCRAT. New
York: King's Crown Press, 1952. 246 p.

> Biography of Wise (1652-1725), long-time minister in Ipswich,
> Massachusetts. Depicts him as a liberal, democratic thinker.
> Another view in Stearns (517).

506 Foner, Eric. TOM PAINE AND REVOLUTIONARY AMERICA. New
York: Oxford University Press, 1976. xx, 326 p.

Study of the interaction between Paine's ideas and the societies in which he lived. More interest in Paine's political ideas than in his religious beliefs. Traces his radicalism to his nonconformist Protestant background.

507   Hawke, David Freeman. PAINE. New York: Harper and Row, 1974. 500 p. 25 illus., bibliog.

A beautifully designed and well-written biography of Tom Paine.

508   Hornberger, Theodore. "Benjamin Colman and the Enlightenment." NEW ENGLAND QUARTERLY 12 (1939): 227-40.

A brief discussion of Colman's theology.

509   Koch, Gustav Adolf. REPUBLICAN RELIGION: THE AMERICAN REVOLUTION AND THE CULT OF REASON. New York: Henry Holt and Co., 1933. 334 p.

Limited description of attempts to establish Deism as a religious cult. Tells what happened when Deism spread from people like Thomas Jefferson to others, such as Ethan Allen and Elihu Palmer (both of whom are discussed in separate chapters). Ends with a discussion of the success of the evangelical revival, which is entitled "the triumph of fidelity." A paperback reprint of the book appeared as RELIGION OF THE AMERICAN ENLIGHTENMENT (New York: Thomas Y. Crowell Co., 1968).

510   Luebke, Fred C. "The Origins of Thomas Jefferson's Anti-Clericalism." CHURCH HISTORY 32 (1963): 344-56.

Jefferson's antagonism toward the clergy traced to his unfair treatment in the election of 1800, from the evidence of his correspondence.

511   Marty, Martin E. THE INFIDEL: FREETHOUGHT AND AMERICAN RELIGION. Cleveland, Ohio: World Publishing Co., 1961. 224 p.

A fascinating study of controversies surrounding such atheists as Robert Ingersoll and other "infidels" in the nineteenth century. Also an analysis of contemporary indifference to religious infidelity.

512   Morais, Herbert M. DEISM IN EIGHTEENTH-CENTURY AMERICA. New York: Columbia University Press, 1934. 203 p.

History of Deism from 1713 to 1805. Background of thought from Lord Herbert of Cherbury to Robespierre.

513 Morgan, Edmund S. THE GENTLE PURITAN: A LIFE OF EZRA STILES, 1727-1795. New Haven, Conn.: Yale University Press, for the Institute of Early American History and Culture, 1962. 490 p.

> Biography of one of New England's leading eighteenth-century intellectuals and a president of Yale. A model of intellectual history.

514 Nash, Gary B. "The American Clergy and the French Revolution." WILLIAM AND MARY QUARTERLY 22 (1965): 392-412.

> Notes that ministerial opposition to the revolution in France began only in 1795. Early reaction uniformly favorable, but when radical republicanism and infidelity (epitomized by Tom Paine) began to champion the cause, the churchmen began to oppose it.

515 Paine, Thomas. COMPLETE WRITINGS OF THOMAS PAINE. Edited by Philip S. Foner. 2 vols. New York: Citadel Press, 1945.

> The best modern edition of Paine's writings, although the editing of the correspondence is not up to scholarly standards.

516 _____. THOMAS PAINE: REPRESENTATIVE SELECTIONS. Edited by Harry Hayden Clark. Rev. ed. New York: Hill and Wang, 1961. clxiii, 436 p.

> A handy and frequently-used collection of his writings.

517 Stearns, Raymond P. "John Wise of Ipswich Was No Democrat in Politics." ESSEX INSTITUTE HISTORICAL COLLECTIONS 97 (1961): 2-18.

> An excellent discussion of the historiography of John Wise and analysis of his thought. Disputes the claim frequently made by scholars such as Cook (505) that Wise taught political democracy.

518 Tucker, Louis Leonard. PURITAN PROTAGONIST: PRESIDENT THOMAS CLAP OF YALE COLLEGE. Chapel Hill: University of North Carolina Press for the Institute of Early American History and Culture, 1962. 283 p.

> A biography of a little-known Yale president whose tenure dated from 1740 to 1766. May overestimate Clap's importance.

519 Van de Wetering, John E. "God, Science and the Puritan Dilemma." NEW ENGLAND QUARTERLY 38 (1965): 494-507.

Analysis of the thought of Thomas Prince (1687-1758), minister at Old South Church, Boston, showing how his appreciation of Newton led him very close to Deism.

RELIGION AND THE AMERICAN REVOLUTION

See also Heimert (272).

520 Albanese, Catherine L. SONS OF THE FATHERS: THE CIVIL RELIGION OF THE AMERICAN REVOLUTION. Philadelphia: Temple University Press, 1976. 288 p.

Examines the "invisible religion" created by America's founding fathers. An imaginative exploration of the founding of the nation as a religious creation.

521 Bailyn, Bernard. THE IDEOLOGICAL ORIGINS OF THE AMERICAN REVOLUTION. Cambridge, Mass.: Harvard University Press, 1967. xiii, 335 p.

A most influential book about the Revolution, giving prominent place to religious issues and the role of the clergy in the coming of the conflict.

522 _____. THE ORDEAL OF THOMAS HUTCHINSON. Cambridge, Mass.: Harvard University Press, 1974. 441 p.

Discussion of the role played by Hutchinson from 1758 to 1770, as lieutenant governor of Massachusetts, and from 1770 to 1774, as the governor. Gives a good deal of attention to this loyalist's religion, a sincere but liberal Calvinism.

523 Brauer, Jerald C., ed. RELIGION AND THE AMERICAN REVOLUTION. Philadelphia: Fortress Press, 1976. 73 p.

Contains three unconnected essays: editor Brauer discusses the contribution of Puritanism and revivalism to the Revolution, Sidney Mead restates his thesis concerning the role of the Enlightenment in creating the religious genius of America, and Robert Bellah writes again about civil religion.

524 Carroll, Peter N., ed. RELIGION AND THE COMING OF THE AMERICAN REVOLUTION. Waltham, Mass.: Ginn-Blaisdell, 1970. 173 p.

Sixteen documents and a brief introduction comprise this volume, which is aimed at helping undergraduates discover how religious leaders and institutions contributed to the coming revolution.

525   Hanley, Thomas O'Brien. THE AMERICAN REVOLUTION AND RELI-
       GION: MARYLAND, 1770-1800. Washington, D.C.: Catholic Uni-
       versity of America Press, 1971. 260 p.

       Attempts to undermine the commonly-held hypothesis that
       the cause of religion suffered during the Revolution. Argues
       that in Maryland, religion prospered during these years and
       there was born there an aspiration to construct a Christian
       state. Unfortunately, poorly written and argument difficult
       to follow.

526   Hatch, Nathan O. THE SACRED CAUSE OF LIBERTY: REPUBLICAN
       THOUGHT AND THE MILLENNIUM IN REVOLUTIONARY NEW EN-
       GLAND. New Haven, Conn.: Yale University Press, 1977. xi, 197 p.

       Discusses the transformation of evangelical millennial expec-
       tations in the early eighteenth century into a secularized
       "civil millennialism" during the American Revolution.
       Finds the change occurring during the war with France and
       documents his findings ably.

527   Ireland, Owen S. "The Ethnic-Religious Dimension of Pennsylvania
       Politics, 1778-1779." WILLIAM AND MARY QUARTERLY 30 (1973):
       423-48.

       Attempts to reassert the importance of ethnic-religious (more
       specifically, Scotch-Irish Calvinist) factions within the poli-
       tics of Pennsylvania by close analysis of their election and
       voting pattern.

528   James, Sydney V. "The Impact of the American Revolution on Quakers'
       Ideas about Their Sect." WILLIAM AND MARY QUARTERLY 19
       (1962): 360-82.

       Article concludes: "Revolutionary events and ideology not
       only revealed both the inadequacy and the inconsistency of
       a long-held group of ideas about the church but also re-
       quired their revision. . . . The Revolution challenged the
       Quakers either to find a new role in American Society or
       to accept a futile isolation from it." Thorough and illumina-
       ting.

529   Kurtz, Stephen, and Hutson, James, eds. ESSAYS ON THE AMERICAN
       REVOLUTION. Chapel Hill: University of North Carolina Press and
       New York: W.W. Norton Co., 1973. 331 p.

       Very distinguished collection of essays. Includes two that
       are appropriately noted in this volume: William G. Mc-
       Loughlin, "The Role of Religion in the Revolution: Liberty
       of Conscience and Cultural Cohesion in the New Nation";
       and Rowland Bertoff and John W. Murrin, "Feudalism, Com-

munalism, and the Yeoman Farmer: The American Revolution Considered as a Social Accident. "

530 Metzger, Charles H. CATHOLICS AND THE AMERICAN REVOLUTION:
A STUDY IN RELIGIOUS CLIMATE. Chicago: Loyola University Press,
1962. 306 p.

Seeks to demonstrate that a strong anti-Catholic climate of
opinion existed in eighteenth-century America, but that, in
spite of this animosity, most Roman Catholics supported the
Revolution. An uneven study but a valuable work, none-
theless.

531 Morgan, Edmund S. "The Puritan Ethic and the American Revolution. "
WILLIAM AND MARY QUARTERLY 24 (1967): 3-43.

A helpful discussion of the ambivalent character of the Puritan ethic and a suggestive interpretation of the manner in
which that set of attitudes affected the Revolution. Reprinted in Vaughan and Bremer (171).

532 Noll, Mark A. "Ebenezer Devotion: Religion and Society in Revolutionary Connecticut." CHURCH HISTORY 45 (1976): 293-307.

Analysis of career of Devotion, a mid-eighteenth-century
Congregational minister in Windham, Connecticut. Uses this
man's life and thought as occasion for a useful discussion of
recent historical literature relating religion and the Revolution.

533 Rezneck, Samuel. UNRECOGNIZED PATRIOTS: THE JEWS IN THE
AMERICAN REVOLUTION. Westport, Conn.: Greenwood Press, 1975.
xiv, 299 p.

Not only catalogs the involvement of Jews in the military
and financial operations of the Revolution, but also discusses
the considerable impact of the American way of life upon
Jews of that generation.

534 Sweet, Douglas H. "Church Vitality and the American Revolution:
Historiographical Consensus and Thoughts Towards a New Perspective. "
CHURCH HISTORY 45 (1976): 341-57.

An excellent survey of the problem of religion in the American Revolution. Discusses the current literature and the
consensus of historians about the role of religion (there is
greater awareness of religious sources of Revolutionary thought).
Like Hanley (525), disputes the widely-accepted generaliza-
tion that religion declined as a result of the Revolution.
The entire September number of CHURCH HISTORY, volume

45, devoted to religion in the American Revolution.

535   Wood, Gordon S. THE CREATION OF THE REPUBLIC, 1776-1787.
       Chapel Hill: University of North Carolina Press for the Institute of
       Early American History and Culture, 1969. 653 p.

       A magisterial survey of the political thought of the revolu-
       tionary generation that gives some attention to religion.

SEPARATION OF CHURCH AND STATE

General

See also Mead (16) and McLoughlin (273).

536   Marnell, William H. THE FIRST AMENDMENT; THE HISTORY OF RE-
       LIGIOUS FREEDOM IN AMERICA. Garden City, N.Y.: Doubleday,
       1964. xiv, 247 p.

       A narrative account of the coming of religious freedom in
       the United States, useful only for a brief introduction.

537   Miller, Glenn T. RELIGIOUS LIBERTY IN AMERICA, HISTORY AND
       PROSPECTS. Philadelphia: Westminster Press, 1976. 156 p.

       Reads more like an outline of the history of religious liberty
       than an introductory essay. So much material condensed
       and digested that no one topic is well developed.

538   Pfeffer, Leo. CHURCH, STATE, AND FREEDOM. Rev. ed. Boston:
       Beacon Press, 1967. xiii, 832 p.

       One of the best books in the field; thorough and scholarly.
       Surveys historic background in Europe and America to the
       passage of the First Amendment. Goes on to discuss vir-
       tually every aspect of church-state relations, including re-
       leased-time religious education, the Bible and prayer in
       public schools, and state aid to religious education.

539   Smith, Elwyn A. RELIGIOUS LIBERTY IN THE UNITED STATES: THE
       DEVELOPMENT OF CHURCH-STATE THOUGHT SINCE THE REVOLU-
       TIONARY ERA. Philadelphia: Fortress Press, 1972. 400 p.

       A comprehensive survey of the subject, organized around
       three headings: first, the separatist or Protestant tradition,
       with emphasis on the colonial experience; second, the Catho-
       lic tradition with essays devoted to Catholic apologists from
       John Carroll to John Courtney Murray; and third, the con-

stitutional tradition with six chapters devoted to legal-constitutional issues.

540   Stokes, Anson Phelps. CHURCH AND STATE IN THE UNITED STATES. 3 vols. New York: Harper and Brothers, 1950.

A comprehensive historical survey and a source book for the churches' relationship to both state and federal governments. A revised one-volume edition by Stokes and Leo Pfeffer published in 1964. Can find longer estimates of this most important book in Sidney E. Mead's review in RELIGION IN LIFE 20 (1950-51): 36-46; and in John Tracy Ellis's review in CATHOLIC HISTORICAL REVIEW 38 (1952): 285-316.

Anthologies

541   Howe, Mark De Wolfe, ed. CASES ON CHURCH AND STATE IN THE UNITED STATES. Cambridge, Mass.: Harvard University Press, 1952. 393 p.

Contains the texts of legal decisions.

542   Tussman, Joseph, ed. THE SUPREME COURT ON CHURCH AND STATE. New York: Oxford University Press, 1962. 305 p.

Contains the texts of legal decisions.

543   Wilson, John F., ed. CHURCH AND STATE IN AMERICAN HISTORY. Boston: D.C. Heath Co., 1965. xxiii, 227 p. Bibliog.

A useful and well-edited anthology containing primary source material and comment from later historians. Surveys the whole of U.S. history.

Special Aspects

544   Adams, William C. "American Public Opinion in the 1960's on Two Church-State Issues." JOURNAL OF CHURCH AND STATE 17 (1975): 477-94.

A statistical study of public opinion regarding prayer in public schools and governmental aid to parochial schools.

545   Boles, Donald E. THE BIBLE, RELIGION, AND THE PUBLIC SCHOOLS. 2d ed. Ames: Iowa State University Press, 1963. 341 p.

A thorough but pedestrian survey of the question of the use of the Bible in public education. Summarizes much state and federal court action in relation to the issue.

546   Cushing, John D. "Notes on Disestablishment in Massachusetts, 1780–1833. " WILLIAM AND MARY QUARTERLY 26 (1969): 169–90.

Tells the same story as McLoughlin, NEW ENGLAND DISSENT (273), but a bit more succinctly.

547   Handy, Robert T. A CHRISTIAN AMERICA: PROTESTANT HOPES AND HISTORICAL REALITIES. New York: Oxford University Press, 1971. 282 p.

Argues that American Protestants did not accept religious pluralism along with the First Amendment but worked to produce a Protestant version of a Christian America. States that they nearly succeeded in the late nineteenth century but have now had to come to terms with a second disestablishment.

548   Healey, Robert M. JEFFERSON ON RELIGION IN PUBLIC EDUCATION. New Haven, Conn.: Yale University Press, 1962. 294 p.

Explores the ambiguities of Jefferson's views on separation of church and state, making the point that Jefferson had no hesitation about teaching quite specific ethical precepts and rationalistic dogmas in the schools although disallowing specific theological positions.

549   Howe, Mark De Wolf. THE GARDEN AND THE WILDERNESS: RELIGION AND GOVERNMENT IN AMERICAN CONSTITUTIONAL HISTORY. Chicago: University of Chicago Press, 1965. 180 p.

An important book by a Harvard law professor. Argues that the purpose of separation of church and state was the protection of the church from the state and that, therefore, the First Amendment should not be used, as has been the practice of the Supreme Court, to outlaw state aid to religious institutions where that aid will not curtail religious liberty.

550   Huegli, Albert G., ed. CHURCH AND STATE UNDER GOD. St. Louis, Mo.: Concordia Publishing House, 1964. 516 p.

A collection of essays on church–state problems written by Lutheran scholars, such as Lewis Spitz, Carl S. Meyer, and Martin E. Marty.

551   Konvitz, Milton R. RELIGIOUS LIBERTY AND CONSCIENCE: A CONSTITUTIONAL INQUIRY. New York: Viking Press, 1968. 116 p.

Published version of a series of lectures in which author, who has written much on civil rights and liberty, muses about the manner in which recent changes in the nature of religious expression affect church-state relations.

552 Kurland, Philip B., ed. CHURCH AND STATE: THE SUPREME COURT AND THE FIRST AMENDMENT. Chicago: University of Chicago Press, 1975. 272 p.

Six scholarly essays reprinted from the SUPREME COURT RE-VIEW by editor Kurland, E.J. Brown, P.G. Kauper, W.G. Katz, K. Greenwalt, and R.E. Morgan.

553 Michaelsen, Robert. PIETY IN THE PUBLIC SCHOOL: TRENDS AND ISSUES IN THE RELATIONSHIP BETWEEN RELIGION AND THE PUBLIC SCHOOL IN THE UNITED STATES. New York: Macmillan Co., 1970. xiii, 274 p.

Argues that the public schools have been acting like established churches and functioning as the chief disseminators of public piety. Advocates a more pluralistic approach in the future.

554 Morgan, Richard E. THE POLITICS OF RELIGIOUS CONFLICT: CHURCH AND STATE IN AMERICA. New York: Pegasus, 1968. xv, 156 p.

Primarily devoted to the question of public education. After surveying pressure and interest groups lobbying for and against aid to parochial education, gives a brief analysis of national issues and a case study of conflict in New York.

555 _____. THE SUPREME COURT AND RELIGION. New York: Free Press, 1972. 216 p.

Topical discussion of some key issues, such as the Jehovah's Witnesses, public prayer, and changing interpretations of the establishment clause.

556 Murray, John Courtney. WE HOLD THESE TRUTHS: CATHOLIC RE-FLECTIONS ON THE AMERICAN PROPOSITION. New York: Sheed and Ward, 1960. 336 p.

A collection of essays on church and state, religion and so-ciety, by the outstanding American Catholic scholar in this field.

557 Norman, Edward R. CONSCIENCE OF THE STATE IN NORTH AMERI-CA. London: Cambridge University Press, 1968. 200 p.

A rare example of a comparative study of American and British history, in this case the question of separation of

church and state. Surveys the contrasting history of separation, the effects of separation, and the problem of education.
Concludes that the effect of the First Amendment in the
United States was not so great as American historians have
assumed.

558   Pratt, John Webb. RELIGION, POLITICS, AND DIVERSITY: THE
CHURCH-STATE THEME IN NEW YORK HISTORY. Ithaca, N.Y.:
Cornell University Press, 1967. 327 p.

Treats the whole history of church-state relations, dealing at
length with the period since religious freedom was guaranteed
in the state constitution of 1777.

559   Rice, Charles E. THE SUPREME COURT AND PUBLIC PRAYER: THE
NEED FOR RESTRAINT. New York: Fordham University Press, 1964.
xiii, 202 p.

A study of recent Supreme Court decisions regarding public
prayer, arguing that the Court has mistakenly gone too far
in eliminating religion from public life.

560   Smith, Elwyn A., ed. THE RELIGION OF THE REPUBLIC. Philadelphia:
Fortress Press, 1971. 296 p.

A useful collection of essays, including J.F. Wilson, "The
Status of 'Civil Religion' in America"; R. Michaelsen, "Is
the Public School Religious or Secular?"; T.T. McAvoy,
"American Cultural Impacts on Catholicism"; D. Dohen,
"The New Quest of American Catholicism"; J. Agus, "Jeru-
salem in America"; J.H. Smylie, "Protestant Clergy, the
First Amendment, and Beginnings of a Constitutional Debate,
1781-91"; E.A. Smith, "The Voluntary Establishment of Re-
ligion"; J.F. Maclear, "The Republic and the Millennium";
J.L. Adams, "The Voluntary Principle in the Forming of
American Religion"; S.E. Mead, "The Fact of Pluralism and
the Persistence of Sectarianism"; and J.E. Thompson, Jr.,
"The Reform of the Racist Religion of the Republic."

CIVIL RELIGION

561   Bellah, Robert N. THE BROKEN COVENANT: AMERICAN CIVIL RE-
LIGION IN THE TIME OF TRIAL. New York: Seabury Press, 1975.
172 p.

Analyzes some of the most important parts of Americans' historic creed--the myth of origins, the idea of a chosen people,
success, nativism, and the taboo on socialism. Originally
delivered in 1971 as a series of lectures.

562   Cherry, Conrad. "Nation, Church, and Private Religion: The Emergence of an American Pattern." JOURNAL OF CHURCH AND STATE 14 (1972): 223-33.

> Discusses the impact of individualism in the disintegration of traditional religion and the growth of personal approaches to faith. Argues that this trend is stronger than the group impulse of "civil religion."

563   Curti, Merle E. THE ROOTS OF AMERICAN LOYALTY. New York: Columbia University Press, 1946. 267 p.

> Describes the forces, personalities, symbols, and events that have formed historical expressions of American patriotism. Patriotism seen as an individualistic and self-contradictory expression of loyalty.

564   Endy, Melvin B., Jr. "Abraham Lincoln and American Civil Religion." CHURCH HISTORY 44 (1975): 229-41.

> Views Lincoln as the high priest of civic piety and argues that Lincoln's understanding of revelation and providence and his attitudes toward the Negro and slavery compromised his prophetic role.

565   McLoughlin, William G., and Bellah, Robert N., eds. RELIGION IN AMERICA. Boston, Mass.: Houghton Mifflin Co., 1968. xxiv, 433 p.

> Nineteen essays exploring the contemporary state of religion in the United States, divided into four sections: "General Evaluations," "Contemporary Issues," "Pluralism and Its Problems," and "Predictions and Reorientations." Contains Robert N. Bellah's controversial "Civil Religion in America." First appearance of seven of the essays here, the remainder appeared originally in DAEDALUS (Winter 1967).

566   Mead, Sidney E. THE NATION WITH THE SOUL OF A CHURCH. New York: Harper and Row, 1975. 158 p.

> Seven provocative essays have been collected here, mostly related to church-state themes.

567   Richey, Russell E., and Jones, Donald G., eds. AMERICAN CIVIL RELIGION. New York: Harper and Row, 1974. 289 p.

> Collection of twelve contributions, the best reader on the subject of this debate. Includes Robert Bellah's 1967 article, which opened the discussion of civil religion, and essays by Sidney E. Mead, Will Herberg, W. Lloyd Warner, John F. Wilson, Martin E. Marty, Herbert Richardson, David Little, Charles Long, and Leo Marx.

Chapter 8

THE CATHOLIC CHURCH IN THE NINETEENTH CENTURY

The division of this chapter into sections devoted to biographies and parochial studies on the one hand and social history on the other corresponds to the development of Catholic historiography. Traditionally, Catholic history has concentrated upon lives of influential bishops and archbishops, diocesan histories, and, more rarely, histories of religious orders. This preoccupation was understandable, perhaps necessary, but it did tend to produce a picture of the church which overemphasized the clergy and the bureaucracy. Recently a kind of social history of the church has appeared that focuses upon parish life and ethnicity.

For works relating to Orestes A. Brownson, see Lapati (907), Leliaert (908), and Ryan (910). See also Rahill (128), Blied (1055), Bowden (1147), and Ranaghan (1269).

BIOGRAPHIES AND PAROCHIAL STUDIES

568   Ahern, Patrick H. THE LIFE OF JOHN J. KEANE, EDUCATOR AND ARCHBISHOP, 1839-1918. Milwaukee, Wis.: Bruce Publishing Co., 1955. 396 p. Bibliog.

        A well-documented biography of this Irish-born archbishop of Dubuque, founder of the Catholic University of America, and advocate of Catholic assimilation in the United States.

569   Bell, Stephen. REBEL, PRIEST, AND PROPHET: A BIOGRAPHY OF DR. EDWARD MCGLYNN. New York: Devin-Adair Co., 1937. 303 p.

        Standard biography of this Catholic priest (1837-1900), who opposed parochial schools, supported Henry George, founded the Anti-Poverty Society, and was once temporarily excommunicated.

570   Callan, Louise. PHILLIPPINE DUCHESNE: FRONTIER MISSIONARY
        OF THE SACRED HEART, 1759-1852. Westminster, Md.: Newman
        Press, 1957. xiii, 805 p.

        A hagiographic biography of a French nun in early Missouri,
        stressing her role in the development of Catholicism in the
        Mississippi Valley.

571   Ellis, John Tracy. THE LIFE OF JAMES CARDINAL GIBBONS, ARCH-
        BISHOP OF BALTIMORE, 1834-1921. 2 vols. Milwaukee, Wis.: Bruce
        Publishing Co., 1952.

        Exhaustive and sympathetic biography of the famous "Ameri-
        canist" clergyman, providing insight into the problems faced
        in a rapidly-changing America.

572   Faherty, William Barnaby. DREAM BY THE RIVER: TWO CENTURIES
        OF SAINT LOUIS CATHOLICISM, 1766-1967. St. Louis, Mo.: Piraeus
        Publishers, 1973. 246 p.

        A good, scholarly history of an important diocese.

573   Gaffey, James P. "Patterns of Ecclesiastical Authority: The Problem of
        Chicago Succession, 1865-1881." CHURCH HISTORY 42 (1973): 257-70.

        Analyzes a long dispute over the leadership of Bishop James
        Duggan.

574   Gallagher, John P. A CENTURY OF HISTORY: THE DIOCESE OF
        SCRANTON, 1869-1968. Scranton, Pa.: Diocese of Scranton, 1968.
        xiv, 615 p.

        Contains a discussion of the Hodur schism which eventually
        led to the formation of the Polish National Catholic Church.
        Detailed and well documented.

575   Galush, William. "The Polish National Catholic Church: A Survey of
        Its Origins, Development and Missions." RECORDS OF THE AMERICAN
        CATHOLIC HISTORICAL SOCIETY OF PHILADELPHIA 83 (1972): 131-49.

576   Garraghan, Gilbert J. THE JESUITS IN THE MIDDLE UNITED STATES.
        3 vols. New York: America Press, 1938.

        A detailed and scholarly history of the Missouri Province
        Jesuits, with emphasis on the period 1830-70. Splendid
        portrayal of Jesuit missions, parochial work, and education.

577   Guilday, Peter. A HISTORY OF THE COUNCILS OF BALTIMORE.
        New York: Macmillan Co., 1932. 291 p.

A dated but able study of church legislation passed in Catholic national assemblies from 1791 until 1884. Valuable for understanding how the American hierarchy came to grips with problems facing the Catholic Church in a frequently hostile environment.

578   _____. THE LIFE AND TIMES OF JOHN ENGLAND, FIRST BISHOP OF CHARLESTON, 1786-1842. 2 vols. New York: America Press, 1927. Bibliog.

An exhaustive biography of the democratic Irish-born bishop, educator, spokesman for Irish rights, and defender of American Catholicism.

579   Hassard, John R.G. LIFE OF THE MOST REVEREND JOHN HUGHES, D.D., FIRST ARCHBISHOP OF NEW YORK. New York: Arno Press, 1969. 519 p.

A reprint of the 1866 edition of this detailed and important biography. Contains extracts from many of Hughes's letters.

580   Holden, Vincent F. THE YANKEE PAUL: ISAAC THOMAS HECKER. Milwaukee, Wis.: Bruce Publishing Co., 1958. xx, 508 p.

Comprehensive and well-documented biography of Hecker (1819-88), a convert to Catholicism who founded the Paulist Fathers.

581   Horgan, Paul. LAMY OF SANTA FE: HIS LIFE AND TIMES. New York: Farrar, Straus, and Giroux, 1975. 523 p.

Detailed and beautifully written biography of Lamy (1814-88), who was Willa Cather's model for DEATH COMES FOR THE ARCHBISHOP (New York: A.A. Knopf, 1927).

582   Johnson, Peter L. CROSIER ON THE FRONTIER: A LIFE OF JOHN MARTIN HENNI, ARCHBISHOP OF MILWAUKEE. Madison: State Historical Society of Wisconsin, 1959. xiii, 240 p.

Life of the Swiss-born priest who served first in the diocese of Cincinnati and became the first bishop of Milwaukee.

583   Leonard, Henry B. "Ethnic Conflict and Episcopal Power: The Diocese of Cleveland, 1847-1870." CATHOLIC HISTORICAL REVIEW 62 (1976): 388-407.

An excellent article on the difficulties encountered by a French-born bishop in dealing with immigrant Catholics of Irish and German background.

584   Lord, Robert H.; Sexton, John E.; and Harrington, Edward T. HISTORY
        OF THE ARCHDIOCESE OF BOSTON IN THE VARIOUS STAGES OF
        ITS DEVELOPMENT, 1604-1943. 3 vols. New York: Sheed and Ward,
        1944.

> The most comprehensive and scholarly of all of the diocesan
> histories.

585   McGloin, John Bernard. CALIFORNIA'S FIRST ARCHBISHOP: THE
        LIFE OF JOSEPH SADOC ALEMANY, C.P., 1814-1888. New York:
        Herder and Herder, 1966. 412 p.

> A well-written but narrowly focused biography, including
> many documents but lacking bibliography.

586   McNamara, Robert F. THE DIOCESE OF ROCHESTER 1868-1968. Roches-
        ter, N.Y.: Diocese of Rochester, 1968. 638 p.

> Shows an awareness of the relationship of church and society,
> which earns it a better rating than most of the diocesan his-
> tories.

587   McSorley, Joseph. FATHER HECKER AND HIS FRIENDS; STUDIES AND
        REMINISCENCES. St. Louis, Mo.: Herder Book Co., 1952. 304 p.

> Ably traces the life of Isaac Hecker (1819-88) and the nine
> other men responsible for founding the Paulist Fathers.

588   Melville, Annabelle M. ELIZABETH BAYLEY SETON, 1774-1821. New
        York: Charles Scribner's Sons, 1951. xvii, 411 p. Bibliog.

> A sympathetic well-documented biography of the foundress
> of the Sisters of Charity, an educator, and the first American-
> born individual to be canonized by the Roman Catholic church.
> Complete with a bibliography of archival and printed sources
> as well as an adequate index.

589   Moynihan, James H. THE LIFE OF ARCHBISHOP JOHN IRELAND.
        New York: Harper and Row, 1953. 441 p. Bibliog.

> A well-documented, sympathetic biography of this Irish-born
> archbishop of Saint Paul (1838-1918), with special attention
> paid to his role as an advocate of assimilation, educator,
> and social reformer.

590   Nolan, Hugh J. THE MOST REVEREND FRANCIS PATRICK KENDRICK,
        THIRD BISHOP OF PHILADELPHIA, 1830-1851. Washington, D.C.:
        Catholic University of America Press, 1948. xv, 502 p. Bibliog.

> Detailed biography of the Irish immigrant theologian and
> participant in ecclesiastical councils (1796-1863). Reprints
> many documents.

591   Oetgen, Jerome. AN AMERICAN ABBOT: BONIFACE WIMMER, O.S.B., 1809–1887. Latrobe, Pa.: Archabbey Press, 1976.

Life of the founder of the Benedictine monks in the United States.

592   Prockho, Bohdan P. "Soter Ortynsky: First Ruthenian Bishop in the United States, 1907–1916." CATHOLIC HISTORICAL REVIEW 58 (1973): 513–33.

593   _____. "The Establishment of the Ruthenian Church in the United States, 1884–1907." PENNSYLVANIA HISTORY 42 (1975): 137–54.

Two articles dealing with a group of immigrants, often called Ukrainians, who belonged to the Byzantine–Slavic rite.

594   Radzialowski, Thaddeus. "Reflections on the History of the Felicians in America." POLISH–AMERICAN STUDIES 32 (1975): 19–28.

A thoughtful and suggestive essay on the American experience of the most important community of religious women among the Polish–Americans, an order devoted mainly to teaching.

595   Rippinger, Joel. "Some Historical Determinants of American Benedictine Monasticism, 1846–1900." AMERICAN BENEDICTINE REVIEW 27 (1976): 63–84.

An interpretive essay on the European background and American influences on Benedictine monasticism in the United States. Reviews much of the literature.

596   Roemer, Theodore. TEN DECADES OF ALMS. St. Louis, Mo.: B. Herder, 1942. 322 p.

Study of financial assistance to the American Catholic Church from mission societies in Europe, especially France.

597   Schauinger, J. Herman. CATHEDRALS IN THE WILDERNESS. Milwaukee, Wis.: Bruce Publishing Co., 1952. xiii, 334 p.

Biography of Benedict Joseph Flaget, first Catholic bishop of Bardstown, Kentucky. Best introduction to Catholicism in the early nineteenth–century West.

598   Shannon, James P. CATHOLIC COLONIZATION OF THE WESTERN FRONTIER. New Haven, Conn.: Yale University Press, 1957. xiii, 302 p.

A thorough study of Archbishop John Ireland's efforts to colonize Roman Catholic immigrants in ten rural villages and farming communities of Minnesota.

599   Spalding, Thomas W. MARTIN JOHN SPALDING: AMERICAN CHURCH-
       MAN. Washington, D.C.: Catholic University of America Press, 1973.
       373 p.

       Excellent study of an important leader (1810-72), who was
       archbishop of Baltimore.

600   Sweeney, David F. THE LIFE OF JOHN LANCASTER SPALDING. New
       York: Herder and Herder, 1965. 384 p.

       A good biography of the bishop of Peoria, who defended
       many late nineteenth-century efforts to adapt Catholicism
       to its American environment but remained conservative on
       most other issues.

601   Trisco, Robert F. THE HOLY SEE AND THE NASCENT CHURCH OF
       THE MIDDLE WESTERN UNITED STATES, 1826-1850. Rome: Gregorian
       University Press, 1962. 408 p.

       Based upon manuscript sources, provides a rich variety of
       material for the early nineteenth century.

602   Weber, Francis J. CALIFORNIA'S RELUCTANT PRELATE: THE LIFE
       AND TIMES OF RIGHT REVEREND THADDEUS AMAT, C.M. (1811-
       1878). Los Angeles: Dawson Book Shop, 1964. 234 p.

       A well-documented study of the life of Bishop Amat.

603   Weber, Ralph E. NOTRE DAME'S JOHN ZAHM. Notre Dame, Ind.:
       University of Notre Dame Press, 1961. 214 p. Bibliog.

       A biography of John Zahm, a Catholic priest of German
       ancestry who sought to accommodate much of Darwin's
       thought in a theory of theistic evolution. Bibliography of
       archival materials and Zahm's works.

SOCIAL HISTORY

604   Abell, Aaron I. AMERICAN CATHOLICISM AND SOCIAL ACTION:
       A SEARCH FOR SOCIAL JUSTICE, 1865-1950. Garden City, N.Y.:
       Hanover House, 1960. 306 p.

       Comprehensive survey of Catholic involvement in social wel-
       fare activities from the mid-nineteenth to mid-twentieth cen-
       tury. A very important study.

605   Barry, Colman. THE CATHOLIC CHURCH AND GERMAN AMERICANS.
       Washington, D.C.: Catholic University of America Press, 1953. 348 p.
       Appendixes.

A thoroughly documented study of German-American Catholicism in the nineteenth century, stressing the efforts of Peter Paul Cahensly and the St. Raphael Society to assist German immigrants. Describes manuscript depositories.

606 Browne, Henry J. THE CATHOLIC CHURCH AND THE KNIGHTS OF LABOR. Washington, D.C.: Catholic University of America Press, 1949. xix, 415 p.

A well-documented study of Catholic participation in and clerical opposition to this early American labor movement, 1879-91.

607 Daley, John M. GEORGETOWN UNIVERSITY: ORIGIN AND EARLY YEARS. Washington, D.C.: Georgetown University Press, 1957. 324 p.

Good history of this earliest Catholic college; covers the period from 1780 to the 1840s.

608 Dolan, Jay P. CATHOLIC REVIVALISM: THE AMERICAN EXPERIENCE, 1830-1900. Notre Dame, Ind.: University of Notre Dame Press, 1977.

A study of the Catholic parish mission movement, pointing out the similarities with Protestant revivalism and analyzing the movement's significance.

609 _____. THE IMMIGRANT CHURCH: NEW YORK'S IRISH AND GERMAN CATHOLICS, 1815-1865. Foreword by Martin E. Marty. Baltimore, Md.: Johns Hopkins University Press, 1975. xiv, 221 p.

Documents the religious practices of parishes dominated by the Irish and Germans, chronicles their conflicts and concludes that their religious practice was not so fervent as might have been expected but was marked by great conservatism. A summary of this book's conclusions published by the author in CHURCH HISTORY 41 (1972): 354-68.

610 Ellis, John Tracy. THE FORMATIVE YEARS OF THE CATHOLIC UNIVERSITY OF AMERICA. Washington, D.C.: Catholic University of America Press, 1946. 415 p.

Important study of the movement to create a European-style university of strictly graduate-level studies during the 1870s and 1880s.

611 Gleason, Philip. THE CONSERVATIVE REFORMERS: GERMAN-AMERICAN CATHOLICS AND THE SOCIAL ORDER. Notre Dame, Ind.: University of Notre Dame Press, 1968. 272 p.

Interpretive study of the Roman Catholic Centralverein, a

federation of mutual aid societies for German-American
Catholics. Describes its activities after 1900 in the field
of social justice.

612 Greene, Victor R. FOR GOD AND COUNTRY: THE RISE OF POLISH
AND LITHUANIAN ETHNIC CONSCIOUSNESS IN AMERICA, 1860-
1910. Madison: State Historical Society of Wisconsin, 1975. 202 p.

Excellent treatment of the development of Polish-American
Catholicism based primarily upon analysis of the Chicago
archdiocese. Lithuanians treated more briefly.

613 Lannie, Vincent P. "Alienation in America: The Immigrant Catholic
and Public Education in Pre-Civil War America." REVIEW OF POLI-
TICS 32 (1970): 503-21.

Analysis of Catholic schools during their formative period,
the 1840s and 1850s.

614 _____. PUBLIC MONEY AND PAROCHIAL EDUCATION: BISHOP
HUGHES, GOVERNOR SEWARD, AND THE NEW YORK SCHOOL
CONTROVERSY. Cleveland, Ohio: Press of Case Western Reserve
University, 1968. 282 p.

A well-researched study of the controversy of 1840-41 surrounding the efforts of Bishop John Hughes to obtain funds
from the state of New York to support parochial education.

615 McAvoy, Thomas T. THE FORMATION OF THE AMERICAN CATHO-
LIC MINORITY, 1820-1860. Philadelphia: Fortress Press, 1967. 37 p.

A Facet book reprint of an article first appearing in REVIEW
OF POLITICS 10 (1948): 13-34.

616 Merwick, Donna. BOSTON PRIESTS, 1848-1910: A STUDY OF SO-
CIAL AND INTELLECTUAL CHANGE. Cambridge, Mass.: Harvard
University Press, 1973. 276 p.

A valuable scholarly study that revises the older view of
Boston's later nineteenth-century priests as Irishmen who
never really became a part of Boston culture.

617 Messbarger, Paul R. FICTION WITH A PAROCHIAL PURPOSE: SO-
CIAL USES OF AMERICAN CATHOLIC LITERATURE, 1884-1900. Boston: Boston University Press, 1971. 179 p.

An excellent study of novels written by and for Catholics.
Shows how a body of literature that is almost without literary merit nevertheless can tell the historian a great deal
about Catholicism in the late nineteenth century.

618   Potter, George. TO THE GOLDEN DOOR: THE STORY OF THE
       IRISH IN IRELAND AND AMERICA. Boston: Little, Brown, and Co.,
       1960. 631 p.

       A sympathetic, popularly written history, based upon original
       research but without notes or bibliography.

619   Reilly, Daniel F. THE SCHOOL CONTROVERSY, 1891-1893. Wash-
       ington, D.C.: Catholic University of America Press, 1943. 302 p.

       Detailed study of the bitter controversy that erupted in the
       American hierarchy over financing parochial schools and the
       possibility of obtaining public funding.

620   Sanders, James W. THE EDUCATION OF AN URBAN MINORITY:
       CATHOLICS IN CHICAGO, 1833-1965. New York: Oxford University
       Press, 1977. 278 p.

       Study of Chicago's parochial schools. Credits part of their
       success to positive attitudes toward ethnic and cultural dis-
       tinctiveness. Best study of its kind.

621   Sanfilippo, M. Helena. "Personal Religious Expressions of Roman Ca-
       tholicism: A Transcendental Critique." CATHOLIC HISTORICAL RE-
       VIEW 62 (1976): 366-87.

       Well-documented study of the interest of American Transcen-
       dentalists in the Catholic religion.

622   Spalding, David. "The Negro Catholic Congresses, 1889-1894." CA-
       THOLIC HISTORICAL REVIEW 55 (1969): 337-57.

       Reviews the movement that resulted in three national meet-
       ings of black Catholics.

623   Tomasi, Silvano M. PIETY AND POWER: THE ROLE OF ITALIAN
       PARISHES IN THE NEW YORK METROPOLITAN AREA, 1880-1930.
       New York: Jerome S. Ozer Publishing Co., for the Center for Migra-
       tion Studies of New York, 1975. 201 p.

       Argues that the parishes functioned to buffer both the immi-
       grants from American culture and the Roman Catholic Church
       as a whole, but that they also eased Italian assimilation into
       both.

VATICAN I AND THE AMERICANIST HERESY

624   Cross, Robert D. THE EMERGENCE OF LIBERAL CATHOLICISM IN
       AMERICA. Cambridge, Mass.: Harvard University Press, 1958. 328 p.
       Bibliog.

A sympathetic analysis of the policies of liberal churchmen, such as Gibbons, Ireland, and Keane, and of the conservative opposition that they met.

625 Fogarty, Gerald P. THE VATICAN AND THE AMERICANIST CRISIS: DENIS J. O'CONNELL, AMERICAN AGENT IN ROME, 1885-1903. Rome: Gregorian University Press, 1974. 369 p.

Biography of O'Connell, concentrating upon his career as rector of the North American College in Rome where he represented the Americanist cause to the Vatican.

626 Hennesey, James. THE FIRST COUNCIL OF THE VATICAN: THE AMERICAN EXPERIENCE. New York: Herder and Herder, 1963. 341 p.

Study of the roles of the American bishops at the council (1869-70), focusing on their opposition to the doctrine of papal infallibility.

627 Killen, David P. "Americanism Revisited: John Spalding and Testem Benevolentiae." HARVARD THEOLOGICAL REVIEW 66 (1973): 413-54.

A revisionist study that argues that the charge of theological Americanism had more substance than older historians, such as McAvoy (628), recognized.

628 McAvoy, Thomas T. THE AMERICANIST HERESY IN ROMAN CATHOLICISM, 1895-1900. Notre Dame, Ind.: University of Notre Dame Press, 1963. 322 p.

First published in 1957 as THE GREAT CRISIS IN AMERICAN CATHOLIC HISTORY. One of the standard works on this important controversy. Pro-liberal stance, however, recently challenged.

629 Reher, Margaret M. "Pope Leo XIII and Americanism." THEOLOGICAL STUDIES 34 (1973): 679-89.

Challenge to older liberal interpretations in this revisionist article.

630 Sewrey, Charles L. "Infallibility, the American Way, and Catholic Apologetics." JOURNAL OF CHURCH AND STATE 15 (1973): 293-302.

Analyzes how U.S. Catholic clergy responded to charges that the doctrine of papal infallibility threatened a growth of papal political power.

631   Wangler, Thomas E.   "John Ireland and the Origins of Liberal Catholicism in the United States." CATHOLIC HISTORICAL REVIEW 56 (1971): 617-29.

632   _____.   "The Birth of Americanism: 'Westward the Apocalyptic Candle-stick.'"   HARVARD THEOLOGICAL REVIEW   65 (1972): 415-36.

633   _____.   "The Emergence of John J. Keane as a Liberal Catholic and Ameri-canist (1878-1887)." AMERICAN ECCLESIASTICAL REVIEW 166 (1972): 457-78.

Three revisionist articles that challenge the older liberal view of the controversy.

NATIVISM

634   Billington, Ray A.   THE PROTESTANT CRUSADE 1800-1860: A STUDY OF THE ORIGINS OF AMERICAN NATIVISM. New York: Macmillan Co., 1938. 514 p.

A pioneering study dealing with antebellum anti-Catholic agi-tation, such as the burning of the Charlestown, Massachusetts convent and the proliferation of spurious exposes of monastic life, rather than with the origins of American nativism in general.

635   Davis, David Brion.   "Some Themes of Counter-Subversion: An Analy-sis of Anti-Masonic, Anti-Catholic, and Anti-Mormon Literature." MIS-SISSIPPI VALLEY HISTORICAL REVIEW (1960): 205-24.

An unusually influential article that describes the three groups as archetypal subversives, although they were seen by con-temporaries as a mirror image of Jacksonian democracy.

636   Hueston, Robert F.   THE CATHOLIC PRESS AND NATIVISM, 1840-1860. New York: Arno Press, 1976.

Most of the English-language Catholic press Irish in orienta-tion during the nineteenth century. Focuses on the role of the Irish in evoking nativism and their reaction to it in this 1972 doctoral dissertation.

637   Kinzer, Donald L. AN EPISODE IN ANTI-CATHOLICISM: THE AMERI-CAN PROTECTIVE ASSOCIATION. Seattle: University of Washington Press, 1964. 342 p.

A well-documented study of this Midwestern nativist association in the 1890s, superseding Humphrey Desmond's THE A.P.A. MOVEMENT: A SKETCH (Washington, D.C.: New Century Press, 1912).

Chapter 9

JUDAISM

Jewish historiography is poorly integrated into the history of religion in America. Some pioneering work has proven valuable, such as Herberg (1088), Glazer (645), and Rischin (667). New studies seem promising, for example, Jick (665). See also Rezneck (533) and the section in chapter 18 devoted to Protestant-Catholic-Jewish dialogue.

BIBLIOGRAPHIES

638 Marcus, Jacob R. AN INDEX TO SCIENTIFIC ARTICLES ON AMERICAN JEWISH HISTORY. Cincinnati, Ohio: American Jewish Archives, 1971. 240 p.

An exhaustive but unannotated bibliography.

639 Rischin, Moses. AN INVENTORY OF AMERICAN JEWISH HISTORY. Cambridge, Mass.: Harvard University Press, 1954. 66 p.

A bibliographical essay listing sources of American Jewish history from the seventeenth until the mid-twentieth century.

GENERAL WORKS

640 Blau, Joseph L., ed. REFORM JUDAISM: A HISTORICAL PERSPECTIVE. New York: KTAV Publishing House, 1973. 529 p.

Twenty-four essays on the Reform wing of American Judaism, grouped under seven headings: "On the Nature of the Reform Movement," "Liberal Judaism in a Reactionary World," "Theological Speculations," "On Ritual and Worship," "On Law and Authority," "On People and Land [Zionism]," and "Some Unusual Themes."

641   Feingold, Henry L. ZION IN AMERICA: THE JEWISH EXPERIENCE FROM COLONIAL TIMES TO THE PRESENT. New York: Twayne Publishers, 1974. 357 p. Bibliog.

        A general synthesis of American Jewish history, relying on the works of Jacob Marcus, Bertram Korn, and other historians.

642   Fredman, J. George, and Falk, Louis A. JEWS IN AMERICAN WARS. New York: Jewish War Veterans of the U.S., 1942. 118 p.

        A sketch of Jewish participation in American international conflicts from the Revolutionary War to World War II.

643   Friedman, Lee M. JEWISH PIONEERS AND PATRIOTS. Philadelphia: Jewish Publication Society of America, 1942. xvii, 430 p. Bibliog.

        A filiopietistic account of Jewish contributions to the development of American society since Christopher Columbus.

644   Glanz, Rudolf. STUDIES IN JUDAICA AMERICANA. New York: KTAV Publishing House, 1970. 407 p.

        Fifteen articles on German Jews in the United States, including such topics as their relations with Chinese, Yankees, German gentiles, and Eastern European Jews, Jewish life in New York City, and German-Jewish names.

645   Glazer, Nathan. AMERICAN JUDAISM. Rev. ed. Chicago: University of Chicago Press, 1972. 210 p. Bibliog.

        A brief historical survey of Judaism in America since the seventeenth century written by a prominent sociologist. Helpful for understanding Jews' renewed interest in their heritage since the 1940s. Useful only as an introduction, but complete with a short annotated bibliography.

646   Handlin, Oscar. ADVENTURE IN FREEDOM: THREE HUNDRED YEARS OF JEWISH LIFE IN AMERICA. New York: McGraw-Hill Book Co., 1954. xiii, 282 p. Bibliog.

        A brief survey of American Jewish life, stressing the acceptance of Jews by the host society.

647   Howe, Irving. WORLD OF OUR FATHERS. New York: Harcourt Brace Jovanovich, 1976. xx, 714 p. Bibliog.

        A comprehensive history of Jews of Eastern European descent in the United States.

648   Karp, Abraham J., ed. THE JEWISH EXPERIENCE IN AMERICA: SE-LECTED STUDIES FROM THE PUBLICATIONS OF THE AMERICAN JEWISH HISTORICAL SOCIETY. 5 vols. New York: KTAV Publishing House, 1969.

> Covers the colonial period, the early republic, the emerging community, the era of assimilation, and at home in America.

649   Marcus, Jacob R., ed. CRITICAL STUDIES IN AMERICAN JEWISH HISTORY. 3 vols. Cincinnati: American Jewish Archives, 1971.

> Thirty-six articles excerpted from AMERICAN JEWISH AR-CHIVES, illuminating various aspects of Judaism in the United States since the seventeenth century.

650   Neusner, Jacob, ed. UNDERSTANDING AMERICAN JUDAISM: TO-WARD THE DESCRIPTION OF A MODERN RELIGION. 2 vols. New York: KTAV Publishing House, 1975.

> An anthology of twenty-nine essays written by scholars of American Judaism and covering the topics of the American synagogue, the American rabbi, and Conservative, Orthodox, Reform, and Reconstructionist Judaism.

651   Schappes, Morris U., ed. A DOCUMENTARY HISTORY OF THE JEWS IN THE UNITED STATES, 1654-1875. 3d ed. New York: Schocken Books, 1971. 780 p.

> A valuable and critically edited collection, the first edition of which appeared in 1950. Covers all aspects of Jewish life.

652   Sklare, Marshall. CONSERVATIVE JUDAISM. Rev. ed. New York: Schocken Books, 1972. 330 p.

> A sociological study of the American synthesis of Orthodox and Reform Jewish elements, including sections on change in the Jewish-American community, the travail of Orthodoxy, the rise of Conservatism, the Conservative rabbinate, the ideology of Conservatism, and recent developments in Conservatism.

653   _____ , ed. THE JEW IN AMERICAN SOCIETY. New York: Behrman House, 1974. 404 p.

> A collection of contributed chapters that together give an overview of Jewish society and its historic development in America. Includes chapters by Sidney Goldstein and Calvin Goldscheider on Jewish religiosity and another by Charles S. Liebman on the religion of the American Jews.

654 _____. THE JEWS; SOCIAL PATTERNS OF AN AMERICAN GROUP.
Glencoe, Ill.: Free Press, 1958. 669 p.

A collection of essays, one group of which is devoted to
Jewish religion: Polsky, "A Study of Orthodoxy in Milwau-
kee"; Rosen, "A Study of Adolescent Religious Conviction
and Conduct"; Warner and Srole, "A Crisis in the Jewish
Community of Yankee City"; Sklare, "Aspects of Religious
Worship in the Contemporary Conservative Synagogue"; Car-
lin and Mendlovitz, "The American Rabbi"; and Glick, "The
Hebrew Christians."

655 Sklare, Marshall, and Greenblum, Joseph, eds. JEWISH IDENTITY ON
THE SUBURBAN FRONTIER: A STUDY OF GROUP SURVIVAL IN THE
OPEN SOCIETY. New York: Basic Books, 1967. xviii, 362 p.

A sociological study of the kind that always sets historians'
teeth on edge: suburb under study was given the anonymous
name "Lakeville," thus making it impossible to criticize author's conclusions or to check on their accuracy. Chapters
3-5 devoted to discussion of Jewish religion.

656 Yaffe, James. THE AMERICAN JEWS: PORTRAIT OF A SPLIT PER-
SONALITY. New York: Random House, 1968. 338 p.

An introduction to the group personality of Jews in the
United States, revealing their frequently contradictory attitudes toward other ethnic groups, the economy, and themselves.

JUDAISM IN THE COLONIAL PERIOD

657 Goodman, Abram Vossen. AMERICAN OVERTURE: JEWISH RIGHTS
IN COLONIAL TIMES. Philadelphia: Jewish Publication Society of
America, 1947. xiv, 265 p. Bibliog.

An older study of the varying degrees of acceptance of Jews
in the American colonies.

658 Hershkowitz, Leo, and Meyer, Isidore S., eds. THE LEE MAX FRIED-
MAN COLLECTION OF AMERICAN JEWISH COLONIAL CORRESPOND-
ENCE: LETTERS OF THE FRANKS FAMILY (1733-1748). Waltham,
Mass.: American Jewish Historical Society, 1968. 171 p.

The record of one of the few Jewish families prominent in
colonial American society.

659 Marcus, Jacob R. THE COLONIAL AMERICAN JEW, 1492-1776. 3 vols.
Detroit: Wayne State University Press, 1970. Bibliog.

Contents of the first volume, Jewish history in New Spain, South America, Mexico, the West Indies, New Netherlands, and British North America; the second volume, economic, religious, social, welfare, and educational activities in British North America; the third volume, a summary of Jewish activities in the American colonies.

660 _____, ed. AMERICAN JEWRY: DOCUMENTS, EIGHTEENTH CENTURY. Cincinnati, Ohio: Hebrew Union College Press, 1959. xix, 492 p.

A well-edited compilation of 196 documents arranged under four headings: personal life, religious life, general community, and commerce and trade.

NINETEENTH-CENTURY JUDAISM

661 Blau, Joseph L., and Baron, Salo W., eds. THE JEWS OF THE UNITED STATES, 1790-1840: A DOCUMENTARY HISTORY. 3 vols. New York: Columbia University Press, 1963.

A well-edited collection of documents illuminating political, cultural, and religious aspects of Jewish life during the early national period when Jews were still a tiny minority.

662 Davidson, Gabriel. OUR JEWISH FARMERS AND THE STORY OF THE JEWISH AGRICULTURAL SOCIETY. New York: L.B. Fischer, 1943. 280 p.

A general history of the Jewish Agricultural Society and its very limited success in turning immigrants from European ghettos into American farmers.

663 Heller, James G. ISAAC M. WISE: HIS LIFE, WORK, AND THOUGHT. New York: Union of American Hebrew Congregations, 1965. xxi, 819 p. Bibliog.

Comprehensive biography of Isaac Wise (1819-1900), the Bohemian rabbi who became the central figure in Reform Judaism in nineteenth-century America. Detailed analysis of Wise's thought.

664 Higham, John. SEND THESE TO ME: JEWS AND OTHER IMMIGRANTS IN URBAN AMERICA. New York: Atheneum, 1975. 259 p.

Eleven essays on ethnic groups in the United States, including several dealing with nativism, anti-Semitism, and other topics relevant to American Jewry.

665   Jick, Leon A. THE AMERICANIZATION OF THE SYNAGOGUE, 1820–
       1870. Hanover, N.H.: University Press of New England, 1976. Bibliog.

       A study of approximately two hundred thousand German Jew-
       ish immigrants and their religious attitudes and practices in
       the New World. Valuable for the background of Reform
       Judaism.

666   Korn, Bertram Wallace. EVENTFUL YEARS AND EXPERIENCES: STUDIES
       IN NINETEENTH CENTURY JEWISH HISTORY. Cincinnati, Ohio:
       American Jewish Archives, 1954. 249 p.

       Eight essays on the Jewish experience in nineteenth-century
       America, focusing on Jews from Germany.

667   Rischin, Moses. THE PROMISED CITY: NEW YORK'S JEWS, 1870–
       1914. Cambridge, Mass.: Harvard University Press, 1962. 342 p.
       14 illus.

       A valuable scholarly study of the city of New York, the
       traditions of the Eastern European Jews who began to flood
       into New York in the 1870s, and the friction that developed
       between these new immigrants and the German Jews of an
       earlier generation.

668   Urofsky, Melvin I. AMERICAN ZIONISM FROM HERZL TO THE
       HOLOCAUST. Garden City, N.Y.: Doubleday, 1975. 538 p.

       Narrative history of Zionism since 1914 with a brief back-
       ward glance at the nineteenth century. Argues that Ameri-
       can Zionism has not been an exclusively Jewish movement,
       but has been closely linked to the dominant trends in America.

LOCAL STUDIES

669   Brooks, Juanita. HISTORY OF THE JEWS IN UTAH AND IDAHO.
       Salt Lake City: Western Epics, 1973. 252 p.

       A sketch of Jewish life in the Mormon strongholds of Utah
       and southern Idaho from 1864 until the 1960s.

670   Dinnerstein, Leonard, and Palsson, Mary Dale, eds. JEWS IN THE
       SOUTH. Baton Rouge: Louisiana State University Press, 1973. 392 p.

       A well-edited compilation of twenty-one documents and
       articles illuminating the history of Jews in the South from
       the antebellum period to the 1960s. Emphasis on the twen-
       tieth century. Bibliographical essay.

671   Evans, Eli N. THE PROVINCIALS: A PERSONAL HISTORY OF JEWS IN THE SOUTH. New York: Atheneum, 1973. xiv, 369 p. Bibliog.

A commendable study of Jews outside the geographical mainstream of American Jewry, covering their relations with white and black gentiles, their struggle against coerced assimilation, and other topics.

672   Ginsberg, Louis. CHAPTERS ON THE JEWS OF VIRGINIA, 1658-1900. Richmond, Va.: Cavalier Press, 1969. 108 p.

A brief study sketching the history of Jews in Virginia during the colonial and antebellum periods, their social structures, and roles they played in the development of several cities.

673   Grinstein, Hyman B. THE RISE OF THE JEWISH COMMUNITY OF NEW YORK, 1654-1860. Philadelphia: Jewish Publication Society of America, 1947. xiii, 645 p. Bibliog.

A thorough study of Jewish life in New York City prior to the flood of Eastern European Jews. Covers such topics as synagogue organization, social welfare, society and culture, religious practice, and religious dissent.

674   Gutstein, Morris A. A PRICELESS HERITAGE: THE EPIC GROWTH OF NINETEENTH CENTURY CHICAGO JEWRY. New York: Bloch Publishing Co., 1953. 488 p. Bibliog.

A general synthesis including discussion of the synagogue, education, immigration, relations with gentiles, beneficence, and Zionism.

675   Kohn, S. Joshua. THE JEWISH COMMUNITY OF UTICA, NEW YORK, 1847-1848. New York: American Jewish Historical Society, 1959. xvi, 221 p.

A well-documented history of Jewish life in this community, covering organizations, immigration, reaction to National Socialism, Zionism, education, and relations with the city as a whole. Emphasis on the twentieth century.

676   Korn, Bertram Wallace. THE EARLY JEWS OF NEW ORLEANS. Waltham, Mass.: American Jewish Historical Society, 1969. xxi, 382 p.

A well-documented study of Jewry in New Orleans during the eighteenth and nineteenth centuries, covering both religious and secular life.

677   Plaut, W. Gunther. THE JEWS IN MINNESOTA: THE FIRST SEVENTY-FIVE YEARS. New York: American Jewish Historical Society, 1959. 347 p. Bibliog.

A thorough study of Jewry in this Midwestern state from the 1840s to the 1920s.

678   Reznikoff, Charles, and Engelman, Uriah Z. THE JEWS OF CHARLES-TON: A HISTORY OF AN AMERICAN JEWISH COMMUNITY. Philadelphia: Jewish Publication Society of America, 1950. 343 p.

A well-documented if brief history of the Jews in this old South Carolina city from colonial days until the twentieth century, stressing secular life and political problems.

679   Rosenberg, Stuart E. THE JEWISH COMMUNITY IN ROCHESTER, 1843-1925. New York: American Jewish Historical Society and Columbia University Press, 1954. xv, 325 p. Bibliog.

A solid study of the German and Eastern European Jews in Rochester, New York. Covers such topics as private life, relations with gentiles, economic activities, religious life, and Zionism.

680   Rudolph, B.G. FROM A MINYAN TO A COMMUNITY: A HISTORY OF THE JEWS OF SYRACUSE. Syracuse, N.Y.: Syracuse University Press, 1970. xix, 314 p.

A solid treatment of various aspects of the religious and secular life of Jews in this upstate New York community from the first half of the nineteenth century to the 1960s.

681   Shinedling, Abraham I. WEST VIRGINIA JEWRY: ORIGINS AND HISTORY, 1850-1958. 3 vols. Philadelphia: Press of Maurice Jacobs, 1963.

A detailed chronicle containing many documents and countless trivial facts of little use to most readers. Little analysis of Jewish history in this state.

682   Shuman, Bernard. A HISTORY OF THE SIOUX CITY JEWISH COM-MUNITY, 1869 TO 1969. Sioux City, Iowa: Bolstein Creative Printers, 1969. 209 p.

A chronicle of a century of Jewish life in this Iowa city, lacking analysis and not meeting the standards set by many other local Jewish histories.

683   Silverman, Morris. HARTFORD JEWS, 1659-1970. Hartford: Connecti-cut Historical Society, 1970. 448 p. Photos.

A detailed chronicle of prominent Jews in the city, providing trivial data of little interest to most readers, and little historical or sociological analysis.

684   Stern, Norton B., ed.   CALIFORNIA JEWISH HISTORY: A DESCRIP-
TIVE BIBLIOGRAPHY.   Glendale, Calif.: Arthur H. Clark Co., 1967.
175 p.

> A well-annotated bibliography with over five hundred entries
> of books, articles, and unpublished materials. Occasionally
> covers other parts of the American West. Includes list of
> Jewish newspapers in California.

685   Swichow, Louis J., and Gartner, Lloyd P.   THE HISTORY OF THE
JEWS OF MILWAUKEE.   Philadelphia: Jewish Publication Society of
America, 1963.   xix, 533 p.   Bibliog.

> A well-documented history covering the period from 1844 to
> 1950. Analyzes both religious and secular life, Zionism,
> socialism, beneficence, and other topics.

686   Vorspan, Max, and Gartner, Lloyd P.   HISTORY OF THE JEWS OF
LOS ANGELES.   San Marino, Calif.: Huntington Library, 1970.   362 p.

> A study of Jewish life in the Los Angeles area from the days
> of the Gold Rush until the 1960s, covering economic activity,
> religious life, relations with other ethnic groups, and the prob-
> lems posed by urban culture.

687   Watters, Leon L.   THE PIONEER JEWS OF UTAH.   New York: American Jewish Historical Society, 1952.   199 p.   Bibliog.

> A well-documented study of Jewish life in this Mormon Zion
> during the nineteenth century, shedding light on the interest-
> ing relations between Jews and Latter-Day Saints.

ANTI-SEMITISM

688   Dinnerstein, Leonard, ed.   ANTISEMITISM IN THE UNITED STATES.
New York: Holt, Rinehart and Winston, 1971.   140 p.

> Sixteen essays and excerpts from longer works exploring four
> areas: roots of anti-Semitism, anti-Semitism in the Gilded
> Age, twentieth-century manifestations of anti-Semitism, and
> black anti-Semitism. Bibliographical essay.

689   Higham, John.   STRANGERS IN THE LAND: PATTERNS OF AMERICAN
NATIVISM, 1850-1925.   New Brunswick, N.J.: Rutgers University
Press, 1955.   431 p.

> Classical history of nativism and the campaign to restrict
> immigration from the Civil War through the enactment of the
> quota systems in the 1920s. Essential for understanding anti-
> Semitism in the United States. Bibliographical essay.

690   Katz, Shlomo. NEGRO AND JEW: AN ENCOUNTER IN AMERICA.
       New York: Macmillan Co., 1967. xvi, 141 p.

       Twenty-seven American Jews and Negroes discuss relations
       between the two ethnic groups. Emphasis is on Negro anti-
       Semitism.

691   Selznick, Gertrude J., and Steinberg, Stephen. THE TENACITY OF
       PREJUDICE: ANTI-SEMITISM IN CONTEMPORARY AMERICA. New
       York: Harper and Row, 1969. xxi, 248 p. 59 statistical tables.

       A sociological study of the extent, nature, and locus of anti-
       Jewish prejudice in the United States.

692   Stark, Rodney, and Glock, Charles Y. CHRISTIAN BELIEFS AND ANTI-
       SEMITISM. New York: Harper and Row, 1966. xxi, 266 p.

       Results of a survey regarding the relationship of Christian
       beliefs and anti-Semitic prejudice. Interviews with San Fran-
       cisco-area Protestants and Catholics and supplemented by
       others taken with a national sample of the population.

693   Stark, Rodney, et al. WAYWARD SHEPHERDS: PREJUDICE AND THE
       PROTESTANT CLERGY. New York: Harper and Row, 1971. 138 p.

       A sociological study of anti-Semitism among Protestant minis-
       ters, arguing that the Christian faith continues to generate
       hostility to Jews.

694   Strong, Donald S. ORGANIZED ANTI-SEMITISM IN AMERICA: THE
       RISE OF GROUP PREJUDICE DURING THE DECADE 1930-40. Washing-
       ton, D.C.: American Council on Public Affairs, 1941. 191 p. Bibliog.

       A survey of anti-Semitic organizations in the United States
       during the 1930s, such as the German-American Bund, the
       Paul Reveres, and the Silver Shirts.

Chapter 10

DENOMINATIONALISM IN THE NINETEENTH CENTURY

SECOND GREAT AWAKENING

695   Birdsall, Richard D. "The Second Great Awakening and the New England Social Order." CHURCH HISTORY 39 (1970): 345-64.

        Suggests that the Awakening played a role in supporting a lagging and undermined confidence among New Englanders.

696   Boles, John B. THE GREAT REVIVAL, 1787-1805: THE ORIGINS OF THE SOUTHERN EVANGELICAL MIND. Lexington: University Press of Kentucky, 1972. 236 p.

        Combines a useful analysis and description of the influential Kentucky revival with a more questionable attempt to explain the character of southern evangelicalism on the basis of that experience.

697   Cleveland, Catharine C. THE GREAT REVIVAL IN THE WEST, 1797-1805. Chicago: University of Chicago Press, 1916. 269 p. Appendix.

        Description of the revival now superseded by many other fuller and more recent narratives, but the appendix contains valuable primary documents describing the revival.

698   Johnson, Charles A. THE FRONTIER CAMP MEETING: RELIGION'S HARVEST TIME. Dallas, Tex.: Southern Methodist University Press, 1955. 325 p. Bibliog.

        An excellent description of the camp meeting, including chapters devoted to preachers, hymns, general organization of the site, and fraternizing at the meetings.

699   Mathews, Donald G. "The Second Great Awakening as an Organizing Process, 1780-1830." AMERICAN QUARTERLY 21 (1969): 23-43.

        A useful review of the literature related to the Second Great

Awakening combined with a provocative new approach to
the examination of this revival. Essential reading for religious and social historians.

700   Weisberger, Bernard A. THEY GATHERED AT THE RIVER: THE STORY
       OF THE GREAT REVIVALISTS AND THEIR IMPACT UPON RELIGION
       IN AMERICA. Boston: Little, Brown, and Co., 1958. 345 p.

       A narrative history of revivalism from the camp meetings to
       the twentieth century. Uniformly enjoyable book for begin-
       ning students. A good introduction to subject, but other
       works necessary to fill out the critical history.

REVIVALISM

General

McLoughlin (703) offers the best discussion of revivalism as a national phenomenon. See also Hudson (1081), Smith (1186), Thompson (1199), Roberts (1270),
Thomas (1257), and Harrell (1263).

701   Hall, Gordon Langley. THE SAWDUST TRAIL: THE STORY OF AMERI-
       CAN EVANGELISM. Philadelphia: Macrae Smith Co., 1964. 249 p.

       A popular version of the history of revivalism told through
       the biographies of such evangelists as Father Dyer, a revival-
       ist on skis; D.L. Moody; "Gypsy" Smith; Billy Sunday; Evangeline
       Booth, a leader of the Salvation Army; Daddy Grace; Father
       Divine; Aimee Semple McPherson, Reba Crawford; and Billy
       Graham.

702   Hofstadter, Richard. ANTI-INTELLECTUALISM IN AMERICAN LIFE.
       New York: Alfred A. Knopf, 1963. xiii, 434 p.

       Describes in part 2 of this book, entitled "The Religion of
       the Heart," the development of the evangelical spirit (by
       which author means revivalism) from earliest times into the
       twentieth century as an example of anti-intellectualism. A
       very popular and widely read book, although author quite
       perverse in his comments on religion: work is less than
       helpful, not so much because of his contempt for religion,
       but because his contempt leads him into superficiality.

703   McLoughlin, William G. MODERN REVIVALISM: CHARLES GRANDI-
       SON FINNEY TO BILLY GRAHAM. New York: Ronald Press, 1959.
       551 p.

       A well-researched study of revivalism in the United States

since the 1820s, focusing on the most prominent Protestant evangelists. Bibliographical essay.

704 _____, ed. THE AMERICAN EVANGELICALS, 1800-1900; AN AN-THOLOGY. New York: Harper and Row, 1968. 213 p.

Excerpts from Baird (721), Cartwright (752), Bushnell, Beecher, Wayland, Phillips Brooks, D.L. Moody, and Strong's OUR COUNTRY (1094).

705 Sweet, William W. REVIVALISM IN AMERICA, ITS ORIGIN, GROWTH AND DECLINE. New York: Charles Scribner's Sons, 1944. 192 p.

A series of eight lectures, comprising an interpretation and appraisal of the movement.

Charles G. Finney

706 Finney, Charles G. LECTURES ON REVIVALS OF RELIGION. Edited by William G. McLoughlin. John Harvard Library. Cambridge, Mass.: Belknap Press of Harvard University Press, 1950. lix, 470 p.

Set of lectures by Finney (1792-1875), the greatest preacher and one of the most important and influential men of the early nineteenth century. Contains his most coherent defense of revivalism and is the best expression of his characteristic mind-set. Helpful introduction by McLoughlin.

707 Johnson, James E. "Charles G. Finney and a Theology of Revivalism." CHURCH HISTORY 38 (1969): 338-58.

A useful summary of his career and brief summary of his teachings, which does not challenge the accepted views of Finney's place in nineteenth-century religious history.

708 _____. "Charles G. Finney and Oberlin Perfectionism." JOURNAL OF PRESBYTERIAN HISTORY 46 (1968): 42-57, 128-38.

A good analysis of Finney's pilgrimage toward Perfectionism, illustrating the often neglected mystical side of the great revivalist.

709 Sweet, Leonard I. "The View of Man Inherent in New Measures Revivalism." CHURCH HISTORY 45 (1976): 206-21.

Argues that Finney, as some historians claim for many "Jacksonians," was not so optimistic about human nature as has been supposed. Shows him to be status-conscious and conservative in his revivalism.

Late Nineteenth Century

710   Findlay, James F., Jr. DWIGHT L. MOODY: AMERICAN EVAN-
        GELIST, 1837–1899. Chicago: University of Chicago Press, 1969.
        440 p.

>   Excellent biography of the renowned evangelist of the Gilded
>   Age, tracing his formative years, career in Britain and the
>   United States, and seeking to appraise his impact on religious
>   life. Bibliographical essay.

711   _____. "Moody, 'Gapmen,' and the Gospel: The Early Days of
        Moody Bible Institute." CHURCH HISTORY 31 (1962): 322–35.

>   Describes the founding of Moody Bible Institute in Chicago
>   in the 1880s and its purpose of training lay evangelists, or
>   "gapmen," to carry on the revival work of Dwight L. Moody.

712   Pollock, John C. MOODY: A BIOGRAPHICAL PORTRAIT OF THE
        PACESETTER IN MODERN MASS EVANGELISM. New York: Macmil-
        lan Co., 1963. 336 p. Bibliog.

>   A readable biography of Dwight L. Moody, written without
>   footnotes and, therefore, of less value for research purposes
>   than Findlay (710).

713   Ruffin, Bernard. FANNY CROSBY. Philadelphia: United Church Press,
        1976. 370 p.

>   A soundly researched, straightforward life of the famous
>   blind songwriter (1820–1915) whose sentimental and lachry-
>   mose hymns may quite possibly have been the best-known
>   literature of the nineteenth century.

Twentieth Century

714   High, Stanley. BILLY GRAHAM, THE PERSONAL STORY OF THE MAN,
        HIS MESSAGE AND HIS MISSION. New York: McGraw-Hill Book
        Co., 1956. 274 p.

>   A journalistic account of the early career, and glimpses into
>   the private life, of the most successful revivalist of the
>   twentieth century.

715   McLoughlin, William G. BILLY GRAHAM: REVIVALIST IN A SECU-
        LAR AGE. New York: Ronald Press, 1960. 269 p.

>   A leading historian of revivalism analyzes Billy Graham's
>   crusades of the 1950s and places them in the context of
>   Anglo-American revivalism.

716   ____. BILLY SUNDAY WAS HIS REAL NAME. Chicago: University of Chicago Press, 1955. 324 p.

> Excellent biography and analysis of the flamboyant revivalist (1865-1935) whose preaching against drink and in favor of patriotism and World War I made him the most popular Protestant of that era.

717   Morris, James. THE PREACHERS. New York: St. Martin's Press, 1973. 418 p.

> A study of several of the best-known American religious figures and analyses of their ministries, including A.A. Allen, Oral Roberts, C.W. Burpo, Reverend Ike, Carl McIntire, Kathryn Kuhlman, Billy James Hargis, Garner Ted and Herbert W. Armstrong, and Billy Graham.

718   Orr, James Edwin. THE FLAMING TONGUE: THE IMPACT OF TWENTIETH CENTURY REVIVALS. Chicago: Moody Press, 1973. 241 p.

> A description of what the author contends was a Third Great Awakening in Western history, a documented revival that began in Wales in 1905 and spread around the world. A work not damaged by the author's acknowledged purpose of hoping to spark yet another Great Awakening.

719   Pollock, John Charles. BILLY GRAHAM: THE AUTHORIZED BIOGRAPHY. New York: McGraw-Hill Book Co., 1966. 277 p.

> A highly sympathetic and selective biography based on interviews and private papers.

720   Ramsay, John Cummins. JOHN WILBUR CHAPMAN, THE MAN, HIS METHODS, AND HIS MESSAGE. Boston: Christopher Publishing House, 1962. 230 p.

> Life of a second-rank revivalist (1859-1918).

THE DENOMINATIONAL PATTERN

William Warren Sweet and Sidney E. Mead, both professors at the University of Chicago Divinity School for the greatest part of their careers, were the scholars preeminently responsible for establishing the conceptual framework used by most historians in interpreting this period. Sweet presented his views succinctly in RELIGION IN THE DEVELOPMENT OF AMERICAN CULTURE (727) and left a monument to his industry in four volumes of source materials (728-31). Mead's most influential work has appeared in the form of essays, especially in THE LIVELY EXPERIMENT (16). Richey (725) has edited a useful collection of writings on denominationalism. See also Mead (45) and Sandeen (46).

721   Baird, Robert. RELIGION IN AMERICA. 1844. Reprint. Abridged
       and edited by Henry W. Bowden. New York: Harper and Row, 1970.
       xxxvii, 314 p.

       Baird (1798–1863) attempted to explain American Protestant-
       ism to Europeans. Described by Sidney Mead as being "a
       classic account not only of religion and the churches of the
       period but also the general social and political atmosphere
       that prevailed. I think it belongs in a class with Tocque-
       ville and Philip Schaff's AMERICA."

722   Cross, Whitney R. THE BURNED–OVER DISTRICT: THE SOCIAL AND
       INTELLECTUAL HISTORY OF ENTHUSIASTIC RELIGION IN WESTERN
       NEW YORK, 1800–1850. Ithaca, N.Y.: Cornell University Press,
       1950. 383 p.

       Influential and important, a pioneering interdisciplinary study
       that attempted to integrate religious, economic, and geogra-
       phic data, but see De Pillis (775) for a thorough critique.

723   Miller, Perry. THE LIFE OF THE MIND IN AMERICA: FROM THE
       REVOLUTION TO THE CIVIL WAR. New York: Harcourt, Brace, and
       World, 1965. 338 p.

       The last of Miller's books, and one of the greatest. Of
       nine proposed sections, only two completed at the time of
       his death--long essays on the evangelical spirit, with special
       attention to Charles G. Finney, and on the law. Like all
       of his writing, not easy to read, but is rewarding.

724   Miyakawa, T. Scott. PROTESTANTS AND PIONEERS: INDIVIDUAL-
       ISM AND CONFORMITY ON THE AMERICAN FRONTIER. Chicago:
       University of Chicago Press, 1964. 306 p.

       Sociological analysis, concentrating on Methodist, Presby-
       terian, Quaker, and Baptist denominations. States that these
       Protestants were members of disciplined religious groups in
       an increasingly organized society, and they created a social
       order in which people resorted to voluntary associations to
       achieve objectives unattainable by individuals.

725   Richey, Russell, ed. DENOMINATIONALISM. Nashville: Abingdon
       Press, 1977. 288 p.

       An anthology of scholarly articles, including contributions
       from Richey, Sidney E. Mead, W.S. Hudson, T.L. Smith,
       E.A. Smith, F.J. Hood, E.F. Frazier, H.R. Niebuhr, and
       M.E. Marty.

726   Sandeen, Ernest R. "The Distinctiveness of American Denominationalism: A Case Study of the 1846 Evangelical Alliance." CHURCH HISTORY 45 (1976): 222–34.

      Analyzes the representation of American and British delegations to the meeting of the Alliance in London, finding British groups responding to and organizing against the same problems and looking very denominational. Raises a question about the distinctiveness of the American church–state relationship as a causative factor in historical interpretation.

727   Sweet, William W. RELIGION IN THE DEVELOPMENT OF AMERICAN CULTURE, 1765–1840. New York: Charles Scribner's Sons, 1952. xiv, 338 p.

      Traces the state of the churches at the time of the American Revolution denomination by denomination, and then examines the manner in which they expanded or failed to expand into the West. Focus in later chapters on college and seminary founding, the revolt against Calvinism, and missions. As in so much of author's work, the emphasis placed on the Northwest Territory.

728   _____, ed. THE BAPTISTS, 1783–1830, A COLLECTION OF SOURCE MATERIAL. Vol. 1. RELIGION ON THE AMERICAN FRONTIER. New York: Henry Holt and Co., 1931. 652 p.

      A series of documents chiefly from Illinois and Kentucky, that are primarily church records and minutes. Also, an extract from a short history and the entire autobiography of Jacob Bower, an Illinois Baptist preacher. Preceded by over one hundred pages of introduction.

729   _____. THE PRESBYTERIANS, A COLLECTION OF SOURCE MATERIALS. Vol. 2. RELIGION ON THE AMERICAN FRONTIER, 1783–1840. New York: Harper and Brothers, 1936. Reprint. New York: Cooper Square Publishers, 1964. xii, 939 p.

      The documents introduced by a narrative of over one hundred pages, explaining the denomination's history from 1783–1837. Followed by a series of extracts from the minutes of presbyteries and sessions records in Kentucky and Ohio, records of the operation of the Plan of Union, and documents relating to discipline, Indian missions, licensing and call of ministers. Closes with several autobiographical sketches and documents relating to the Old School–New School schism in 1837.

730   _____. THE CONGREGATIONALISTS, A COLLECTION OF SOURCE MATERIALS. Vol. 3. RELIGION ON THE AMERICAN FRONTIER, 1783–1850. Chicago: University of Chicago Press, 1939. 435 p.

A general introduction of sixty-three pages. Followed by documents illustrating missions to the Indians, work in Michigan, Illinois, and Wisconsin, and examples of church records. Also reprints a portion (1833-40) of the autobiography of Flavel Pascom, a preacher who served the American Home Missionary Society in Illinois.

731 _____. THE METHODISTS, A COLLECTION OF SOURCE MATERIALS. Vol. 4. RELIGION ON THE AMERICAN FRONTIER, 1783-1840. Chicago: University of Chicago Press, 1946. 800 p.

Illustrates the activities of the Methodist circuit rider and includes primarily journals and letters from Methodist preachers on circuit. Has a seventy-page introduction.

ADVENTISTS

732 Froom, Leroy E. THE PROPHETIC FAITH OF OUR FATHERS. 4 vols. Washington, D.C.: Review and Herald Publishing Association, 1946-54.

A monumental, scholarly, but strongly prejudiced, denominational history. Defends Adventist doctrines as apostolic truth and openly champions the cause of historicist premillennialism. Provides an invaluable reference service and is completely accurate in citations of books and events. American scene covered in volume 4.

733 Gaustad, Edwin S[cott]., ed. THE RISE OF ADVENTISM: RELIGION AND SOCIETY IN MID-NINETEENTH-CENTURY AMERICA. New York: Harper and Row, 1975. 329 p. Bibliog.

A well-edited collection of ten addresses delivered in Loma Linda, California, during 1972-73. Although essays delivered to an Adventist audience, are only partly denominational history, and when Adventist themes are addressed, the treatment is not at all sectarian. Contributors and their subjects: W.S. Hudson, "A Time of Religious Ferment"; T.L. Smith, "Social Reform"; J.B. Blake, "Health Reform"; J.C. Greene, "Science and Religion"; R.L. Moore, "Spiritualism"; E.R. Sandeen, "Millennialism"; W.G. McLoughlin, "Revivalism"; D.T. Arthur, "Millerism"; and J.M. Butler, "Adventism and the American Experience." Concludes with the best bibliography of Adventist materials available--over one hundred pages.

734 Nichol, Francis David. THE MIDNIGHT CRY: A DEFENSE OF THE CHARACTER AND CONDUCT OF WILLIAM MILLER AND THE MILLERITES. Washington, D.C.: Review & Herald Publishing Association, 1944. 560 p.

An Adventist historian's attempt to vindicate the followers of William Miller from the charge that belief in the second coming of Christ fostered insanity and appealed to persons of fanatical disposition. Retells the story of Miller's ministry. Ironically, after acceptance by most secular historians for a generation, Adventist historians have now begun to question whether author was completely correct in his assessment.

735   Numbers, Ronald L. PROPHETESS OF HEALTH: A STUDY OF ELLEN G. WHITE. New York: Harper and Row, 1976. xiv, 271 p.

A soundly researched, well-written study of the most important figure in the history of the Seventh-Day Adventist denomination and one of the most important women of the nineteenth century. Although author an Adventist, provides a critical portrait of this leader, showing how she was inconsistent and confused at certain points in her life. Excellent on health reform movement of the era.

736   Spaulding, Arthur Whitefield. ORIGIN AND HISTORY OF SEVENTH-DAY ADVENTISTS. 4 wols. Washington, D.C.: Review & Herald Publishing Association, 1961-62.

A reissue of the two-volume 1949 edition which appeared under the titles, CAPTAINS OF THE HOST, 1845-1900, and CHRIST'S LAST LEGION, 1901-1948. An "official" chronicle and catalog of leaders, missions, publications.

DISCIPLES OF CHRIST

See also Tucker (1109) and Garrison (1318)

737   Beazley, George B., Jr., ed. THE CHRISTIAN CHURCH (DISCIPLES OF CHRIST): AN INTERPRETATIVE EXAMINATION IN THE CULTURAL CONTEXT. St. Louis, Mo.: Bethany Press, 1973. 417 p.

A collection of essays on Disciples' history, emphasizing the role of the denomination in ecumenical enterprises.

738   Boren, Carter E. RELIGION ON THE TEXAS FRONTIER. San Antonio, Tex.: Naylor Co., 1968. 390 p.

A history of the Disciples of Christ denomination in Texas, from territory's admission to the Union to 1906.

739   DeGroot, Alfred Thomas. NEW POSSIBILITIES FOR DISCIPLES AND INDEPENDENTS, WITH A HISTORY OF THE INDEPENDENTS, CHURCH OF CHRIST NUMBER TWO. St. Louis, Mo.: Bethany Press, 1963. 112 p.

An account of the forces behind a schism among the Disciples of Christ, which culminated in the organization of the second group in 1955.

740   Garrison, Winfred E., and DeGroot, Alfred T. THE DISCIPLES OF CHRIST, A HISTORY. Rev. ed. St. Louis, Mo.: Bethany Press, 1958. 592 p. Bibliog.

The standard denominational history of the Disciples of Christ denomination written by two recognized historians of the church.

741   Harrell, David Edwin, Jr. QUEST FOR A CHRISTIAN AMERICA: THE DISCIPLES OF CHRIST AND AMERICAN SOCIETY TO 1866. Vol. 1. A SOCIAL HISTORY OF THE DISCIPLES OF CHRIST. Nashville: Disciples of Christ Historical Society, 1966. 256 p.

Annotation in next entry.

742   _____. THE SOCIAL SOURCES OF DIVISION IN THE DISCIPLES OF CHRIST, 1865-1900. Vol. 2. A SOCIAL HISTORY OF THE DISCIPLES OF CHRIST. Atlanta, Ga.: Publishing Systems, 1973. 458 p.

Important and valuable history of the denomination, which includes churches known both as Disciples of Christ and Churches of Christ. A model study that might well be emulated by other denominational traditions.

743   Lindley, Denton Ray. APOSTLE OF FREEDOM. St. Louis, Mo.: Bethany Press, 1957. 264 p.

An exposition and description of Alexander Campbell's conception of the structure and function of the church, as revealed in his writings. Campbell (1788-1866) a founder of the Disciples of Christ.

744   McAllister, Lester G. THOMAS CAMPBELL: MAN OF THE BOOK. St. Louis, Mo.: Bethany Press, 1954. 294 p.

A competent biography of Thomas Campbell (1763-1854), one of the founders of the Disciples denomination and father of Alexander Campbell.

745   McAllister, Lester G., and Tucker, William E. JOURNEY IN FAITH: A HISTORY OF THE CHRISTIAN CHURCH (DISCIPLES OF CHRIST). St. Louis, Mo.: Bethany Press, 1975. 505 p. Bibliog.

A recent history of the denomination that improves on Garrison and DeGroot (740) in its coverage of the post-Civil War period.

746   West, Robert F. ALEXANDER CAMPBELL AND NATURAL RELIGION.
       New Haven, Conn.: Yale University Press, 1948. 250 p.

> Scholarly, well-written treatment of Campbell's role in com-
> batting the liberal-deist philosophy of the early nineteenth
> century. Recounts Campbell's attack upon ecclesiasticism,
> his defense of revealed religion, and his philosophy of his-
> tory in three separate sections of the book.

747   West, William G. BARTON WARREN STONE; EARLY AMERICAN AD-
       VOCATE OF CHRISTIAN UNITY. Nashville: Disciples of Christ His-
       torical Society, 1954. 245 p.

> A narrative biography of Stone (1772-1844), one of the
> founders of the Disciples denomination.

GERMAN METHODISTS

748   Albright, Raymond W. A HISTORY OF THE EVANGELICAL CHURCH.
       Harrisburg, Pa.: Evangelical Press, 1942. 501 p.

> Standard history for this denomination.

749   Drury, Augustus W. HISTORY OF THE CHURCH OF THE UNITED
       BRETHREN IN CHRIST. Dayton, Ohio: Otterbein Press, 1924. 821 p.

> Encyclopaedic treatment includes the author's nineteenth-
> century life of Philip Wilhelm Otterbein.

750   O'Malley, J. Steven. PILGRIMAGE OF FAITH: THE LEGACY OF
       THE OTTERBEINS. American Theological Library Association Mono-
       graph Series, no. 4. Metuchen, N.J.: Scarecrow Press, 1973. 225 p.

> Biography of Philip Wilhelm Otterbein (1726-1813), a Ger-
> man reformed pietist who came to the Middle Colonies in
> America as a missionary and remained to found the United
> Brethren Church. This analysis of the family theological
> legacy especially valuable since it provides one of the few
> historical accounts of the pietist tradition outside New Eng-
> land and Britain.

METHODISTS

See also Sweet (731), Keller (966), Gravely (964), Mathews (968), Culver (981),
Posey (999), Sweet (1062), Mann (1074), Jones (1251), MacKenzie (1291), and
Dabney (1563).

751   Byrne, Donald E., Jr. NO FOOT OF LAND: FOLKLORE OF AMERI-
       CAN METHODIST ITINERANTS. ATLA Monograph Series, no. 6. Me-
       tuchen, N.J.: Scarecrow Press, 1975. xvi, 354 p.

       A catalogue of Methodist folk tales, summarized and sorted,
       but not well related to the literature or theory of folklore.

752   Cartwright, Peter. AUTOBIOGRAPHY. Edited by Charles L. Wallis.
       Nashville: Abingdon Press, 1956. 349 p.

       Most famous of all the narratives of the Methodist circuit
       riders by a preacher who ranged all over the Upper Missis-
       sippi Valley in the decades before the Civil War, spent
       much time preaching in Indiana and Illinois, and really knew
       how to tell a story. Republished one hundred years after its
       first appearance.

753   Finley, James B. SKETCHES OF WESTERN METHODISM: BIOGRAPHI-
       CAL, HISTORICAL, AND MISCELLANEOUS. Edited by W.P. Strick-
       land. Cincinnati, Ohio: Methodist Book Concern, 1854. Reprint.
       New York: Arno Press, 1969. 551 p.

       About thirty thumbnail sketches of Methodist preachers com-
       prise the bulk of this volume.

754   Peters, John L. CHRISTIAN PERFECTION AND AMERICAN METHOD-
       ISM. New York: Abingdon Press, 1956. 252 p.

       Analyzes Wesley's doctrine of perfection and traces its trans-
       plantation to and modification in America up to 1900.

PRESBYTERIANS AND CONGREGATIONALISTS

See also Sweet (729, 730), Sherrill (813), Meredith (969), Thompson (976), Murray (987), Posey (1000), Vander Velde (1063), McLoughlin (1089), Loetscher
(1105), and Hinckley (1283).

755   Henry, Stuart C. UNVANQUISHED PURITAN: A PORTRAIT OF LY-
       MAN BEECHER. Grand Rapids, Mich.: William B. Eerdmans Publish-
       ing Co., 1973. 299 p.

       A biography of Beecher (1775-1863), New School Presbyterian
       revivalist and controversialist, concentrating upon his career
       up to the 1837 schism in the Presbyterian denomination.

756   McKinney, William Wilson, ed. THE PRESBYTERIAN VALLEY. Pitts-
       burgh, Pa.: Davis and Warde, 1958. 639 p.

       Account of the development of the Presbyterian churches in

the Upper Ohio River Valley (Western Pennsylvania, Eastern Ohio, and Western West Virginia) by a group of seven authors. Fragmentary, hagiographic treatment concentrating on institutional development.

757 Marsden, George M. THE EVANGELICAL MIND AND THE NEW SCHOOL PRESBYTERIAN EXPERIENCE: A CASE STUDY OF THOUGHT AND THEOLOGY IN NINETEENTH-CENTURY AMERICA. New Haven, Conn.: Yale University Press, 1970. 293 p.

Quite useful as a history of the New School movement from about 1800 until 1869, but attempt to connect the New School experience with the "evangelical mind" has not proven so successful.

758 Melton, Julius. PRESBYTERIAN WORSHIP IN AMERICA: CHANGING PATTERNS SINCE 1787. Richmond, Va.: John Knox Press, 1967. 173 p.

Vivid descriptions of a variety of services, ranging from frontier sacramental seasons to the elegance of wealthy city parishes. Best for the nineteenth-century worship.

759 Opie, John, Jr. "James McGready: Theologian of Frontier Revivalism." CHURCH HISTORY 34 (1965): 455-56.

Shows that this early-nineteenth-century Kentucky Presbyterian not only had a theology but a conservative one at that.

760 Pearson, Samuel C., Jr. "From Church to Denomination: American Congregationalism in the Nineteenth Century." CHURCH HISTORY 38 (1969): 67-87.

A detailed study illustrating Elwyn Smith's thesis (762) for the Congregationalist churches.

761 Rudolph, L.C. HOOSIER ZION: THE PRESBYTERIANS IN EARLY INDIANA. New Haven, Conn.: Yale University Press, 1963. 218 p.

An excellent local history study that is not only detailed but interesting as well. Includes analysis of early settlers, leading preachers, church organization, and intellectual developments. Emphasizes the clash of sectional interests (Hoosiers and Yankees) in the churches.

762 Smith, Elwyn A. "The Forming of a Modern American Denomination." CHURCH HISTORY 31 (1962): 74-99.

Discusses the formation of the Old School Presbyterians into

a denomination according to a definition of denominationalism
that extends and helpfully clarifies S.E. Mead's formulation
(16).

PROTESTANT EPISCOPAL CHURCH

See also Cheshire (1056) and Albright (1086).

763   Loveland, Clara Olds. THE CRITICAL YEARS: THE RECONSTITUTION
       OF THE ANGLICAN CHURCH IN THE UNITED STATES OF AMERICA:
       1780-1789. Greenwich, Conn.: Seabury Press, 1956. 311 p. Bibliog.

       A useful monograph that surveys the process of reconstitution
       on a year-by-year basis in its separate chapters.

764   Manross, William W. THE EPISCOPAL CHURCH IN THE UNITED STATES,
       1800-1840: A STUDY IN CHURCH LIFE. Reprint. 1938. New
       York: Morehouse Gorham, 1959. 270 p. Bibliog.

       A thematic discussion of church life including chapters on
       the rector, missionary, parish, services, and layman.

765   Shepherd, Massey H.   THE REFORM OF LITURGICAL WORSHIP: PER-
       SPECTIVES AND PROSPECTS. New York: Oxford University Press,
       1961. 118 p.

       A brief interpretation of liturgical reforms in American Prot-
       estantism in the nineteenth and twentieth centuries, focusing
       on movements in the Protestant Episcopal Church.

766   Skardon, Alvin W. WILLIAM AUGUSTUS MUHLENBERG: CHURCH
       LEADER IN THE CITIES. Philadelphia: University of Pennsylvania
       Press, 1971. 343 p.

       A good biography of Muhlenberg (1796-1877), one of the
       most influential Episcopalians of the nineteenth century, who
       founded many institutions in Philadelphia and possessed a
       good sense of the problems of his denomination and of the
       urban areas of Philadelphia and New York.

OTHER GROUPS

767   Block, Marguerite. THE NEW CHURCH IN THE NEW WORLD: A
       STUDY OF SWEDENBORGIANISM IN THE NEW WORLD. New York:
       Henry Holt and Co., 1932. 464 p.

       A general history of this denomination by a nonmember.

768   Kern, Richard. JOHN WINEBRENNER: NINETEENTH CENTURY RE-
       FORMER. Harrisburg, Pa.: Central Publishing House, 1974. xii, 226 p.

      Biography of Winebrenner (1797-1860), a German Reformed
      minister who separated from that denomination and created
      a small sect called the General Eldership of the Churches
      of God which, like the Disciples, emphasized the restoration
      of primitive Christianity.

769   Post, Albert. POPULAR FREE THOUGHT IN AMERICA, 1825-1850.
       New York: Columbia University Press, 1943. 258 p.

      Religious aspects of this movement during its most influential
      years; discusses adherents' disbelief in divine revelation and
      emphasis on natural law and human reason.

770   Wilson, Bryan R. SECTS AND SOCIETY: A SOCIOLOGICAL STUDY
       OF THE ELIM TABERNACLE, CHRISTIAN SCIENCE, AND CHRISTADEL-
       PHIANS. Berkeley and Los Angeles: University of California Press,
       1961. 397 p.

      An analysis of the Christadelphians, founded during the 1860s
      by Dr. John Thomas Convers, in pages 219-314, but con-
      centrates upon the British side of the sect.

THE MORMONS, THE CHURCH OF JESUS CHRIST OF LATTER-DAY SAINTS

771   Anderson, Nels. DESERT SAINTS: THE MORMON FRONTIER IN
       UTAH. Chicago: University of Chicago Press, 1942. xxxviii, 459 p.

      A good volume of frontier history, narrated without bias by
      a trained sociologist who had in his possession many pre-
      viously unused community records, diaries, and Mormon church
      documents.

772   Anderson, Richard. JOSEPH SMITH'S NEW ENGLAND HERITAGE.
       Salt Lake City: Deseret Book Co., 1971.

      Careful research by a trained historian who is a Mormon.
      Emphasizes the importance of New England culture on Smith's
      thought.

773   Arrington, Leonard J. GREAT BASIN KINGDOM: AN ECONOMIC
       HISTORY OF THE LATTER-DAY SAINTS, 1830-1900. Cambridge, Mass.:
       Harvard University Press, 1958. 534 p.

      Well-organized, standard scholarly treatment. Covers gold
      rush, immigration, railroads, co-op movement, and attacks
      upon Mormon practices.

774 Brodie, Fawn. NO MAN KNOWS MY HISTORY: THE LIFE OF JO-
SEPH SMITH, THE MORMON PROPHET. 2d ed. New York: Alfred
A. Knopf, 1971. 476 p.

> The standard biography of Smith and the most influential book
> on early Mormonism, but see also Marvin S. Hill, "Secular
> or Sectarian History? A Critique of NO MAN KNOWS
> MY HISTORY," CHURCH HISTORY 43 (1974): 78-96.

775 De Pillis, Mario S. "The Social Sources of Mormonism." CHURCH
HISTORY 37 (1968): 50-79.

> Begins with a critique of Cross (722) and, to a lesser extent
> Davis (635), fundamentally discussing the intriguing problem
> of how to characterize Mormon origins---as New England or
> frontier. Argues that the question of the frontier in Cross
> has obscured the real context of Mormon development. In
> addition, states that Cross was guilty of scholarly mistakes,
> especially in his poor use of maps and charts.

776 Ericksen, Ephraim E. THE PSYCHOLOGICAL AND ETHICAL ASPECTS
OF MORMON GROUP LIFE. Chicago: University of Chicago Press,
1922. Reprint. Salt Lake City: University of Utah, 1974. 101 p.

> Traces Mormon values back to crises endured in the history
> of the denomination.

777 Flanders, Robert Bruce. NAUVOO: KINGDOM ON THE MISSISSIPPI.
Urbana: University of Illinois Press, 1965. 364 p.

> Urban history and religious history combined: a valuable
> account of the critical period in Mormon development from
> 1839 to 1846 when Smith came closest to establishing a
> physical location for the kingdom.

778 Hansen, Klaus. QUEST FOR EMPIRE: THE POLITICAL KINGDOM OF
GOD AND THE COUNCIL OF FIFTY IN MORMON HISTORY. East
Lansing: Michigan State University, 1967. 237 p.

> The Council of Fifty, a secret Mormon organization, attempted
> to institute a literal and political kingdom of God in Ameri-
> ca during the nineteenth century.

779 Hill, Marvin S. "The Historiography of Mormonism." CHURCH HIS-
TORY 28 (1959): 418-26.

> A thorough examination of the sources of Mormon history by
> the best-known Mormon expert and scholar. Especially good
> for the older sources.

780 _____. "The Shaping of the Mormon Mind in New England and New York." BRIGHAM YOUNG UNIVERSITY STUDIES 9 (1969): 351-72.

Takes issue with De Pillis's western approach to the origins of Mormonism.

781 Hill, Marvin S., and Allen, James B., eds. MORMONISM AND AMERICAN CULTURE. New York: Harper and Row, 1972. 189 p. Bibliog.

An extremely valuable reprinting of ten scholarly articles, including David B. Davis, "New England Origins of Mormonism," and "Some Themes of Counter-Subversion" (635); Mario S. De Pillis, "Quest for Religious Authority and the Rise of Mormonism"; and other articles by Arrington, Huntress, Mulder, Ivins, Hansen, Lamar, and O'Dea. Bibliography alone worth the price of the book.

782 Hunter, Milton R. BRIGHAM YOUNG, THE COLONIZER. Salt Lake City: Deseret News Press, 1940. xvi, 383 p.

The best treatment of the Mormon settlement of the Great Basin following the migration from Illinois in 1846.

783 McMurrin, Sterling M. THEOLOGICAL FOUNDATIONS OF THE MORMON RELIGION. Salt Lake City: University of Utah Press, 1965. 151 p.

The most significant book available on Mormon metaphysics and theology.

784 Mulder, William. HOMEWARD TO ZION: THE MORMON MIGRATION FROM SCANDINAVIA. Minneapolis: University of Minnesota Press, 1957. 375 p.

Describes the immigration of thousands of Scandinavian converts from their homeland to Utah.

785 Mulder, William A., and Mortensen, A. Russell, eds. AMONG THE MORMONS; HISTORIC ACCOUNTS BY CONTEMPORARY OBSERVERS. New York: Alfred A. Knopf, 1958. Reprint. Lincoln: University of Nebraska Press, 1973. 482 p.

A careful selection of original source material that captures the drama of Mormon history.

786 Oaks, Dallin H., and Hill, Marvin S. CARTHAGE CONSPIRACY: THE TRIAL OF THE ACCUSED ASSASSINS OF JOSEPH SMITH. Urbana: University of Illinois Press, 1975. xiv, 248 p.

A meticulous and exhaustive analysis and recreation of the

trial that followed the murder of the Smith brothers in the Carthage jail in 1844. Questionable whether the trial (in which the verdict of not guilty was a foregone conclusion) worth such expenditure of energy.

787   O'Dea, Thomas [F.]. THE MORMONS. Chicago: University of Chicago Press, 1957. 288 p.

A useful introduction to Mormon thought and theology by a sympathetic non-Mormon scholar. Not a history of the denomination.

788   Roberts, Brigham H. A COMPREHENSIVE HISTORY OF THE CHURCH OF JESUS CHRIST OF LATTER DAY SAINTS. 1909-15. Reprint. 6 vols. Salt Lake City: Deseret New Press, 1930.

Old-fashioned denominational epic by a Mormon leader. Because of its detail and scope, the work is recognized by Mormons as the standard comprehensive history of the early Latter Day Saints Church.

789   Smith, Joseph. HISTORY OF THE CHURCH OF JESUS CHRIST OF LATTER-DAY SAINTS. 8 vols. Salt Lake City: Deseret Book Co., 1971.

An important documentary source by the founder of the Latter Day Saints Church.

790   Taylor, Philip A.M. EXPECTATIONS WESTWARD: THE MORMONS AND THE EMIGRATION OF THEIR BRITISH CONVERTS IN THE NINETEENTH CENTURY. Ithaca, N.Y.: Cornell University Press, 1966. 277 p.

An excellent work by a non-Mormon British historian who emphasizes the incredible job of organization, the "masterly job of planning," done by the Mormons to transport their British converts from Liverpool to Salt Lake City, Utah. Useful as immigration history as well as religious history.

791   West, Ray B. KINGDOM OF THE SAINTS: THE STORY OF BRIGHAM YOUNG AND THE MORMONS. New York: Viking Press, 1957. 389 p.

A well-written, good general account of Mormon history.

792   Young, Kimball. ISN'T ONE WIFE ENOUGH? New York: Henry Holt and Co., 1954. 476 p.

Rather a better study of Mormon polygamy than the title suggests.

Chapter 11

PHILOSOPHY, THEOLOGY, AND REFORM BEFORE 1865

MORAL PHILOSOPHY

See also Howe (845).

793   Madden, Edward H. CIVIL DISOBEDIENCE AND MORAL LAW IN
       NINETEENTH-CENTURY AMERICAN PHILOSOPHY. Seattle: Univer-
       sity of Washington Press, 1968. 214 p. Bibliog.

       Analysis of moral philosophers from Francis Wayland, Asa
       Mahan, and James H. Fairchild to George William Curtis,
       Chauncey Wright, and Charles Eliot Norton; Transcenden-
       talists are touched on only briefly.

794   Meyer, Donald H. THE INSTRUCTED CONSCIENCE: THE SHAPING
       OF THE AMERICAN NATIONAL ETHIC. Philadelphia: University of
       Pennsylvania Press, 1972. 234 p.

       A discussion of some of the principal moral philosophers of
       the mid-nineteenth century (Francis Wayland of Brown, Mark
       Hopkins of Williams, Francis Bowen of Harvard, and James
       McCosh and Archibald Alexander of Princeton), who are
       described as inhabiting a half-way house on the road between
       the worlds dominated by theology and science.

795   Smith, Wilson. PROFESSORS AND PUBLIC ETHICS: STUDIES IN
       NORTHERN MORAL PHILOSOPHERS BEFORE THE CIVIL WAR. Ithaca,
       N.Y.: Cornell University Press, 1956. 244 p.

       Begins with a discussion of Paley's influence and goes on to
       treat John Gros, Francis Lieber, Charles Haddock, and Fran-
       cis Wayland, concluding with a chapter on James Walker.

MERCERSBURG THEOLOGY

796   Binkley, Luther J. THE MERCERSBURG THEOLOGY. Lancaster, Pa.:
       Franklin and Marshall, 1953. 156 p.

       Topical analysis including chapters on Christology, doctrine
       of the church, sin and salvation, and liturgy.

797   Nevin, John W. THE MYSTICAL PRESENCE AND OTHER WRITINGS.
       Lancaster Series on the Mercersburg Theology, vol. 4. Edited by Bard
       W. Thompson and George H. Bricker. Philadelphia: United Church
       Press, 1966. 431 p. Bibliog.

       A republication of THE MYSTICAL PRESENCE: A VINDICA-
       TION OF THE REFORMED OR CALVINISTIC DOCTRINE OF
       THE HOLY EUCHARIST (1846), and THE DOCTRINE OF THE
       REFORMED CHURCH ON THE LORD'S SUPPER (1850). In-
       cludes a short introduction.

798   Nichols, James Hastings. ROMANTICISM IN AMERICAN THEOLOGY:
       NEVIN AND SCHAFF AT MERCERSBURG. Chicago: University of
       Chicago Press, 1961. 322 p.

       A masterful narrative and analytical treatment of this semi-
       nary's most influential figures.

799   Nichols, James Hastings, ed. THE MERCERSBURG THEOLOGY. Library
       of Protestant Thought. New York: Oxford University Press, 1966.
       384 p.

       Contains some material from John W. Nevin and Philip Schaff
       not republished in the Lancaster Series on the Mercersburg
       Theology, including some of Nevin's sermons and an excerpt
       from his ANTICHRIST, OR THE SPIRIT OF SECT AND SCHISM;
       and from Schaff's THESES FOR THE TIME and sections from
       his general introduction to church history.

800   Schaff, Philip. AMERICA: A SKETCH OF ITS POLITICAL, SOCIAL,
       AND RELIGIOUS CHARACTER. Edited by Perry Miller. John Harvard
       Library. Cambridge, Mass.: Belknap Press of Harvard University Press,
       1961. xxxv, 241 p.

       Interprets American religion to foreigners in a very percep-
       tive work. Author (1815-93), a German-born and trained
       historian who spent his active professional life in the United
       States.

801   _____. THE PRINCIPLE OF PROTESTANTISM. Lancaster Series on
       the Mercersburg Theology, vol. 1. Philadelphia: United Church Press,
       1964. 268 p.

A scholarly edition of the 1845 English translation of this address, which touched off the great controversy over the Mercersburg Theology.

HORACE BUSHNELL

See also Thompson (1199) and Kirschenmann in Brauer (39).

802   Cross, Barbara M. HORACE BUSHNELL: MINISTER TO A CHANG-
ING AMERICA. Chicago: University of Chicago Press, 1958.   xv,
201 p. Bibliog.

A good, scholarly analysis of the thought of Bushnell (1802-
76), who has been called the most important theologian in
American history between Jonathan Edwards and Reinhold
Niebuhr. Emphasizes how Bushnell met the challenge of
the mid-nineteenth century to become a dynamic force in
the transformation of American Protestantism.

803   Johnson, William A. NATURE AND THE SUPERNATURAL IN THE
THEOLOGY OF HORACE BUSHNELL. Lund, Sweden: C.W.K. Glee-
rup, 1963.   276 p.

Useful, though the author struggles too much to interpret all
of Bushnell's thought through the concepts of nature and the
supernatural.

804   Smith, Hilrie Shelton, ed. HORACE BUSHNELL. New York: Oxford
University Press, 1965. 407 p.

An excellent collection of extracts from the work of Horace
Bushnell.

HENRY JAMES, SR.

See also Block (767).

805   James, Henry, Sr. HENRY JAMES, SENIOR: A SELECTION OF HIS
WRITINGS. Edited by Giles Gunn. Chicago: American Library Association, 1974.   312 p.

A collection of excerpts from the works of the elder Henry
James (1811-82), along with an autobiographical sketch and
brief selections by his sons assessing his work.

806   Hoover, Dwight W. HENRY JAMES, SR. AND THE RELIGION OF
COMMUNITY. Grand Rapids, Mich.: William B. Eerdmans Publishing Co., 1969. 152 p. Bibliog.

A brief analysis of the writings of the elder Henry James.

807   Young, Frederic H. THE PHILOSOPHY OF HENRY JAMES, SR. New York: Bookman Associates, 1951. xiv, 338 p. Bibliog.

A penetrating analysis of the spiritual philosphy of the elder Henry James.

EDUCATION

808   Brown, Jerry W. THE RISE OF BIBLICAL CRITICISM IN AMERICA, 1800-1870: THE NEW ENGLAND SCHOLARS. Middletown, Conn.: Wesleyan University Press, 1969. 212 p.

Discusses from previously unpublished sources the development of biblical criticism, as well as the careers of Joseph Stevens Buckminster, Edward Everett, George Bancroft, Andrews Norton, Moses Stuart, Edward Robinson, Josiah Willard Gibbs, George R. Noyes, and Theodore Parker.

809   Godbold, Albea. THE CHURCH COLLEGE OF THE OLD SOUTH. Durham, N.C.: Duke University Press, 1944. 221 p.

Briefly describes the founding of colleges and the motives of the denominations that established them. Discusses their relationship to state universities of the same region.

810   Hislop, Codman. ELIPHALET NOTT. Middletown, Conn.: Wesleyan University Press, 1971. 674 p.

A biography of the man who was president of Union College from 1804 to 1866. Useful, although one learns more than he ever thought he might want to know about Nott.

811   Lynn, Robert W., and Wright, Elliot. THE BIG LITTLE SCHOOL: SUNDAY CHILD OF AMERICAN PROTESTANTISM. New York: Harper and Row, 1971. 108 p.

An essay about, rather than the history of, the Sunday School, this book is, nevertheless, interesting and provocative. The Sunday School viewed as the fount of reform movements.

812   Rice, Edwin W. THE SUNDAY-SCHOOL MOVEMENT, 1780-1917, AND THE AMERICAN SUNDAY-SCHOOL UNION, 1817-1917. Philadelphia: American Sunday-School Union, 1917. 501 p.

Thorough treatment by a man who spent over fifty years in the Sunday school movement.

813   Sherrill, Lewis J. PRESBYTERIAN PAROCHIAL SCHOOLS, 1846-70. New Haven, Conn.: Yale University Press, 1932. xv, 261 p.

Description and analysis of the stillborn attempt of Presbyterians to create their own system of private schools.

814 Tewksbury, Donald G. THE FOUNDING OF AMERICAN COLLEGES AND UNIVERSITIES BEFORE THE CIVIL WAR, WITH PARTICULAR REFERENCE TO THE RELIGIOUS INFLUENCES BEARING ON THE COLLEGE MOVEMENT. New York: Columbia University Press, 1932. 254 p.

Analytical and historical work. Studies eighty-two colleges and finds that most of them were denominational.

815 Welch, Claude. PROTESTANT THOUGHT IN THE NINETEENTH CENTURY. Vol. I, 1799-1870. New Haven, Conn.: Yale University Press, 1972. 325 p.

A commendable study of the main currents of Protestant theology in the nineteenth century, especially valuable for revealing parallel developments in Europe and the United States.

816 Wilson, Major L. "Paradox Lost: Order and Progress in Evangelical Thought of Mid-Nineteenth-Century America." CHURCH HISTORY 44 (1975): 352-66.

Argues that the liberal evangelical of the mid-nineteenth century paradoxically affirmed both the freedom to move toward perfection and the need for order and stability. Based on analysis of four denominational periodicals from the period, representing Baptist, Disciple, Methodist, and Presbyterian points of view. Analysis combines with a useful summary of recent work in intellectual history.

REFORM

See as well the sections devoted to Temperance and Pacifism in chapter 21, and also Smith (1186) and Wyatt-Brown (978).

817 Banner, Lois W. "Religious Benevolence as Social Control: A Critique of an Interpretation." JOURNAL OF AMERICAN HISTORY 60 (1973): 23-41.

Accuses Bodo (818), Cole (819), Foster (820), and Griffin (821) of creating a new-style muckraking historiography by claiming that the social reformers of the early nineteenth century were using benevolence only as a form of social control.

818   Bodo, John R. THE PROTESTANT CLERGY AND PUBLIC ISSUES, 1812-
        1848. Princeton, N.J.: Princeton University Press, 1954. xiv, 291 p.

        Analysis of the same problem covered by Cole (819) and
        Griffin (821). Discusses the northern clergy's plan for a
        godly America (which author calls the "theocratic pattern"),
        and the manner in which that plan was applied to Catho-
        lics, Indians, slaves and free blacks, territorial expansion,
        and America's world role.

819   Cole, Charles C., Jr. THE SOCIAL IDEAS OF THE NORTHERN EVAN-
        GELISTS, 1826-1860. New York: Columbia University Press, 1954.
        268 p.

        An unsophisticated but useful discussion of social reform activ-
        ities and the political thought of a rather miscellaneous
        group of northern clergymen that includes two Beechers,
        Finney, Cartwright, Wayland, and Bushnell.

820   Foster, Charles I. AN ERRAND OF MERCY: THE EVANGELICAL
        UNITED FRONT, 1790-1837. Chapel Hill: University of North Caro-
        lina Press, 1960. 320 p.

        An excellent study of voluntary societies of Britain and the
        United States, exploring the manner in which the machinery
        of benevolence was developed in Britain and the manner in
        which this organization was utilized in America. Good dis-
        cussion of various American societies.

821   Griffin, Clifford S. THEIR BROTHERS' KEEPERS: MORAL STEWARD-
        SHIP IN THE UNITED STATES, 1800-1865. New Brunswick, N.J.:
        Rutgers University Press, 1960. xv, 332 p.

        The central document in what has become known (from author's
        title) as the moral stewardship controversy. Thesis is that
        the great wave of social reform during this period was gener-
        ated by benevolence certainly, but by benevolence acting as
        an agent of social control. Argues that the great societies
        which sponsored these benevolences were really seeking to
        sustain their own class interests and uphold their own social
        status. The best counter-argument found in Banner (817).
        Contains good descriptions of groups such as the American
        Bible Society, American Home Missionary Society, and the
        American Tract Society.

822   Keller, Charles Roy. THE SECOND GREAT AWAKENING IN CON-
        NECTICUT. New Haven, Conn.: Yale University Press, 1942. 275 p.

        Argues that the revival, which is not well treated, produced
        a burgeoning reform movement manifested in the growth of
        missionary societies and other reform-minded voluntary asso-
        ciations.

823   Ludlum, David M. SOCIAL FERMENT IN VERMONT, 1791-1850.
       New York: Columbia University Press, 1939. 305 p.

> Traces careers of reform movements in Vermont, including the
> temperance crusade, antislavery, anti-Masonry, and what
> the author calls the "Puritan counterrevolution."

824   Ratner, Lorman, ed. ANTIMASONRY: THE CRUSADE AND THE PARTY.
       Englewood Cliffs, N.J.: Prentice-Hall, 1969. 100 p.

> A collection of primary documents focused upon the famous
> case of William Morgan, a Mason who was abducted from a
> New York prison in 1826 just as he was about to reveal the
> secret of the society.

825   Rosenberg, Carroll Smith. RELIGION AND THE RISE OF THE AMERI-
       CAN CITY: THE NEW YORK CITY MISSION MOVEMENT, 1812-1870.
       Ithaca, N.Y.: Cornell University Press, 1971. 300 p.

> A two-part scholarly study, divided at 1837, which covers
> early societies, such as the Tract Society, Moral Reform
> Society and Episcopal City Mission in the first half; and,
> in the second half, emphasizes problems relating to poverty,
> especially around the Five Points area.

826   Tyler, Alice F. FREEDOM'S FERMENT: PHASES OF AMERICAN SO-
       CIAL HISTORY TO 1860. Minneapolis: University of Minnesota Press,
       1944. 608 p.

> Although an old book and in some ways not very satisfactory,
> remains one of the most useful surveys of the reform move-
> ments of the era. The author's tone on religious movements
> often flippant as she tends to dismiss groups with which she
> has no personal sympathy.

ROLE OF WOMEN

See also Fuller (905-6) and Hovet (965).

827   Beaver, R. Pierce. ALL LOVES EXCELLING: AMERICAN PROTES-
       TANT WOMEN IN WORLD MISSION. Grand Rapids, Mich.: William
       B. Eerdmans Publishing Co., 1968. 227 p.

> A competent survey that does not, however, relate the his-
> tory of women in missions to the history of feminism generally.

828   Cott, Nancy F. THE BONDS OF WOMANHOOD: "WOMAN'S SPHERE"
       IN NEW ENGLAND, 1780-1835. New Haven, Conn.: Yale Univer-
       sity Press, 1977.

Analyzes work, domesticity, education, religion, and sister-
hood, arguing that their "bonds" functioned both to restrict
women and also to unite them, creating the basis upon which
nineteenth-century feminism would rise.

829   Daly, Mary. BEYOND GOD THE FATHER; TOWARD A PHILOSOPHY
OF WOMEN'S LIBERATION. Boston: Beacon Press, 1973. 225 p.

A set of essays so pervaded by the author's breathless description of what is happening at "this" moment that, since
that moment is already some years past, the book has become a kind of fossil--a monument to the state of mind that
existed in 1973.

830   Doely, Sarah Bentley, ed. WOMEN'S LIBERATION AND THE CHURCH;
THE NEW DEMAND FOR FREEDOM IN THE LIFE OF THE CHRISTIAN
CHURCH. New York: Association Press, 1970. 158 p. Appendix,
bibliog.

A not-very-distinguished collection of essays on women's liberation, but containing some interesting material in the appendix
about the position of the Protestant denominations on women.

831   Drury, Clifford M., ed. FIRST WHITE WOMEN OVER THE ROCKIES:
DIARIES, LETTERS, AND BIOGRAPHICAL SKETCHES OF THE SIX WOMEN
OF THE OREGON MISSION WHO MADE THE OVERLAND JOURNEY
IN 1836 AND 1838. 3 vols. Glendale, Calif.: Arthur H. Clark Co.,
1963-66.

A marvelous collection of primary material relating to cultural
conflict, sex roles, religious vocation, and racial stereotypes.

832   Kraditor, Aileen S., ed. UP FROM THE PEDESTAL: SELECTED WRIT-
INGS IN THE HISTORY OF AMERICAN FEMINISM. Chicago: Quadrangle Books, 1968. 372 p. Bibliog.

A very fine collection of sources for American feminism,
including a great many relating to religion and the churches.

833   O'Neill, William L. EVERYONE WAS BRAVE: A HISTORY OF FEMI-
NISM IN AMERICA. 2d ed. .Chicago: Quadrangle Books, 1971. 379 p.

Although written before the revival of the feminist movement in the early seventies, does provide a scholarly treatment of the history of feminism in the United States.

834   Sklar, Kathryn Kish. CATHARINE BEECHER: A STUDY IN AMERICAN
DOMESTICITY. New Haven, Conn.: Yale University Press, 1973.
xv, 356 p.

Biography of Catharine Beecher (1800-78), daughter of Lyman Beecher, a leader in the education of women and representative nineteenth-century woman. Not merely a biography, but also an important representative of the new genre of family and feminist studies.

835   Stanton, Elizabeth Cady, ed. THE WOMAN'S BIBLE. 2 vols. New York: European Publishing Co., 1895-98. Reprint. New York: Arno Press, 1972.

Edited by a leading nineteenth-century feminist, who judged organized religion to be one of the strongest opponents of female emancipation. Organized a committee of like-minded women to edit this collection of biblical texts pertaining to the status of women; the resulting volume appalled and alarmed even some supporters of the feminist crusade.

836   Tavard, George H. WOMAN IN CHRISTIAN TRADITION. Notre Dame, Ind.: University of Notre Dame Press, 1973. 257 p.

Only marginally related to American studies, but a worthwhile contribution to women's studies. Discussion in the first part of the book of the biblical tradition about women, beginning with the divergent double tradition in the first few chapters of Genesis--a tradition that so early a feminist as Elizabeth Cady Stanton was well aware of. Examines Catholic, Greek Orthodox, and Protestant traditions concerning women in the second part.

837   Ulrich, Laurel Thatcher. "Vertuous Women Found: New England Ministerial Literature, 1668-1735." AMERICAN QUARTERLY 38 (1976): 20-40.

An examination of sermons and pious literature that shows the virtuous woman of the period studied to have been prayerful, industrious, and charitable, but not to have been distinguishable from the virtuous man who shared the same ideal virtues. Notes that only late in the century were ministers willing to begin dealing in sexual stereotypes.

838   Welter, Barbara. "The Cult of True Womanhood, 1820-1860." AMERICAN QUARTERLY 18 (1966): 151-74.

An influential article often anthologized in which the author creates a paradigm for the model woman of that period--piety, purity, submissiveness, and domesticity.

Chapter 12

FROM UNITARIANISM TO TRANSCENDENTALISM

UNITARIANISM

See also Bolster (900), Persons (1157), and Tapp (1614).

839   Chadwick, John White. WILLIAM ELLERY CHANNING. Boston: Houghton, Mifflin, and Co., 1903. xvii, 463 p.

> As Conrad Wright notes in "The Rediscovery of Channing" (852), there has been a great number of recent biographies of Channing (1780-1842), the "father" of American Unitarianism, all based upon the same nineteenth-century sources to which all serious students of Channing will want ultimately to turn. Chadwick's biography, although old, still better than any of the recent attempts.

840   Channing, William Ellery. UNITARIAN CHRISTIANITY AND OTHER ESSAYS. Edited by Irving H. Bartlett. New York: Liberal Arts Press, 1957. xxxii, 121 p.

> The text of his famous 1819 sermon and four other well-known works.

841   Crompton, Arnold. UNITARIANISM ON THE PACIFIC COAST; THE FIRST SIXTY YEARS. Boston: Beacon Press, 1957. 182 p.

> A thin narrative account of the establishment of Unitarianism in the far West that ends its coverage in 1900.

842   Edgell, David P. WILLIAM ELLERY CHANNING: AN INTELLECTUAL PORTRAIT. Boston: Beacon Press, 1955. 264 p.

> A short biographical sketch followed by a topical assessment of Channing's contributions. Fair and judicious.

843   Geffen, Elizabeth M. PHILADELPHIA UNITARIANISM, 1796-1861.
       Philadelphia: University of Pennsylvania Press, 1961. 323 p.

       A good scholarly study.

844   Greeley, Dana McLean. 25 BEACON STREET AND OTHER RECOL-
       LECTIONS. Boston: Beacon Press, 1971. 232 p.

       A refreshing, well-written autobiography and recollection of
       more than a decade in the presidency of the Unitarian Uni-
       versalist Association, from 1957 to 1970.

845   Howe, Daniel W. THE UNITARIAN CONSCIENCE: THE HARVARD
       MORAL PHILOSOPHERS, 1805-1861. Cambridge, Mass.: Harvard Uni-
       versity Press, 1970. 398 p.

       A superb study of the intellectual climate in and around
       Harvard during the early nineteenth century. Necessary for
       understanding of Transcendentalism and illuminating in re-
       gard to the climate of opinion during the late eighteenth
       century.

846   Hunter, Edith F. SOPHIA LYON FAHS, A BIOGRAPHY. Boston:
       Beacon Press, 1966. 276 p.

       Experiences of Sophia Fahs (1876-1966), a leader in Unitarian
       religious education. Provides many interesting insights into
       the history of the Student Volunteer Movement and the So-
       cial Gospel.

847   Kring, Walter Donald. LIBERALS AMONG THE ORTHODOX: UNI-
       TARIAN BEGINNINGS IN NEW YORK CITY, 1819-1839. Boston:
       Beacon Press, 1974. 278 p.

       A readable parish history, quite a bit better than one usually
       finds in this genre, and a useful addition to the story of
       Unitarianism outside New England.

848   Lyttle, Charles H. FREEDOM MOVES WEST: A HISTORY OF THE
       WESTERN UNITARIAN CONFERENCE, 1852-1952. Boston: Beacon
       Press, 1952. 298 p. 16 illus.

       Notes that Unitarianism outside of Massachusetts lost the
       glamor of its Transcendentalist-Brahmin associations and
       played a role similar to that of most other Protestant sects.
       Perhaps not surprising, then, that this history of Unitarian
       expansion into the Mississippi Valley suffers from a great
       many of the limitations of old-fashioned denominational his-
       tory; it is self-congratulatory and bureaucracy-centered.

849   McGiffert, Arthur Cushman, Jr.   PILOT OF A LIBERAL FAITH: SAMUEL
       ATKINS ELIOT, 1862-1950.   Boston: Beacon Press, 1976.   321 p.

>   Narrative biography of a leading Unitarian minister of the
>   twentieth century and president of the American Unitarian
>   Association, 1900-1927.

850   Wilbur, Earl M.   A HISTORY OF UNITARIANISM IN TRANSYLVANIA,
       ENGLAND, AND AMERICA.   Boston: Beacon Press, 1952.   518 p.

>   Only the last four of twenty-three chapters devoted to
>   America, but the extensive materials on England are essen-
>   tial for understanding American Unitarianism.

851   Wright, Conrad.   THE BEGINNINGS OF UNITARIANISM IN AMERI-
       CA.   Boston: Beacon Press, 1955.   305 p.

>   An excellent narrative history of two generations of liberals
>   who, from 1735 to 1805, struggled to enunciate a new set
>   of assumptions about human nature.   Led ultimately to the
>   creation of the Unitarian movement.   Actually serves as an
>   intellectual history of eighteenth-century New England.

852   _____.   THE LIBERAL CHRISTIANS: ESSAYS ON AMERICAN UNI-
       TARIAN HISTORY.   Boston: Beacon Press, 1970.   147 p.

>   Contains six essays: "Rational Religion in Eighteenth-Century
>   America"; "The Rediscovery of Channing"; "Emerson, Barzil-
>   lai Frost, and the Divinity School Address"; "The Minister
>   as Reformer"; "Henry W. Bellows and the Organization of
>   the National Conference"; and "From Standing Order to
>   Secularism."   The work of a master.

853   _____, ed.   A STREAM OF LIGHT, A SESQUICENTENNIAL HISTORY
       OF AMERICAN UNITARIANISM.   Boston: Unitarian-Universalist Asso-
       ciation, 1975.   xiv, 178 p.

>   A collaboratively written history of the denomination with
>   five chapters covering major events and personalities.   Ex-
>   hibits a welcome critical spirit.

UNIVERSALISM

854   Cassara, Ernest.   HOSEA BALLOU: THE CHALLENGE TO ORTHODOXY.
       Boston: Beacon Press, 1961.   226 p.

>   The only modern life of Ballou (1771-1852), the nineteenth-
>   century champion of Universalism and a cousin of Adin Bal-
>   lou (970).

855 _____, ed. UNIVERSALISM IN AMERICA: A DOCUMENTARY
HISTORY. Boston: Beacon Press, 1971. 290 p.

A serviceable collection.

856 Seaburg, Alan. "Recent Scholarship in American Universalism: A Bibliographic Essay." CHURCH HISTORY 41 (1972): 513-23.

A good survey of a thin field.

857 Williams, George Huntston. AMERICAN UNIVERSALISM: A BICEN-
TENNIAL ESSAY. Raleigh, N.C.: Universalist Historical Society,
1971. 94 p. Also published in JOURNAL OF THE UNIVERSALIST
HISTORICAL SOCIETY 9 (1971): 1-94.

A brilliant study and the most significant work on the Universalists in this century. First analyzes the Universalist General Convention of 1870, which was held at the one hun-
dredth anniversary of the founding of the denomination, and
then turns to a more general discussion of events crucial to
the development of Universalism in its second century.

TRANSCENDENTALISM

See as well the appropriate essays in Miller (177); works on Brook Farm by
Codman (943), Curtis (944), and Swift (948); and Sanfilippo (621).

858 Barbour, Brian M., ed. AMERICAN TRANSCENDENTALISM: AN AN-
THOLOGY OF CRITICISM. Notre Dame, Ind.: University of Notre
Dame Press, 1973. xiii, 302 p.

A collection of seventeen essays including six from intellectual historians' perspectives, including Perry Miller's well-
known "From Edwards to Emerson," three on religious issues,
and three on Emerson.

859 Boller, Paul F., Jr. AMERICAN TRANSCENDENTALISM, 1830-1860:
AN INTELLECTUAL INQUIRY. New York: G.P. Putnam's Sons, 1974.
243 p.

A summary of recent scholarly work rather than a monograph.
Should prove very useful to students of Transcendentalism.
Emphasis in the well-written work on the religious views of
these thinkers. Begins with a discussion of the radicalism
of Transcendentalists and describes their philosophy of in-
tuitionism and idealism. Also discusses their relationship to
social reform.

860 Buell, Lawrence. LITERARY TRANSCENDENTALISM: STYLE AND VISION IN THE AMERICAN RENAISSANCE. Ithaca, N.Y.: Cornell University Press, 1973. 350 p.

> An analysis of the transformation of the Puritan and Unitarian into the Transcendentalist, done on the basis of rhetoric-- the conversation and sermonic style of these New England leaders. A well-written and useful study.

861 Frothingham, Octavius Brooks. TRANSCENDENTALISM IN NEW ENG- LAND: A HISTORY. New York: G.P. Putnam's Sons, 1876. 386 p.

> Considered the standard history of the movement as a whole. Also, an insider's story since author was himself at one time a Transcendentalist. A primary document tracing the Euro- pean background and the careers of the major American thinkers, but ignores Henry David Thoreau completely.

862 Hockfield, George, ed. SELECTED WRITINGS OF THE AMERICAN TRANSCENDENTALISTS. New York: New American Library, 1966. xxx, 432 p.

> Concentrates upon writers other than Emerson and Thoreau and is divided into four main sections--the Vanguard, de- voted to the religious and philosophic background; the New School; the Voice of the Dial; and Brook Farm.

863 Hutchison, William R. THE TRANSCENDENTALIST MINISTERS: CHURCH REFORM IN THE NEW ENGLAND RENAISSANCE. New Haven, Conn.: Yale University Press, 1959. xvii, 240 p. 6 illus.

> A reassessment of the role of Transcendentalist ministers in the Unitarian church. In many ways, the best treatment of Transcendentalism considered as an episode in American re- ligious history. Treats Ripley, Emerson, Parker, Frederic Hedge, James Freeman Clarke, Orestes Brownson, and Wil- liam H. Channing.

864 Koster, Donald N. TRANSCENDENTALISM IN AMERICA. New York: Twayne Publishers, 1975. 126 p. Bibliog.

> A good guide for beginning students. A useful and balanced overview.

865 Matthiessen, Francis O. THE AMERICAN RENAISSANCE; ART AND EXPRESSION IN THE AGE OF EMERSON AND WHITMAN. New York: Oxford University Press, 1941. 678 p.

> A work in literary criticism, but so influential and widely- known as to affect everyone's treatment of the Transcendent- alists. Examines literary theories of Emerson, Thoreau, Mel-

ville, Hawthorne, and Whitman. Draws conclusions about the dilemma of American culture from the literary problems of the writers.

866   Miller, Perry, ed. THE AMERICAN TRANSCENDENTALISTS: THEIR PROSE AND POETRY. Garden City, N.Y.: Doubleday and Co., 1957. 388 p.

An anthology designed for the undergraduate college market, but not simply an abridgement of Miller (867). Contains material other than that found in his earlier work.

867   _____, ed. THE TRANSCENDENTALISTS: AN ANTHOLOGY. Cambridge, Mass.: Harvard University Press, 1950. xvii, 521 p.

A valuable, superbly edited collection of more than one hundred documents selected from authors and essays not generally available in print. Organized around headings entitled "Forerunners," "Impact," "Emergence," "Annus Mirabilis," "Miracles" (27 documents), "Manifestos," "Statements" (40 documents), and "Recollections."

RALPH WALDO EMERSON

See also "Emerson, Barzillai Frost, and the Divinity School Address," in Wright (852).

868   Emerson, Ralph Waldo. COMPLETE WORKS OF RALPH WALDO EMERSON. Edited by Edward Waldo Emerson. 12 vols. Boston: Houghton, Mifflin, and Co., 1903-4.

One volume of a new edition of THE COLLECTED WORKS has appeared edited by Alfred E. Ferguson and Robert E. Spiller (Cambridge, Mass.: Harvard University Press, 1972--).

869   _____. EARLY LECTURES OF RALPH WALDO EMERSON. Edited by Stephen E. Whicher et al. 3 vols. Cambridge, Mass.: Harvard University Press, 1959-72.

A critical edition of the surviving lectures from 1833-47.

870   _____. JOURNALS OF RALPH WALDO EMERSON. Edited by Edward Waldo Emerson and Waldo Emerson Forbes. 10 vols. Boston: Houghton, Mifflin, and Co., 1909-14.

A new edition of the JOURNALS AND MISCELLANEOUS NOTEBOOKS, edited by William H. Gilman et al. (Cambridge, Mass.: Harvard University Press, 1960--). Projected to be 16 volumes, of which over half have already appeared.

871 _____ . LETTERS OF RALPH WALDO EMERSON. Edited by Ralph L. Rusk. 6 vols. New York: Columbia University Press, 1939.

The standard edition of Emerson's correspondence.

872 Berry, Edmund G. EMERSON'S PLUTARCH. Cambridge, Mass.: Harvard University Press, 1961. 337 p.

Explores the extent of Plutarch's influence on Emerson, concluding that it was great. Originated as much from Plutarch's MORALS as his LIVES, and had an effect upon Emerson's literary form.

873 Bishop, Jonathan. EMERSON ON THE SOUL. Cambridge, Mass.: Harvard University Press, 1964. 248 p.

A powerful and challenging book. Argues that only through a direct response to Emerson's major prose works (not through a synopsis or paraphrase but through his tone, metaphors and prose rhythms) can one grasp his central emphasis—the act of experiencing, which is the fundamental aspect of the concept of the soul. After analysis of this idea, turns to examination of Emerson's prose style.

874 Brooks, Van Wyck. THE LIFE OF EMERSON. New York: E.P. Dutton and Co., 1932. 315 p.

Biography a kind of literary classic in its own right. Makes much use of Emerson's words and presents a sympathetic portrait of the man.

875 Carpenter, Frederic I. EMERSON AND ASIA. Cambridge, Mass.: Harvard University Press, 1930. 282 p.

Treats Emerson's relationship to Eastern thought. Shows how Emerson's early acquaintance with neoplatonic thought opened him to the influence of thinkers from Asia; however, was never fundamentally converted to Eastern thought but only used those parts he found acceptable.

876 _____ . EMERSON HANDBOOK. New York: Hendricks House, 1957. xiv, 268 p. Bibliog.

A most useful summary of information, both biographical and critical.

877 Cowan, Michael H. CITY OF THE WEST: EMERSON, AMERICA, AND URBAN METAPHOR. New Haven, Conn.: Yale University Press, 1967. xiv, 284 p.

Attempts to demonstrate the importance of urban material to

Emerson, the writer (which author succeeds in doing), and
to show that Emerson was not an opponent of cities (which
he does not prove so conclusively).

878   Holmes, Oliver Wendell. RALPH WALDO EMERSON. Boston: Houghton, Mifflin, and Co., 1885. Reprint. Detroit: Gale Research Co.,
1967. 441 p.

Another classic life of Emerson, recommended by Carpenter
(875) for its treatment of Emerson's later years but not for
its criticism.

879   Konvitz, Milton R., and Whicher, Stephen E., eds. EMERSON: A
COLLECTION OF CRITICAL ESSAYS. Englewood Cliffs, N.J.: Prentice-
Hall, 1962. 184 p.

A collection of essays by Robert Frost, William James, John
Dewey, George Santayana, Stephen Whicher, Newton Arvin,
Henry Nash Smith, Perry Miller, Daniel Aaron, F.O. Matthiessen, Norman Foerster, Henry B. Parkes, Charles Feidel-
son, and Sherman Paul.

880   Levin, David, ed. EMERSON: PROPHECY, METAMORPHOSIS, AND
INFLUENCE. New York: Columbia University Press, 1975. 181 p.

An excellent collection of scholarly essays, including Daniel
B. Shea's discussion of the significance of the recent re-
publication of Emerson's works; James M. Cox discussing
Emerson's famous transparent eyeball metaphor; Sacvan Bercovitch on "Emerson and the Prophet: Romanticism, Puritanism,
and Auto-American-Biography"; and other essays by Bloom,
Gelpi, Cole, and Gonnaud.

881   Paul, Sherman. EMERSON'S ANGLE OF VISION: MAN AND NA-
TURE IN AMERICAN EXPERIENCE. Cambridge, Mass.: Harvard University Press, 1952. 268 p.

A complex, more difficult book than many, it does, however,
seek to explicate a central problem in Emerson's thought--
the relation of man and nature. Concentrates upon the
Emersonian category of "correspondence," which served as
the bridge between the separate entities, man and nature.

882   Rusk, Ralph L. THE LIFE OF RALPH WALDO EMERSON. New York:
Charles Scribner's Sons, 1949. 592 p.

Generally considered to be the best modern biography of
Emerson. Based upon thorough study of manuscript and
printed sources.

883   Staebler, Warren.   RALPH WALDO EMERSON.   New York: Twayne
       Publishers, 1973.   268 p.   Bibliog.

       A short, eclectic introduction to Emerson, perhaps the best
       first book for the beginning student.

884   Whicher, Stephen E.   FREEDOM AND FATE: AN INNER LIFE OF
       RALPH WALDO EMERSON.   Philadelphia: University of Pennsylvania
       Press, 1953.   xvi, 203 p.

       A very important scholarly study, sensitive and well written.
       Analyzes the progress of Emerson's ideas through his youth
       and maturity, emphasizing that Emerson did indeed possess a
       tragic sense.

HENRY DAVID THOREAU

885   Thoreau, Henry David.   THE WRITINGS OF HENRY DAVID THOREAU.
       20 vols.   Boston: Houghton, Mifflin, and Co., 1906.

       The standard edition.   Of course, virtually all of Thoreau's
       works available in a wide variety of editions which there is
       no point in listing.

886   _____.   THE CORRESPONDENCE OF HENRY DAVID THOREAU.
       Edited by Walter Harding and Carl Bode.   New York: New York Uni-
       versity Press, 1958.   xxi, 665 p.

       A well-edited presentation of Thoreau's letters with some
       written to him as well.

887   _____.   THOREAU'S WORLD: MINIATURES FROM HIS JOURNAL.
       Edited by Charles R. Anderson.   Englewood Cliffs, N.J.:   Prentice-
       Hall, 1971.   370 p.

       A beautifully edited selection of passages from Thoreau's
       journals collected under such headings as people, places,
       wildlife, and seasons.

888   Canby, Henry Seidel.   THOREAU.   Boston: Houghton, Mifflin, and
       Co., 1939.   xx, 508 p.   16 illus.

       A standard modern biography of Thoreau, based upon a great
       deal of serious scholarship and understanding of Thoreau's
       writings.   Not completely acceptable to Thoreau scholars,
       especially because of the treatment of Thoreau's relation-
       ship with Lidian Emerson and the scant attention paid to
       Thoreau's days at Harvard.

889   Harding, Walter. THE DAYS OF HENRY THOREAU. New York: Alfred A. Knopf, 1965. xvi, 488 p. 35 illus.

A modern biography by the foremost Thoreau scholar of this
era. Probably the best account of his life. Based upon an
exceptionally thorough understanding of the literature by
and about Thoreau.

890   _____. A THOREAU HANDBOOK. New York: New York University
Press, 1959. xviii, 229 p. Bibliog.

An immensely useful work that gives facts and bibliography
under the headings of Thoreau's life, works, sources, ideas,
and fame. An absolutely indispensable tool for anyone work-
ing with Thoreau or trying to make a knowledgeable beginning.

891   _____, ed. HENRY DAVID THOREAU; A PROFILE. New York: Hill
and Wang, 1971. xxiii, 260 p.

A collection of essays divided into, first, eight contemporary
descriptions of Thoreau and, second, eight critical essays
about Thoreau, including Charles Ives's interesting criticism.

892   _____. THOREAU, MAN OF CONCORD. New York: Holt, Rinehart and Winston, 1960. xx, 251 p.

A collection of over one hundred contemporary reactions to
or descriptions of Thoreau.

893   Hicks, John H., ed. THOREAU IN OUR SEASON. Amherst: University of Massachusetts Press, 1962. 176 p.

A collection of critical essays.

894   Krutch, Joseph Wood. HENRY DAVID THOREAU. New York: William Sloane Associates, 1948. xiii, 298 p.

A critical treatment of Thoreau, set in a very spare biographical setting. A balanced discussion useful to beginning
students.

895   Paul, Sherman. THE SHORES OF AMERICA: THOREAU'S INWARD
EXPLORATION. Urbana: University of Illinois Press, 1958. 433 p.

A connected narrative of Thoreau's intellectual pilgrimage
based upon close reading and detailed exposition of Thoreau's
published and unpublished writings. A book that can be
read with pleasure by both the beginning and advanced student.

896   Porte, Joel. EMERSON AND THOREAU: TRANSCENDENTALISTS IN
      CONFLICT. Middletown, Conn.: Wesleyan University Press, 1965.
      226 p.

> In an effort to demonstrate the falsity of the largely nineteenth-
> century notion that Thoreau was only a pint-size version of
> Emerson, explores the relationship of these two leading Trans-
> cendentalists to document their lack of agreement. Book,
> however, organized into three early chapters on Emerson and
> two later ones on Thoreau—not a very dialectical format.

897   Wolf, William J. THOREAU: MYSTIC, PROPHET, ECOLOGIST. Phil-
      adelphia: United Church Press, 1974. 223 p.

> A serious work based upon primary sources that does a great
> deal to set Thoreau in his historic context and to emphasize
> the basic Judeo-Christian tradition behind his teachings.
> However, neglects or underestimates some aspects of Thoreau's
> thought.

OTHER TRANSCENDENTALISTS

898   Alcott, A. Bronson. THE JOURNALS OF BRONSON ALCOTT. Edited
      by Odell Shepard. Boston: Little, Brown, and Co., 1938. xxx, 559 p.

> A selection of material from the fifty volumes of manuscript
> journals which Alcott kept between 1826 and 1882.

899   _____. THE LETTERS OF A. BRONSON ALCOTT. Edited by Richard
      L. Herrnstadt. Ames: Iowa State University Press, 1969. xxxvii,
      846 p. Genealogical table, 8 illus.

> A massive and magnificent publication of virtually all of
> Alcott's letters, but unfortunately none of the letters written
> to him, so that it seems to be only one side of the conversa-
> tion.

900   Bolster, Arthur S. JAMES FREEMAN CLARKE, DISCIPLE TO ADVANC-
      ING TRUTH. Boston: Beacon Press, 1954. 373 p.

> Readable biography of Clarke (1810-88), Unitarian minister,
> sometime Transcendentalist, and outspoken opponent of slavery.

901   Commager, Henry S. THEODORE PARKER. Boston: Little, Brown, and
      Co., 1936. 339 p.

> Standard life of Parker (1810-60), Boston Transcendentalist
> minister, prominent abolitionist, and reformer. Seen through
> his own eyes and those of his contemporaries.

902 Crowe, Charles. GEORGE RIPLEY: TRANSCENDENTALIST AND UTO-PIAN SOCIALIST. Athens: University of Georgia Press, 1967. 316 p.

> Biography stressing the public career of Ripley (1802-80). Concentrates upon Brook Farm, in which Ripley was the moving spirit, in last half of the book.

903 Dirks, John E. THE CRITICAL THEOLOGY OF THEODORE PARKER. New York: Columbia University Press, 1948. 173 p.

> Exposition of Parker's philosophy, his methods of biblical and historical criticism, and his examination of the basis of religious truth.

904 Duffy, John J., ed. COLERIDGE'S AMERICAN DISCIPLES: THE SELECTED CORRESPONDENCE OF JAMES MARSH. Amherst: University of Massachusetts Press, 1973. 296 p.

> A well-edited collection of letters written between 1819 and 1842 by James Marsh, who was president of the University of Vermont, a leader among the early Transcendentalists, and an interpreter of S.T. Coleridge to Americans. Does a good deal to establish the significance of Marsh himself as well as to explain the manner in which Coleridge's thought was transmitted to America.

905 Fuller, Margaret. MARGARET FULLER, AMERICAN ROMANTIC; A SELECTION FROM HER WRITINGS AND CORRESPONDENCE. Edited by Perry Miller. New York: Doubleday and Co., 1963. 319 p.

> Sixty, mostly brief selections from all periods of Fuller's life (1810-50) with notes and introduction by Perry Miller.

906 _____. WOMAN IN THE NINETEENTH CENTURY. Edited by Bernard Rosenthal. New York: W.W. Norton and Co., 1971. 212 p.

> An eloquent appeal for the emancipation of women that illustrates the problem better than the solution.

907 Lapati, Americo D. ORESTES A. BROWNSON. New York: Twayne Publishers, 1965. 159 p. Bibliog.

> Designed as a primer on Brownson (1803-76), seeks to treat his thought as well as events in his life and to give just emphasis to his Catholicism.

908 Leliaert, Richard M. "The Religious Significance of Democracy in the Thought of Orestes A. Brownson." REVIEW OF POLITICS 38 (1976): 3-26.

> Representative of recent scholarship on Brownson, written by a Catholic theologian.

909 Parker, Theodore. THEODORE PARKER, AN ANTHOLOGY. Edited by
Henry S. Commager. Boston: Beacon Press, 1960. 391 p.

A good collection from the writings of Parker, whose works
were edited in 15 volumes in 1907.

910 Ryan, Thomas R. ORESTES A. BROWNSON. Huntington, Ind.: Our
Sunday Visitor, 1976.

A detailed and comprehensive new biography of the leading
Catholic intellectual of the nineteenth century.

911 Shepard, Odell. PEDLAR'S PROGRESS: THE LIFE OF BRONSON ALCOTT.
Boston: Little, Brown, and Co., 1937. xvii, 546 p.

The standard, scholarly life of Alcott (1799-1888), who left
unusually full manuscript letters and journals upon which the
author has drawn extensively.

912 Wells, Ronald Vale. THREE CHRISTIAN TRANSCENDENTALISTS: JAMES
MARSH, CALEB SPRAGUE HENRY, FREDERIC HENRY HEDGE. New
York: Columbia University Press, 1943. Rev. ed. New York: Octa-
gon Books, 1972. 314 p.

Essentially a reprinting of a 1943 Columbia University Press
edition of this book with some new introductory material
added. Each of the persons treated separately with little
synthesis attempted. Half of the pages given over to reprinting original source material, mostly letters.

Chapter 13

UTOPIAN AND COMMUNITARIAN GROUPS

GENERAL WORKS

See in addition works on modern communitarianism by Roberts (1628) and Veysey (1631).

913   Egbert, Donald Drew, and Persons, Stow, eds. SOCIALISM AND AMERI-CAN LIFE. 2 vols. Princeton, N.J.: Princeton University Press, 1952. Bibliog.

> A collaborative seminar lecture series and reading list. Largely devoted to forms of socialism irrelevant to this bibliography. Provides a general overview of the communitarian movement of the nineteenth century in volume 1, chapters 4 and 5, although overemphasizing the secular character of the Owenites. Many pages of bibliography in volume 2 on Ephrata, Amana, Rappites, Shakers, Mormons, Oneida, Owenites, Fourierists, and Icarians (pp. 106–40).

914   Fellman, Michael. THE UNBOUNDED FRAME: FREEDOM AND COM-MUNITY IN NINETEENTH CENTURY AMERICAN UTOPIANISM. Westport, Conn.: Greenwood Press, 1973. 223 p.

> More successful as a series of sketches of notable reformers than as a survey of utopian thought. Covers the careers of such figures as Albert Brisbane, Josiah Warren, Isaac T. Hecker, John Humphrey Noyes, Horace Mann, Margaret Fuller, Edward Bellamy, and Ignatius Donnelly.

915   Fogarty, Robert S., ed. AMERICAN UTOPIANISM. Itasca, Ill.: F.E. Peacock, 1972. 175 p.

> A collection of thirty-two short selections from primary documents illustrating the history of communities from the Shakers and Ephrata to those of the 1960s.

916   Hinds, William A.   AMERICAN COMMUNITIES AND COOPERATIVE
       COLONIES.   3d ed.   Chicago: C.H. Kerr and Co., 1908.   608 p.

       Includes descriptions of the Shakers, the Owenite communities,
       Brook Farm, Fourieristic phalanxes, Icaria, the Oneida com-
       munity, the Theosophist colony (Point Loma), Single Tax So-
       ciety (Fairhope, Alabama), Ruskin commonwealth, Helicon
       home colony, the Straight Edge, and numerous less-known
       settlements.   Written by a resident of Oneida from 1847 who
       visited the other communities. A valuable primary document.
       Reprinted in various editions, most recently in 1975.

917   Hine, Robert V.   CALIFORNIA'S UTOPIAN COLONIES.   San Marino,
       Calif.: Huntington Library, 1953.   209 p.   Bibliog.

       A good, scholarly treatment of Fountain Grove, Point Loma,
       Icaria Speranza, Kaweah, Altruria, Llano del Rio, and another
       ten communities of less significance.

918   Holloway, Mark.   HEAVENS ON EARTH: UTOPIAN COMMUNITIES
       IN AMERICA, 1680-1880.   2d ed.   New York: Dover Publications,
       1966.   246 p.

       A competent survey covering the Shakers, Rappites, Zoarites,
       Owen and New Harmony, the Fourierists, Bethel, Aurora,
       Oneida, and Icaria.

919   Kanter, Rosabeth Moss.   COMMITMENT AND COMMUNITY, COMMUNES
       AND UTOPIAS IN SOCIOLOGICAL PERSPECTIVE.   Cambridge, Mass.:
       Harvard University Press, 1972.   303 p.

       A well-designed, powerful analytical essay that utilizes data
       from both nineteenth- and twentieth-century communities. Fo-
       cuses throughout on how groups are built and maintained,
       and constructs criteria for judging the success of a communal
       endeavor.

920   Muncy, Raymond Lee.   SEX AND MARRIAGE IN UTOPIAN COM-
       MUNITIES: NINETEENTH CENTURY AMERICA.   Bloomington: Indiana
       University Press, 1973.   297 p.

       Includes sectarian communities in the survey, which is some-
       times helpful but often pedestrian.

921   Nordhoff, Charles.   THE COMMUNISTIC SOCIETIES OF THE UNITED
       STATES; FROM PERSONAL VISIT AND OBSERVATION.   New York:
       Harper and Brothers, 1875.   Reprint.   New York: Hillary House, 1960.
       439 p.

       A valuable old work that retains its usefulness while more
       recent treatments become outdated in a few years.   Includes

descriptions of Amana, Harmonists at Economy, Separatists of Zoar, Shakers, Oneida, Aurora and Bethel, Icarians, Bishop Hill, Cedar Vale, and Social Freedom.

922 Noyes, John Humphrey. HISTORY OF AMERICAN SOCIALISMS. Philadelphia: J.B. Lippincott and Co., 1870. 678 p.

Narrative based upon the manuscript collection of A.J. MacDonald, an inveterate commune-visitor whose intention of writing a history of the communitarian movement was cut short by cholera in 1854 (the MacDonald MSS still exist at Yale University). MacDonald's materials fleshed out by author with his own broad knowledge and this account printed first serially in his newspaper, then later as a book. Main emphasis on the Fourierist phalanxes.

923 Webber, Everett. ESCAPE TO UTOPIA; THE COMMUNAL MOVEMENT IN AMERICA. New York: Hastings House Publishing, 1959. 444 p.

A popularized history of the most important communal experiments in which the author has felt obliged to sacrifice any semblance of serious scholarship or even accuracy in order to simplify and sensationalize his material. Very poor book.

SHAKERS

924 Andrews, Edward Deming. THE COMMUNITY INDUSTRIES OF THE SHAKERS. Albany: New York State Museum, 1932. 322 p. Bibliog.

The earliest of the author's writings on the Shakers, it is also the most concerned with their material culture. Contains much factual data.

925 _____. THE GIFT TO BE SIMPLE; SONGS, DANCES AND RITUALS OF THE AMERICAN SHAKERS. New York: J.J. Augustin, 1940. Reprint. New York: Dover Publications, 1962. 170 p., 17 illus.

A good analysis of this side of Shaker life including the words and music for many hymns.

926 _____. THE PEOPLE CALLED SHAKERS: A SEARCH FOR THE PERFECT SOCIETY. New York: Oxford University Press, 1953. 309 p.

A complete, chronological history. The society described by author as "the purest, most successful and in many respects most creative of new world socialisms."

927 Andrews, Edward Deming, and Andrews, Faith. RELIGION IN WOOD; A BOOK OF SHAKER FURNITURE. Introduction by Thomas Merton.

Bloomington: Indiana University Press, 1966. xxi, 106 p. Illus., bibliog.

Primarily a series of over seventy-five captioned photographs of Shaker furniture.

928 _____. VISIONS OF THE HEAVENLY SPHERE; A STUDY IN SHAKER RELIGIOUS ART. Charlottesville: University Press of Virginia for the Henry Francis du Pont Winterthur Museum, 1969. xiv, 138 p. Illus.

Analysis of the few examples of Shaker graphic art to survive from the period of "Mother Ann's work" (1830s).

929 Cook, Harold E. SHAKER MUSIC: A MANIFESTATION OF AMERICAN FOLK CULTURE. Lewisburg, Pa.: Bucknell University Press, 1973. 312 p.

A more thorough and technically-oriented treatment of Shaker music than in Andrews (925). A fundamental work for anyone concerned with Shaker music.

930 Desroche, Henri. THE AMERICAN SHAKERS; FROM NEO-CHRISTIANITY TO PRESOCIALISM. Translated and edited by John Savacol. Amherst: University of Massachusetts Press, 1971. 357 p.

Marvelous as the historiographical legacy of the Andrewses may be, is refreshing to find the author analyzing the Shakers from a different perspective. Not at all a perfect book, either in research or in argument, but it is provocative and takes Shaker millenarianism seriously.

931 Melcher, Marguerite Fellows. THE SHAKER ADVENTURE. Princeton, N.J.: Princeton University Press, 1941. Reprint. Cleveland: Press of Western Reserve University, 1960. 319 p.

A useful narrative history of the Shakers, now superseded by Andrews (926).

932 Quimby, Ian M.G., ed. WINTERTHUR PORTFOLIO 8. Charlottesville: Henry Francis du Pont Winterthur Museum by the University Press of Virginia, 1973. 246 p.

Two of the articles in this collection of essays devoted to the Shakers: Edward D. Andrews and Faith Andrews discuss the Children's Order; Mary Lyn Ray examines Shaker furniture design, arguing for more secular influence in its style than was ordinarily believed. In the third article on communities, Charles Morse Stotz writes about Economy.

933   Thomas, Samuel W., and Thomas, James C.   THE SIMPLE SPIRIT: A
PICTORIAL STUDY OF THE SHAKER COMMUNITY AT PLEASANT HILL,
KENTUCKY.   Harrodsburg, Ky.:   Pleasant Hill Press, 1973.   128 p.

>A photographic essay describing the material culture, princi-
>pally the architecture, of this most western Shaker community.
>A handsome book.

OWENITES

934   Arndt, Karl J.R.   GEORGE RAPP'S HARMONY SOCIETY, 1785-1847.
Rev. ed.   Rutherford, N.J.:   Fairleigh Dickinson University Press, 1972.
713 p.   Bibliog., appendixes.

>The definitive study of the Harmonists of Harmony, Pennsyl-
>vania; New Harmony, Indiana; and Economy, Pennsylvania.

935   _____.   GEORGE RAPP'S SUCCESSORS AND MATERIAL HEIRS, 1847–
1916.   Rutherford, N.J.:   Fairleigh Dickinson University Press, 1971.
445 p.

>Continuation of Arndt's earlier work (934).   Takes the story
>of the Harmony Society from the date of the founder's death
>to the dissolution of the Society.

936   Bestor, Arthur Eugene, Jr.   BACKWOODS UTOPIAS: THE SECTARIAN
AND OWENITE PHASES OF COMMUNITARIAN SOCIALISM IN AMERI-
CA, 1663-1829.   2d ed.   Philadelphia: University of Pennsylvania
Press, 1970.   330 p.   Bibliog.

>The best book on the Owenite phase of communitarianism.
>Contains much good material on earlier movements, such as
>the Shakers and Harmonists, and an indispensable checklist
>of communities in an appendix.

937   Harrison, John F.C.   QUEST FOR THE MORAL WORLD; ROBERT OWEN
AND THE OWENITES IN BRITAIN AND AMERICA.   New York: Charles
Scribner's Sons, 1969.   392 p.   40 illus.

>An ably researched but densely written treatment of Robert
>Owen.   Devoted more to his British than his American ven-
>tures, which is only right in view of the fact that Owen spent
>only a few years in America.   Chapter on millennialism a
>noteworthy contribution.

938   Kring, Hilda Adam.   THE HARMONISTS, A FOLK-CULTURAL APPROACH.
ATLA Monograph Series, no. 3.   Metuchen, N.J.:   Scarecrow Press and
American Theological Library Association, 1973.   240 p.

>Although neither written nor printed attractively, will pro-

vide material of interest to students of the Rappite Harmony Society.

939   Leopold, Richard W. ROBERT DALE OWEN; A BIOGRAPHY. Cambridge, Mass.: Harvard University Press, 1940. 470 p.

An old but serviceable full-length life (1801-77) of the son and heir of Robert Owen, whose career included much more than the early excitement of New Harmony.

940   Wilson, William E. THE ANGEL AND THE SERPENT: THE STORY OF NEW HARMONY. Bloomington: Indiana University Press, 1964. xiv, 222 p.

A good description of the various communal experiments at New Harmony based upon thorough research but lacking notes.

941   Young, Marguerite. ANGEL IN THE FOREST; A FAIRY TALE OF TWO UTOPIAS. New York: Reynal and Hitchcock, 1945. 313 p.

A facile and simplistic description of New Harmony, Indiana, under the Rappites and Owenites.

FOURIER AND HIS AMERICAN FOLLOWERS

942   Brisbane, Albert. SOCIAL DESTINY OF MAN: OR, ASSOCIATION AND REORGANIZATION OF INDUSTRY. Philaladelphia: C.F. Stoll-meyer, 1840. 480 p.

Fourier's ideas popularized in the United States by author after his having been introduced to, and subsequently tutored by, Fourier in Paris. Really edited for American tastes, eliminating those parts of Fourier's teachings (e.g., his sexual theories) which author judged might offend Americans.

943   Codman, John Thomas. BROOK FARM: HISTORIC AND PERSONAL MEMOIRS. Boston: Arena Publishing Co., 1894. 335 p.

The good old days at Brook Farm as fondly recalled by the author, who lived there nearly half a century before he penned these memoirs.

944   Curtis, Edith Roelker. A SEASON IN UTOPIA; THE STORY OF BROOK FARM. New York: Thomas Nelson and Sons, 1961. 346 p.

A narrative of events described carefully, and presented with the rhetorical trappings of a historical novel without any critical or analytical problems raised.

945   Fourier, Francois Marie Charles. DESIGN FOR UTOPIA; SELECTED
        WRITINGS OF CHARLES FOURIER. 1901. Reprint. Introduction by
        Charles Gide, new foreword by Frank Manuel, translated by Julia Frank-
        lin. New York: Schocken Books, 1971. 208 p.

        Probably provides a large enough sample of his work for any-
        one but a scholar, who will want to read the French original
        anyway.

946   _____. THE UTOPIAN VISION OF CHARLES FOURIER; SELECTED
        TEXTS ON WORK, LOVE, AND PASSIONATE ATTRACTION. Transla-
        ted and edited by Jonathan Beecher and Richard Bienvenu. Boston:
        Beacon Press, 1971. xiv, 427 p. Bibliog.

        Second anthology of Fourier's work. Contains more of the
        master's words, is freshly translated, and includes a seventy-
        five page introduction and headnotes.

947   Riasanovsky, Nicholas V. THE TEACHING OF CHARLES FOURIER.
        Berkeley and Los Angeles: University of California Press, 1969. xii,
        256 p.

        A brief account of Fourier (1772-1837), followed by a de-
        scription of the basic elements of his schemata, a more
        general discussion of Fourier's critique of civilization, his
        place in Socialist thought, and his psychological vision. The
        best book in English on Fourier.

948   Swift, Lindsay. BROOK FARM: ITS MEMBERS, SCHOLARS, AND
        VISITORS. New York: Macmillan Co., 1900. Reprint. Secaucus,
        N.J.: Citadel Press, 1973. 303 p.

        A delightful sketchbook containing dozens of vignettes of
        the people who lived at or passed through Brook Farm, but
        not to be taken seriously as a history of the experiment.

JOHN HUMPHREY NOYES AND THE ONEIDA COMMUNITY

949   Carden, Maren Lockwood. ONEIDA: UTOPIAN COMMUNITY TO
        MODERN CORPORATION. Baltimore, Md.: Johns Hopkins Press,
        1969. Bibliog.

        The best single volume treatment of John Humphrey Noyes
        and Oneida. Although devoted especially to the last years
        of the community, is excellent in what it discloses of the
        early years. Based upon sound research, some of it in new
        sources.

950   Noyes, George Wallingford.   JOHN HUMPHREY NOYES, THE PUTNEY
      COMMUNITY.   Oneida, N.Y.:   N.p., 1931.   393 p.

951   _____.   THE RELIGIOUS EXPERIENCE OF JOHN HUMPHREY NOYES.
      New York: Macmillan Co., 1923.   416 p.

      The best two volumes on the life of John Humphrey Noyes.
      Voluminous collection of sources stitched together with brief
      narrative passages.

952   Parker, Robert A.   A YANKEE SAINT: JOHN HUMPHREY NOYES
      AND THE ONEIDA COMMUNITY.   New York: G.P. Putnam's Sons,
      1935.   322 p.

      The only full-length biography of Noyes, but one whose value
      is limited by the author's attempt to picture Noyes as a
      suitable ancestor for conservative Republicans of the 1930s
      and by the fact that the author trusts Noyes's own late-life
      recollections of his youth too much.

953   Robertson, Constance Noyes.   ONEIDA COMMUNITY; THE BREAKUP,
      1876-1881.   Syracuse, N.Y.:   Syracuse University Press, 1972.   xv,
      327 p.   58 illus.

      Retells the story of the dissolution of the community.   Use-
      ful for the ample quotations from sources.   A better analysis
      of the struggle found in Carden's work (949).

954   _____.   ONEIDA COMMUNITY: AN AUTOBIOGRAPHY, 1851-1876.
      Syracuse, N.Y.:   Syracuse University Press, 1970.   xvi, 364 p.   42 illus.,
      bibliog.

      A collection of articles culled from the Oneida community
      newspapers and organized under such topical headings as
      criticism, health, education, complex marriage, and stirpi-
      culture.

955   Sandeen, Ernest R.   "John Humphrey Noyes as the New Adam."   CHURCH
      HISTORY   40 (1971):   82-90.

      Raises questions about the pathological side of Noyes's early
      development and relates the founding of the Putney and
      Oneida communities to Noyes's resolution of some of his
      personal problems.

OTHER COMMUNITIES

See, in addition, references to the Amish and Hutterites in chapter 6.

956　Schneider, Herbert W., and Lawton, George. A PROPHET AND A PIL-
GRIM: BEING THE INCREDIBLE HISTORY OF THOMAS LAKE HARRIS
AND LAURENCE OLIPHANT. New York: Columbia University Press,
1942. 589 p.

> Narrative of a Utopian community near Santa Rosa, Cali-
> fornia.

957　Shambaugh, Bertha M. AMANA THAT WAS AND AMANA THAT IS.
Iowa City: State Historical Society of Iowa, 1932. 502 p.

> Reprints Shambaugh's AMANA, THE COMMUNITY OF TRUE
> INSPIRATION (Iowa City: State Historical Society of Iowa,
> 1908), and adds new material about changes in the community
> since its constitution was altered in 1932.

958　Wisbey, Herbert A., Jr. PIONEER PROPHETESS: JEMIMA WILKINSON,
THE PUBLICK UNIVERSAL FRIEND. Ithaca, N.Y.: Cornell University
Press, 1964. 232 p.

> The best account that probably can be written from the scant
> and difficult sources remaining for the life of the founder of
> this obscure sect.

959　Yambura, Barbara S., and Bodine, Eunice W. A CHANGE AND A
PARTING: MY STORY OF AMANA. Illustrated by Dale Ballantyne.
Ames: Iowa State University Press, 1960. 361 p.

> An anecdotal first-person recollection of an Amana childhood.
> Uncritical but filled with interesting details.

960　Zablocki, Benjamin David. THE JOYFUL COMMUNITY; AN ACCOUNT
OF THE BRUDERHOF, A COMMUNAL MOVEMENT NOW IN ITS THIRD
GENERATION. Baltimore, Md.: Penguin Books, 1971. 362 p.

> A good description drawn partly from first-hand knowledge
> of the Bruderhof, a twentieth-century community that origi-
> nated in Germany and is located today in Connecticut, New
> York, and Pennsylvania.

Chapter 14

SLAVERY, BLACK RELIGION, AND THE SOUTH

ABOLITIONISM AND THE CHURCHES

See as well Stein (288), Bolster (900), Commager (901), and Parker (909).

961   Barnes, Gilbert H. THE ANTI-SLAVERY IMPULSE, 1830-1844. New
York: D. Appleton-Century Co., 1933. Reprint. New York: Harcourt,
Brace, and World, 1964. 298 p.

> A classic study of the impact of the Second Great Awaken-
> ing upon the abolitionist movement, undertaken when the
> author discovered the long-lost papers of Theodore D. Weld
> and Angelina Grimke Weld. Showed, for the first time in
> the twentieth century, that abolitionism had another face
> than that given it by the Garrisonians, that it was rooted
> in revivalistic concerns and not anti-Christian.

962   Davis, David Brion. THE PROBLEM OF SLAVERY IN THE AGE OF
REVOLUTION, 1770-1823. Ithaca, N.Y.: Cornell University Press,
1975. 576 p.

> Volume 2 in author's history of antislavery. Chapter 5 de-
> voted to the Quaker initiative for emancipation, and chapter
> 11 discusses the place of the Bible in enslavement and emanci-
> pation.

963   _____. THE PROBLEM OF SLAVERY IN WESTERN CULTURE. Ithaca,
N.Y.: Cornell University Press, 1966. xiv, 505 p.

> The introductory volume in author's projected history of the
> antislavery movement. This magnificent book relevant to
> the problem of religion in America at many points: the
> question of slavery and sin (chapter 2), the legitimacy of
> slavery and the ideal of the Christian servant (chapters 6-7),
> and the religious sources of antislavery thought (chapters
> 10-12).

964   Gravely, William B. GILBERT HAVEN, METHODIST ABOLITIONIST.
       Nashville: Abingdon Press, 1973. 272 p.

       A sound and useful biography of a northern Methodist who
       attempted to use his denomination as a center for public re-
       form on race and slavery. Notes that Haven was a radical
       but opposed William Lloyd Garrison during much of his ca-
       reer.

965   Havet, Theodore R. "Christian Revolution: Harriet Beecher Stowe's
       Response to Slavery and the Civil War." NEW ENGLAND QUARTERLY
       46 (1974): 535–49.

       A broad-ranging article that includes analysis of Stowe's
       novel DRED (1856) as well as her familiar UNCLE TOM'S
       CABIN. Concludes that the study of Stowe's views shows
       her becoming increasingly radical in the 1850s but also re-
       veals the reasons for the failure of that radicalism.

966   Keller, Ralph A. "Methodist Newspapers and the Fugitive Slave Law:
       A New Perspective for the Slavery Crisis in the North." CHURCH HIS-
       TORY 43 (1974): 319–39.

       Appears that author's "new" perspective is really rather old-
       fashioned. Summarizes the views of five Methodist news-
       papers in regard to the Fugitive Slave Law and finds them
       divided and frequently compromising.

967   McPherson, James M. THE STRUGGLE FOR EQUALITY; ABOLITIONISTS
       AND THE NEGRO IN THE CIVIL WAR AND RECONSTRUCTION.
       Princeton, N.J.: Princeton University Press, 1964. 474 p.

       Traces the role of the abolitionists during the Civil War and
       Reconstruction, showing that, contrary to popular opinion,
       they did not disappear as soon as the war broke out. De-
       votes some attention to the work of religiously inspired
       abolitionists and missionary groups.

968   Mathews, Donald G. SLAVERY AND METHODISM: A CHAPTER IN
       AMERICAN MORALITY, 1780–1845. Princeton, N.J.: Princeton Uni-
       versity Press, 1965. 329 p.

       The best treatment of the slavery question in any American
       denomination. Equally good on southern and northern atti-
       tudes. Well-researched and written.

969   Merideth, Robert. THE POLITICS OF THE UNIVERSE: EDWARD BEECHER,
       ABOLITION, AND ORTHODOXY. Nashville: Vanderbilt University
       Press, 1968. 274 p.

       An interesting study of one of Lyman Beecher's sons, who

moved between Illinois Congregational pastorates, a college
presidency, and Boston pulpits. A controversial figure because of his theological views on sin and the soul and his
political views on abolitionism.

970   Perry, Lewis. "Adin Ballou's Hopedale Community and the Theology of
        Antislavery." CHURCH HISTORY 39 (1970): 372-89.

        Argues that antislavery became a religious movement perhaps
        even more than a practical reform movement. Illustrates his
        argument from the career of Adin Ballou.

971   _____. RADICAL ABOLITIONISM: ANARCHY AND THE GOVERN-
        MENT OF GOD IN ANTISLAVERY THOUGHT. Ithaca, N.Y.: Cor-
        nell University Press, 1973. 344 p.

        An important book for understanding the mentality of reform
        in the early nineteenth century. Discussion focused on the
        work of abolitionists such as Henry C. Wright, Adin Ballou,
        and William Lloyd Garrison, but the analysis goes beyond
        the question of the Negro to illuminate the era's thought on
        anarchy, the millennium, non-resistance, and perfectionism.

972   Staudenraus, P.J. THE AFRICAN COLONIZATION MOVEMENT, 1816-
        1865. New York: Columbia University Press, 1961. 323 p.

        The best history of this movement and the society that at-
        tempted to carry out its aims--the return of all Afro-Americans
        to Africa. Provides evidence to refute the notion that this
        was a quixotic endeavor, showing how serious and well-
        intentioned Americans could join and support such a move-
        ment.

973   Thomas, Benjamin P. THEODORE WELD, CRUSADER FOR FREEDOM.
        New Brunswick, N.J.: Rutgers University Press, 1950. xii, 307 p.

        A vivid biography of the leader of the evangelical faction
        of the antislavery movement, which gives more of the details
        of Weld's life than does the earlier treatment by Barnes
        (961).

974   Thomas, John L. THE LIBERATOR: WILLIAM LLOYD GARRISON, A
        BIOGRAPHY. Boston: Little, Brown, and Co., 1963. 502 p.

        The best life of the greatest of the abolitionists--a man who
        finally concluded that both the churches and the Constitution
        ought to be destroyed if they insisted on upholding the slavery
        of the black man.

975 Thompson, J. Earl, Jr. "Abolitionism and Theological Education at Andover." NEW ENGLAND QUARTERLY 47 (1974): 238-61.

A good discussion of life and education at Andover in the 1830s. Illustrates the manner in which the faculty were able to discourage ministerial candidates from joining the abolitionist crusade.

976 _____. "Lyman Beecher's Long Road to Conservative Abolitionism." CHURCH HISTORY 42 (1973): 89-109.

Attempts to refurbish Beecher's reputation, arguing that, rather than being simply a "trimmer," he moved in a consistent fashion to ultimately become a conservative abolitionist.

977 Walter, Ronald. THE ANTISLAVERY APPEAL: ABOLITIONISM SINCE 1830. Baltimore, Md.: Johns Hopkins Press, 1977. 196 p.

Treats antislavery as a coherent religious movement, emphasizing the religious climate of opinion which all abolitionists shared regardless of their faction.

978 Wyatt-Brown, Bertram. LEWIS TAPPAN AND THE EVANGELICAL WAR AGAINST SLAVERY. Cleveland, Ohio: Case Western Reserve University, 1969. 376 p.

The life of Lewis Tappan (1788-1873) proves to be broad enough in scope to touch virtually every important aspect of abolitionism from the 1830s to the Civil War. This excellent study ranks as one of the best introductions to this subject; it is also just plain good reading.

979 Zilversmit, Arthur. THE FIRST EMANCIPATION: THE ABOLITION OF SLAVERY IN THE NORTH. Chicago: University of Chicago Press, 1967. 262 p.

Traces the end of slavery in the northern states during the last years of the eighteenth century, arguing that ferment of the Revolution and not the unprofitability of slavery brought an end to the institution.

RACISM AND RELIGION

980 Chalmers, David M. HOODED AMERICANISM: THE FIRST CENTURY OF THE KU KLUX KLAN, 1865-1965. Garden City, N.Y.: Doubleday and Co., 1965. xii, 420 p. 26 illus.

A popularly written but well-researched study of the Klan, which after describing the origin of the Klan in the Reconstruction period, surveys its activities in virtually all of the states.

981   Culver, Dwight W. NEGRO SEGREGATION IN THE METHODIST
       CHURCH. New Haven, Conn.: Yale University Press, 1953. xii,
       218 p.

       More a description of the segregated condition of Methodism
       immediately following World War II than a historical study
       of the development of that practice. Based on a 1948 dis-
       sertation in sociology.

982   Glock, Charles Y., and Siegelman, Ellen, eds. PREJUDICE U.S.A.
       New York: Frederick A. Praeger, 1969. xxii, 194 p.

       Nine essays on the nature of prejudice and its impact on
       churches, education, the mass media, and economics in the
       United States.

983   Gossett, Thomas F. RACE: THE HISTORY OF AN IDEA IN AMERICA.
       Dallas, Tex.: Southern Methodist University Press, 1963. 512 p.

       A survey of racial theories and the misinformation upon which
       those theories were based. Carried out on a wide front, in-
       cluding chapters on Social Darwinism, the Social Gospel and
       race, Indians, and immigrants, as well as a great deal of
       material on anti-black racial theories and stereotypes.

984   Jackson, Kenneth T. THE KU KLUX KLAN IN THE CITY, 1915-1930.
       New York: Oxford University Press, 1967. xv, 326 p.

       Notes that, contrary to popular consensus, the Klan flourished
       in cities as well as in the countryside in the 1920s. Treats
       Klan activities in Atlanta, Memphis, Knoxville, Dallas, Chi-
       cago, Detroit, Indianapolis, Portland, and Denver.

985   Jordan, Winthrop D. WHITE OVER BLACK: AMERICAN ATTITUDES
       TOWARD THE NEGRO, 1550-1812. Chapel Hill: Institute of Early
       American History and Culture by the University of North Carolina Press,
       1968. xx, 651 p.

       Perhaps the finest book in a generation of fine scholarship
       that has transformed the historiography of black-white rela-
       tions. Relevance for the student of religion in virtually all
       of this book, but of special note are chapters 1, with its
       comments upon defective religion; 5, "The Souls of Men: The
       Negro's Spiritual Nature"; and 9, devoted to antislavery
       thought.

986   Loescher, Frank S. THE PROTESTANT CHURCH AND THE NEGRO: A
       PATTERN OF SEGREGATION. New York: Association Press, 1948.
       159 p. 6 tables.

       Analyzes the pattern of racial segregation in church and

school as it existed during the period 1930 to 1948 in the fifteen largest Protestant denominations affiliated with the Federal Council of Churches.

987   Murray, Andrew E. PRESBYTERIANS AND THE NEGRO: A HISTORY. Philadelphia: Presbyterian Historical Society, 1966. 270 p.

A survey, through the entire history of America, of the role of the Presbyterian church in relation to blacks.

988   Orser, W. Edward. "Racial Attitudes in Wartime: The Protestant Churches During the Second World War." CHURCH HISTORY 41 (1972): 337–53.

Traces dawning recognition of black inequalities of opportunity and white racism in the pronouncements of the major Protestant denominations.

989   Reimers, David M. WHITE PROTESTANTISM AND THE NEGRO. New York: Oxford University Press, 1965. 227 p.

A survey of the Protestant churches throughout American history in their relation to black Americans, with the exception of the Baptists who are unaccountably ignored. Fairly thin analysis.

990   Smith, Hilrie Shelton. IN HIS IMAGE, BUT . . . . : RACISM IN SOUTHERN RELIGION, 1780–1910. Durham, N.C.: Duke University Press, 1972. 318 p.

Described by reviewers as "dramatic, powerful, and indispensable," deals more with the intellectual side of religion than the popular, with the leaders rather than the rank-and-file in the churches.

991   Trelease, Allen W. WHITE TERROR: THE KU KLUX KLAN, CONSPIRACY AND SOUTHERN RECONSTRUCTION. New York: Harper and Row, 1971. xlviii, 557 p. 17 illus.

Thorough, scholarly study of the Klan immediately after its inception in the wake of the Civil War. Extensive notes and bibliographical essay.

992   Twomby, Robert C., and Moore, Robert H. "Black Puritan: The Negro in Seventeenth Century Massachusetts." WILLIAM AND MARY QUARTERLY 24 (1967): 224–42.

A study of the treatment of blacks, especially their handling in the courts. Judges that blacks were treated fairly. Article reprinted in Vaughan and Bremer (171).

CHURCHES IN THE ANTE-BELLUM SOUTH

See also Thompson (436).

993 Barnes, William Wright. THE SOUTHERN BAPTIST CONVENTION, 1845-1953. Nashville: Broadman Press, 1954. 330 p. Bibliog.

An official denominational history but done with scholarly care from primary sources. Provides extensive notes.

994 Bruce, Dickson D., Jr. AND THEY ALL SANG HALLELUJAH: PLAIN-FOLK CAMP-MEETING RELIGION, 1800-1845. Knoxville: University of Tennessee Press, 1974. 160 p.

Argues that antebellum Southern townspeople and small farmers who owned few slaves defended the southern social system but were frustrated by it. Notes that camp meetings helped these plain folk to deal with the gap between image and reality in their lives.

995 Eaton, Clement. THE MIND OF THE OLD SOUTH. Rev. ed. Baton Rouge: Louisiana State University Press, 1967. 348 p.

Emphasizes economic, social, and institutional developments --not the political. Deals extensively with the "plain folk of the Old South" and the pro-slavery argument.

996 Mathews, Donald G. RELIGION IN THE OLD SOUTH. Chicago History of American Religion, edited by Martin E. Marty. Chicago: University of Chicago Press, 1977. 288 p.

Presents a series of hypotheses about the nature of southern guilt, the place of antislavery and proslavery ideas in shaping white and black southerners' sensibilities, the role of religion in the life of southern women, and the impact of evangelical values and institutions on race relations.

997 _____. "Religion in the Old South: Speculation on Methodology." SOUTH ATLANTIC QUARTERLY 73 (1974): 34-52.

A stimulating discussion that would repay reading even for those not interested in the South.

998 Posey, Walter B. THE BAPTIST CHURCH IN THE LOWER MISSISSIPPI VALLEY, 1776-1830. Lexington: University of Kentucky Press, 1957. 166 p.

999 _____. THE DEVELOPMENT OF METHODISM IN THE OLD SOUTHWEST, 1783-1824. Tuscaloosa, Ala.: Weatherford Printing Co., 1933. 151 p.

1000 _____. THE PRESBYTERIAN CHURCH IN THE OLD SOUTHWEST, 1778-1838. Richmond, Va.: John Knox Press, 1952. 192 p.

The same treatment of these denominations in all three books. Each chapter devoted to a separate topic, with attention given to missionary efforts, Indian and Negro relations, education, and the ministry.

1001 _____. FRONTIER MISSION: A HISTORY OF RELIGION WEST OF THE SOUTHERN APPALACHIANS TO 1861. Lexington: University of Kentucky Press, 1966. 436 p.

Touches on a wide variety of topics, including revivals, splintering, local denominational practices, Indians, education, slavery, and moral codes. Broad cross-denominational treatment includes Catholics. Summarizes the author's earlier works.

1002 _____. RELIGIOUS STRIFE ON THE SOUTHERN FRONTIER. Baton Rouge: Louisiana State University Press, 1965. xviii, 112 p.

Surveys the facts and sporadic character of religious controversy but does not explain why it occurred when it did.

1003 Wyatt-Brown, Bertram. "The Antimission Movement in the Jacksonian South: A Study in Regional Folk Culture." JOURNAL OF SOUTHERN HISTORY 36 (1970): 501-29.

Argues that the antimission spirit represents the persistent southern struggle to preserve old values.

BLACK RELIGION

General

1004 Bradley, David M. A HISTORY OF THE A.M.E. CHURCH. 2 vols. Nashville: Parthenon Press, 1956-70. Bibliog.

A good denominational history of the second largest black denomination in the United States.

1005 Frazier, Edward Franklin. THE NEGRO CHURCH IN AMERICA. New York: Schocken Books, 1963. xii, 92 p.

A short but most influential book divided into sections on the religion of the slaves, the institutional church of the free Negroes, the Negro church: a nation within a nation, Negro religion in the city, and the Negro church and assimilation. Argues in the first chapter that the slave lost contact with his African heritage and retained no basis of social cohesion; Christianity provided the new basis of social cohesion. An opposing view in Mitchell (1009).

1006   Hamilton, Charles V. THE BLACK PREACHER IN AMERICA. New York: William Morrow and Co., 1972. 246 p.

An excellent study of the black minister based upon a large number of interviews. Combines discussion of historical development, as in the chapter on the ministry during slavery, with analysis of the problems of the education of the ministry, political activism, and conflicts between congregations and their ministers. Especially well-written and engaging.

1007   Lincoln, Charles Eric. THE BLACK CHURCH SINCE FRAZIER. New York: Schocken Books, 1974. 216 p.

Reprints the text of Edward Franklin Frazier's book, THE NEGRO CHURCH IN AMERICA, and adds three more essays by Lincoln entitled, "The Power of the Black Church," "The New Black Theology," and "The Nation of Islam: An Alternative Expression of Black Religion."

1008   Mays, Benjamin E. THE NEGRO'S GOD, AS REFLECTED IN HIS LITERATURE. Boston: Chapman and Grimes, 1938. 269 p.

Book's purpose to trace historically the development of the idea of God in "mass" and "classical" Negro literature from 1760 to 1937. Written by a liberal black theologian, who has little sympathy for the religion of the Negro "masses," feeling that it leaves them passive and complacent.

1009   Mitchell, Henry H. BLACK BELIEF: FOLK BELIEFS OF BLACKS IN AMERICA AND WEST AFRICA. New York: Harper and Row, 1975. xiii, 175 p.

Argues that African religious patterns have survived in black American religion and that religion is not something inflicted upon blacks by whites but a part of their African heritage.

1010   Nelsen, Hart M.; Nelsen, Anne K.; and Yokley, Raytha L., eds. THE BLACK CHURCH IN AMERICA. New York: Basic Books, 1971. 375 p.

A miscellany of thirty-three readings selected from source material and journal articles and loosely organized around a series of questions and issues. Not too well-organized collection as a whole, but individual contributions may be valuable.

1011   Walls, William J. THE AFRICAN METHODIST EPISCOPAL ZION CHURCH. Charlotte, N.C.: A.M.E. Zion Publishing House, 1974. 669 p.

Denominational history written by a bishop of the church who was ordained in 1903 and in his nineties when this book was published. A substantial contribution to understanding one of the most significant of the black denominations.

1012   Washington, Joseph R., Jr. BLACK RELIGION. Boston: Beacon Press, 1964. 308 p.

An interpretive essay rather than a narrative history of black religion. Argues that black churches have never been theology-centered but express a folk faith that emphasizes freedom and justice.

1013   _____. BLACK SECTS AND CULTS. Garden City, N.Y.: Double-day and Co., 1972. 188 p.

A useful description of black sects tied to the thesis that all of these expressions of black religion share a common core or essence that unifies their otherwise very different forms.

1014   Young, Henry J. MAJOR BLACK RELIGIOUS LEADERS: 1755-1940. Nashville: Abingdon Press, 1977.

Examines the theologies and contributions of twelve leaders, including David Walker, Henry H. Garnet, Richard Allen, Nat Turner, and Marcus Garvey.

Ante-Bellum Period

1015   Cone, James H. THE SPIRITUALS AND THE BLUES: AN INTERPRETA-TION. New York: Seabury Press, 1972. 152 p.

A concise introduction to the development and meaning of the sacred and secular music of Afro-Americans.

1016   Genovese, Eugene D. ROLL, JORDAN, ROLL; THE WORLD THE SLAVES MADE. New York: Pantheon Books, 1974. xxii, 823 p.

A reassessment of American Negro slavery that pays significant attention to slave religion. Discusses the entire spectrum of black religion in the antebellum South in the section entitled, "Of the God of the Living" (pp. 161-284).

1017   George, Carol V.R. SEGREGATED SABBATHS: RICHARD ALLEN AND THE EMERGENCE OF INDEPENDENT BLACK CHURCHES, 1760-1840. New York: Oxford University Press, 1973. 205 p.

A scholarly study of Richard Allen (1769-1831), the founder of the African Methodist Episcopal denomination, which is also a valuable contribution to understanding black self-consciousness in antebellum America.

1018 Goodwin, Mary F. "Christianizing and Educating the Negro in Colonial Virginia." HISTORICAL MAGAZINE OF THE PROTESTANT EPISCOPAL CHURCH 1 (1932): 143–52.

Description chiefly of Anglican efforts, emphasizing the role of the SPCK (Society for Promoting Christian Knowledge) and "Dr. Brays Associates".

1019 Jones, Jerome W. "The Established Virginia Church and the Conversion of Negroes and Indians." JOURNAL OF NEGRO HISTORY 46 (1961): 12–23.

Describes the failure of the Virginia–established church to evangelize either Indians or Negroes.

1020 Johnson, Clifton H., ed. GOD STRUCK ME DEAD: RELIGIOUS CON-VERSION EXPERIENCES AND AUTOBIOGRAPHIES OF EX-SLAVES. Philadelphia: Pilgrim Press, 1969. xix, 171 p.

Publication of over thirty conversion stories and six auto-biographical fragments, which relate experiences of the middle–nineteenth century that were transcribed in 1927.

1021 Litwack, Leon F. NORTH OF SLAVERY; THE NEGRO IN THE FREE STATES, 1790–1860. Chicago: University of Chicago Press, 1961.

The "Church and the Negro" examined in chapter 6 of this study of the Negro in the North. Traces the role of the church among northern Negroes and the establishment of various black denominations.

1022 Moore, LeRoy, Jr. "The Spiritual: Soul of Black Religion." CHURCH HISTORY 40 (1971): 79–81.

A useful summary with extensive bibliographic citations re-lating to the question of African influence in the creation of the Negro spiritual.

1023 Richardson, Harry V. DARK SALVATION: THE STORY OF METHOD-ISM AS IT DEVELOPED AMONG BLACKS IN AMERICA. C. Eric Lincoln Series on Black Religion. Garden City, N.Y.: Anchor-Press, 1976. 324 p.

A good, readable history of black Methodists with notes and index.

1024 Sernett, Milton C. BLACK RELIGION AND AMERICAN EVANGELI-CALISM: WHITE PROTESTANTS, PLANTATION MISSIONS AND THE

FLOWERING OF NEGRO CHRISTIANITY, 1787-1865. American Theological Library Association Monograph Series. Metuchen, N.J.: Scarecrow Press, 1975. 320 p. Bibliog.

> A wide-ranging and loosely organized study of many aspects of black religion in the antebellum period. Strongest contribution in discussing black Methodism.

1025 Smith, Timothy L. "Slavery and Theology: The Emergence of Black Christian Consciousness in Nineteenth-Century America." CHURCH HISTORY 41 (1972): 497-512.

> Argues that Christianity provided the slave with a moral ideal that allowed endurance without acquiescence and submission and which also carried with it a moral judgment.

Post- Civil War Period

See also Spalding (622).

1026 Cronon, E. David. BLACK MOSES: THE STORY OF MARCUS GARVEY AND THE UNIVERSAL NEGRO IMPROVEMENT ASSOCIATION. Madison: University of Wisconsin Press, 1955. xxiii, 278 p. Bibliog.

> Study of this controversial Jamaican Negro leader (1887-1940) and his efforts to encourage Afro-Americans to emigrate to Africa.

1027 Drake, St. Clair, and Cayton, Horace E. BLACK METROPOLIS: A STUDY OF NEGRO LIFE IN A NORTHERN CITY. New York: Harcourt, Brace, and Co., 1945. xxxiv, 809 p. Bibliog.

> A comprehensive sociological study of the Chicago Negro community in the 1940s, especially its internal structure and relationship to the rest of the metropolis. Gives some attention to Negro churches. Antiquated bibliography.

1028 Fauset, Arthur H. BLACK GODS OF THE METROPOLIS: NEGRO CULTS IN THE URBAN NORTH. Philadelphia: University of Pennsylvania Press, 1944. 126 p.

> Concise analysis of five Negro religious cults in Philadelphia.

1029 Mays, Benjamin E., and Nicholson, Joseph W. THE NEGRO'S CHURCH. New York: Institute of Social and Religious Research, 1933. xiii, 321 p.

> A critical assessment of black churches, based upon a sample of 609 urban and 185 rural churches surveyed by the two authors. Situation concluded to be rather bleak, with the

weak academic and theological background of the pastors, high church debt, and little concern by members of black churches with social problems being among the most serious difficulties discovered.

1030 Pelt, Owen D., and Smith, Ralph Lee. THE STORY OF THE NATIONAL BAPTISTS. New York: Vantage Press, 1960. 272 p. Appendixes.

Old-fashioned denominational history, heavily anecdotal, containing the charter and constitution of the church in appendixes.

1031 Redkey, Edwin S. BLACK EXODUS: BLACK NATIONALIST AND BACK-TO-AFRICA MOVEMENTS, 1890-1910. New Haven, Conn.: Yale University Press, 1969. 319 p.

A look at the origins of several black nationalist movements (especially under the leadership of Bishop Henry M. Turner), which desired to return to Africa to escape poverty and discrimination in the United States. Comparison of this movement to European emigration to the United States during the same period.

1032 Rose, Arnold. THE NEGRO IN AMERICA. Boston: Beacon Press, 1956. xvii, 325 p.

A condensation of THE AMERICAN DILEMMA (1944), the classic sociological analysis of the American Negro situation by Swedish sociologist Gunnar Myrdal.

Father Divine

1033 Harris, Sara, and Crittenden, Harriet. FATHER DIVINE, HOLY HUSBAND. Garden City, N.Y.: Doubleday and Co., 1953. 320 p.

A biography of the Negro preacher Father Divine and a loose study of the Peace Mission movement he founded.

1034 Hoshor, J. GOD IN A ROLLS ROYCE: THE RISE OF FATHER DIVINE. New York: Hillman-Carl, 1936. 272 p.

A poorly edited study of the prosperous Negro preacher of the 1930s.

Albert Cleage

1035 Cleage, Albert B., Jr. THE BLACK MESSIAH. New York: Sheed and Ward, 1968. 278 p.

Twenty sermons by Albert Cleage, pastor of the Shrine of the Black Madonna in Detroit and noted black power advocate.

1036   Ward, Hiley H.   PROPHET OF THE BLACK NATION.   Philadelphia: Pilgrim Press, 1969.   xviii, 222 p.

A study of Albert Cleage.

Martin Luther King, Jr.

1037   Bennett, Lerone, Jr.   WHAT MANNER OF MAN: A BIOGRAPHY OF MARTIN LUTHER KING, JR.   Introduction by Benjamin E. Mays.   Chicago: Johnson Publishing Co., 1964.   237 p.

An insider's view of King, written before the noted civil-rights leader's assassination.   Had the help and cooperation of many around King as well as King himself.

1038   Bishop, Jim.   THE DAYS OF MARTIN LUTHER KING, JR.   New York: G.P. Putnam's Sons, 1971.   516 p.

A well-written journalistic account of King's life by the author of a great many best-selling biographies.

1039   Lincoln, C. Eric, ed.   MARTIN LUTHER KING, JR.: A PROFILE. New York: Hill and Wang, 1970.   xix, 232 p.

Thirteen essays on King by Ralph Abernathy, James Baldwin, Lerone Bennett, Haig Bosmajian, Reese Cleghorn, David Halberstam, Vincent Harding, Louis Lomax, August Meier, William Miller, Lawrence Reddick, Carl Rowan, and Jerry Tallmer.

1040   Reddick, L.D.   CRUSADER WITHOUT VIOLENCE: A BIOGRAPHY OF MARTIN LUTHER KING, JR.   New York: Harper and Brothers, 1959. 243 p.

An early biography written with the cooperation of the King family from a perspective of a man who lived in Atlanta and Montgomery.

1041   Schulke, Flip, ed.   MARTIN LUTHER KING, JR.: A DOCUMENTARY, MONTGOMERY TO MEMPHIS.   Introduction by Coretta Scott King. New York: W.W. Norton and Co., 1976.   224 p.

A beautifully edited collection of photographs, many by the editor, which gives a vivid account of King's critical years in public life.

1042 Walton, Hanes, Jr. THE POLITICAL PHILOSOPHY OF MARTIN LUTHER
KING, JR. Introduction by Samuel D. Cook. Westport, Conn.: Greenwood Publishing Co., 1971. xxxviii, 137 p. Bibliog.

> Brief but useful analysis of King's political philosophy, with
> one chapter devoted to his nonviolence beliefs. Includes
> references to all of King's published work.

Black Muslims

1043 Breitman, George. THE LAST YEAR OF MALCOLM X: THE EVOLU-
TION OF A REVOLUTIONARY. New York: Merit Publishers, 1967.
169 p. Bibliog.

> Sequel to THE AUTOBIOGRAPHY OF MALCOLM X. Ex-
> amines Malcolm's leadership characteristics and answers
> critics of this apostate Black Muslim.

1044 _____, ed. MALCOLM X SPEAKS. New York: Grove Press, 1965.
226 p.

> Selected speeches of Malcolm X, accompanied by brief intro-
> ductions.

1045 Essien-Udom, E.U. BLACK NATIONALISM: A SEARCH FOR AN
IDENTITY IN AMERICA. Chicago: University of Chicago Press, 1962.
xiii, 367 p. Bibliog.

> A study of efforts of Black Americans to recapture their
> African heritage, focusing on the Nation of Islam. Treats
> the ideology, leaders, programs, and organizations of the
> Black Muslims.

1046 Lincoln, C. Eric. THE BLACK MUSLIMS IN AMERICA. Boston: Beacon Press, 1961. 276 p.

> A well-documented analysis of the history, structure, ideol-
> ogy, and practices of the Nation of Islam.

1047 Malcolm X. THE AUTOBIOGRAPHY OF MALCOLM X. Edited by
Alex Haley. New York: Grove Press, 1965. xvi, 455 p.

> Revealing autobiography of this black Muslim who left the
> Nation of Islam. Written shortly before his murder in 1965.

In Contemporary Times

1048 Ahmann, Mathew, and Roach, Margaret, eds. THE CHURCH AND THE
URBAN RACIAL CRISIS. Techny, Ill.: Divine Word Publications, 1967.
262 p.

Thirteen essays focusing on Roman Catholic social work among
Afro-Americans in metropolitan areas.

1049 Bracey, John H., Jr.; Meier, August; and Rudwick, Elliott, eds. BLACK
NATIONALISM IN AMERICA. Indianapolis: Bobbs-Merrill Co., 1970.
lxx, 568 p.

A well-edited collection of documents illuminating various
aspects of Black nationalism, including the roles of the Black
churches and the Nation of Islam in the movement.

1050 Fullinwider, S. P. THE MIND AND MOOD OF BLACK AMERICA.
Homewood, Ill.: Dorsey Press, 1969. 255 p. Bibliog.

A brief, historical study, giving some attention to Negro religious thought.

1051 Gardiner, James J., and Roberts, J. Deotis, Sr., eds. QUEST FOR A
BLACK THEOLOGY. Philadelphia: Pilgrim Press, 1971. xiii, 111 p.

A collection of addresses delivered at a conference in 1969,
including those by Albert B. Cleage, Jr., "The Black Mes-
siah and the Black Revolution"; Joseph R. Washington, Jr.,
"How Black Is Black Religion?"; Walter L. Yates, "The
God-Consciousness of the Black Church"; J. Deotis Roberts,
Sr., "Black Consciousness in Theological Perspective"; Pres-
ton N. Williams, "The Ethics of Black Power"; and Joseph
A. Johnson, Jr., "Jesus, the Liberator."

1052 Nelsen, Hart M., and Nelsen, Anne K. BLACK CHURCHES IN THE
SIXTIES. Lexington: University of Kentucky Press, 1975. 172 p.

A concise, sociological analysis of Afro-American Christianity, both past and present.

1053 Williams, Melvin D. COMMUNITY IN A BLACK PENTECOSTAL
CHURCH: AN ANTHROPOLOGICAL STUDY. Pittsburgh: University
of Pittsburgh Press, 1974. 202 p. Bibliog.

An intensive study of one Pentecostal congregation in Pittsburgh.

1054 Wright, Nathan, Jr. BLACK POWER AND URBAN UNREST. New
York: Hawthorne Books, 1967. 200 p.

Contains a chapter on the significance of the black power
movement for American Christianity.

THE CIVIL WAR AND THE CHURCHES

1055   Blied, Benjamin J. CATHOLICS AND THE CIVIL WAR. Milwaukee,
        Wis.: Privately printed, 1945. 162 p. Bibliog.

        Ten essays exploring such topics as the positions of the Roman
        Catholic priests in the Union and the Confederacy on seces-
        sion and war, the Catholic press, and Catholicism and abo-
        litionism.

1056   Cheshire, Joseph Blount. THE CHURCH IN THE CONFEDERATE STATES:
        A HISTORY OF THE PROTESTANT EPISCOPAL CHURCH IN THE CON-
        FEDERATE STATES. New York: Longmans, Green, 1912. 291 p.

        Covers Episcopal loyalty to the Confederacy, chaplaincy work
        during the Civil War, ministries to Negroes, and the reunion
        of the Episcopal Church after the Civil War.

1057   Clebsch, William A. "Christian Interpretations of the Civil War."
        CHURCH HISTORY 30 (1961): 212-22.

        Focuses on interpretations by Horace Bushnell, Congrega-
        tionalist minister in New Haven, and Philip Schaff, Reformed
        immigrant minister from Switzerland. Reveals how the Civil
        War could be interpreted by various Christians to fit their
        theologies and prejudices.

1058   Dunham, Chester Forrester. THE ATTITUDE OF THE NORTHERN CLERGY
        TOWARD THE SOUTH, 1860-1865. Toledo, Ohio: Gray Co., 1942.
        258 p. Bibliog.

        Focusing on the larger Protestant denominations, discusses
        attitudes of their ministers toward slavery, southern customs,
        warfare, nationalism, and plans for restructuring the South
        after the war.

1059   Dybvig, Paul S. "Lutheran Participation in the Civil War." LUTHERAN
        QUARTERLY 14 (1962): 294-300.

        Discusses the willingness of Lutherans in the Confederacy
        and in the Union to fight in the Civil War, and the limited
        relief work which Lutheran bodies undertook during and after
        that war.

1060   Fredrickson, George M. THE INNER CIVIL WAR; NORTHERN INTEL-
        LECTUALS AND THE CRISIS OF THE UNION. New York: Harper
        and Row, 1965. 277 p.

        A study of the response of northern intellectuals, especially
        Bostonians like Oliver Wendell Holmes, Sr. and Jr., Thomas

and Henry Higginson, Ralph Waldo Emerson, Henry and William James, to the problems of suffering, the horrors of war, and the emancipation of the Negro.

1061   Silver, James W. CONFEDERATE MORALE AND CHURCH PROPA-
        GANDA. New York: W.W. Norton, 1967. 120 p. Bibliog.

        A brief study of the role of the churches in prodding the
        South to secede.

1062   Sweet, William W. THE METHODIST EPISCOPAL CHURCH AND THE
        CIVIL WAR. Cincinnati, Ohio: Methodist Book Concern, 1912.
        228 p. Bibliog.

        A pioneering study of Methodists in both the Union and the
        Confederacy during the Civil War, treating their missions,
        periodicals, chaplains, bishops, and interdenominational activ-
        ities in the war effort. Antiquated bibliography.

1063   Vander Velde, Lewis G. THE PRESBYTERIAN CHURCHES AND THE
        FEDERAL UNION, 1861-1869. Cambridge, Mass.: Harvard University
        Press, 1932. xv, 575 p. Bibliog.

        A brief survey of American Presbyterian history before the
        Civil War and a detailed treatment of the conservative "Old
        School" wing of the denomination (less attention given the
        "New School") and the problems posed by the Civil War.

1064   Wolf, William J. THE ALMOST CHOSEN PEOPLE: A STUDY OF THE
        RELIGION OF ABRAHAM LINCOLN. Garden City, N.Y.: Double-
        day and Co., 1959. 215 p.

        A valuable and insightful treatment of Lincoln's spiritual de-
        velopment that quotes extensively from Lincoln's writings.
        Republished in 1963 by Seabury Press under the title THE
        RELIGION OF ABRAHAM LINCOLN.

SOUTHERN CHURCHES SINCE THE CIVIL WAR

See also Kendall (377), Baker (373), Ryland (382), Thompson (436), Anderson
(1113), Gatewood (1176-77), and Eighmy (1189).

1065   Bailey, Kenneth K. "Southern White Protestantism at the Turn of the
        Century." AMERICAN HISTORICAL REVIEW 68 (1963): 618-35.

        Analyzes several characteristics of Southern Protestantism sup-
        posedly descended from frontier revivalism, including an em-
        phasis on individual repentance, biblical literalism, and overt
        expression of religious emotions.

1066 _____. SOUTHERN WHITE PROTESTANTISM IN THE TWENTIETH
CENTURY. New York: Harper and Row, 1964. 180 p.

Concise but illuminating study, focusing on Baptists, Methodists, and Presbyterians, and countering the misperception of
Southern Protestantism as anti-intellectual and socially reactionary. Bibliographical essay.

1067 Bode, Frederick A. PROTESTANTISM AND THE NEW SOUTH: NORTH
CAROLINA BAPTISTS AND METHODISTS IN POLITICAL CRISIS, 1894-
1903. Charlottesville: University Press of Virginia, 1975. 171 p.

Shows how the leadership of these two denominations, particularly Methodist John C. Kilgo and Baptist Josiah W.
Bailey, adopted and promoted progressive capitalism in the
new South. A study of the social philosophy and political
activities of a handful of denominational leaders.

1068 Dabbs, James McBride. HAUNTED BY GOD. Richmond, Va.: John
Knox Press, 1972. 255 p.

A very personal set of reflections on the American South,
especially southern religion. Emphasis on the impact of
slavery, plantation, and the family in the South today.

1069 Dorough, C. Dwight. THE BIBLE BELT MYSTIQUE. Philadelphia:
Westminster Press, 1974. 217 p.

An attempt to understand the religious mind of the rural
South, but the author uncritically reproduces many time-
honored perceptions, ignores recent scholarship, and fails to
demonstrate regional uniqueness.

1070 Eighmy, John Lee. CHURCHES IN CULTURAL CAPTIVITY: A HISTORY
OF THE SOCIAL ATTITUDES OF SOUTHERN BAPTISTS. Knoxville:
University of Tennessee Press, 1972. xvii, 249 p. Bibliog.

A survey of Southern Baptists' responses to social issues from
the antebellum period until the middle of the twentieth century, arguing that the Social Gospel made a noticeable, if
circumscribed, impact in the South.

1071 Harrell, David Edwin, Jr. WHITE SECTS AND BLACK MEN IN THE
RECENT SOUTH. Nashville: Vanderbilt University Press, 1971. 180 p.

Argues that the racial views of white southerners are more de-
termined by social class than by theological tenets. Concludes with a good bibliographic essay.

1072 Hill, Samuel S., Jr. SOUTHERN CHURCHES IN CRISIS. New York: Holt, Rinehart and Winston, 1967. 252 p.

Finds southern churches unable to deal with current social problems due to their emphasis on emotional conversion, "narrow piety," and dependence on surrounding "folk culture." Main focus on the development of Baptist and Methodist denominations.

1073 Hill, Samuel S., Jr., et al. RELIGION AND THE SOLID SOUTH. Nashville: Abingdon Press, 1972. 208 p.

Six essays from a symposium on "The 'Bible Belt' in Continuity and Change," including "The South's Two Cultures," "God and the Southern Plantation System," "Women, Religion, and Social Change in the South, 1830-1930," "The Structure of a Fundamentalist Christian Belief-System," "Religious Demography of the South," and "Toward a Charter for a Southern Theology."

1074 Mann, Harold W. ATTICUS GREENE HAYGOOD: METHODIST BISHOP, EDITOR, AND EDUCATOR. Athens: University of Georgia Press, 1965. 254 p.

This life of a late-nineteenth-century figure gives some good insights into the social history of the postwar Deep South.

1075 Spain, Rufus B. AT EASE IN ZION: SOCIAL HISTORY OF SOUTHERN BAPTISTS, 1865-1900. Nashville: Vanderbilt University Press, 1967. xiii, 247 p.

A study of Southern Baptist attitudes toward segregation, temperance, economic problems, and other social issues, arguing that the predominant pattern in this denomination was one of noninvolvement. Bibliographical essay.

1076 Weatherford, Willis D., and Brewer, Earl D.C. LIFE AND RELIGION IN SOUTHERN APPALACHIA. New York: Friendship Press, 1962. 165 p.

Second section by Brewer devoted to religion, including a discussion of churches, beliefs, and leadership.

1077 Woodward, C. Vann. ORIGINS OF THE NEW SOUTH, 1877-1913. Baton Rouge: Louisiana State University Press, 1951. 542 p.

A comprehensive study of the South after the Reconstruction period, focusing on the rapidly changing social environment and discussing briefly the position of the churches in the emerging new South. Bibliographical essay.

Chapter 15

RELIGION IN THE GILDED AGE

GENERAL WORKS

1078 Atkins, Gaius Glenn. RELIGION IN OUR TIMES. New York: Round
Table Press, 1932. 330 p.

A survey of Protestant history from the Civil War to the
1920s, covering topics such as the "twilight" of revivalism,
Social Gospel, the institutional church, liberalism, and the
conflict between science and religion. Still a useful book
for its presentation of these themes from the perspectives of
American liberal Protestantism unshaken by self-doubts.

1079 Carter, Paul A. THE SPIRITUAL CRISIS OF THE GILDED AGE. De-
Kalb: Northern Illinois University Press, 1971. 308 p.

A good series of essays that attempts to document the earnest
struggle and agony of this age through reproductions of pictorial material, analysis of novels, and discussion of the formal religious thought of the day.

1080 Garrison, Winfred E. THE MARCH OF FAITH; THE STORY OF RELI-
GION IN AMERICA SINCE 1865. New York: Harper and Brothers,
1933. 332 p.

A lively historical narrative by the Disciples historian and
long-time editor of CHRISTIAN CENTURY.

1081 Hudson, Winthrop S. THE GREAT TRADITION OF THE AMERICAN
CHURCHES. New York: Harper and Brothers, 1953. 282 p.

Argues that despite the legal separation of church and state,
American churches in the nineteenth century prospered to
the point where they upset their balanced relationship with
society, thereby becoming institutional ends in themselves
and surrendering their prophetic voice. Especially good for
treatment of important urban ministers, "princes of the pulpit."

1082   Jensen, Richard J. THE WINNING OF THE MIDWEST: SOCIAL AND POLITICAL CONFLICT, 1888–96. Chicago: University of Chicago Press, 1971. 374 p.

>Argues, in this study in local political history, that religion was the fundamental source of political conflict in the region.

1083   Kleppner, Paul. THE CROSS OF CULTURE: A SOCIAL ANALYSIS OF MIDWESTERN POLITICS, 1850–1900. Rev. ed. New York: Free Press, 1970. 402 p. Bibliog.

>A controversial study seeking to analyze statistically the correlations between religion, ethnicity, and voting patterns in the Midwest.

1084   Weisenburger, Francis P. ORDEAL OF FAITH: THE CRISIS OF CHURCH-GOING AMERICA, 1865–1900. New York: Philosophical Library, 1959. 380 p.

>A broad and bland survey of social, intellectual, and theological problems faced by certain Protestant and Catholic churches during the Gilded Age.

1085   _____. TRIUMPH OF FAITH: CONTRIBUTIONS OF THE CHURCH TO AMERICAN LIFE, 1865–1900. Richmond, Va.: William Byrd Press, 1962. 221 p.

>A formless catalogue of aspects of the religious scene during the Gilded Age. May be useful as a reference tool, but offers no interpretation.

SPECIAL ASPECTS OF THE GILDED AGE

1086   Albright, Raymond W. FOCUS ON INFINITY: A LIFE OF PHILLIPS BROOKS. New York: Macmillan Co., 1961. 464 p.

>A thorough but narrowly defined study, which does not relate Brooks to his culture very perceptively.

1087   Boyer, Paul S. PURITY IN PRINT; THE VICE SOCIETY MOVEMENT AND BOOK CENSORSHIP IN AMERICA. New York: Charles Scribner's Sons, 1968. xxi, 362 p.

>A good historical treatment of the censorship movement from its origin in the 1870s up to the 1930s. Based upon primary research including interviews with individuals involved in censorship battles in the 1920s and 1930s.

1088   Herberg, Will. PROTESTANT, CATHOLIC, JEW: AN ESSAY IN AMERI-
        CAN RELIGIOUS SOCIOLOGY. Rev. ed. Garden City, N.Y.:
        Doubleday and Co., 1960. 309 p.

> An exceptionally important and influential book. Argues
> that three religiously-determined social groupings emerged
> in the early twentieth century to replace ethnic boundary
> lines, but that all three groups have come to accept a vague
> ideology called the American Way of Life.

1089   McLoughlin, William G. THE MEANING OF HENRY WARD BEECHER;
        AN ESSAY ON THE SHIFTING VALUES OF MID-VICTORIAN AMERICA,
        1840-1870. New York: Alfred A. Knopf, 1970. xiii, 276 p.

> An attempt to clarify how and why Beecher became the most
> respected and best known clergyman of the Civil War era.
> Argues, perhaps correctly, that Beecher was the spokesman
> for the period 1840-70 and must be judged by what he said
> and wrote at that time, especially by his novel NORWOOD.

1090   Meyer, Paul R. "The Fear of Cultural Decline: Josiah Strong's Thought
        about Reform and Expansion." CHURCH HISTORY 42 (1973): 396-405.

> A useful summary, emphasizing a decline in Strong's optimism
> after the publication of his book OUR COUNTRY in 1885.

1091   Morrison, Theodore. CHAUTAUQUA: A CENTER FOR EDUCATION,
        RELIGION, AND THE ARTS IN AMERICA. Chicago: University of
        Chicago Press, 1974. 351 p. Illus.

> A well-written and beautifully printed account of the summer
> conference in southwestern New York, which became a cen-
> ter for cultural and religious enrichment for thousands in the
> late nineteenth and early twentieth centuries.

1092   Muller, Dorothea R. "Josiah Strong and American Nationalism: A
        Reevaluation." JOURNAL OF AMERICAN HISTORY 53 (1966):
        487-503.

> Raises doubts about the extent of the influence of Strong's
> OUR COUNTRY (1094), rather than reassessing Strong him-
> self.

1093   Pivar, David J. PURITY CRUSADE: SEXUAL MORALITY AND SOCIAL
        CONTROL, 1868-1900. Westport, Conn.: Greenwood Press, 1973.
        308 p.

> Describes several dimensions of this Victorian campaign, and
> its connections with other reform movements in rapidly urban-
> izing American society. Bibliographical essay.

1094   Strong, Josiah. OUR COUNTRY. 1885. John Harvard Library. Reprint. Cambridge, Mass.: Harvard University Press, 1963. xxvi, 265 p.

    Argued that the United States, although destined to lead the world, was imperiled by immigration, Catholicism, secularization of the public schools, Mormonism, intemperance, socialism, poor distribution of wealth, and urbanization.

1095   Walters, Ronald G., ed. PRIMERS FOR PRUDERY: SEXUAL ADVICE TO VICTORIAN AMERICA. Englewood Cliffs, N.J.: Prentice-Hall, 1974. xiv, 175 p.

    A compilation of excerpts from various nineteenth-century sources of advice on sexual topics. Touches on such religious phenomena as Mormon polygamy, communitarianism, perfectionism, and revivalism. Bibliographical essay.

RELIGION AND THE RISE OF THE CITIES

See as well Abell (604) and many of the other entries in that section devoted to Catholic social history.

1096   Abell, Aaron I. THE URBAN IMPACT ON AMERICAN PROTESTANTISM, 1865-1900. Cambridge, Mass.: Harvard University Press, 1943. 275 p.

    A pioneering analysis of the changes which urbanization wrought in American Protestantism during the second half of the nineteenth century, focusing especially on the institutional church movement and the Social Gospel. Bibliographical essay.

1097   Cross, Robert D., ed. THE CHURCH AND THE CITY, 1865-1910. Indianapolis: Bobbs-Merrill Co., 1967. xlv, 359 p.

    A well-edited anthology of selections from the works of Protestants and Roman Catholics, pertaining to the churches during this period of rapid urbanization. A very good book for group discussion because of the juxtaposition of sources.

1098   Gutman, Herbert G. "Protestantism and the American Labor Movement: The Christian Spirit in the Gilded Age." AMERICAN HISTORICAL REVIEW 72 (1966): 74-101.

    A highly regarded essay argues that Protestantism penetrated American society more deeply in the Gilded Age than is usually recognized, and that it had a profound impact on the spirit of the labor reform movements.

1099   Mann, Arthur. YANKEE REFORMERS IN THE URBAN AGE. Cambridge, Mass.: Harvard University Press. 1954. 314 p.

        A microcosmic study of progressive social reform in Boston, 1880-1900, paying considerable attention to the variety of responses within Roman Catholic, Jewish, and Protestant groups. Bibliographical essay.

1100   May, Henry F. PROTESTANT CHURCHES AND INDUSTRIAL AMERICA. New York: Harper and Brothers, 1949. 297 p. Bibliog.

        An important and basic work that analyzes the increasing awareness of some Protestant denominations to the social problems of the Gilded Age. Emphasis on Presbyterians, Congregationalists, Baptists, Methodists, and Episcopalians.

1101   Schlesinger, Arthur M. THE AMERICAN AS REFORMER. Cambridge, Mass.: Harvard University Press, 1950. 127 p.

        Three provocative essays portraying moderate social reform as a continuing theme in American history. Bibliographical essay.

1102   _____. THE RISE OF THE CITY, 1878-1898. New York: Macmillan Co., 1933. xvi, 494 p.

        A pioneering study of urbanization as a profound social force during the Gilded Age, exploring its impact on such topics as the churches, education, politics, and the arts. Bibliographical essay.

DENOMINATIONS IN THE GILDED AGE

1103   Davis, Lawrence B. IMMIGRANTS, BAPTISTS, AND THE PROTESTANT MIND IN AMERICA. Urbana: University of Illinois, 1973. 230 p.

        Analysis of Northern Baptist views concerning late nineteenth-century immigrants. Based on material published in regional and national Baptist publications, including discussion of the role of Baptists in the anti-Chinese agitation of the 1880s, attitudes of Baptist clergymen toward the "new immigrants" of the 1880s and 1890s, and Baptist work among these recent arrivals. Argues that Baptists began to favor immigrant exclusion when it became clear that the new immigrants were not susceptible to evangelization.

1104   Kromminga, John Henry. THE CHRISTIAN REFORMED CHURCH: A STUDY IN ORTHODOXY. Grand Rapids, Mich.: Baker Book House, 1949. 241 p. Bibliog.

A defensive history of this conservative, Netherlandic–American denomination, stressing its adherence to Calvinist orthodoxy in an American environment where Calvinism was almost extinct.

1105   Loetscher, Lefferts A.   THE BROADENING CHURCH: A STUDY OF THEOLOGICAL ISSUES IN THE PRESBYTERIAN CHURCH SINCE 1869. Philadelphia: University of Pennsylvania Press, 1954.   195 p.

A masterful and penetrating treatment of this denomination after the reunion of 1869.   One of the best discussions in print of the impact of liberalism and biblical criticism upon a denomination.   Perceptive analysis of liberals and Fundamentalists and of the structure of the denomination.

1106   Olsson, Karl A.   BY ONE SPIRIT.   Chicago: Covenant Press, 1962. xiv, 811 p.

A well–researched and sensitively written history of the Evangelical Mission Covenant Church.   Published by the denomination on the occasion of the seventy–fifth anniversary of its founding in America by Swedish immigrants.   No bibliography, but most of the important sources for this group cited in the extensive notes.

1107   Smith, Timothy L.   CALLED UNTO HOLINESS.   Kansas City, Mo.: Nazarene Publishing House, 1962.   413 p.

An official denominational history of the Church of the Nazarene, but entirely an exception to the rule that such works must be uncritical and self–congratulatory.   A sound work of research.

1108   _____.   "Religious Denominations as Ethnic Communities: A Regional Case Study."   CHURCH HISTORY 35 (1966):   207–26.

Analyzes the religious history of the communities of Minnesota's Iron Range, especially the Finns.

1109   Tucker, William E.   J.H. GARRISON AND DISCIPLES OF CHRIST. St. Louis, Mo.:   Bethany Press, 1964.   278 p.

Scholarly biography of Garrison, an editor for one of the Disciples' denominational papers.   Shows how he exerted influence in the history of that denomination in the half century after the Civil War.

1110   Wardin, Albert W.   BAPTISTS IN OREGON.   Portland, Oreg.:   Judson Baptist College, 1969.   635 p.

An unusually well-researched and valuable study in regional religious history, especially valuable for its treatment of the Social Gospel and Fundamentalism in Oregon.

1111 Zwaanstra, Henry. REFORMED THOUGHT AND EXPERIENCE IN A NEW WORLD: A STUDY OF THE CHRISTIAN REFORMED CHURCH AND ITS AMERICAN ENVIRONMENT, 1890-1918. Grand Rapids, Mich.: William B. Eerdmans Publishing Co., 1974. 331 p.

Praised as a distinctive contribution to religious and immigration history, concentrates on the period in which the small Michigan-centered Netherlandic-American denomination struggled to enunciate what it might mean to bring proper Calvinism to America.

AMERICAN LUTHERANS: GENERAL

See also Dybvig (1059) and Jorstad (1264). References to colonial Lutheranism are located in chapter 6.

1112 Ahlstrom, Sydney E. "The Lutheran Church and American Culture: A Tercentenary Report." LUTHERAN QUARTERLY 9 (1957): 321-42.

An analysis of the history of the ever-changing relationship between Lutheran churches and their environment in the United States, which is interpreted as essentially one of tension.

1113 Anderson, Hugh George. LUTHERANISM IN THE SOUTHEASTERN STATES, 1860-1886: A SOCIAL HISTORY. The Hague, Netherlands: Mouton Publishers, 1969. 276 p. Bibliog.

A well-documented, if narrowly focused, history of Lutheranism below the Mason-Dixon Line from 1860 until the establishment of the United Synod of the South in 1886.

1114 Ferm, Vergilius. THE CRISIS IN AMERICAN LUTHERAN THEOLOGY: A STUDY OF THE ISSUE BETWEEN AMERICAN LUTHERANISM AND OLD LUTHERANISM. New York: Century Co., 1927. xiii, 409 p. Bibliog.

An excellent analysis of the syncretistic American Lutheranism associated with Samuel Schmucker and the triumph of conservative, confessional Lutheranism in the nineteenth century. Helpful chart of Lutheran synods.

1115 Kersten, Lawrence K. THE LUTHERAN ETHIC: THE IMPACT OF RELIGION ON LAYMEN AND CLERGY. Detroit: Wayne State University Press, 1970. 309 p.

A statistical study of the beliefs, attitudes, political activity and personal morals of Lutherans in the United States.

1116   Marty, Myron A. LUTHERANS AND ROMAN CATHOLICISM: THE CHANGING CONFLICT, 1917–1963. Notre Dame, Ind.: University of Notre Dame Press, 1968. 245 p.

A study of American Lutherans' changing attitudes toward the Roman Catholic Church. Emphasis on the Missouri Synod.

1117   Nelson, E. Clifford. LUTHERANISM IN NORTH AMERICA, 1914–1970. Minneapolis, Minn.: Augsburg Publishing House, 1972. xvi, 315 p. Graphs, maps.

A well-documented history of the several Lutheran synods in the United States and Canada during the twentieth century. Includes a timeline helpful for tracing these synods and their antecedents.

1118   _____, ed. THE LUTHERANS IN NORTH AMERICA. Philadelphia: Fortress Press, 1975. 541 p.

Excellent general history of Lutheranism in the United States and Canada from the seventeenth century to the 1970s. Synthesizes, with the research of earlier historians, writings of Theodore Tappert, H. George Anderson, August Suelflow, E. Clifford Nelson, Eugene Fevold, and Fred Meuser.

1119   Reed, Luther D. THE LUTHERAN LITURGY. Rev. ed. Philadelphia: Fortress Press, 1947. xxiii, 824 p. Bibliog.

A detailed study of Lutheran worship in Europe and the United States. Includes discussion of its medieval and early church antecedents and an analysis of more recent phenomena, such as the SERVICE BOOK AND HYMNAL of 1958.

1120   Schmucker, Samuel S. FRATERNAL APPEAL TO THE AMERICAN CHURCHES. Philadelphia: Fortress Press, 1965. 229 p.

A new edition of the call, issued in the 1830s, for American Protestants to unite on apostolic principles. Written by a German-American Lutheran, who was educated at Princeton Theological Seminary and rejected much traditional Lutheran confessionalism.

1121   Strommen, Merton P., et al. A STUDY OF GENERATIONS. Minneapolis, Minn.: Augsburg Publishing House, 1972. 411 p. Bibliog.

A comprehensive, statistical study of the beliefs, values, attitudes, and behavior of members of the American Lutheran Church, the Lutheran Church in America, and the Lutheran Church—Missouri Synod.

1122   Tappert, Theodore G., ed. LUTHERAN CONFESSIONAL THEOLOGY IN AMERICA, 1840-1880. New York: Oxford University Press, 1972. 364 p. Bibliog.

        A well-edited collection of excerpts from the works of C.F.W. Walther, Charles Porterfield Krauth, and other conservative Lutherans, illuminating their theological stance which ended the "American Lutheranism" of Samuel Schmucker. Bibliography of theological journals, church newspapers, and secondary works.

1123   Wentz, Frederick K. LUTHERANS IN CONCERT: THE STORY OF THE NATIONAL LUTHERAN COUNCIL, 1918-1966. Minneapolis, Minn.: Augsburg Publishing House, 1968. 221 p.

        A brief survey of intersynodical Lutheran ventures since World War I, stressing social work and missionary ventures.

1124   Wolf, Richard C., ed. DOCUMENTS OF LUTHERAN UNITY IN AMERICA. Philadelphia: Fortress Press, 1966. xxvii, 672 p.

        A well-edited collection of 250 documents revealing both the successes and failures of ethnically and doctrinally heterogeneous Lutherans to unite from the eighteenth century to the 1960s.

DANISH-AMERICAN LUTHERANS

1125   Jensen, John M. THE UNITED EVANGELICAL LUTHERAN CHURCH: AN INTERPRETATION. Minneapolis, Minn.: Augsburg Publishing House for the Institute for Danish Church History, 1964. 311 p.

        A poorly written, derivative history of the pietistic Danish Lutheran tradition in the United States. A companion piece to Enok Mortensen (1126).

1126   Mortensen, Enok. THE DANISH LUTHERAN CHURCH IN AMERICA. Philadelphia: Board of Publication, Lutheran Church in America, 1967. xiv, 320 p.

        A history of high-church, Grundtvigian Danish Lutherans in the United States from the 1870s until their merger with the Lutheran Church in America in 1962. A companion piece to John M. Jensen (1125).

1127   Nyholm, Paul C. THE AMERICANIZATION OF THE DANISH LUTHERAN CHURCHES IN AMERICA. Minneapolis, Minn.: Augsburg Publishing House for the Institute for Danish Church History, 1963. 480 p. Maps.

        A well-documented account of two small Danish synods from

the 1870s until they merged with other Lutheran groups in
the 1960s. Contains some demographic data.

1128   Skarsten, Trygve R. "Danish Contributions to Religion in America."
        LUTHERAN QUARTERLY 25 (1973): 42–53.

        A concise survey of Lutheranism among Danish immigrants,
        but virtually ignoring the Mormons and other religious bodies
        which were fairly well represented among Danes on both
        sides of the Atlantic.

THE LUTHERAN CHURCH—MISSOURI SYNOD

See also Rudnick (1578).

1129   Baepler, Walter A. A CENTURY OF GRACE: A HISTORY OF THE
        MISSOURI SYNOD, 1847–1947. St. Louis, Mo.: Concordia Publishing
        House, 1947. 408 p.

        A chronology tracing Saxon confessional Lutheranism from
        Germany to the Midwest and the growth of the Missouri
        Synod since the 1840s. Useful only as an uncritical intro-
        duction to the subject.

1130   Forster, Walter O. ZION ON THE MISSISSIPPI: THE SETTLEMENT
        OF THE SAXON LUTHERANS IN MISSOURI 1839–1841. St. Louis,
        Mo.: Concordia Publishing House, 1953. xiv, 606 p. Illus., bibliog.

        A very thorough study of the migration of followers of Mar-
        tin Stephan from Saxony to Missouri, where they became one
        root of the Missouri Synod. Complete with many documents
        and an extensive bibliography of primary and secondary ma-
        terials in English and German.

1131   Graebner, Alan. UNCERTAIN SAINTS: THE LAITY IN THE LUTHERAN
        CHURCH—MISSOURI SYNOD, 1900–1970. Westport, Conn.: Green-
        wood Press, 1975. xiii, 284 p.

        A good study of emerging lay roles in a denomination heavily
        dominated by its clergy.

1132   Jordahl, Leigh D. "The Theology of Franz Pieper: A Resource for
        Fundamentalistic Thought Modes Among American Lutherans." LUTHERAN
        QUARTERLY 23 (1971): 118–37.

        An attempt to define Fundamentalism and differentiate it
        from theology of the Missouri Synod theologian Franz Pieper.

1133   Lueking, F. Dean.   MISSION IN THE MAKING: THE MISSIONARY
ENTERPRISE AMONG MISSOURI SYNOD LUTHERANS, 1846-1963.   St.
Louis, Mo.: Concordia Publishing House, 1964.   354 p.

A scholarly study of the Missouri Synod's missions among immigrants and Negroes in the United States and to India,
China, and other foreign fields. Finds the missionary moti-
vation in "American evangelicalism" and Lutheran confessionalism.

1134   Meyer, Carl S.   LOG CABIN TO LUTHER TOWER.   St. Louis, Mo.:
Concordia Publishing House, 1965.   322 p.

A history of the Missouri Synod Lutheran Concordia Seminary,
showing that the early history of the institution was as much
marred by disputes and difficulties as has been the case in
the 1970s.

1135   _____.   MOVING FRONTIERS: READINGS IN THE HISTORY OF
THE LUTHERAN CHURCH--MISSOURI SYNOD.   St. Louis, Mo.: Concordia Publishing House, 1964.   500 p.

A reader in the sources of the Missouri Synod, containing a
balanced selection of official documents, contemporary accounts, and personal narratives. Translation of German sources
into English.

1136   _____, ed.   LETTERS OF C.F.W. WALTHER: A SELECTION.   Philadelphia: Fortress Press, 1969.   167 p.

A translation and editing of twenty-four letters of this significant nineteenth-century leader of the Missouri Synod Lutheran denomination.

NORWEGIAN-AMERICAN LUTHERANS

1137   Fevold, Eugene L.   THE LUTHERAN FREE CHURCH IN AMERICA.   Minneapolis, Minn.: Augsburg Publishing House, 1969.   342 p.

An excellent treatment of one wing of Norwegian-American
Lutheranism, which rejected Lutheran confessionalism and
much of the traditional liturgy and polity in favor of congregational polity and low church worship.

1138   Hamre, James S.   "Georg Sverdrup's Concept of Theological Education
in the Context of a Free Church." LUTHERAN QUARTERLY 22
(1970): 199-209.

A concise analysis of the Norwegian-American Lutheran
Georg Sverdrup's (1848-1907) ideal of a restored apostolic

church and the role of theological education in it.

1139 _____. "Georg Sverdrup's Defense of Secular Education." LUTHERAN QUARTERLY 17 (1965): 143-50.

An analysis of the advocacy of public schools of Georg Sver-drup (1848-1907), Norwegian-American Lutheran and champion of the free church ideal.

1140 Helland, Melvin A., ed. THE HERITAGE OF FAITH: SELECTIONS FROM THE WRITINGS OF GEORG SVERDRUP. Minneapolis, Minn.: Augsburg Publishing House, 1969. 136 p.

Selections from the six-volume untranslated corpus of this leader of the Norwegian-American Lutheran Free Church in the nineteenth century.

1141 Nelson, E. Clifford, and Fevold, Eugene L. THE LUTHERAN CHURCH AMONG NORWEGIAN-AMERICANS. 2 vols. Minneapolis, Minn.: Augsburg Publishing House, 1960.

A comprehensive, well-documented history of the various Lutheran synods among Norwegian immigrants from the 1820s until 1960. Special emphasis given to relations among these denominations and the mergers that consolidated most of them.

OTHER LUTHERAN SYNODICAL TRADITIONS

1142 Arden, G. Everett. AUGUSTANA HERITAGE: A HISTORY OF THE AUGUSTANA LUTHERAN CHURCH. Rock Island, Ill.: Augustana Press, 1963. 424 p.

A good history of the largest Swedish-American denomina-tion, which in 1962 became part of the Lutheran Church in America.

1143 Jalkanen, Ralph J., ed. THE FAITH OF THE FINNS: HISTORICAL PERSPECTIVES ON THE FINNISH LUTHERAN CHURCH IN AMERICA. East Lansing: Michigan State University Press, 1972. xvi, 360 p.

A miscellany of twenty articles illuminating Finnish-American Lutheranism since the end of the nineteenth century, includ-ing the social context of this smaller Lutheran tradition.

1144 Koehler, John Philipp. THE HISTORY OF THE WISCONSIN SYNOD. Edited by Leigh Jordahl. St. Cloud, Minn.: Sentinel Publishing Co., 1970. xxix, 260 p.

An updated edition of author's 1925 chronicle of this conservative, German-American Lutheran synod.

1145   Schneider, Carl E. THE GERMAN CHURCH ON THE AMERICAN
        FRONTIER: A STUDY IN THE RISE OF RELIGION AMONG THE
        GERMANS OF THE WEST, BASED ON THE HISTORY OF THE EVAN-
        GELISCHER KIRCHENVEREIN DES WESTENS, 1840-1866. St. Louis,
        Mo.: Eden Publishing House, 1939. xx, 579 p.

        Case study of a single sect of German Lutherans, die Kir-
        chenverein, and its work in the western United States.
        Gives background of religious and social conditions of their
        immigrant congregations.

Chapter 16

LIBERALISM, SCIENCE, AND THE SOCIAL GOSPEL

LIBERALISM

See as well Brown (808) on the history of biblical criticism.

1146 Averill, Lloyd J. AMERICAN THEOLOGY IN THE LIBERAL TRADI-
TION. Philadelphia: Westminster Press, 1967. 173 p.

> Presents a profile of the movement from 1879 to 1917 and
> a discussion of tensions within liberalism. Good as an
> introductory study.

1147 Bowden, Henry W. CHURCH HISTORY IN THE AGE OF SCIENCE:
HISTORIOGRAPHICAL PATTERNS IN THE UNITED STATES, 1876-1918.
Chapel Hill: University of North Carolina Press, 1971. xvi, 269 p.
Bibliog.

> Essays on efforts to apply principles of scientific objectivity
> to church historiography by both American Protestant and
> Roman Catholic scholars.

1148 Cauthen, Kenneth. THE IMPACT OF AMERICAN RELIGIOUS LIBERAL-
ISM. New York: Harper and Row, 1962. 290 p.

> Much narrower study than the title indicates. Divides
> liberalism into two camps: the "evangelical liberalism" of
> such men as Walter Rauschenbusch and Harry Emerson Fos-
> dick, and the "modernistic liberalism" of Shailer Mathews,
> Douglas Clyde MacIntosh, and Henry Nelson Wieman.

1149 Fosdick, Harry Emerson. THE LIVING OF THESE DAYS. New York:
Harper and Brothers, 1956. 324 p.

> Memoirs of a noted American preacher (1878-1969), with a
> lengthy description of his childhood and youth. A lovely
> recreation of the nineteenth century, giving good evidence

from which to judge how one man's liberalism developed.

1150   Foster, Frank H. THE MODERN MOVEMENT IN AMERICAN THEOL-
        OGY. New York: Fleming H. Revell Co., 1939. 219 p.

        Continuation of an earlier work (331) discusses Protestant
        thought from the Civil War to World War I. Based on lec-
        tures at Andover Newton Theological School in 1934.

1151   Hutchison, William R. "Cultural Strain and Protestant Liberalism."
        AMERICAN HISTORICAL REVIEW 76 (1971): 386-411.

        A study of 250 American Protestant leaders of the 1875-
        1914 period, designed to determine the influence of their
        social and intellectual backgrounds on their eventual theo-
        logical stances.

1152   _____. "Disapproval of Chicago: The Symbolic Trial of David Swing."
        CHURCH HISTORY 59 (1972): 30-47.

        A study of the heresy trial of the Presbyterian theology
        professor, David Swing, in Chicago in 1874. Argues against
        the tendency in much Protestant historiography to regard
        "liberalism" as something that emigrated from New England
        into the supposedly conservative Midwest.

1153   _____. THE MODERNIST IMPULSE IN AMERICAN PROTESTANTISM.
        Cambridge, Mass.: Harvard University Press, 1976. 347 p. Bibliog.

        The best book in this field. Excellent analysis of the de-
        velopment of liberalism in American Protestant theology
        during the nineteenth and early twentieth centuries.

1154   _____, ed. AMERICAN PROTESTANT THOUGHT: THE LIBERAL ERA.
        New York: Harper and Row, 1968. 243 p.

        A paperback book of twenty-three readings taken from works
        of the period. Organized into five sections: the setting,
        characteristic ideas, implications, complications, and recon-
        struction.

1155   Larson, Orvin. AMERICAN INFIDEL: ROBERT G. INGERSOLL.   New
        York: Citadel Press, 1962. 316 p. Bibliog.

        Biography of the notorious, flamboyant American atheist,
        Robert Ingersoll (1833-99), resting upon extensive research
        and analyzing Ingersoll's rhetoric.

1156   Marty, Martin E. THE MODERN SCHISM: THREE PATHS TO THE
        SECULAR. New York: Harper and Row, 1969. 191 p.

Study of secularization in Great Britain, continental Europe, and America during the period 1830-70. A provocative essay that utilizes a much-needed comparative approach.

1157　Persons, Stow. FREE RELIGION: AN AMERICAN FAITH. New Haven, Conn.: Yale University Press, 1947. 168 p.

A brief but illuminating study of the Free Religious Association and its roots in American Unitarianism, stressing its democratic character and advocacy of social reform. Bibliographical essay.

1158　Radest, Howard B. TOWARD COMMON GROUND: THE STORY OF THE ETHICAL SOCIETIES IN THE UNITED STATES. New York: Frederick Ungar Co., 1969. 348 p.

Relates that the Ethical Societies are the outgrowth of the Society for Ethical Culture founded in 1876 by Felix Adler in New York City. Story carried up to 1969 in this history, which shows this group to have been roughly equivalent to the British Fabians.

1159　Shriver, George H., ed. AMERICAN RELIGIOUS HERETICS: FORMAL AND INFORMAL TRIALS. Nashville: Abingdon Press, 1966. 240 p.

Describes the trials of five Protestant ministers in the period 1845-1906: Philip Schaff, German Reformed; Crawford H. Toy, Southern Baptist; Charles A. Briggs, Presbyterian; Borden Parker Bowne, Methodist; and Algernon S. Crapsey, Episcopal. Useful both for its discussion of the image of the heretic in American life and for its analysis of the controversy over biblical authority and liberal theology.

1160　Wieman, Henry Nelson. THE EMPIRICAL THEOLOGY OF HENRY NELSON WIEMAN. Edited by Robert W. Bretall. Library of Living Theology Series, vol. 4. Carbondale: Southern Illinois University Press, 1969. 423 p.

Includes an autobiographical essay, nineteen other essays on Wieman's theology with his brief responses to each, and a bibliography of his works up to 1961.

1161　Williams, Daniel Day. THE ANDOVER LIBERALS: A STUDY IN AMERICAN THEOLOGY. New York: King's Crown Press, 1941. 203 p.

A study of "Progressive Orthodoxy," a moderately liberal, post-Calvinist school of Protestant theology identified with Andover Theological Seminary in the 1880s.

SCIENCE AND RELIGION

See also Wiener (1342) and Weber (603).

1162   Bledstein, Burton J. "Noah Porter Versus William Graham Sumner."
CHURCH HISTORY 43 (1974): 340–49.

An analysis of the controversy in 1879–80 between the aging
president of Yale and a young professor of political and social science, who insisted on his right to use Herbert Spencer's STUDY OF SOCIOLOGY as a textbook. Concludes
that Sumner was not so clearly the victim of a witch-hunt
as has been supposed.

1163   Boller, Paul F., [Jr.]. AMERICAN THOUGHT IN TRANSITION: THE IM-
PACT OF EVOLUTIONARY NATURALISM, 1865–1900. Chicago: Rand
McNally and Co., 1969. xiii, 271 p.

A synthesis of American thought in the Gilded Age, stressing
evolutionary thought in both its progressive and naturalistic
manifestations as a unifying theme. Bibliographical essay.

1164   Brown, Ira V. LYMAN ABBOTT, CHRISTIAN EVOLUTIONIST. Cambridge, Mass.: Harvard University Press, 1953. 303 p. Bibliog.

An excellent biography of this liberal Congregationalist
minister, educator, and champion of evolutionary thought.

1165   Dupree, A. Hunter. ASA GRAY, 1810–1888. Cambridge, Mass.:
Harvard University Press, 1959. 505 p. Illus.

A thorough and well-documented biography of this theistic
botanist and Harvard professor who defended many of Darwin's theories. Contains a description of archival materials.

1166   Gillespie, Neal C. THE COLLAPSE OF ORTHODOXY: THE INTEL-
LECTUAL ORDEAL OF GEORGE FREDERICK HOLMES. Charlottesville:
University Press of Virginia, 1972. 273 p.

Traces the reaction of one scholar and educator to the tide
of scientific change during the late nineteenth century.
Holmes (1820–97) was long-time professor of history and
political economy at the University of Virginia.

1167   Greene, John C. DARWIN AND THE MODERN WORLD VIEW. Baton
Rouge: Louisiana State University Press, 1961. 141 p.

A series of essays on "Darwin and the Bible," "Darwin and
Natural Theology," and "Darwin and Social Science," tracing
in broad strokes the impact of evolutionary thought on these

areas of religion and scholarship.

1168 _____. THE DEATH OF ADAM: EVOLUTION AND ITS IMPACT ON
WESTERN THOUGHT. Ames: Iowa State University Press, 1959. 388 p.
Illus.

Traces the development of evolutionary thought from the
seventeenth century through Darwin. Thoroughly documented.

1169 Hofstadter, Richard. SOCIAL DARWINISM IN THE UNITED STATES,
1860-1915. Philadelphia: University of Pennsylvania Press, 1945.
191 p. Bibliog.

An important and well-documented study of social Darwinism,
as interpreted by such Americans as William Graham Sumner
and Lester Frank Ward, and its impact on social theory, racism, and imperialism.

1170 Loewenberg, Bert James. "The Controversy over Evolution in New England, 1835-1873. NEW ENGLAND QUARTERLY 8 (1935): 232-57.

A brief analysis of the initially hostile attitude of Americans
in New England and elsewhere to Darwinian evolution.

1171 Lurie, Edward. LOUIS AGASSIZ: A LIFE IN SCIENCE. Chicago:
University of Chicago Press, 1960. xiv, 449 p. Bibliog.

An excellent biography of Jean Louis Rodolphe Agassiz
(1807-73), the Swiss-born naturalist who, as a professor at
Harvard, became the most prominent scientific opponent of
Darwin's theory of natural selection.

1172 Persons, Stow, ed. EVOLUTIONARY THOUGHT IN AMERICA. New
Haven, Conn.: Yale University Press, 1950. 462 p.

Eleven essays exploring the development of evolutionary
thought and its impact on philosophy, political theory, sociology, psychology, literature, economics, architecture, and
theology in the United States.

1173 White, Andrew Dickson. A HISTORY OF THE WARFARE OF SCIENCE
WITH THEOLOGY IN CHRISTENDOM. 2 vols. New York: D. Apple-
ton and Co., 1896.

Perhaps the most forceful and dauntless expression of the late-
nineteenth-century liberal view that science would soon replace religion as an ultimate explanation of the nature of
the cosmos. Makes quaint reading nearly a century later.

1174   White, Edward A. SCIENCE AND RELIGION IN AMERICAN THOUGHT: THE IMPACT OF NATURALISM. Stanford, Calif.: Stanford University Press, 1952. 117 p.

> A very brief analysis of the thought of such liberal thinkers as John William Draper, Andrew Dickson White, John Fiske, William James, David Starr Jordan, and John Dewey on the relationship of religion and science.

THE ANTI-EVOLUTION MOVEMENT

1175   De Camp, L. Sprague. THE GREAT MONKEY TRIAL. Garden City, N.Y.: Doubleday and Co., 1968. 538 p. Bibliog.

> Lively account of the 1925 trial of John Scopes in Dayton, Tennessee, for violating a statute prohibiting teaching Darwinian evolution in the public schools of that state.

1176   Gatewood, Willard B., Jr. PREACHERS, PEDAGOGUES AND POLITICIANS: THE EVOLUTION CONTROVERSY IN NORTH CAROLINA, 1920-1927. Chapel Hill: University of North Carolina Press, 1966. 268 p. Bibliog.

> A detailed monographic study of the efforts and failure to enact a statute banning the teaching of evolution in North Carolina.

1177   _____, ed. CONTROVERSY IN THE TWENTIES: FUNDAMENTALISM, MODERNISM, AND EVOLUTION. Nashville: Vanderbilt University Press, 1969. 459 p.

> A useful anthology that concentrates on southern sources and contains some fiction. Consists of a collection of documents relating to several controversies involving church leaders and others over the teaching of evolution and on other scientific issues that rocked many Protestant denominations and state legislatures during the 1920s. Bibliographic essay.

1178   Ginger, Ray. SIX DAYS OR FOREVER? TENNESSEE V. JOHN THOMAS SCOPES. Boston: Beacon Press, 1958. 258 p. Bibliog.

> Analysis of the cultural and political climate of the Scopes "monkey trial," which tested the legality of teaching Darwinian evolution in Tennessee in 1925.

1179   Grebstein, Sheldon Norman, ed. MONKEY TRIAL: THE STATE OF TENNESSEE VS. JOHN THOMAS SCOPES. Boston: Houghton Mifflin Co., 1960. xiv, 221 p.

> A sourcebook that contains the text of the Tennessee statute

forbidding the teaching of evolution, selections from Genesis and from Darwin's ORIGIN OF THE SPECIES and DESCENT OF MAN, selections from the biology textbook used by Scopes, and the entire transcript of the 1925 trial.

1180 Levine, Lawrence W. DEFENDER OF THE FAITH, WILLIAM JENNINGS BRYAN: THE LAST DECADE, 1915–1925. New York: Oxford University Press, 1965. 386 p.

Biography of "the great commoner" will delight the reader and provide him with a discerning and finely detailed portrait based upon sound scholarship. Description of the part Bryan played in the Scopes trial done well, although author does not have a clear understanding of Fundamentalism.

1181 Scopes, John T., and Presley, James. CENTER OF THE STORM: MEMOIRS OF JOHN T. SCOPES. New York: Holt, Rinehart and Winston, 1967. 277 p.

Serves only to indicate that John Scopes was unnecessary to the 1925 Dayton, Tennessee, trial, as biography retells the story without adding anything to the well-known case. Admission by Scopes that he was not a regular biology teacher in Dayton, and had no recollection of actually teaching about evolution.

SOCIAL GOSPEL

General

1182 Dombrowski, James. THE EARLY DAYS OF CHRISTIAN SOCIALISM IN AMERICA. New York: Columbia University Press, 1936. 208 p.

An early study of the liberal wing of the Social Gospel, examining Stephen Colwell, Richard Ely, George D. Herron, and others. Superseded by Hopkins' work (1184).

1183 Handy, Robert T., ed. THE SOCIAL GOSPEL IN AMERICA, 1870–1920: GLADDEN, ELY, RAUSCHENBUSCH. Library of Protestant Thought. New York: Oxford University Press, 1966. 399 p. Bibliog.

A well-edited but narrowly focused collection of writings by these three exponents of the Social Gospel. Bibliography listing works by these men as well as secondary material.

1184 Hopkins, Charles Howard. THE RISE OF THE SOCIAL GOSPEL IN AMERICAN PROTESTANTISM, 1865–1915. New Haven, Conn.: Yale University Press, 1940. 342 p.

A standard but dated history of the Social Gospel, arguing that the movement went hand-in-hand with the proliferation of liberalism and evolutionary thought. Emphasis on individuals who fit this thesis.

1185 Hutchison, William R. "The Americanness of the Social Gospel; An Inquiry in Comparative History." CHURCH HISTORY 44 (1975): 367-81.

Examines the basis for the commonly-held European and American notion that the Social Gospel was a peculiarly American phenomenon and that it became the characteristic expression of most main-line American denominations by the 1920s. Finds little evidence to support either hypothesis. In the process of discussing these issues, raises crucial questions about comparative history and points at new directions to follow.

1186 Smith, Timothy L. REVIVALISM AND SOCIAL REFORM IN MID-NINETEENTH-CENTURY AMERICA. New York: Abingdon Press, 1957. 253 p.

Argues that revivalism was "the cutting edge" of American Protestantism in the 1850s, that it was predominantly an urban phenomenon, and that it was the chief root of the later Social Gospel. Bibliographic essay.

1187 Visser't Hooft, Willem A. THE BACKGROUND OF THE SOCIAL GOSPEL IN AMERICA. Haarlem, Netherlands: H.D. Tjeenk Willink and Zoon, 1928. 187 p.

A pioneering Netherlandic study of the Social Gospel in the United States, examining its roots in Puritanism, the Enlightenment, revivalism, modern science, and theologies stressing divine immanence.

Special Aspects

1188 Dorn, Jacob H. WASHINGTON GLADDEN: PROPHET OF THE SOCIAL GOSPEL. Athens: Ohio State University Press, 1967. 489 p. Bibliog.

A solid biography of this leading Congregationalist advocate of the Social Gospel (1836-1918).

1189 Eighmy, John Lee. "Religious Liberalism in the South during the Progressive Era." CHURCH HISTORY 38 (1969): 359-72.

Describes the impact of the Social Gospel on the South.

1190   Ely, Richard T. GROUND UNDER OUR FEET: AN AUTOBIOGRAPHY. New York: Macmillan Co., 1938. 330 p.

> The autobiography of this institutional economist who applied Christianity to social reform.

1191   Everett, John Rutherford. RELIGION IN ECONOMICS: A STUDY OF JOHN BATES CLARK, RICHARD T. ELY, SIMON N. PATTEN. New York: King's Crown Press, 1946. xiii, 160 p. Bibliog.

> A brief but well-documented study of the relationship between religion and economic theory in the work of these three American economists. Bibliography focusing on published works of other social commentators.

1192   Griffen, Clyde C. "Rich Laymen and Early Social Christianity." CHURCH HISTORY 36 (1967): 45-65.

> A case study of the small group of wealthy Protestant laymen in New York City who approved of their ministers' participation in the Social Gospel, even if they did not always concur with the social criticism that flowed from many pulpits during the Gilded Age.

1193   Jensen, Billie Barnes. "A Social Gospel Experiment in Newspaper Reform: Charles M. Sheldon and the TOPEKA DAILY CAPITAL." CHURCH HISTORY 33 (1964): 74-83.

> Describes the efforts of Charles Sheldon, exponent of the Social Gospel and author of the best seller IN HIS STEPS, to manage the CAPITAL for one week on exclusively Christian principles.

1194   Hopkins, Charles H. A HISTORY OF THE YMCA IN NORTH AMERICA. New York: Association Press, 1951. 818 p.

> A comprehensive and well-documented history of the YMCA in Canada and the United States, 1851-1951.

1195   Huggins, Nathan Irvin. PROTESTANTS AGAINST POVERTY: BOSTON'S CHARITIES, 1870-1900. Westport, Conn.: Greenwood Publishing Co., 1971. 239 p.

> Monographic treatment of Protestant reformers who created a series of voluntary associations to combat poverty among immigrants and victims of industrialism. Their efforts judged to have been conservative and simplistic.

1196   Knudten, Richard D. THE SYSTEMATIC THOUGHT OF WASHINGTON GLADDEN. New York: Humanities Press, 1969. 301 p.

An analysis of the religious and social thought of this Congregationalist exponent of the Social Gospel (1836–1918). Less useful than Dorn's work (1188).

1197   Nicholl, Grier. "The Image of the Protestant Minister in the Christian Social Novel." CHURCH HISTORY 37 (1968): 319–34.

On the basis of a survey of one hundred novels published between 1865 and 1918, argues that the minister's role in relationship to social change during the period was often more positively presented in the fiction than historians have been willing to admit was true in actuality.

1198   Sims, Mary S.S. THE YWCA: AN UNFOLDING PURPOSE. New York: Woman's Press, 1950. xv, 157 p.

Chronological history in which material is related to the social background of the period.

1199   Thompson, Ernest Trice. CHANGING EMPHASES IN AMERICAN PREACHING. The Stone Lectures for 1943. Philadelphia: Westminster Press, 1943. 234 p.

Essays on Horace Bushnell, Henry Ward Beecher, Dwight L. Moody, Washington Gladden, and Walter Rauschenbusch, tracing a transition from individual evangelization to the Social Gospel in one stream of American Protestantism.

1200   Wisbey, Herbert A. SOLDIERS WITHOUT SWORDS: A HISTORY OF THE SALVATION ARMY IN THE UNITED STATES. New York: Macmillan Co., 1955. 242 p. Bibliog.

A standard but poorly documented history covering the period from 1880 until the 1950s.

Walter Rauschenbusch

1201   Rauschenbusch, Walter. CHRISTIANITY AND THE SOCIAL CRISIS. 1907. Reprint. Edited by Robert Cross. New York: Harper and Row, 1964. xxv, 429 p.

A new edition of author's demand for increased social action by churchmen to ameliorate the material ills of modern civilization.

1202   _____. A RAUSCHENBUSCH READER. Edited by Benson Y. Landis. New York: Harper and Brothers, 1957. 167 p.

About half the collection drawn from author's major works, CHRISTIANITY AND THE SOCIAL CRISIS, CHRISTIANIZING

THE SOCIAL ORDER, and A THEOLOGY FOR THE SOCIAL GOSPEL.

1203 Aiken, John R. "Walter Rauschenbusch and Education for Reform." CHURCH HISTORY 36 (1967): 456-69.

Examines the contradictions that existed between Rauschenbusch's elitist theories of education and his social reform policies. Valuable.

1204 Bodein, Vernon Parker. THE SOCIAL GOSPEL OF WALTER RAUSCHENBUSCH AND ITS RELATION TO RELIGIOUS EDUCATION. New Haven, Conn.: Yale University Press, 1944. 168 p. Bibliog.

A brief pioneering study of the thought of this Baptist exponent of the Social Gospel and pacifism. Contains little on religious education.

1205 Schneider, Carl E. "Americanization of Karl August Rauschenbusch, 1816-1899." CHURCH HISTORY 24 (1955): 3-14.

A brief but illuminating look at this leader of German-American Baptists, concentrating on the interplay of German pietism and American religious factors in him.

1206 Sharpe, Dores R. WALTER RAUSCHENBUSCH. New York: Macmillan Co., 1942. xiii, 463 p.

A sympathetic biography of Rauschenbusch (1861-1918), the Baptist exponent of the Social Gospel and pacifism, written by the man who served as his secretary.

Twentieth Century

1207 Carter, Paul A. THE DECLINE AND REVIVAL OF THE SOCIAL GOSPEL: SOCIAL AND POLITICAL LIBERALISM IN AMERICAN PROTESTANT CHURCHES, 1920-1940. Ithaca, N.Y.: Cornell University Press, 1954. 265 p. Bibliog.

Argues that the social conscience of certain Protestant denominations in the United States waned during the 1920s but was revived during the years of the New Deal.

1208 Handy, Robert T. "Christianity and Socialism in America, 1900-1920." CHURCH HISTORY 21 (1952): 39-54.

A stimulating analysis of Protestant involvement in the Socialist Party before and during World War I.

1209   Hughley, J. Neal. TRENDS IN PROTESTANT SOCIAL IDEALISM.
        Freeport, N.Y.: Books for Libraries Press, 1948. xiii, 184 p. Bibliog.

> A very brief study of mid-twentieth-century American Protes-
> tant social thought, focusing on E. Stanley Jones, Charles A.
> Ellwood, Francis J. McConnell, Kirby Page, Harry F. Ward,
> and Reinhold Neibuhr. Bibliography listing several works by
> each of these persons.

1210   Meyer, Donald B. THE PROTESTANT SEARCH FOR POLITICAL REALISM,
        1919-1941. Berkeley and Los Angeles: University of California Press,
        1960. 482 p.

> A well-written scholarly analysis of a small group of Protes-
> tant leaders who struggled to carry on the traditions of the
> Social Gospel after 1918. Emphasis upon the Niebuhrs,
> Charles C. Morrison, Harry F. Ward, Francis J. McConnell,
> and A.J. Muste.

1211   Miller, Robert Moats. AMERICAN PROTESTANTISM AND SOCIAL
        ISSUES, 1919-1939. Chapel Hill: University of North Carolina Press,
        1958. xiv, 385 p. Bibliog.

> An examination of the attitudes of several denominations to
> civil liberties, labor problems, race relations, pacifism, and
> international military intervention during these two decades
> of prosperity and depression.

1212   Quinley, Harold E. THE PROPHETIC CLERGY: SOCIAL ACTIVISM
        AMONG PROTESTANT MINISTERS. New York: John Wiley and
        Sons, 1974. 369 p.

> A detailed analysis, resting largely on statistical findings, of
> the social activism of clergymen in nine Protestant denomina-
> tions. Reveals a polarization of "traditionalists" and "mod-
> ernists." Compiled data in California.

Chapter 17

NEW RELIGIOUS MOVEMENTS

OF THE NINETEENTH CENTURY

GENERAL WORKS

1213   Bach, Marcus. STRANGE SECTS AND CURIOUS CULTS. New York:
Dodd, Mead and Co., 1962. 277 p.

> A study of American and foreign cults, divided into three
> sections: the sex sects, the conscience cults, and the search
> for Utopia. Includes, in addition to the groups found in
> many similar books, chapters on Voodoo and the Doukhobors.

1214   _____. THEY HAVE FOUND A FAITH. Indianapolis: Bobbs-Merrill
Co., 1946. 300 p.

> An informal and sympathetic treatment of Jehovah's Witnesses,
> Spiritualism, Baha'i, and other late nineteenth and early twen-
> tieth century groups.

1215   Braden, Charles S. THESE ALSO BELIEVE: A STUDY OF MODERN
AMERICAN CULTS AND MINORITY RELIGIOUS MOVEMENTS. New
York: Macmillan Co., 1949. xv, 491 p. Bibliog.

> An investigation of the history and doctrines of thirteen re-
> ligious groups and movements that stand outside the "main-
> stream" of American religion. Capsule descriptions of several
> other minor groups.

1216   Clark, Elmer T. THE SMALL SECTS IN AMERICA. Rev. ed. New
York: Abingdon-Cokesbury Press, 1949. 256 p.

> A detailed but outdated, and in places unreliable, encyclo-
> pedia of dozens of Pentecostal, Adventist, communitarian, and
> other small religious groups in the United States.

1217   Zaretsky, Irving I., and Leone, Mark P., eds. RELIGIOUS MOVE-
MENTS IN CONTEMPORARY AMERICA. Princeton, N.J.: Princeton
University Press, 1974. xxxvi, 837 p.

A well-edited collection of twenty-seven scholarly essays devoted to the analysis of "marginal" religious movements, both those which, like Christian Science and Pentecostalism, originated outside mainstream religion in the nineteenth century and have since moved toward acceptance, and those which have recently been founded or imported from abroad, such as Scientology or Hare Krishna. An extraordinary collection, containing more good articles on these groups than does virtually any other source.

SPIRITUALISM AND THEOSOPHY

1218   Braden, Charles S.   SPIRITS IN REBELLION: THE RISE AND DEVELOPMENT OF NEW THOUGHT.   Dallas, Tex.:   Southern Methodist University Press, 1963.   571 p.

A sound, scholarly analysis of New Thought, with particular attention given to the International New Thought Alliance, the Unity School of Christianity, Divine Science, and Religious Science.

1219   Cunningham, Raymond J.   "From Holiness to Healing: The Faith Cure in America, 1872-1892."   CHURCH HISTORY 43 (1974):   499-513.

A useful and interestingly written summary of the faith-cure teachings of a number of evangelical Protestant ministers in the generation after the Civil War, including Charles Cullis, William E. Boardman, Albert B. Simpson, and Adoniram J. Gordon.

1220   Dresser, Horatio W.   HISTORY OF THE NEW THOUGHT MOVEMENT. New York: Thomas Y. Crowell Co., 1919.   131 p.

A study of Phineas Quimby, the origins of Christian Science, and other healing movements in the United States.

1221   Eek, Sven, and Zirkoff, Boris de, eds.   WILLIAM QUAN JUDGE, 1851-1896: THE LIFE OF A THEOSOPHICAL PIONEER AND SOME OF HIS OUTSTANDING ARTICLES.   Wheaton, Ill.:   Theosophical Publishing House, 1969.   96 p.

Brief excerpts from the works of this Irish-American colleague of Madame Blavatsky.   Judge was among the founders of the Theosophical Society.

1222   Fornell, Earl Wesley.   THE UNHAPPY MEDIUM: SPIRITUALISM AND THE LIFE OF MARGARET FOX.   Austin: University of Texas Press, 1964.   204 p.

Biography of Margaret Fox, who was one, and perhaps the most notorious, participant in a Spiritualist movement in the late 1840s. The movement given a bad name for a generation by her confession that her communications were fraudulent. Details but not much analysis or historical background provided in this account.

1223 Frazier, Claude A., ed. FAITH HEALING: FINGER OF GOD OR SCIENTIFIC CURIOSITY? New York: Thomas Nelson, 1973. 192 p.

Twenty essays by medical doctors examining faith healing and the role of Christianity in medical practice.

1224 Gordon, Arthur. ONE MAN'S WAY: THE STORY AND MESSAGE OF NORMAN VINCENT PEALE. Englewood Cliffs, N.J.: Prentice-Hall, 1972. 324 p.

Sympathetic, informal biography of Peale, minister of Marble Collegiate Church in New York City and exponent of "positive thinking."

1225 Kerr, Howard. MEDIUMS, AND SPIRIT-RAPPERS, AND ROARING RADICALS: SPIRITUALISM IN AMERICAN LITERATURE, 1850-1900. Urbana: University of Illinois Press, 1972. 261 p.

Traces briefly the history of the spiritualist movement, but is mostly concerned with the reaction to spiritualism of writers such as William Dean Howells, Mark Twain, and Henry James.

1226 Kuhn, Alvin Boyd. THEOSOPHY: A MODERN REVIVAL OF ANCIENT WISDOM. New York: Henry Holt and Co., 1930. 381 p. Bibliog.

A scholarly study of the recrudescence of interest in theosophy, especially in the United States during the nineteenth century.

1227 Meyer, Donald B. THE POSITIVE THINKERS: A STUDY OF THE AMERICAN QUEST FOR HEALTH, WEALTH AND PERSONAL POWER FROM MARY BAKER EDDY TO NORMAN VINCENT PEALE. New York: Doubleday and Co., 1965. 342 p.

A popular account of the mind-healers in the era of Mary Baker Eddy, and of Norman Vincent Peale, connected by a desultory narrative of the intervening years.

1228 Nelson, Geoffrey K. SPIRITUALISM AND SOCIETY. New York: Schocken Books, 1969. 307 p.

Sociological and historical analysis of the origins of spiritualism in Britain and America. A good treatment although better for Britain than for America.

1229 Parker, Gail Thain. MIND CURE IN NEW ENGLAND: FROM THE CIVIL WAR TO WORLD WAR I. Hanover, N.H.: University Press of New England, 1973. 197 p.

A stimulating and perceptive series of psychobiographical sketches on leaders of the New Thought or mental healing movement of the late nineteenth century. Includes chapters on Emerson, Swedenborg, Mary Baker Eddy, Horatio Dresser, and William James. In contrast to Meyer (1227), finds a good deal to praise in the mind-cure movement, describing advocates as "at their best . . . among the most honest Americans of their generation."

CHRISTIAN SCIENCE

1230 Bates, Ernest Sutherland, and Dittemore, John V. MARY BAKER EDDY: THE TRUTH AND THE TRADITION. New York: Alfred A. Knopf, 1932. 510 p.

Although this work written by authors who were one-time leaders of the Mother Church in Boston and based upon archival material that has been authenticated by church historians, is rejected as unacceptable by Christian Scientist denominational leaders because of its criticism of Mary Baker Eddy.

1231 Braden, Charles S. CHRISTIAN SCIENCE TODAY: POWER, POLICY, PRACTICE. Dallas, Tex.: Southern Methodist University Press, 1958. xvi, 432 p. Bibliog.

An objective and very useful treatment of the origins of Christian Science and its members, internal power struggles, doctrines, and organization in the twentieth century.

1232 Clemens, Samuel L. [Mark Twain]. CHRISTIAN SCIENCE. New York: Harper and Brothers, 1907. 362 p.

An example of Twain at his most cantankerous. Not good Twain and not good criticism. Amounts, at best, to an illustration of the kind of objections raised against Christian Science in the early decades of its existence.

1233 Cunningham, Raymond J. "The Impact of Christian Science on the American Churches, 1880-1910." AMERICAN HISTORICAL REVIEW 72 (1967): 885-905.

Focuses on the initially hostile reaction of several Protestant denominations to the emergence of Christian Science, and their gradual adoption of the "gospel of health."

1234 Dakin, Edwin F. MRS. EDDY: THE BIOGRAPHY OF A VIRGINAL MIND. New York: Charles Scribner's Sons, 1929. 553 p.

An example of the rashly psychoanalytic, debunking biographies popular during the 1920s. Although based upon extensive research, is vitiated by its pervasive antagonism toward Mary Baker Eddy. The object of a long-lived campaign of suppression by Christian Scientists.

1235 Gottschalk, Stephen. THE EMERGENCE OF CHRISTIAN SCIENCE IN AMERICAN RELIGIOUS LIFE. Berkeley and Los Angeles: University of California Press, 1973. xxix, 305 p.

A study of the early years of Christian Science in the United States, placing this movement in the context of American Protestantism and analyzing how it differed from mainstream Protestant denominations on one hand, and occult movements on the other.

1236 Kennedy, Hugh A. Studdert. MRS. EDDY: HER LIFE, HER WORK AND HER PLACE IN HISTORY. San Francisco: Farallon Press, 1947. 507 p.

A largely successful attempt at a balanced biography of Mary Baker Eddy.

1237 Peel, Robert. CHRISTIAN SCIENCE: ITS ENCOUNTER WITH AMERICAN CULTURE. New York: Holt, Rinehart and Winston, 1958. xiv, 239 p.

An analysis of Christian Science's links with and separation from other aspects of American intellectual life, both in the nineteenth century when it was formulated, and in the twentieth century. Short bibliographical essay.

1238 _____. MARY BAKER EDDY: THE YEARS OF DISCOVERY. New York: Holt, Rinehart and Winston, 1966. 372 p.

1239 _____. MARY BAKER EDDY: THE YEARS OF TRIAL. New York: Holt, Rinehart and Winston, 1971. 391 p.

The best biography of Mary Baker Eddy certainly comprised in these two volumes.

1240   Wilbur, Sibyl. THE LIFE OF MARY BAKER EDDY. Boston: Christian Science Publishing Co., 1907. xvi, 425 p.

>   The earliest "official" biography and a book still popular among Christian Scientists. An example of Christian Scientist hagiography.

JEHOVAH'S WITNESSES

1241   Beckford, James A. THE TRUMPET OF PROPHECY: A SOCIOLOGICAL STUDY OF JEHOVAH'S WITNESSES. New York: John Wiley and Sons, 1975. 244 p. Bibliog.

>   A penetrating sociological analysis of the development of the Jehovah's Witnesses, with discussion of their theology, organization, publications, membership, proselytizing, and morality.

1242   Cole, Marley. JEHOVAH'S WITNESSES: THE NEW WORLD SOCIETY. New York: Vantage Press, 1955. 229 p.

>   A sympathetic introduction to the Jehovah's Witnesses, attempting to place this denomination in the perspective of church history and American society. Of some value for understanding its members' conflicts with other Christians and civil governments.

1243   Gruss, Edmond Charles. THE JEHOVAH'S WITNESSES AND PROPHETIC SPECULATION. Nutley, N.J.: Presbyterian and Reformed Publishing Co., 1974.

>   A poorly edited attack on the eschatology of the Jehovah's Witnesses.

1244   Stroup, Gerbert Hewitt. THE JEHOVAH'S WITNESSES. New York: Columbia University Press, 1945. 180 p.

>   The first scholarly and objective study, still useful for its treatment of the early history of the movement and the struggles that occurred after the death of founder Charles Taze Russell (1853-1916).

1245   White, Timothy. A PEOPLE FOR HIS NAME: A HISTORY OF JEHOVAH'S WITNESSES AND AN EVALUATION. New York: Vantage Press, 1968. 418 p.

>   Probably the best, detailed history of the movement, especially its recent history under president Nathan H. Knorr.

1246   Zygmunt, Joseph F.   "Prophetic Failure and Chiliastic Identity: The
       Case of Jehovah's Witnesses."   AMERICAN JOURNAL OF SOCIOLOGY
       75 (1970):   926-48.

         Analyzes the failure of several Witness predictions, showing
         how the group reacted to these disappointments and used
         them as "identity confirmations."

PENTECOSTALISM

General Works

See also Williams (1053), and Smith (1107).

1247   Bloch-Hoell, Nils.   THE PENTECOSTAL MOVEMENT: ITS ORIGIN,
       DEVELOPMENT, AND DISTINCTIVE CHARACTER.   Oslo, Norway:
       Universitetsforlaget, 1964.   256 p.

         The abbreviated, English version of author's book PINSEBEV-
         EGELSEN.   Traces the history of Pentecostalism in the
         United States and, to a lesser extent, in Norway, from the
         beginning of the twentieth century until the 1950s.   Ana-
         lyzes Pentecostal theology and phenomena.

1248   Brumback, Carl.   SUDDENLY . . . FROM HEAVEN: A HISTORY OF
       THE ASSEMBLIES OF GOD.   Springfield, Mo.:   Gospel Publishing
       House, 1961.   380 p.   Appendixes.

         An unsophisticated narrative account of denominational his-
         tory from 1875 to 1960.   A statement of belief, lists of de-
         nominational officials, and statistics of membership in ap-
         pendixes.

1249   Hollenweger, Walter J.   THE PENTECOSTALS: THE CHARISMATIC
       MOVEMENT IN THE CHURCHES.   Translated from the German by
       R.A. Wilson.   Minneapolis, Minn.:   Augsburg Publishing House, 1972.
       592 p.

         An excellent study that places Pentecostalism into a world-
         wide context.   Written by a former member of a Pentecostal
         group and later administrator for the World Council of Churches.

1250   Jones, Charles Edwin.   A GUIDE TO THE STUDY OF THE HOLINESS
       MOVEMENT.   American Theological Library Association Bibliography
       Series, vol. 1.   Metuchen, N.J.:   Scarecrow Press, 1974.   918 p.

         First volume in a series that promises to offer great help to
         students of American religion.   In addition to lists of sources,
         contains thumbnail sketches of holiness denominations.

1251 _____. PERFECTIONIST PERSUASION: THE HOLINESS MOVEMENT AND AMERICAN METHODISM, 1867-1936. American Theological Association Monograph Series. Metuchen, N.J.: Scarecrow Press, 1974. xx, 242 p. Appendixes.

> Traces the development of several holiness denominations (i.e., Church of the Nazarene, Pilgrim Holiness Church) out of Methodism into middle-class churches in the 1930s. Based upon a large amount of demographic data.

1252 Menzies, William W. ANOINTED TO SERVE: THE STORY OF THE ASSEMBLIES OF GOD. Springfield, Mo.: Gospel Publishing House, 1971. 436 p.

> Although this is essentially an official, insider's glorification of denominational success, does have some value as a reference work for the largest Pentecostal group in the United States.

1253 Nichol, John Thomas. PENTECOSTALISM. New York: Harper and Row, 1966. xvi, 264 p. Bibliog.

> A brief but far-ranging history of the Pentecostal movement, tracing its course from the United States to Europe, the Orient, Africa, and Latin America, from the beginning of the twentieth century until the 1960s.

1254 Synan, Vinson. THE HOLINESS-PENTECOSTAL MOVEMENT IN THE UNITED STATES. Grand Rapids, Mich.: William B. Eerdmans Publishing Co., 1971. 248 p. Bibliog.

> A general history of Pentecostalism and holiness movements in the United States, especially in the South and among Negroes, arguing that they stem primarily from the Wesleyan tradition.

1255 _____. THE OLD-TIME POWER. Franklin Springs, Ga.: Advocate Press, n.d. 296 p.

> A history of the denomination called the Pentecostal Holiness Church. Developed from dissertation of the author, a life-long member of the denomination.

1256 _____, ed. ASPECTS OF PENTECOSTAL-CHARISMATIC ORIGINS. Plainfield, N.J.: Logos International, 1973. 252 p.

> A collection of papers delivered at a symposium on the history of the Pentecostal movement.

1257   Thomas, Lately. STORMING HEAVEN. New York: Ballantine Books, 1970. 305 p. Bibliog.

A popular biography of Aimee Semple McPherson (1890-1944), the Pentecostal revivalist of California.

Contemporary Charismatic Revival

1258   Agrimson, J. Elmo, ed. GIFTS OF THE SPIRIT AND THE BODY OF CHRIST. Minneapolis, Minn.: Augsburg Publishing House, 1974. 112 p.

Modern Pentecostalism and charismatic movements, and their biblical and historical backgrounds, as interpreted by six Lutheran theologians.

1259   Durasoff, Steve. BRIGHT WIND OF THE SPIRIT: PENTECOSTALISM TODAY. Englewood Cliffs, N.J.: Prentice-Hall, 1972. 277 p. Bibliog.

An introduction to the history and current state of the Pentecostal movement, examining such leaders as Aimee Semple McPherson and Oral Roberts, and the various structures in which the movement is manifested.

1260   Goodman, Felicitas D. SPEAKING IN TONGUES: A CROSS-CULTURAL STUDY OF GLOSSOLALIA. Chicago: University of Chicago Press, 1972. xxii, 175 p. Bibliog.

An analysis of glossolalia employing the methodology of physiological psychology.

1261   Gromacki, Robert Glenn. THE MODERN TONGUES MOVEMENT. Philadelphia: Presbyterian and Reformed Publishing Co., 1967. 165 p. Bibliog.

A poorly-edited and loosely-written analysis of glossolalia in the New Testament and among Christians in the twentieth century.

1262   Hamilton, Michael P., ed. THE CHARISMATIC MOVEMENT. Grand Rapids, Mich.: William B. Eerdmans Publishing Co., 1975. 196 p.

A collection of ten articles especially written for this volume and devoted to psychological and theological analysis, as well as historical treatment, of the phenomenon of tongues speaking in Christian churches. Contains two case studies of American congregations and chapters devoted to black Pentecostalism and the Holiness Movement in Southern Appalachia. Also includes a phonograph record of people speaking in tongues.

1263   Harrell, David Edwin, Jr.   ALL THINGS ARE POSSIBLE: THE HEALING
AND CHARISMATIC REVIVALS IN MODERN AMERICA.   Bloomington:
Indiana University Press, 1975.   304 p.

> Essentially a set of biographical sketches of Pentecostal ministers
> who, beginning in 1947, began to break away from their de-
> nominational ties and to become independent healers.   Treats
> such figures as Oral Roberts, A.A. Allen, and William Bran-
> ham.

1264   Jorstad, Erling.   BOLD IN THE SPIRIT: LUTHERAN CHARISMATIC RE-
NEWAL IN AMERICA TODAY.   Minneapolis, Minn.:   Augsburg Publishing House, 1974.   126 p.

> A brief description of the extent of charismatic renewal in
> American Lutheranism, a survey of the history of Lutheran
> response to this phenomenon, and an attempt to reconcile
> Lutherans to its presence.

1265   _____, ed.   THE HOLY SPIRIT IN TODAY'S CHURCH: A HANDBOOK
OF THE NEW PENTECOSTALISM.   Nashville: Abingdon Press, 1973.
160 p.

> An anthology of twelve essays introducing glossolalia, faith
> healing, and other aspects of contemporary Pentecostalism,
> and including the movement within Roman Catholicism.

1266   Kerr, John Stevens.   THE FIRES FLARE ANEW: A LOOK AT THE NEW
PENTECOSTALISM.   Philadelphia: Fortress Press, 1974.   107 p.

> A superficial introduction to the rise, fall, and resurrection
> of Pentecostalism in church history.

1267   McDonnell, Kilian.   CHARISMATIC RENEWAL AND THE CHURCHES.
New York: Seabury Press, 1976.   202 p.   Bibliog.

> Presents a detailed historical survey of how the historic
> churches have reacted to the presence of Pentecostals in
> their congregations, and then summarizes and analyzes the
> research of the psychological health of people who pray in
> tongues.   A rewarding but not simple study.

1268   Quebedeaux, Richard.   THE NEW CHARISMATICS: THE ORIGINS, DE-
VELOPMENT, AND SIGNIFICANCE OF NEO-PENTECOSTALISM.   New
York: Doubleday and Co., 1976.   252 p.

> A useful summarized collection of elementary information
> about the history and theological tradition of the charismatic
> revival.

1269   Ranaghan, Kevin, and Ranaghan, Dorothy. CATHOLIC PENTECOSTALS.
        Paramus, N. J.: Paulist Press Deus Books, 1969. 266 p. Bibliog.

        A brief, sympathetic introduction to the Pentecostal move-
        ment among American Roman Catholics in the 1960s.

1270   Roberts, Oral. THE CALL: AN AUTOBIOGRAPHY. Garden City,
        N. Y.: Doubleday and Co., 1972. 216 p.

        A loosely written autobiography of the contemporary Oklahoma-
        based Pentecostal revivalist.

1271   Samarin, William J. TONGUES OF MEN AND ANGELS: THE RELI-
        GIOUS LANGUAGE OF PENTECOSTALISM. New York: Macmillan
        Co., 1972. xv, 277 p. Bibliog.

        A sympathetic linguistic analysis of glossolalia, the language
        of Pentecostals, comparing it with magical incantations, jazz,
        and other oral forms of expression.

1272   Sherrill, John L. THEY SPEAK WITH OTHER TONGUES. New York:
        McGraw-Hill Book Co., 1964. 165 p.

        A loosely written account of modern Pentecostalism, attempt-
        ing to understand the reasons for its rapid growth.

Chapter 18

MISSIONS AND THE ECUMENICAL MOVEMENT

MISSIONARY EXPANSION

See also the sections devoted to Indian missions in chapter 2.

1273   Anderson, Courtney. TO THE GOLDEN SHORE: THE LIFE OF ADON-
        IRAM JUDSON. Boston: Little, Brown, and Co., 1956. xiii, 530 p.

> A nicely-written popular account of the life of Judson (1788–
> 1850), one of the earliest Protestant foreign missionaries and
> member of the famous Williams College group; he worked in
> Burma.

1274   Anderson, Rufus. TO ADVANCE THE GOSPEL. Edited by R. Pierce
        Beaver. Grand Rapids, Mich.: William B. Eerdmans Publishing Co.,
        1967. 217 p.

> A compilation of the writings of Rufus Anderson (1796–1880),
> for forty-three years secretary of the American Board of Com-
> missioners for Foreign Missions.

1275   Andrew, John A. III. REBUILDING THE CHRISTIAN COMMON-
        WEALTH: NEW ENGLAND CONGREGATIONALISTS AND FOREIGN
        MISSIONS, 1800–1830. Lexington: University Press of Kentucky,
        1976. 232 p.

> A welcome fresh look at a long-neglected subject. Argues
> the thesis that the foreign mission enterprise was undertaken
> to quiet factionalism within the denomination. Focuses, thus,
> more on New England than on the Sandwich Islands and con-
> centrates on sources of social discord rather than on theologi-
> cal sources of mission activity.

1276   Barr, Pat. TO CHINA WITH LOVE: THE LIVES AND TIMES OF PROT-
        ESTANT MISSIONARIES IN CHINA 1860–1900. Garden City, N.Y.:
        Doubleday and Co., 1973. xiii, 210 p. Bibliog.

A popular history of diverse Protestant missions in China, emphasizing British endeavors, but also considering such American groups as the American Board of Commissioners for Foreign Missions.

1277   Beaver, R. Pierce. THE MISSIONARY BETWEEN THE TIMES. Garden City, N.Y.: Doubleday and Co., 1968. xiii, 196 p. Bibliog.

Lectures on problems confronting Christian missions in a contemporary world of rapid change, that often resents foreign religion as an intrusion.

1278   Dryden, Cecil P. GIVE ALL TO OREGON: MISSIONARY PIONEERS OF THE FAR WEST. New York: Hastings House, 1968. 256 p.

Concise and comprehensive account of Methodist, Presbyterian-Congregational, and Catholic missions to Oregon in the early nineteenth century.

1279   Elsbree, Oliver W. THE RISE OF THE MISSIONARY SPIRIT IN AMERICA, 1790-1815. Williamsport, Pa.: Williamsport Printing Co., 1928. 187 p. Bibliog.

An early study of the missionary spirit handled in a critical manner. Concentrates on New England.

1280   Fairbank, John K., ed. THE MISSIONARY ENTERPRISE IN CHINA AND AMERICA. Cambridge, Mass.: Harvard University Press, 1974. 442 p.

Thirteen essays on religious aspects of Chinese contacts with the United States, arranged under three topics: "Protestant Missions in American Expansion," "Christianity and the Transformation of China," and "China Mission Images and American Policies."

1281   Goodykoontz, Colin B. HOME MISSIONS ON THE AMERICAN FRONTIER, WITH PARTICULAR REFERENCE TO THE AMERICAN HOME MISSIONARY SOCIETY. Caldwell, Idaho: Caxton Printers, 1939. 460 p.

A doctoral dissertation on the history of the AHMS, written at Harvard under the direction of Frederick Jackson Turner. Structured around Turner's frontier thesis, but the body of the book is a state by state, denomination by denomination, description of activities.

1282   Grabill, Joseph L. "The 'Invisible' Missionary: A Study in American Foreign Relations." JOURNAL OF CHURCH AND STATE 14 (1972): 93-105.

Argues that historians of American foreign policy have tended to neglect the role of missionaries in shaping public opinion of events and peoples overseas, and that greater attention to their role would enhance our knowledge of how foreign policy is formed.

1283   Hinckley, Ted C. "The Presbyterian Leadership in Pioneer Alaska."
        JOURNAL OF AMERICAN HISTORY 52 (1966): 742-56.

        A study of missionary policies in this generally neglected field, revealing that they reflected the Social Gospel, the quest for civil service, the temperance movement, and other currents in contemporary life in the United States.

1284   Hocking, William Ernest, ed. RE-THINKING MISSIONS: A LAYMEN'S INQUIRY AFTER ONE HUNDRED YEARS. New York: Harper and Brothers, 1932. xv, 349 p.

        The report of commissioners representing the Baptist (Northern), Congregational, Methodist Episcopal, Presbyterian Church in the U. S. A., Protestant Episcopal, Reformed Church in America, and United Presbyterian denominations. An assessment of their accomplishments and suggestions for future foreign missions, with re-emphasis on the importance of social work in the mission field.

1285   Horner, Norman A., ed. PROTESTANT CROSSCURRENTS IN MISSION: THE ECUMENICAL-CONSERVATIVE ENCOUNTER. Nashville: Abingdon Press, 1968. 224 p.

        Missionary strategies and interdenominational relations in this regard discussed by seven Americans from "evangelical" and "ecumenical" perspectives.

1286   Hudson, Winthrop S. "Protestant Clergy Debate the Nation's Vocation, 1898-1899." CHURCH HISTORY 42 (1973): 110-18.

        A very helpful article tracing the part played by several influential clergymen in the American involvement in the Spanish-American War and the occupation of the Philippines.

1287   Iglehart, Charles W. A CENTURY OF PROTESTANT CHRISTIANITY IN JAPAN. Rutland, Vt.: Charles E. Tuttle Co., 1959. 384 p.

        A detailed chronicle of Protestantism in Japan since Perry "opened" that country. Provides many facts about American missionary involvement but lacks footnotes and a bibliography.

1288 Kent, Graeme. COMPANY OF HEAVEN: EARLY MISSIONARIES IN SOUTH SEAS. Nashville: Thomas Nelson, 1972. 230 p. Bibliog.

A brief look at Protestant and Roman Catholic missions in the Pacific since the seventeenth century, focusing on British endeavors but also taking into account American missionaries.

1289 Latourette, Kenneth Scott. A HISTORY OF CHRISTIAN MISSIONS IN CHINA. New York: Macmillan Co., 1929. 930 p. Bibliog.

A well-researched, comprehensive history of Roman Catholic, Protestant, and other missions in China from the seventeenth century until the 1920s. An excellent study, but does not include developments after 1926.

1290 _____. A HISTORY OF THE EXPANSION OF CHRISTIANITY. 7 vols. New York: Harper and Brothers, 1937-45.

Exhaustive chronicle of missionary activities throughout the history of Christianity. Volumes 4-6, covering the nineteenth century, and volume 7, the twentieth century, of little relevance today and, save for occasional reference service, now stand on library shelves as a historical monument to a kind of Christian imperialism that is now defunct.

1291 MacKenzie, Kenneth M. THE ROBE AND THE SWORD: THE METHODIST CHURCH AND THE RISE OF AMERICAN IMPERIALISM. Washington, D.C.: Public Affairs Press, 1961. 128 p.

Argues that Methodist missionaries and their sponsors played an important role in making American imperialism palatable to the public between 1865 and 1900 by helping to create public opinion favorable to further expansion.

1292 Mendelsohn, Jack. THE FOREST CALLS BACK. Boston: Little, Brown, and Co., 1965. 267 p.

An informal account of American and German medical missions in Peru under the auspices of the Binder Schweitzer Amazonian Hospital Foundation.

1293 Mott, John R. ADDRESSES AND PAPERS. 6 vols. New York: Association Press, 1946-47.

The complete writings of Mott (1865-1955), leader of the late-nineteenth-century Student Volunteer Movement for foreign missions and author of the famous call to evangelize the world in this generation.

1294   Reed, James Eldin.   "American Foreign Policy, the Politics of Missions and Josiah Strong, 1890–1900." CHURCH HISTORY 41 (1972): 230–45.

   Describes Strong's part in attempts by the American Board of Commissioners for Foreign Missions to involve the United States in its conflicts with the Turkish sultan.

1295   Strong, William E.   THE STORY OF THE AMERICAN BOARD.   Boston: Pilgrim Press, 1910. Reprint. New York: Arno Press, 1969. xv, 523 p.

   The editorial secretary of the American Board of Commissioners for Foreign Missions describes the beginnings, purposes, and accomplishments of the organization in fields overseas.

1296   Varg, Paul A.   MISSIONARIES, CHINESE, AND DIPLOMATS: THE AMERICAN PROTESTANT MISSIONARY MOVEMENT IN CHINA, 1890–1952.   Princeton, N.J.: Princeton University Press, 1958. 335 p.

   A pioneering study of missions in China from the earliest American contacts until the expulsion of Christian foreigners after Mao Tse-tung came to power.

1297   _____.   "Motives in Protestant Missions, 1890–1917." CHURCH HISTORY 23 (1954): 68–82.

   Sees American Protestant foreign missions as extensions of domestic religious currents, and finds in the revivalism associated with Dwight Moody the chief impetus prior to World War I.

1298   Wu, Chao-Kwang.   THE INTERNATIONAL ASPECT OF THE MISSIONARY MOVEMENT IN CHINA.   Baltimore, Md.: Johns Hopkins Press, 1930. 285 p.

   A study of Chinese hostility to foreign missionaries in the nineteenth and twentieth centuries, emphasizing legal and political ramifications of this international confrontation.

ECUMENISM: GENERAL WORKS

1299   Brown, William Adams.   TOWARD A UNITED CHURCH: THREE DECADES OF ECUMENICAL CHRISTIANITY.   New York: Charles Scribner's Sons, 1946. xvi, 264 p. Bibliog., appendixes.

   A brief history of world Protestant ecumenism from the Edinburgh Conference of 1910 through the 1930s. Emphasis on larger European conferences. Includes affirmations of unity and other statements produced by these conventions in appendixes.

1300   Cavert, Samuel McCrea. THE AMERICAN CHURCHES IN THE ECU-
        MENICAL MOVEMENT, 1900-1968. New York: Association Press,
        1968. 288 p. Bibliog.

        A leading Presbyterian ecumenist sketches interchurch relations
        in nineteenth-century America and describes in greater depth
        such twentieth-century phenomena as the Federal and National
        Councils of Churches. Emphasis on Protestant denominations.

1301   _____, ed. CHURCH COOPERATION AND UNITY IN AMERICA: A
        HISTORICAL REVIEW, 1900-1970. New York: Association Press, 1970.
        400 p. Bibliog.

        Examination by editor and a group of collaborators of spe-
        cific areas of ecumenical activity, such as world missions,
        higher education, evangelism, race relations, women, mass
        communications, and church mergers. Includes chronology of
        ecumenical events.

1302   Fey, Harold E. A HISTORY OF THE ECUMENICAL MOVEMENT, 1948-
        1968. Philadelphia: Westminster Press, 1970. xvii, 524 p. Bibliog.

        A sequel to Rouse and Neill (1304), analyzing many aspects
        of interchurch relations since the founding of the World Coun-
        cil of Churches.

1303   MacFarland, Charles S. CHRISTIAN UNITY IN THE MAKING: THE
        FIRST TWENTY-FIVE YEARS OF THE FEDERAL COUNCIL OF THE
        CHURCHES OF CHRIST IN AMERICA, 1905-1930. New York: Federal
        Council of Churches of Christ in America, 1948. 376 p. Bibliog.

        An "official" history.

1304   Rouse, Ruth, and Neill, Stephen Charles, eds. A HISTORY OF THE
        ECUMENICAL MOVEMENT, 1517-1948. Rev. ed. Philadelphia:
        Westminster Press, 1967. xxiv, 838 p. Bibliog.

        Comprehensive history of interdenominational relations in
        Europe, the Americas, and elsewhere, from the Reformation
        to the founding of the World Council of Churches. Sixteen
        chapters by specialists in church history and ecumenics. In-
        cludes glossary of ecumenical nomenclature.

PROTESTANT-CATHOLIC-JEWISH DIALOGUE

See also Marty (1116).

1305   Brown, Robert McAfee. THE ECUMENICAL REVOLUTION: AN INTER-
        PRETATION OF THE CATHOLIC-PROTESTANT DIALOGUE. Garden

City, N.Y.: Doubleday and Co., 1967. xix, 388 p. Bibliog.

A leading Presbyterian ecumenist interprets various aspects of Protestant-Catholic relations, focusing on the Second Vatican Council and its impact on the ecumenical movement.

1306 Brown, Robert McAfee, and Weigel, Gustave. AN AMERICAN DIALOGUE: A PROTESTANT LOOKS AT CATHOLICISM AND A CATHOLIC LOOKS AT PROTESTANTISM. Garden City, N.Y.: Doubleday and Co., 1960. 216 p.

A Presbyterian and a Catholic examine each other's faiths before the Second Vatican Council.

1307 Eckardt, A. Roy. ELDER AND YOUNGER BROTHERS: THE ENCOUNTER OF JEWS AND CHRISTIANS. New York: Charles Scribner's Sons, 1967. xx, 188 p. Bibliog.

Discussion of anti-Semitism and continuities and discontinuities between these two faiths, with a view toward theological-ethical reconstruction to mediate their differences.

1308 Empie, Paul C., and Murphy, T. Austin. PAPAL PRIMACY AND THE UNIVERSAL CHURCH: LUTHERANS AND CATHOLICS IN DIALOGUE. Minneapolis, Minn.: Augsburg Publishing House, 1974. 255 p.

Dialogue between a Lutheran and a Roman Catholic theologian. Discuss dimensions of the papacy, particularly the doctrine of papal infallibility, and place this obstacle to Christian unity in historical perspective.

1309 Handy, Robert T. "Studies in the Interrelationships between America and the Holy Land: A Fruitful Field for Interdisciplinary and Interfaith Cooperation." JOURNAL OF CHURCH AND STATE 13 (1971): 283-301.

Investigates American Christians' attitudes toward Palestine and the role of the Zion motif in American religious rhetoric.

1310 Hargrove, Katharine T., ed. THE STAR AND THE CROSS: ESSAYS ON JEWISH-CHRISTIAN RELATIONS. Milwaukee, Wis.: Bruce Publishing Co., 1966. 318 p.

Seventeen essays on various aspects of Jewish-Catholic relations, including intermarriage, anti-Semitism, and mutual images of the two groups.

1311 Miller, Samuel H., and Wright, G. Ernest. ECUMENICAL DIALOGUE AT HARVARD: THE ROMAN CATHOLIC-PROTESTANT COLLOQUIUM. Cambridge, Mass.: Harvard University Press, 1964. 385 p.

Addresses and papers on various theological topics given by

Protestant and Roman Catholic scholars at Harvard University in 1963.

1312   Scharper, Philip, ed. TORAH AND GOSPEL: JEWISH AND CATHOLIC THEOLOGY IN DIALOGUE. New York: Sheed and Ward, 1966. xiii, 305 p.

A symposium presenting one Jewish and one Roman Catholic essay on each of six topics: "Evaluating the Past," "The Bond or Barrier?" "Freedom of Conscience," "Religion and the Public Order," and "Israel as Idea and Reality."

SPECIAL STUDIES IN THE HISTORY OF ECUMENISM

1313   Beaver, R. Pierce. ECUMENICAL BEGINNINGS IN PROTESTANT WORLD MISSION: A HISTORY OF COMITY. New York: Thomas Nelson and Sons, 1962. 356 p. Bibliog.

A commendable history of cooperative missionary ventures among Protestants in several fields. Emphasis on the twentieth century.

1314   Brown, Robert McAfee, and Scott, David H., eds. THE CHALLENGE TO REUNION. New York: McGraw-Hill Book Co., 1963. 292 p.

Essays on the subject of church union, past and present, by Protestant scholars of several denominations, and reactions to the "Blake Proposal" of 1960 to merge many of the larger American Protestant denominations.

1315   Crow, Paul A., and Boney, William J., eds. CHURCH UNION AT MIDPOINT. New York: Association Press, 1972. 253 p. Bibliog.

A compendium of eighteen essays on the Consultation on Church Union, an effort begun in the early 1960s to unite ten American Protestant denominations.

1316   Ernst, Eldon G. MOMENT OF TRUTH FOR PROTESTANT AMERICA: INTERCHURCH CAMPAIGNS FOLLOWING WORLD WAR ONE. AAR Disssertation Series. Missoula, Mont.: Scholars Press, 1974. vii, 197 p.

Narrates the sad tale of the Interchurch World Movement, which was born in the misplaced optimism of the 1918 armistice when Protestant leaders, following Wilson's crusading lead, felt that they could contribute to the salvation of the world by spreading American religion abroad. Tells how, after early successes, financing dried up and the movement collapsed.

1317   Estep, William R.   BAPTISTS AND CHRISTIAN UNITY.   Nashville:
       Broadman Press, 1966.   199 p.   Bibliog.

       A brief sketch of the ecumenical movement in historical per-
       spective and a description of Baptist participation in, and
       aloofness from, such organizations as the National and World
       Councils of Churches.

1318   Garrison, Winfred E.   CHRISTIAN UNITY AND DISCIPLES OF CHRIST.
       St. Louis, Mo.:   Bethany Press, 1955.   286 p.   Bibliog.

       A historical treatment of the interdenominational relations of
       this American communion, founded in the nineteenth century
       in an effort to overcome sectarianism by emphasizing apos-
       tolic principles.   Poorly edited bibliography.

1319   Glock, Charles Y., and Stark, Rodney.   RELIGION AND SOCIETY IN
       TENSION.   Chicago: Rand McNally Co., 1965.   316 p.

       A sociological study of religion in the United States during
       the 1960s, exploring such diverse topics as the political in-
       volvement of the clergy, the incompatibility of religion and
       science, and trends in denominationalism.   Counters Robert
       Lee's thesis that social forces are gradually uniting American
       Protestantism (1320).

1320   Lee, Robert.   THE SOCIAL SOURCES OF CHURCH UNITY.   New York:
       Abingdon Press, 1960.   238 p.   Bibliog.

       Argues that there is a homogenizing trend in American so-
       ciety that is bringing Christians of diverse cultural back-
       grounds closer together.   Written by a sociologist of religion.

1321   Lowell, C. Stanley.   THE ECUMENICAL MIRAGE.   Grand Rapids, Mich.:
       Baker Book House, 1967.   205 p.

       A critical look at the ecumenical movement by a conservative
       Protestant who contends that "the ecumenical obsession of our
       time is leading Protestantism to a dead end" and that Roman
       Catholicism is making inroads into the American political sys-
       tem.

1322   Mackay, John A.   ECUMENICS: THE SCIENCE OF THE CHURCH UNI-
       VERSAL.   Englewood Cliffs, N.J.: Prentice-Hall, 1964.   294 p.   Bib-
       liog.

       A general study of the background of ecumenism, analyzing
       the subject from a historical context, as well as describing
       the role of other academic disciplines, and the nature, role,
       and social setting of the church.

1323   Mathews, Basil. ` JOHN R. MOTT, WORLD CITIZEN.   New York:
        Harper and Brothers, 1934.   xiii, 469 p.   Bibliog.

> A biography of John Raleigh Mott (1865-1955), renowned stu-
> dent leader and missionary, who chaired the Student Volun-
> teer Movement, the World Missionary Conference at Edinburgh
> in 1910, and the International Missionary Council.   Received
> the Nobel Peace Prize in 1946.

1324   Nichols, James Hastings.   EVANSTON: AN INTERPRETATION.   New
        York: Harper and Brothers, 1954.   155 p.

> A discussion of the Second Assembly of the World Council
> of Churches held in Evanston, Illinois, in 1954.   Emphasis
> on interpretation of social action and missionary ventures.

1325   Smith, John Abernathy.   "Ecclesiastical Politics and the Founding of
        the Federal Council of Churches."   CHURCH HISTORY 43 (1974):
        350-65.

> An able summary of the elaborate intra- and interdenomina-
> tional maneuverings that preceded the formation of the FCC.

Chapter 19

FROM PRAGMATISM TO CONTEMPORARY PHILOSOPHY

LATE NINETEENTH-CENTURY PHILOSOPHY

1326   Easton, Lloyd D. HEGEL'S FIRST AMERICAN FOLLOWERS: THE OHIO HEGELIANS. Athens: Ohio University Press, 1966. 353 p.

Analyzes the reception of Hegelianism in the United States by examining the works of John B. Stallo, Peter Kaufmann, Moncure Conway, and August Willich from the middle of the nineteenth century.

1327   Goetzmann, William H., ed. THE AMERICAN HEGELIANS; AN IN-TELLECTUAL EPISODE IN THE HISTORY OF WESTERN AMERICA. New York: Alfred A. Knopf, 1973. 397 p.

A beautifully edited and printed collection of philosophical writings from Hegel's largely German followers, who settled in Cincinnati, Chicago, and (especially) St. Louis in the late nineteenth century.

1327A   Kuklick, Bruce. THE RISE OF AMERICAN PHILOSOPHY: CAMBRIDGE, MASSACHUSETTS, 1860-1930. New Haven, Conn.: Yale University Press, 1977. xxvii, 674 p. Illus. bibliog.

Monumental study. Reinterpretation of American intellectual history organized around the philosophers of Harvard: William James, Josiah Royce, George Santayana, Alfred North Whitehead, and C.I. Lewis.

1328   White, Morton G. SOCIAL THOUGHT IN AMERICA: THE REVOLT AGAINST FORMALISM. New York: Viking Press, 1949. 260 p.

A penetrating analysis of liberal social philosophy in the United States from the late nineteenth century to the 1920s, focusing on such figures as John Dewey, Thorstein Veblen, Charles Beard, James Harvey Robinson, and Oliver Wendell Holmes, Jr.

THORSTEIN VEBLEN

1329   Dorfman, Joseph. THORSTEIN VEBLEN AND HIS AMERICA. New York: Viking Press, 1940. 556 p.

        A well-researched, comprehensive biography of Thorstein Bunde Veblen (1857-1929), the Norwegian-American economist, social philosopher, and author of THE THEORY OF THE LEISURE CLASS, who is remembered for his concept of "conspicuous consumption."

1330   Qualey, Carlton C., ed. THORSTEIN VEBLEN. New York: Columbia University Press, 1968. 170 p. Bibliog.

        Five essays, including "Veblen on the Future of American Capitalism," by Charles B. Friday; "Business in Veblen's America," by Thomas C. Cochran; "The Sacred and the Profane: The Theology of Thorstein Veblen," by David W. Noble; and "Recollections of Veblen," by Isador Lubin.

1331   Riesman, David. THORSTEIN VEBLEN: A CRITICAL INTERPRETATION. New York: Charles Scribner's Sons, 1953. xiii, 221 p.

        A penetrating analysis of Thorstein Veblen, examining the biographical sources of his thought and criticizing his failure to participate actively in reform movements. Bibliographical essay.

1332   Schneider, Louis. THE FREUDIAN PSYCHOLOGY AND VEBLEN'S SOCIAL THEORY. New York: King's Crown Press, 1948. 270 p.

        A scholarly study of relationships between the psychoanalytical theories of Sigmund Freud and the social theories of Thorstein Veblen.

PRAGMATISM

1333   Ayer, A.J. THE ORIGINS OF PRAGMATISM, STUDIES IN THE PHILOSOPHY OF CHARLES SANDERS PEIRCE AND WILLIAM JAMES. San Francisco: Freeman, Cooper and Co., 1968. 336 p.

        Analysis of the two founding fathers of pragmatism by a well-known contemporary British philosopher. States: "I tried to make up my own mind about what Peirce and James were saying and I have also felt free to develop my own theories on some of the main issues which they raise."

1334   Fisch, Max H., ed. CLASSIC AMERICAN PHILOSOPHERS: PEIRCE, JAMES, ROYCE, SANTAYANA, DEWEY, WHITEHEAD. New York: Appleton-Century-Crofts, 1951. 493 p.

Covers virtually the same ground as Frankel (1335), which is more readily available. Some of the selections are not repeated; therefore, the student or teacher will want to check the tables of contents if he is looking for specific essays.

1335 Frankel, Charles, ed. THE GOLDEN AGE OF AMERICAN PHILOSOPHY. New York: George Braziller, 1960. 534 p.

Substantial excerpts from the writings of Chauncey Wright, Charles Peirce, William James, Josiah Royce, George Santayana, John Dewey, and short excerpts from Ralph Barton Perry, Clarence Lewis, and Morris Cohen.

1336 Kurtz, Paul, ed. AMERICAN PHILOSOPHY IN THE TWENTIETH CENTURY: A SOURCEBOOK FROM PRAGMATISM TO PHILOSOPHICAL ANALYSIS. New York: Macmillan Co., 1966. 573 p. Bibliog.

The first 300 pages given over to the pragmatists. A sampling of the work of eighteen other later men or schools in the last nearly 300 pages, including Sellars, Cohen, Lewis, Carnap, Quine, Tillich, Hook, and Nagel. A bibliography provided for each philosopher.

1337 Miller, Randolph Crump. THE AMERICAN SPIRIT IN THEOLOGY. Philadelphia: United Church Press, 1974. 252 p. Bibliog.

An analysis of the impact on Protestant theology of "the American spirit," here understood to include such currents as pragmatism and radical empiricism, as exemplified by the thought of John Dewey and William James.

1338 Novak, Michael, ed. AMERICAN PHILOSOPHY AND THE FUTURE: ESSAYS FOR A NEW GENERATION. New York: Charles Scribner's Sons, 1968. 367 p.

A collection of essays devoted in large part to discussions of American philosophers James, Peirce, Whitehead, G.H. Mead, Royce, and Brightman.

1339 Smith, John E. SPIRIT OF AMERICAN PHILOSOPHY. New York: Oxford University Press, 1963. 219 p.

Interprets the spirit and basic drift of American philosophy through a series of essays on Peirce, James, Royce, Dewey, and Whitehead.

1340 White, Morton G. THE AGE OF ANALYSIS: TWENTIETH CENTURY PHILOSOPHERS. New York: George Braziller, 1958. 253 p.

Brief introductions to thirteen British, European, and American philosophers. Places the Americans--George Santayana,

Charles Peirce, William James, and John Dewey--in a transatlantic context.

1341 _____. PRAGMATISM AND THE AMERICAN MIND. New York: Oxford University Press, 1973. xiv, 265 p.

Twenty-six essays and reviews exploring the course of prag-
matism and its impact on several aspects of thought in the
United States. Discusses philosophers William James and
John Dewey, and also men of other disciplines, such as
Robert Oppenheimer, Reinhold Niebuhr, and E.H. Carr.

1342 Wiener, Philip P. EVOLUTION AND THE FOUNDERS OF PRAGMA-
TISM. Cambridge, Mass.: Harvard University Press, 1949. xiv, 288 p.

A well-researched study of the roots of American pragmatism
at Harvard University in the 1870s and the impact of evolutionary thought on the formation of this philosophical school.

CHARLES S. PEIRCE

Peirce (1839-1914) is considered to be the founder of pragmatism and one of
the most influential of modern American philosophers.

1343 Peirce, Charles S. COLLECTED PAPERS. Vols. 1-6, edited by Charles
Hartshorne and Paul Weiss. Vols. 7-8, edited by A.W. Burks. Cambridge, Mass.: Harvard University Press, 1931-58.

The standard edition of Peirce's work. A comprehensive bibliography of all his published writings and of his correspondence in volume 8.

1344 _____. THE ESSENTIAL WRITINGS. Edited by Edward C. Moore.
New York: Harper and Row, 1972. 317 p.

A well-edited collection designed for the undergraduate market.
All selections taken from Peirce's COLLECTED PAPERS (1343).

1345 _____. CHARLES S. PEIRCE: SELECTED WRITINGS. Edited by
Philip Wiener. New York: Dover Publications, 1966. xxiv, 446 p.

A well-edited anthology (first published in 1958) illuminating
Peirce's versatility as a thinker and containing several previously unprinted shorter works on the humanistic dimensions
of science and philosophy.

1346 Bernstein, Richard J., ed. CRITICAL ESSAYS ON CHARLES SANDERS
PEIRCE. New Haven, Conn.: Yale University Press, 1965. 148 p.

Five essays by editor Bernstein, Rulon Wells, N.R. Hanson,

J. E. Smith, and Paul Weiss, plus the biographical sketch of Peirce by Weiss from the D.A.B.

1347 Buchler, Justus. CHARLES PEIRCE'S EMPIRICISM. London: Kegan Paul, Trench, Trubner, and Co., 1939. xvii, 275 p.

An analysis limited to the methodological side of Peirce's thought, his empiricism, which is discussed under three headings: critical common-sensism, pragmatism, and the theory of the formal sciences.

1348 Feibleman, James K. AN INTRODUCTION TO THE PHILOSOPHY OF CHARLES S. PEIRCE. New York: Harper and Brothers Publishers, 1946. Reprint. Cambridge, Mass.: M.I.T. Press, 1970. xx, 503 p.

A comprehensive survey tracing the development of Peirce's thought from his encounter with Kant's works through the development of his scientific and pragmatic philosophy, and assessing his place in the history of philosophy and his impact on contemporaries.

1349 Gallie, W.B. PEIRCE AND PRAGMATISM. New York: Dover Publications, 1966. 247 p.

First published in England in 1955, a general introduction to the philosophy of Peirce, analyzing his epistemology, logic, metaphysics, and pragmatism. Short bibliographical essay.

1350 Goudge, Thomas A. THE THOUGHT OF C.S. PEIRCE. Toronto: University of Toronto Press, 1950. 360 p.

An introduction to the philosophy of Charles S. Peirce, exploring his methods of inquiry, logic, and transcendentalism, and briefly describing his career.

1351 Moore, Edward C., and Robin, Richard S., eds. STUDIES IN THE PHILOSOPHY OF CHARLES SANDERS PEIRCE. 2d series. Amherst: University of Massachusetts Press, 1964. 525 p. Bibliog.

A second volume of essays following the pattern of Wiener and Young (1355) and designed to commemorate the fiftieth anniversary of Peirce's death. An updated bibliography in the appendixes.

1352 Murphey, Murray G. THE DEVELOPMENT OF PEIRCE'S PHILOSOPHY. Cambridge, Mass.: Harvard University Press, 1961. 432 p. Appendix.

An important work in which the author has set himself the task of discovering the underlying principles upon which Peirce's work was based, and of showing that those principles bring order to the mass of fragmentary manuscripts remaining today. Several drafts of the "New List of Categories" published in appendix.

1353   Potter, Vincent G. CHARLES S. PEIRCE ON NORMS AND IDEALS. Amherst: University of Massachusetts Press, 1967. xiii, 229 p. Bibliog.

Argues that Peirce's doctrine of the normative sciences and his cosmology must be understood in the context of his pragmatism. Explicates Peirce's understanding of man's participation in his own evolution.

1354   Thompson, Manley. THE PRAGMATIC PHILOSOPHY OF C.S. PEIRCE. Chicago: University of Chicago Press, 1953. xvii, 318 p.

A broad explication and analysis of Peirce's thought following a division of his work into two parts, breaking in the early 1890s.

1355   Wiener, Philip P., and Young, Frederic H., eds. STUDIES IN THE PHILOSOPHY OF CHARLES SANDERS PEIRCE. Cambridge, Mass.: Harvard University Press, 1952. 396 p.

A collection of twenty-four essays on a broad variety of topics by the most eminent Peirce scholars. Volume sponsored by the Peirce Society.

JOSIAH ROYCE

Royce (1855-1916) taught philosophy at the University of California and at Harvard. Much of his work remains unpublished.

1356   Royce, Josiah. THE BASIC WRITINGS OF JOSIAH ROYCE. Edited by John J. McDermott. 2 vols. Chicago: University of Chicago Press, 1969. Bibliog.

Contains an extensive annotated bibliography edited by Ignas Skrupskelis, 2:1167-1226.

1357   _____. THE LETTERS OF JOSIAH ROYCE. Edited by John Clendenning. Chicago: University of Chicago Press, 1970. 696 p.

A comprehensive edition of Royce's letters, covering the period from 1875 until his death in 1916.

1358   _____. THE PHILOSOPHY OF JOSIAH ROYCE. Edited by John K. Roth. New York: Thomas Y. Crowell Co., 1971. 421 p. Bibliog.

A well-edited anthology of selections from his THE RELIGIOUS ASPECT OF PHILOSOPHY; STUDIES OF GOOD AND EVIL; THE WORLD AND THE INDIVIDUAL; THE PHILOSOPHY

OF LOYALTY; THE PROBLEM OF CHRISTIANITY; and THE
HOPE OF THE GREAT COMMUNITY.

1359   Buranelli, Vincent. JOSIAH ROYCE. New York: Twayne Publishers,
1964. 174 p. Bibliog.

A brief introduction to this American idealist, paying attention not only to his philosophy but also to his belletristic
works.

1360   Cotton, James Harry. ROYCE ON THE HUMAN SELF. Cambridge,
Mass.: Harvard University Press, 1954. xiv, 347 p.

A chatty and discursive analysis of Royce's thought, not very
technical, and containing some biographical material. Considered the best introduction to Royce for general readers.

1361   Fuss, Peter. THE MORAL PHILOSOPHY OF JOSIAH ROYCE. Cambridge, Mass.: Harvard University Press, 1965. xv, 272 p.

An explication and, to some extent, reformulation of Royce's
moral philosophy. Discussion divided into three parts, co-
inciding with periods of development in Royce's thought.

1362   Kuklick, Bruce. JOSIAH ROYCE, AN INTELLECTUAL BIOGRAPHY.
Indianapolis: Bobbs-Merrill Co., 1972. 270 p. Bibliog.

Well-written analysis of Royce's thought, tracing the strong
influence of Kant upon him, and the evolution of Royce's
own distinctive idealism.

1363   Mahowald, Mary Briody. AN IDEALISTIC PRAGMATISM: THE DE-
VELOPMENT OF THE PRAGMATIC ELEMENT IN THE PHILOSOPHY OF
JOSIAH ROYCE. The Hague, Netherlands: Martinus Nijhoff, 1972.
186 p. Bibliog.

A discussion of Royce's thought, emphasizing the pragmatic
element during the early, middle, and mature periods of his
career. Based upon a reading of both published and unpublished sources.

1364   Marcel, Gabriel. ROYCE'S METAPHYSICS. Translated by Virginia
and Gordon Ringer. Chicago: Henry Regnery Co., 1956. xix, 180 p.

The translation of the 1918 French edition of an analysis of
Royce's metaphysics. Described by Harvard philosopher William Ernest Hocking as the most substantial discussion available. No index or bibliography.

1365   Robinson, Daniel Sommer. ROYCE AND HOCKING: AMERICAN
IDEALISTS. Boston: Christopher Publishing House, 1968. 175 p.
Bibliog.

Six essays each on Josiah Royce and William Ernest Hocking, Harvard philosophers and founders of American idealism, and a brief collection of letters by and about these two men. Bibliography of bibliographies.

1366   Smith, John E. ROYCE'S SOCIAL INFINITE: THE COMMUNITY OF INTERPRETATION. New York: Liberal Arts Press, 1950. xiii, 176 p.

Uses Royce's conception of the community of interpretation as a starting point to relate to Royce's discussion of the problem of Christianity.

WILLIAM JAMES

James (1842-1910), the best-known of the pragmatists, taught philosophy at Harvard from 1872 to 1907.

1367   James, William. THE MORAL PHILOSOPHY OF WILLIAM JAMES. Edited by John K. Roth. New York: Thomas Y. Crowell Co., 1969. 355 p. Bibliog.

A well-edited collection of selections from the works of William James, illuminating many aspects of his moral philosophy.

1368   _____. THE WRITINGS OF WILLIAM JAMES: A COMPREHENSIVE EDITION. Edited by John J. McDermott. New York: Random House, 1967. li, 858 p.

A very well-edited collection of James's works, making specific reference to individual works unnecessary. Especially noteworthy for the reprinting and updating of Ralph B. Perry's annotated bibliography on pages 811-58.

1369   Allen, Gay Wilson. WILLIAM JAMES, A BIOGRAPHY. New York: Viking Press, 1967. xx, 556 p.

A very full portrait of James, concentrating on depiction of the man in his social setting and not attempting a discussion of his thought.

1370   Brennan, Bernard P. THE ETHICS OF WILLIAM JAMES. New York: Bookman Associates, 1961. 183 p.

A systematic exposition of James's moral thought. Challenging task for author since James never produced such an analysis himself, and especially in view of the popular notion that pragmatists lack an adequate moral philosophy.

1371   _____. WILLIAM JAMES. New York: Twayne Publishers, 1968.
176 p.

> A brief introductory, systematic exposition of the philosophy
> of James, with references to his achievement in psychology
> only in terms of their significance to his philosophy.

1372   Dooley, Patrick Kirian. PRAGMATISM AS HUMANISM: THE PHILOS-
OPHY OF WILLIAM JAMES. Chicago: Nelson-Hall, 1974. 220 p.
Bibliog.

> An analysis of James's early psychological works, arguing that
> humanism was the unifying theme of his philosophy and the
> basis of his pragmatism.

1373   Moore, Edward C. WILLIAM JAMES. New York: Washington Square
Press, 1965. 194 p. Bibliog.

> An introductory treatment of James's philosophy, designed for
> the reader with little training in philosophy.

1374   Morris, Lloyd. WILLIAM JAMES: THE MESSAGE OF A MODERN
MIND. New York: Charles Scribner's Sons, 1950. 98 p. Bibliog.

> A very brief introduction to William James, his pragmatism,
> and other dimensions of his thought.

1375   Perry, Ralph Barton. THE THOUGHT AND CHARACTER OF WILLIAM
JAMES. 2 vols. Boston: Little, Brown, and Co., 1936.

> A Pulitzer Prize-winning study of James and the most thorough
> exposition of James's works. Based largely on, and reprint-
> ing much, correspondence to and from him. An abridgement
> published by Harvard University Press under the same title
> in 1948.

1376   Reck, Andrew J., ed. INTRODUCTION TO WILLIAM JAMES; AN ES-
SAY AND SELECTED TEXTS. Bloomington: Indiana University Press,
1967. 205 p. Bibliog.

> Contains an eighty-page essay, which author admits is drawn
> largely from Ralph Barton Perry's work (1375), and about one
> hundred pages of readings from James. Includes chronology
> of James's life.

1377   Roth, John K. FREEDOM AND THE MORAL LIFE: THE ETHICS OF
WILLIAM JAMES. Philadelphia: Westminster Press, 1969. 157 p.
Bibliog.

> A brief but well-researched introduction to the postulate of
> free will in William James's moral thought.

JOHN DEWEY

Dewey (1859–1952) played an influential role in the history of American philosophy and education primarily at Columbia and the University of Chicago.

1378   Dewey, John. THE EARLY WORKS, 1882–1898. 5 vols. Carbondale:
Southern Illinois University Press, 1967–72.

Elegant and scholarly re-editing of Dewey's early works, including PSYCHOLOGY, THE STUDY OF ETHICS, and OUT-
LINES OF A CRITICAL THEORY OF ETHICS. Also issued in
paperbound format.

1379   _____. JOHN DEWEY; HIS CONTRIBUTION TO THE AMERICAN
TRADITION. Edited by Irwin Edman. Indianapolis: Bobbs-Merrill Co.,
1955. 322 p.

An anthology of Dewey's writings in only seven selections,
all long. Accompanied by an introductory interpretive essay
by the editor.

1380   _____. ON EXPERIENCE, NATURE, AND FREEDOM: REPRESENTATIVE
SELECTIONS. Edited by Richard J. Bernstein. New York: Liberal
Arts Press, 1960. xlix, 292 p.

A selection drawn, with only two exceptions, from Dewey's
post-1925 writings, which, the editor feels, contain more
careful clarification and justification of the central themes
of his philosophy than his pre-1925 writings.

1381   Bernstein, Richard J. JOHN DEWEY. New York: Washington Square
Press, 1966. 213 p.

Not so much a biography, although the events of his life are
covered, as an essay interpreting Dewey's thought in the
framework of his developing philosophy.

1382   Blewett, John. JOHN DEWEY: HIS THOUGHT AND INFLUENCE.
New York: Fordham University Press, 1960. xiv, 242 p.

A compendium of eight essays by Roman Catholics exploring
Dewey's naturalism, view of democracy, theory of knowledge,
philosophy of education, attitudes toward technology and history, and influence in China. Bibliographical essay.

1383   Coughlan, Neil. YOUNG JOHN DEWEY: AN ESSAY IN AMERICAN
INTELLECTUAL HISTORY. Chicago: University of Chicago Press, 1975.
xii, 187 p.

A well-written account of Dewey's intellectual and psychological development. Considerable attention paid to Dewey's relationship with George Herbert Mead and the early days of the Chicago School.

1384 Crosser, Paul K. THE NIHILISM OF JOHN DEWEY. New York: Philosophical Library, 1955. 238 p.

A forthright critique of Dewey's philosophy. Argues that Dewey's philosophy has had a deleterious effect upon educators, artists, and intellectuals, and undertakes to demonstrate the cognitive untenability of Dewey's position.

1385 Dykhuizen, George. THE LIFE AND MIND OF JOHN DEWEY. Carbondale: Southern Illinois University Press, 1973. xxv, 429 p. Illus.

A comprehensive and sympathetic biography of Dewey.

1386 Feldman, W.T. THE PHILOSOPHY OF JOHN DEWEY; A CRITICAL ANALYSIS. Baltimore, Md.: Johns Hopkins Press, 1934. 127 p.

Stated purpose of work to be "an enumeration and analysis of the principal presuppositions which have combined to form the basis of Dewey's philosophical position." These presuppositions discussed and illustrated in succeeding chapters.

1387 Geiger, George R. JOHN DEWEY IN PERSPECTIVE. New York: Oxford University Press, 1958. 248 p.

An influential and sympathetic interpretation of Dewey's thought discussed under such headings as the affirmation of experience, experience as art, the nature of value, and inquiry, knowing, and truth.

1388 Gouinlock, James. JOHN DEWEY'S PHILOSOPHY OF VALUE. New York: Humanities Press, 1972. 377 p.

Attempts to discuss Dewey's philosophy of value in the context of his most fundamental assumptions and to show how his conclusions about value are related to an explicitly elaborated theory concerning the nature of nature.

1389 Gutzke, Manford George. JOHN DEWEY'S THOUGHT AND ITS IMPLICATIONS FOR CHRISTIAN EDUCATION. New York: King's Crown Press, 1956. xv, 270 p.

A study of Dewey's instrumentalism and its applicability to religious education.

1390   Hendel, Charles W., ed. JOHN DEWEY AND THE EXPERIMENTAL
        SPIRIT IN PHILOSOPHY. New York: Liberal Arts Press, 1959. 119 p.

>   Four lectures, including "The New Empiricism and the Phil-
>   osophical Tradition," by Charles W. Hendel; "Education as
>   Social Process," by Nathaniel M. Lawrence; "Knowledge,
>   Value, and Freedom," by Richard J. Bernstein; and "John
>   Dewey: Philosopher of Experience," by John E. Smith.

1391   Hook, Sidney. JOHN DEWEY, AN INTELLECTUAL PORTRAIT. New
        York: John Day Co., 1939. 242 p.

>   Although quite an old book, is still valued highly by Dewey
>   students. An attempt to provide an introduction to Dewey's
>   thought, especially aimed at meeting difficulties likely to
>   arise in the minds of readers first encountering Dewey's phi-
>   losophy.

1392   _____, ed. JOHN DEWEY: PHILOSOPHER OF SCIENCE AND FREE-
        DOM. New York: Dial Press, 1950. 383 p. Bibliog.

>   A symposium of twenty essays analyzing various aspects of
>   John Dewey's philosophy and his impact on education, his-
>   toriography, and other philosophers.

1393   Nathanson, Jerome. JOHN DEWEY: THE RECONSTRUCTION OF THE
        DEMOCRATIC LIFE. New York: Charles Scribner's Sons, 1951. 127 p.
        Bibliog.

>   A brief, general introduction to the philosophy of John Dewey,
>   focusing on his concept of democracy. Useful only as an
>   introduction.

1394   Nissen, Lowell. JOHN DEWEY'S THEORY OF INQUIRY AND TRUTH.
        The Hague, Netherlands: Mouton and Co., 1966. 112 p.

>   A brief analysis of Dewey's account of making scientific
>   methodology available to scholars in other disciplines, es-
>   pecially in the humanities and social sciences.

1395   Ratner, Sidney, ed. THE PHILOSOPHER OF THE COMMON MAN:
        ESSAYS IN HONOR OF JOHN DEWEY TO CELEBRATE HIS EIGHTIETH
        BIRTHDAY. 1940. Reprint. New York: Greenwood Press, 1968.
        228 p.

>   Essays by nine authors on "Freedom and Education," "Dewey's
>   Theory of the Nature and Function of Philosophy," "Dewey's
>   Reconstruction of Logical Theory," "Method in Aesthetics,"
>   "The Religion of Shared Experience," "A Deweyesque Mosaic,"
>   "Pragmatism as a Philosophy of Law," "The Political Philoso-
>   phy of Instrumentalism," and "Creative Democracy--the Task
>   Before Us."

1396 Roth, Robert J. JOHN DEWEY AND SELF-REALIZATION. Englewood Cliffs, N.J.: Prentice-Hall, 1962. 152 p. Bibliog.

Argues that a concern for human self-realization underlay much of Dewey's thought, and explores this theme in his views of science, technology, and naturalism.

1397 Schilpp, Paul Arthur, ed. THE PHILOSOPHY OF JOHN DEWEY. Library of Living Philosophers. Evanston, Ill.: Northwestern University, 1939. xv, 708 p. Bibliog.

Seventeen contemporaries criticize the philosophy of Dewey. Includes Dewey's reply to his critics and a biography.

1398 Thomas, Milton Halsey. JOHN DEWEY: A CENTENNIAL BIBLIOG-RAPHY. Chicago: University of Chicago Press, 1962. xiv, 370 p.

Provides the best introduction to Dewey's writings in the absence of an edition of Dewey's collected works. Also lists reviews of Dewey's works and contains a comprehensive catalogue of work about Dewey.

GEORGE SANTAYANA

Santayana (1863-1952) was born in Spain, taught for many years at Harvard, and then returned to Europe in 1912. His reputation now seems to rest on his ability more as an essayist than as a philosopher.

1399 Santayana, George. ANIMAL FAITH AND SPIRITUAL LIFE. Edited by John Lachs. New York: Appleton-Century-Crofts, 1967. 470 p.

A collection of Santayana's most significant philosophical essays together with critical discussion of aspects of his work by other philosophers, such as J.H. Randall, Jr., Willard Arnett, Justus Buchler, and Sterling Lamprecht.

1400 _____. THE BIRTH OF REASON AND OTHER ESSAYS. Edited by Daniel Cory. New York: Columbia University Press, 1968. xii, 184 p.

A collection of twenty-two essays edited by Santayana's secretary and literary executor, most only a few pages long.

1401 _____. PHYSICAL ORDER AND MORAL LIBERTY: PREVIOUSLY UN-PUBLISHED ESSAYS OF GEORGE SANTAYANA. Edited by John and Shirley Lachs. Nashville: Vanderbilt University Press, 1969. xiv, 322 p.

A collection of fifty-five of Santayana's shorter posthumous works, dealing with causation, sensation and thought, spirituality, ethics, politics, and freedom.

1402 _____. SANTAYANA ON AMERICA: ESSAYS, NOTES, AND LET-TERS ON AMERICAN LIFE, LITERATURE, AND PHILOSOPHY. Edited by Richard C. Lyon. New York: Harcourt, Brace, and World, 1968. xxxvii, 307 p.

Twenty-two essays of varying length and a few letters illuminating George Santayana's perceptions of the United States and American philosophers and writers between 1890 and 1951.

1403 Arnett, Willard E. SANTAYANA AND THE SENSE OF BEAUTY. Bloomington: Indiana University Press, 1955. xv, 252 p.

An attempt to describe the nature of aesthetic values in Santayana's thought, the role he saw these values playing in social and intellectual life, and the influence that the dominance of aesthetic values had on Santayana's thought and writings.

1404 Ashmore, Jerome. SANTAYANA, ART, AND AESTHETICS. Cleveland, Ohio: Press of Western Reserve University, 1966. 139 p.

An explication of the artistic and aesthetic underpinnings of George Santayana's moral philosophy.

1405 Cory, Daniel. SANTAYANA: THE LATER YEARS. A PORTRAIT WITH LETTERS. New York: George Braziller, 1963. 330 p.

Sympathetic portrayal of George Santayana, covering the period from 1927 to 1952 when this Spanish-American philosopher was residing in Europe.

1406 Munitz, Milton Karl. THE MORAL PHILOSOPHY OF SANTAYANA. New York: Columbia University Press, 1939. 116 p.

Discovers a dualism in Santayana and finds grounds for classifying him both as a humanist inquiring into the natural conditions of the good life and as a mystic seeking a paradise.

1407 Schilpp, Paul Arthur, ed. THE PHILOSOPHY OF GEORGE SANTAYANA. Library of Living Philosophers. New York: Tudor Publishing Co., 1951. 710 p. Bibliog.

Eighteen essays exploring various aspects of Santayana's philosophy, and a brief autobiographical statement and replies by Santayana to his critics. Comprehensive annotated bibliography of Santayana's works by Shohig Terzian, pages 609-78.

1408 Singer, Irving. SANTAYANA'S AESTHETICS: A CRITICAL INTRODUCTION. Cambridge, Mass.: Harvard University Press, 1957. 235 p.

Explication of George Santayana's earlier works on art and aesthetics from the viewpoint of his later writings in the areas of epistemology and ontology.

1409 Sprigge, Timothy L. S. SANTAYANA: AN EXAMINATION OF HIS PHILOSOPHY. London: Routledge and Kegan Paul, 1974. 247 p.

A general introduction to George Santayana's thought, analyzing both the central tenets underlying his philosophy and the detailed manifestations in many areas of his thought.

ALFRED NORTH WHITEHEAD

Whitehead (1861-1947) was born in Britain but spent the years 1924-37 teaching at Harvard University.

1410 Whitehead, Alfred North. ALFRED NORTH WHITEHEAD; AN ANTHOLOGY. Edited by F. S. C. Northrop and Mason W. Gross. New York: Macmillan Co., 1953. 928 p.

A group of lengthy selections from Whitehead's most important works, such as "On Mathematical Concepts of the Material World," SCIENCE AND THE MODERN WORLD, PROCESS AND REALITY, and ADVENTURES OF IDEAS.

1411 Christian, William A. AN INTERPRETATION OF WHITEHEAD'S METAPHYSICS. New Haven, Conn.: Yale University Press, 1959. 419 p.

An analytical study of the metaphysical theories advanced in the later writings of Whitehead. Focuses upon Whitehead's theory of actual occasions, his theory of eternal objects, and his theory of God and the world.

1412 Emmet, Dorothy. WHITEHEAD'S PHILOSOPHY OF ORGANISM. 2d ed. New York: St. Martin's Press, 1966. 291 p.

Virtually a reprint of the 1932 edition, which the author herself describes as a juvenile work important for conveying the excitement produced by the first impact of PROCESS AND REALITY.

1413   Hartshorne, Charles. WHITEHEAD'S PHILOSOPHY; SELECTED ESSAYS,
        1935-1970. Lincoln: University of Nebraska Press, 1972. 217 p.

        A collection of thirteen of the author's previously published
        essays on Whitehead, along with a facsimile letter from
        Whitehead to the author.

1414   Johnson, A.H. WHITEHEAD'S THEORY OF REALITY. Boston:
        Beacon Press, 1952. Reprint. New York: Dover Publications, 1962.
        267 p.

        An introduction to Whitehead's theory of actual entities con-
        centrating upon the main aspects of his mature philosophy.

1415   Lango, John W. WHITEHEAD'S ONTOLOGY. Albany: State Univer-
        sity of New York Press, 1972. 102 p.

        A densely-written and complex analysis of the ontology im-
        plicit in Whitehead's metaphysical system. Not recommended
        for introductory reading.

1416   Lawrence, Nathaniel. ALFRED NORTH WHITEHEAD; A PRIMER OF HIS
        PHILOSOPHY. New York: Twayne Publishers, 1974. 192 p.

        Contents of the first three chapters: a biography, a general
        statement of the principal aspects of Whitehead's philosophy
        (ignoring his work in mathematics and logic), and a discussion
        of his concept of the "actual occasion." Discusses PROCESS
        AND REALITY in the remainder of the book.

1417   _____ . WHITEHEAD'S PHILOSOPHICAL DEVELOPMENT; A CRITICAL
        HISTORY OF THE BACKGROUND OF PROCESS AND REALITY. Berke-
        ley and Los Angeles: University of California Press, 1956. xxi, 370 p.

        A book designed to provide non-philosophers, and even phi-
        losophers who have not studied Whitehead's early works, with
        the background to understand his Gifford lectures of 1927-28,
        PROCESS AND REALITY.

1418   Leclerc, Ivor. WHITEHEAD'S METAPHYSICS, AN INTRODUCTORY EX-
        POSITION. New York: Macmillan Co., 1958. xiii, 234 p.

        Thesis is that in developing the system which he elaborated
        in such detail in PROCESS AND REALITY, Whitehead's prob-
        lems were specifically metaphysical. Explanation of how and
        why Whitehead posed his questions in a way that differed
        from the classical tradition of philosophy.

1419   _____ , ed. THE RELEVANCE OF WHITEHEAD. New York: Mac-
        millan Co., 1961. 383 p.

Fourteen essays contributed in commemoration of the centenary of Whitehead's birth. Written by philosophers, most of whom are listed in this section as authors of books on Whitehead.

1420 Lowe, Victor. UNDERSTANDING WHITEHEAD. Baltimore, Md.: Johns Hopkins Press, 1962. xvii, 398 p.

A sympathetic introduction to all of Whitehead's thought designed for the general reader. Treats his metaphysical system and his philosophies of science and religion.

1421 Mays, W. THE PHILOSOPHY OF WHITEHEAD. New York: Macmillan Co., 1959. 259 p.

Illustrates the two principles upon which Whitehead's philosophy of organism is based--its logical or structural side and its physical-experiential side. Book divided into two main sections to reflect this. Not recommended for beginning students.

1422 Schilpp, Paul Arthur, ed. THE PHILOSOPHY OF ALFRED NORTH WHITEHEAD. Vol. 3. Library of Living Philosophers. Evanston, Ill.: Northwestern University Press, 1941. xviii, 745 p. Bibliog.

Contains an autobiographical sketch by Whitehead and eighteen descriptive and critical essays on his philosophy by such writers as Lowe, Dewey, Quine, Northrop, Hocking, and Hartshorne.

CLARENCE IRVING LEWIS

Lewis (1883-1964), a logician, epistemologist, and moral philosopher, taught at Harvard University from 1920 to 1953.

1423 Goheen, John D., and Mothershead, John L., eds. COLLECTED PAPERS OF CLARENCE IRVING LEWIS. Stanford, Calif.: Stanford University Press, 1970. 444 p.

A collection of both previously published and unpublished shorter works by Lewis, covering the years 1912-57.

1424 Saydah, J. Roger. THE ETHICAL THEORY OF CLARENCE IRVING LEWIS. Athens: Ohio University Press, 1969. 171 p. Bibliog.

An analysis of the rational imperatives of Lewis' ethical theory and an investigation of his understanding of value, action, rightness, and knowledge.

1425 Schilpp, Paul Arthur, ed. THE PHILOSOPHY OF C.I. LEWIS. LaSalle, Ill.: Open Court Publishing Co., 1968. xiv, 709 p. Bibliog.

Twenty-four contemporaries criticize the philosophy of Lewis. Includes Lewis' autobiographical statement and his response to his critics.

PHILOSOPHY SINCE 1920

1426   Black, Max., ed. PHILOSOPHY IN AMERICA. Ithaca, N.Y.: Cornell University Press, 1965. 307 p.

Writings by a group of fourteen young American philosophers, who were selected to provide a profile of their work in progress at that time in the middle 1960s.

1427   Donnell, Franklin H., Jr., ed. ASPECTS OF CONTEMPORARY AMERICAN PHILOSOPHY. Wuerzburg, Austria: Physica-Verlag, 1965. 106 p.

A collection of nine essays selected in an effort to provide Europeans (especially students of the Institute for Advanced Studies in Vienna) with an overview of the contemporary American scene.

1428   Hook, Sidney, ed. AMERICAN PHILOSOPHERS AT WORK, THE PHILOSOPHIC SCENE IN THE UNITED STATES. New York: Criterion Books, 1956. 512 p.

A collection of essays by twenty-eight of the best-known philosophers of the early 1950s. Invited to illustrate their current interests and positions.

1429   Krikorian, Yervant Hovhannes. RECENT PERSPECTIVES IN AMERICAN PHILOSOPHY. The Hague, Netherlands: Martinus Nijhoff, 1973. 90 p.

A brief discussion of the following twentieth-century philosophers: Dewey, Cohen, Singer, Hocking, Blanshard, Whitehead, and Sheldon.

1430   Kurtz, Paul, ed. SIDNEY HOOK AND THE CONTEMPORARY WORLD: ESSAYS ON THE PRAGMATIC INTELLIGENCE. New York: John Day Co., 1968. 474 p.

A Festschrift of twenty-four articles by such American philosophers as Morton White and Adolf Berle on Marxism, political philosophy, and other topics of interest to Sidney Hook.

1431   Reck, Andrew J. THE NEW AMERICAN PHILOSOPHERS: AN EXPLORATION OF THOUGHT SINCE WORLD WAR II. Baton Rouge: Louisiana State University Press, 1968. xxi, 362 p.

A sequel to Reck's earlier volume (1432), with essays on

C.I. Lewis, Stephen C. Pepper, Brand Blanshard, Ernest
Nagel, John Herman Randall, Justus Buchler, Sidney Hook,
F.S.C. Northrop, James Kern Feibleman, John Wild, Charles
Hartshorne, and Paul Weiss.

1432 _____. RECENT AMERICAN PHILOSOPHY: STUDIES OF TEN REP-
RESENTATIVE THINKERS. New York: Random House, 1961. xxiii,
343 p.

Essays on philosophers Ralph Barton Perry, William Ernest
Hocking, George Herbert Mead, John Elof Boodin, Wilbur
Marshall Urban, DeWitt H. Parker, Roy Wood Sellars, Arthur
O. Lovejoy, Elijah Jordan, and Edgar Sheffield Brightman.

1433 Smith, John E., ed. CONTEMPORARY AMERICAN PHILOSOPHY. 2d
series. Muirhead Library of Philosophy. New York: Humanities Press,
1970. 351 p.

A reader presenting a cross-section of the philosophical
thinking taking place in the 1960s. Anthology of fifteen
philosophers' work.

Chapter 20

THEOLOGY IN THE TWENTIETH CENTURY

NEO-ORTHODOXY

1434 Ahlstrom, Sydney E. "Continental Influence on American Christian Thought Since World War I." CHURCH HISTORY 27 (1958): 256-72.

A concise analysis of the reception in the United States of the thought of Soren Kierkegaard, Karl Barth, and other European theologians.

1435 Hordern, William. THE CASE FOR A NEW REFORMATION THEOLOGY. Philadelphia: Westminster Press, 1959. 176 p. Bibliog.

Written by a leading Lutheran theologian who, like Karl Barth, argues that certain dimensions of Reformation theology should be reasserted to correct our understanding of revelation, divine transcendence, the sinful nature of man, and salvation.

1436 _____. A LAYMAN'S GUIDE TO PROTESTANT THEOLOGY. Rev. ed. New York: Macmillan Co., 1955. 222 p.

Survey of the main currents in Protestant theology of particular value for understanding Reinhold Niebuhr, Paul Tillich, and neo-orthodoxy, but misrepresents fundamentalism.

1437 Kegley, Charles W. POLITICS, RELIGION AND MODERN MAN: ESSAYS ON REINHOLD NIEBUHR, PAUL TILLICH, AND RUDOLF BULTMANN. Quezon City: University of the Philippines Press, 1969. xiv, 163 p.

An introduction to the theology of these three men, with brief essays criticizing each.

1438 Miller, Alexander. THE RENEWAL OF MAN: A TWENTIETH CENTURY ESSAY ON JUSTIFICATION BY FAITH. Garden City, N.Y.: Doubleday and Co., 1955. 184 p.

An interpretation of the doctrine of justification during the heyday of neo-orthodoxy in the United States. Relies heavily on the thought of Reinhold Niebuhr.

1439   Pittenger, W. Norman. THE HISTORIC FAITH AND A CHANGING WORLD. New York: Oxford University Press, 1950. 181 p.

Argues for the necessity and relevance of orthodox Protestantism to a rapidly-changing American society.

1440   Wieman, Henry N., et al. RELIGIOUS LIBERALS REPLY. Boston: Beacon Press, 1947. 177 p.

Defense by author and six other liberal Protestants of their interpretation of Christianity against the attacks of neo-orthodoxy.

H. RICHARD AND REINHOLD NIEBUHR

The most influential American theologians of the early twentieth century. H. Richard (1894-1962) taught at Yale Divinity School from 1931 until his death; his brother Reinhold (1892-1971) taught at Union Theological Seminary, New York City, 1928-60.

1441   Ahlstrom, Sydney E. "H. Richard Niebuhr's Place in American Thought." CHRISTIANITY AND CRISIS 23 (1963): 213-17.

A brief assessment of the influence of this important historian and theologian (1894-1962).

1442   Bingham, June. COURAGE TO CHANGE: AN INTRODUCTION TO THE LIFE AND THOUGHT OF REINHOLD NIEBUHR. New York: Charles Scribner's Sons, 1961. 414 p. Bibliog.

Selections from several of Niebuhr's works placed into a biographical framework, illuminating the course of this thought and action.

1443   Carnell, Edward John. THE THEOLOGY OF REINHOLD NIEBUHR. Grand Rapids, Mich.: William B. Eerdmans Publishing Co., 1950. 250 p.

A critical evaluation by a noted conservative Protestant theologian.

1444   Davies, David Richard. REINHOLD NIEBUHR: PROPHET FROM AMERICA. New York: Macmillan Co., 1948. 102 p.

A very brief introduction to the theology of Reinhold Niebuhr, tracing the development of his thought from the 1920s to the 1940s.

1445　Fackre, Gabriel. THE PROMISE OF REINHOLD NIEBUHR. Philadelphia: J.B. Lippincott Co., 1970. 101 p. Bibliog.

A very brief but enlightening introduction to several dimensions of Niebuhr's theology.

1446　Fowler, James W. TO SEE THE KINGDOM: THE THEOLOGICAL VISION OF H. RICHARD NIEBUHR. Nashville: Abingdon Press, 1974. xii, 292 p.

A brief biographical sketch and a thorough analysis of the development of the thought and theology of this very influential Evangelical and Reformed minister, who spent the most fruitful years of his life at Yale University.

1447　Hammar, George. CHRISTIAN REALISM IN AMERICAN THEOLOGY: A STUDY OF REINHOLD NIEBUHR, W.M. HORTON, AND H.P. VAN DUSEN. Uppsala, Sweden: Appelbergs Boktryckeriaktiebolag, 1940. 364 p. Bibliog.

Discusses the rise and fall of liberal theology in the United States and the efforts of Niebuhr, Horton, and Van Dusen to replace it with a more realistic theology. Bibliography stressing the works of these and other twentieth-century American theologians.

1448　Hoedemaker, Libertus A. THE THEOLOGY OF H. RICHARD NIEBUHR. Philadelphia: Pilgrim Press, 1970. xix, 204 p. Bibliog.

A general introduction to the theology of Reinhold Niebuhr's less well-known brother, tracing its development partly in a biographical framework.

1449　Kegley, Charles W., and Bretall, Robert W., eds. REINHOLD NIEBUHR: HIS RELIGIOUS, SOCIAL, AND POLITICAL THOUGHT. New York: Macmillan Co., 1956. xiv, 486 p. Bibliog. Paperback.

The best introductory volume on Niebuhr. A short intellectual autobiography by Niebuhr, followed by twenty critical essays on his thought, (most of which are written by well-known theologians), and a reply by Niebuhr to his critics. Niebuhr's published works to 1956 in bibliography.

1450　Ramsey, Paul, ed. FAITH AND ETHICS: THE THEOLOGY OF H. RICHARD NIEBUHR. New York: Harper and Brothers, 1957. xv, 306 p. Bibliog.

A collection of essays on Niebuhr's thought, especially concentrating on his ethics. Contributors include Waldo Beach,

Hans Frei, James Gustafson, Julian Hartt, Robert Michaelsen, Carl Michalson, Raymond P. Morris, Liston Pope, and George Schrader.

1451 Stone, Ronald H. REINHOLD NIEBUHR, PROPHET TO POLITICIANS. Nashville: Abingdon Press, 1972. 272 p.

A brief description of Niebuhr's background, followed by discussion of the development of his thought and (in the last two chapters) an analysis of his perspective on American foreign policy.

1452 Thompson, Dennis L. "The Basic Doctrines and Concepts of Reinhold Niebuhr's Political Thought." JOURNAL OF CHURCH AND STATE 17 (1975): 275-99.

An analysis of Niebuhr's concepts of love, justice, freedom, responsibility, sin, man, power and prestige, society, community, and history, and their dialectic roles in his political thought.

PAUL TILLICH

1453 Tillich, Paul. SYSTEMATIC THEOLOGY. 3 vols. Chicago: University of Chicago Press, 1951-63.

The chief work of this great twentieth-century theologian. His other essays listed in works by Kegley and Bretall (1458) or Hammond (1456).

1454 Adams, James Luther. PAUL TILLICH'S PHILOSOPHY OF CULTURE, SCIENCE, AND RELIGION. New York: Harper and Row, 1965. 313 p. Bibliog.

A study of Tillich's early thought that begins with a discussion of his criticism of traditional religious language and his search for basic concepts, goes on to discuss culture, science, and philosophy. Extensive bibliography of works up to 1945.

1455 Hamilton, Kenneth. THE SYSTEM AND THE GOSPEL: A CRITIQUE OF PAUL TILLICH. New York: Macmillan Co., 1963. 247 p.

A sustained critique of Tillich's SYSTEMATIC THEOLOGY from the perspective of the relation of the system to historic Christianity.

1456 Hammond, Guyton B. THE POWER OF SELF-TRANSCENDENCE: AN INTRODUCTION TO THE PHILOSOPHICAL THEOLOGY OF PAUL TILLICH. St. Louis, Mo.: Bethany Press, 1966. 160 p. Bibliog.

A good introduction to Tillich's thought for those who have had no theological training.

1457 Hopper, David. TILLICH: A THEOLOGICAL PORTRAIT. Philadelphia: J.B. Lippincott Co., 1968. 189 p.

A concise and penetrating analysis of the life and thought of Paul Tillich, revealing that the lineaments of his existential theology were drawn at an early age and that they reflected the theological controversies in which he became embroiled during that time.

1458 Kegley, Charles W., and Bretall, Robert W., eds. THE THEOLOGY OF PAUL TILLICH. New York: Macmillan Co., 1952. xiv, 370 p. Bibliog.

A compendium of fourteen essays on Tillich's thought by such colleagues as Walter Horton, Nels Ferre, Reinhold Niebuhr, James Luther Adams, and Charles Hartshorne, and a brief reply by Tillich.

1459 McKelway, Alexander J. THE SYSTEMATIC THEOLOGY OF PAUL TILLICH, A REVIEW AND ANALYSIS. Richmond, Va.: John Knox Press, 1964. 280 p.

An excellent introduction to the thought of Tillich and the structure of his SYSTEMATIC THEOLOGY, organized helpfully with an elaborate table of contents and good introductory essay.

1460 Macleod, Alistair M. PAUL TILLICH: AN ESSAY ON THE ROLE OF ONTOLOGY IN HIS PHILOSOPHICAL THEOLOGY. London: George Allen and Unwin, 1973. 157 p.

A critique of Tillich's ontology, the question, "What does it mean to be?", which was so important to his theology. Argues that Tillich is not clear in this critical area and that this constitutes an irremediable flaw in his thought.

1461 Mahan, Wayne W. TILLICH'S SYSTEM. San Antonio, Tex.: Trinity University Press, 1974. 148 p.

Argues that Tillich's SYSTEMATIC THEOLOGY does not and cannot hold together due to the failure of his method of correlation; but that there is a true gestalt to the system, which the author can demonstrate.

1462 Martin, Bernard. THE EXISTENTIAL THEOLOGY OF PAUL TILLICH. New York: Bookman Associates, 1963. 221 p.

A good book for the beginning student. Analyzes Tillich's SYSTEMATIC THEOLOGY under the headings of human reason and revelation, structure of man's being, man's estranged existence, and the sources of man's courage and healing.

1463 O'Meara, Thomas A., and Weisser, Celestin D., eds. PAUL TILLICH
IN CATHOLIC THOUGHT. London: Darton, Longman, and Todd, 1965.
xxiii, 323 p.

> Fifteen essays on Tillich by such Catholic scholars as Gus-
> tave Weigel, George Tavard, Kenelm Foster, and George
> McLean.

1464 Pauck, Wilhelm, and Pauck, Marion. PAUL TILLICH: HIS LIFE AND
THOUGHT, vol. 1. LIFE. New York: Harper and Row, 1976. 352 p.

> The first volume in a projected two-volume set. Traces Til-
> lich's life from his early career in Germany, through his ex-
> pulsion by the Nazis, to his successful teaching career in
> the United States. Tillich's thought to be analyzed in the
> second volume.

1465 Rowe, William L. RELIGIOUS SYMBOLS AND GOD: A PHILOSOPHI-
CAL STUDY OF TILLICH'S THEOLOGY. Chicago: University of Chicago Press, 1968. 245 p.

> Focuses on Tillich's doctrine of God and his theory of reli-
> gious symbols, the two primary elements that enter into his
> explanation of man's quest for religion.

1466 Scharlemann, Robert P. REFLECTION AND DOUBT IN THE THOUGHT
OF PAUL TILLICH. New Haven, Conn.: Yale University Press, 1969.
xx, 220 p.

> Traces Tillich's development of reflection and doubting as a
> method that forms a complete but not a closed system of
> thought. Uses this insight to approach such topics in Til-
> lich's thought as the nature of religious symbols, the rela-
> tionship of subjective and objective thinking, and revelation
> and reason.

DEATH OF GOD THEOLOGY

1467 Ahlstrom, Sydney E. "The Moral and Theological Revolution of the
1960s and Its Implications for American Religious History." In THE
STATE OF AMERICAN HISTORY, edited by Herbert J. Bass, pp. 99-118.
Chicago: Quadrangle Books, 1970.

> Argues that such phenomena of the 1960s as the acknowledg-
> ment of secularization, shifts in popular morality, and the
> "death of God" theology will make a major impact on the
> writing of American religious history.

1468 Altizer, Thomas J.J. THE DESCENT INTO HELL: A STUDY OF THE
RADICAL REVERSAL OF THE CHRISTIAN CONSCIOUSNESS. Phila-

delphia: J.B. Lippincott Co., 1970. 217 p.

> Written by the controversial "death of God" theologian, who argues that Christianity can be realized only if mankind rejects the traditional aspiration of ascent into heaven, and embraces the present world ("Hell") with Buddhist-like compassion.

1469 _____. THE GOSPEL OF CHRISTIAN ATHEISM. Philadelphia: Westminster Press, 1966. 157 p.

> A concise statement of the radical pantheism of this leading "death of God" theologian.

1470 _____, ed. TOWARD A NEW CHRISTIANITY: READINGS IN THE DEATH OF GOD THEOLOGY. New York: Harcourt, Brace, and World, 1967. 374 p.

> Includes selections from the works of Blake, Hegel, Kierkegaard, Dostoevski, Nietzsche, Weil, Barth, Buber, Tillich, Bultmann, and Braun as European backgrounds of the "death of God" theology. Also, writings by Taubes, Cobb, Vahanian, Hamilton, Van Buren, Altizer, Mallard, and Kaufman.

1471 Altizer, Thomas J.J., and Hamilton, William. RADICAL THEOLOGY AND THE DEATH OF GOD. Indianapolis: Bobbs-Merrill Co., 1966. xiii, 202 p. Bibliog.

> Eleven essays on radical theology and its supposed precursors by two exponents of the "death of God." Focuses on radical religious thought in the twentieth century in bibliography.

1472 Cobb, John B., ed. THE THEOLOGY OF ALTIZER: CRITIQUE AND RESPONSE. Philadelphia: Westminster Press, 1970. 269 p. Bibliog.

> Protestant, Catholic, and Jewish theologians comment on the "death of God" theology of Thomas J.J. Altizer, and Altizer responds to each critique.

1473 Hamilton, Kenneth. GOD IS DEAD: THE ANATOMY OF A SLOGAN. Grand Rapids, Mich.: William B. Eerdmans Publishing Co., 1966. 86 p.

> Brief discussion of Nietzsche's famous assertion, "God is dead," and its use by radical theologians in the 1960s.

1474 Ice, Jackson Lee, and Carey, John J. THE DEATH OF GOD DEBATE. Philadelphia: Westminster Press, 1967. 267 p.

> Thirteen essays on the "death of God" theology. Includes

letters to two of its leading exponents, William Hamilton and Thomas Altizer, and prognostications for the future of radical theology and religion by Hamilton, Altizer, and Gabriel Vahanian.

1475   Miller, William Robert, ed. THE NEW CHRISTIANITY. New York: Dell Publishing Co., 1967. xxi, 393 p. Bibliog.

An anthology that traces the historical development of the "death of God" theology in the works of Blake, Schleiermacher, Hegel, Kierkegaard, Feuerbach, Renan, Strauss, Nietzsche, Freud, Buber, Tillich, Bultmann, Weil, Bonhoeffer, Robinson, Hamilton, Vahanian, Altizer, and Cox.

1476   Murchland, Bernard, ed. THE MEANING OF THE DEATH OF GOD. New York: Random House, 1967. xv, 265 p.

Protestant, Roman Catholic, and Jewish theologians comment on the "death of God" theology in eighteen essays.

1477   Ogletree, Thomas W. THE DEATH OF GOD CONTROVERSY. Nashville: Abingdon Press, 1966. 127 p. Bibliog.

A very brief introduction to the radical Protestant theology of the 1960s, focusing on William Hamilton, Paul M. Van Buren, and Thomas J.J. Altizer.

1478   Vahanian, Gabriel. THE DEATH OF GOD: THE CULTURE OF OUR POST-CHRISTIAN ERA. New York: George Braziller, 1961. xxxiii, 253 p. Bibliog.

Argues that the intertwining of Christianity and culture has invalidated the former, and that we are now living in an inherently immanentist society that leaves no room for a transcendent God.

Chapter 21

TWENTIETH-CENTURY RELIGIOUS MOVEMENTS

GENERAL WORKS

1479   Carter, Paul A. "The Idea of Progress in Most Recent Protestant Thought, 1930-1960." CHURCH HISTORY 32 (1963): 75-89.

      Offers a graph of the health of the idea of progress on the basis of an excellent bibliographic survey.

1480   Cavert, Samuel M., and Van Dusen, Henry P., eds. THE CHURCH THROUGH HALF A CENTURY. New York: Charles Scribner's Sons, 1936. xii, 426 p.

      A collection of eighteen essays focusing on such aspects of modern Protestantism as liberal theology, social action, and the ecumenical movement.

1481   Ferm, Vergilius, ed. CONTEMPORARY AMERICAN THEOLOGY. New York: Round Table Press, 1932. xx, 376 p.

      Brief theological autobiographies by Edward Scribner Ames, John Baillie, William Adams Brown, Eugene William Lyman, Daniel Arthur McGregor, Shailer Matthews, Frank Chamberlin Porter, Harris Franklin Rall, William L. Sullivan, Luther Allan Weigle, and William Kelley Wright.

1482   Handy, Robert T. "The American Religious Depression, 1925-1935." CHURCH HISTORY 29 (1960): 3-16.

      An influential study, but argues that there was a depression only among main-line Protestants and does not touch on the "fringe" groups that seem to have attracted rather than lost followers during this period.

1483   Miller, William R., ed. CONTEMPORARY AMERICAN PROTESTANT THOUGHT, 1900-1970. Indianapolis: Bobbs-Merrill Co., 1973. xc, 567 p.

A well-edited collection. Generally neglects the conserva-
tive voice in twentieth-century American Protestantism but
includes excerpts from the works of Henry Churchill King,
Josiah Strong, Josiah Royce, William James, Walter Rauschen-
busch, Woodrow Wilson, Harry Emerson Fosdick, Edward Scribner
Ames, Edgar Sheffield Brightman, Walter Lowrie, H. Richard
Niebuhr, Rufus Jones, Charles Hartshorne, H. N. Wieman,
Reinhold Niebuhr, James Gustafson, Thomas Altizer, John
Cobb, Carl Michalson, Martin Luther King, Paul Van Buren,
Peter Berger, and W. Richard Comstock.

1484   Nash, Arnold S., ed. PROTESTANT THOUGHT IN THE TWENTIETH
CENTURY: WHENCE AND WHITHER? New York: Macmillan Co.,
1951. vii, 296 p.

A discussion of trends in most fields of Protestant theology
by Arnold Nash, G. Ernest Wright, Floyd V. Filson, George
F. Thomas, Walter M. Horton, Waldo Beach, John C. Bennett, George Huntston Williams, Seward Hiltner, Charles W.
Gilkey, H. Shelton Smith, H. S. Leiper, and John A. Mackay. Broad thematic scope; theologically, the emphasis is
liberal and neo-orthodox.

1485   Schneider, Herbert W. RELIGION IN TWENTIETH CENTURY AMERICA.
Rev. ed. New York: Atheneum, 1964. 285 p.

A retrospective look at changes in American religious life
since 1900, examining structural changes, moral revolution,
public worship, religious art, intellectual patterns, and new
varieties of religious experience. Well-documented and includes several statistical tables demonstrating longitudinal
changes in religious beliefs and behavior.

CATHOLICISM IN THE TWENTIETH CENTURY

See also Wentz (1553) for Catholic reaction to Nazism and Smith (1605) and
Tull (1607) for the career of Father Coughlin.

1486   Abramson, Harold J. ETHNIC DIVERSITY IN CATHOLIC AMERICA.
New York: John Wiley and Sons, 1973. xvi, 207 p. Bibliog.

A sociological study of the various ethnic groups among
Roman Catholics in the United States, stressing relations
among them and with American society.

1487   Broderick, Francis L. THE RIGHT REVEREND NEW DEALER: JOHN
A. RYAN. New York: Macmillan Co., 1963. 290 p.

A competent, well-researched biography of Ryan (1869-1945),

one of the foremost Catholic crusaders for social justice during the 1930s.

1488 Buczek, Daniel S. IMMIGRANT PASTOR: THE LIFE OF THE RIGHT
REVEREND MONSIGNOR LUCYAN BOJNOWSKI OF NEW BRITAIN,
CONNECTICUT. Waterbury, Conn.: Association of Polish Priests in
Connecticut, 1974. 184 p.

A biography of Bojnowski, a twentieth-century Polish-American
priest, which succeeds in being both an appreciative memoir
and a critical study of one man's and one congregation's
Americanization.

1489 Christ, Frank L., and Sherry, Gerard E., eds. AMERICAN CATHOLI-
CISM AND THE INTELLECTUAL IDEAL. New York: Appleton-Century-
Crofts, 1961. 318 p.

Compiled in reaction to John Tracy Ellis' 1955 article,
"American Catholicism and the Intellectual Life" (an abridgement of which is included in this volume), provides 150 short
excerpts selected to provoke further reflection on the plight
of the American Catholic intellectual.

1490 Cutler, John Henry. CARDINAL CUSHING OF BOSTON. New York:
Hawthorn Books, 1970. 404 p.

A sympathetic but well-documented biography of Richard J.
Cushing (1895-1970).

1491 DeSantis, Vincent P. "American Catholics and McCarthyism."
CATHOLIC HISTORICAL REVIEW 51 (1965): 1-30.

Analyzes Catholic response to Sen. Joseph McCarthy and
discusses sources of Catholic support for him.

1492 Duclos, Warren E. "Crisis of an American Catholic Modernist: Toward
the Moral Absolutism of William L. Sullivan." CHURCH HISTORY 41
(1972): 369-84.

Describes Sullivan's intellectual pilgrimage from the Paulist
priesthood to Unitarianism.

1493 Flynn, George Q. AMERICAN CATHOLICS AND THE ROOSEVELT
PRESIDENCY, 1932-1936. Lexington: University of Kentucky Press,
1968. 272 p.

Argues that during the New Deal, American Catholics first
received recognition as a major social force and were raised
"to a new level of association." Indicates a change in
government attitude toward the church and vice versa.

1494   Fuchs, Lawrence H. JOHN F. KENNEDY AND AMERICAN CATHOLI-CISM. New York: Meredith Press, 1967. xiv, 271 p.

> A good discussion of Kennedy's relationship to the Catholic Church, the effect of anti-Catholic feeling in the 1960 presidential election, and the impact of Kennedy's presidency upon attitudes toward Catholicism.

1495   Gaffey, James. "The Changing of the Guard: The Rise of Cardinal O'Connell of Boston." CATHOLIC HISTORICAL REVIEW 59 (1973): 225-44.

> Background of O'Connell's selection as archbishop in 1907.

1496   Gleason, Philip. "Mass and Maypole Revisited: American Catholics and the Middle Ages." CATHOLIC HISTORICAL REVIEW 57 (1971): 249-74.

> Analyzes background and nature of medievalist enthusiasm that reached a climax among American Catholics from 1920 to 1950. Divides the topic into apologetic, romantic and aesthetic, social reform, neoscholastic, and scholarly motifs.

1497   Greeley, Andrew M. THE CATHOLIC EXPERIENCE: AN INTERPRETA-TION OF THE HISTORY OF AMERICAN CATHOLICISM. Garden City, N.Y.: Doubleday and Co., 1967. 307 p.

> An interpretive study by a sociologist who espoused an "Americanizationist" position but who has subsequently modified his views. See, for example, Andrew M. Greeley, "Catholicism in America: 200 Years and Counting," CRITIC 34 (1976): 14-47 and 54-70.

1498   Koenker, Ernest Benjamin. THE LITURGICAL RENAISSANCE IN THE ROMAN CATHOLIC CHURCH. Rev. ed. St. Louis, Mo.: Concordia Publishing House, 1966. 274 p. Bibliog.

> A study of the various dimensions in the reform of the Roman Catholic liturgy, both before and after the Second Vatican Council.

1499   Linkh, Richard M. AMERICAN CATHOLICISM AND EUROPEAN IM-MIGRANTS, 1900-1924. Staten Island, N.Y.: Center for Migration Studies, 1975. 200 p.

> A study based mainly on secondary sources and concentrating on Italian and Polish immigrants, arguing that the Catholic Church was "not an active force working toward immigrant assimilation."

1500   McAvoy, Thomas T., ed.   ROMAN CATHOLICISM AND THE AMERI-
        CAN WAY OF LIFE.   Notre Dame, Ind.: University of Notre Dame
        Press, 1960.   248 p.

> Catholic problems in the second half of the twentieth cen-
> tury.   Deals with the general position of Roman Catholics
> in the United States in the first half of the work, and in the
> second half, with the adaptation of the Catholic immigrant
> to American life.

1501   McKeown, Elizabeth.   "Apologia for an American Catholicism: the
        Petition and Report of the National Catholic Welfare Council to Pius
        XI, April 25, 1922."   CHURCH HISTORY 43 (1974): 514–28.

> Discusses the National Catholic Welfare Council, an organi-
> zation of Catholic bishops within the United States that at-
> tempted to create policy and articulate a national identity
> for American Catholicism as a whole.   The council ordered
> suppressed by the Pope in 1922, upon the urging of a few
> American bishops.   Reprints the petition (pages 515–22)
> which the council addressed to the papacy in successfully
> arguing its case and analyzes the historical situation and
> the content of the petition.

1502   McNeal, Patricia.   "Catholic Conscientious Objection During World
        War II."   CATHOLIC HISTORICAL REVIEW 61 (1975): 222–42.

> Survey of the history and philosophy of the few Catholic
> conscientious objectors during World War II.

1503   Marx, Paul B.   VIRGIL MICHEL AND THE LITURGICAL MOVEMENT.
        Collegeville, Minn.: Liturgical Press, 1957.   466 p.

> A thorough study of Virgil Michel (1890–1938) and the
> modern liturgical movement in Roman Catholicism, partic-
> ularly at St. John's Abbey in Collegeville, Minnesota.

1504   Merton, Thomas.   THE SEVEN STOREY MOUNTAIN.   New York: Har-
        court, Brace, and Co., 1948.   429 p.

> The popular autobiography of this Trappist monk (1915–68),
> who introduced countless Americans to modern monastic life
> through his writings.

1505   Miller, Robert Moats.   "A Footnote to the Role of the Protestant Churches
        in the Election of 1928."   CHURCH HISTORY 25 (1956): 145–59.

> A re-examination of Protestant rhetoric against Roman Cath-
> olic presidential candidate Al Smith, arguing that the Prot-
> estant clergy did not seek to coerce their flocks to vote for
> Hoover and that their anti-Smith arguments cannot be written
> off as bigotry.

1506   Miller, William D. A HARSH AND DREADFUL LOVE: DOROTHY DAY AND THE CATHOLIC WORKER MOVEMENT. New York: Liveright, 1973. xvi, 370 p.

> Biography of Dorothy Day (b. 1899) that also covers the Catholic Worker Movement and the CATHOLIC WORKER which she founded.

1507   Nolan, Hugh J., ed. PASTORAL LETTERS OF THE AMERICAN HIERARCHY, 1792-1970. Huntington, Ind.: Our Sunday Visitor, 1971. xiv, 785 p.

> Approximately 100 letters to American Catholics. Emphasis on the twentieth century. Chronological table of events in American Catholic history since 1789.

1508   Novitsky, Anthony. "Peter Maurin's Green Revolution: The Radical Implications of Reactionary Social Catholicism." REVIEW OF POLITICS 37 (1975): 83-103.

> Show how Maurin derived his ideas from conservative organicist social thought of European Catholic intellectuals.

1509   O'Brien, David J. AMERICAN CATHOLICS AND SOCIAL REFORM: THE NEW DEAL YEARS. New York: Oxford University Press, 1968. 287 p.

> Analyzes writings of Catholic intellectuals and publicists from 1933 to 1940, particularly those that relate papal encyclicals to problems of the Depression and the New Deal. Little on social reforms other than those pertaining to labor movements.

1510   O'Dea, Thomas F. AMERICAN CATHOLIC DILEMMA: AN INQUIRY INTO THE INTELLECTUAL LIFE. New York: Sheed and Ward, 1958. 173 p.

> A leading Catholic sociologist of religion discusses the participation and failings of Roman Catholics in American intellectual life, a problem that preoccupied many of the church's leaders in the 1950s.

1511   Ong, Walter J. AMERICAN CATHOLIC CROSSROADS. New York: Macmillan Co., 1959. 160 p.

> Six essays on the Roman Catholic Church's encounter with a secularized modern world in the United States.

1512   _____. FRONTIERS IN AMERICAN CATHOLICISM: ESSAYS ON IDEOLOGY AND CULTURE. New York: Macmillan Co., 1957. 125 p.

Six broadly cast essays focusing on Catholicism's confrontation with the modern world.

1513   Sheerin, John B.   NEVER LOOK BACK: THE CAREER AND CONCERNS OF JOHN J. BURKE.   Paramus, N.J.: Paulist Press, 1975.   254 p.

Biographical study of Burke, a Paulist priest, editor of the CATHOLIC WORLD from 1904 to 1922 and a leader in the National Catholic Welfare Conference from 1917 to 1936.

1514   Smylie, James H.   "The Roman Catholic Church, the State and Al Smith."   CHURCH HISTORY   29 (1960): 321-43.

Reviews American Protestant views of the Roman Catholic "threat" during the first quarter of the twentieth century and the role of Smith's candidacy for the presidency in 1928 as a stimulant of further inquiry as well as Catholic arguments against these fears.

1515   VanAllen, Rodger.   THE COMMONWEAL AND AMERICAN CATHOLICISM: THE MAGAZINE, THE MOVEMENT AND THE MEANING.   Philadelphia: Fortress Press, 1974.   218 p.

Traces the fifty-year history of this influential expression of the Catholic laity, including sketches of the people involved in founding the magazine, its editorial policy, and its career.

CATHOLICISM SINCE VATICAN II

1516   Casey, William Van Etten, and Nobile, Philip., eds.   THE BERRIGANS.   New York: Praeger Publishers, 1971.   253 p.

Eighteen diverse essays illuminating the lives of Philip and Daniel Berrigan, two activist Catholic priests who were among leaders of the movement against American military intervention in Southeast Asia.

1517   Gleason, Philip, ed.   CONTEMPORARY CATHOLICISM IN THE UNITED STATES.   Notre Dame, Ind.: University of Notre Dame Press, 1969.   xviii, 385 p.

A collection of fourteen essays, most of which were written by Catholic scholars, on recent trends in Catholic ecumenism, education, social action, lay organizations, and other topics.

1518   Greeley, Andrew M.   THE HESITANT PILGRIM: AMERICAN CATHOLICISM AFTER THE COUNCIL.   New York: Sheed and Ward, 1966.   xxi, 276 p.

A sympathetic study of gradual change and upward social mobility of Catholics in the 1960s.

1519 _____. PRIESTS IN THE UNITED STATES: REFLECTIONS ON A SURVEY. Garden City, N.Y.: Doubleday and Co., 1972. 213 p.

An interpretation of surveys of Roman Catholic priests in the United States, covering such topics as celibacy, acceptance of doctrine, social problems, and decisions to resign from the priesthood.

1520 Hitchcock, James. THE DECLINE AND FALL OF RADICAL CATHOLICISM. New York: Herder and Herder, 1971. 228 p.

A progressive Roman Catholic argues that little has been accomplished in reforming the Church since the Second Vatican Council, 1962-65.

1521 Kavanaugh, James. A MODERN PRIEST LOOKS AT HIS OUTDATED CHURCH. New York: Trident Press, 1967. xiii, 190 p.

Examines the symptoms of disintegration in the Roman Catholic Church in the 1960s and criticizes its doctrines relating to birth control, parochial schools, confession, monasticism, and other controversial topics. A best seller in 1967.

1522 Lapomarda, Vincent A. "A Jesuit Runs for Congress: The Rev. Robert F. Drinan, S.J. and His 1970 Campaign." JOURNAL OF CHURCH AND STATE 15 (1973): 205-22.

An analysis of the Congressional campaign of Drinan, Democrat from eastern Massachusetts, and the implications of his political role for the future of church-state relations in the United States.

1523 O'Brien, David J. "American Catholic Historiography: A Post-Conciliar Evaluation." CHURCH HISTORY 37 (1968): 80-94.

An analysis and assessment of current tendencies in Catholic historiography rather than merely a listing of books.

1524 _____. THE RENEWAL OF AMERICAN CATHOLICISM. New York: Oxford University Press, 1972. xvi, 302 p.

A series of loosely related essays that attempts to describe and assess the nature and origin of the ferment that struck the Catholic church in the 1960s. Arguing that Pope John XXIII and John F. Kennedy affected American Catholicism in fundamental ways, sees the contemporary church involved in a basic redefinition of its faith.

1525   O'Connor, John. THE PEOPLE VERSUS ROME: RADICAL SPLIT IN
        THE AMERICAN CHURCH. New York: Random House, 1969. 223 p.

    A leading Catholic journalist describes the revolt of many
    Roman Catholics against clerical authoritarianism and their
    willingness to act outside of traditional channels to reform
    the Church.

1526   _____, ed. AMERICAN CATHOLIC EXODUS. Washington, D.C.:
        Corpus Publications, 1968. 224 p.

    A compendium of essays supporting the belief that the de-
    cline of traditionalism among American Catholics is more
    accurately described as a projection of faith into new forms
    and social action. Includes "Blood, War and Witness" by
    Philip Berrigan, "The Ecumenical Plateau" by Eugene C.
    Bianchi, "Youth, Schools, and Hope" by William Birming-
    ham, "The Church's Ecumenical Outreach" by Robert McAfee
    Brown, "The Church and the Black Man" by Dennis Clark,
    "Catholic Reaction and the Social Conscience" by A.V.
    Krebs, "Sisters, Celibacy, and Community" by Maryellen
    Mackenhirn, "The Laity and a Moment of Dread" by John
    Mulholland, "Women: the Church's Third Class Citizens"
    by Arlene Swidler, "Schism, Heresy, and a New Guard" by
    Frederick D. Wilhelmsen, and "American Catholic Exodus"
    by John O'Connor.

1527   O'Dea, Thomas F. THE CATHOLIC CRISIS. Boston: Beacon Press,
        1968. 267 p.

    An analysis of the decrees of the Second Vatican Council,
    1962-65, on the Roman Catholic Church in the United States
    and a call for flexibility and willingness to change in order
    to save the Church.

1528   Wills, Garry. BARE RUINED CHOIRS: DOUBT, PROPHECY, AND
        RADICAL RELIGION. Garden City, N.Y.: Doubleday and Co., 1972.
        272 p.

    A biting if loosely-written analysis of the disarray of Roman
    Catholicism since Vatican II, 1962-65, by a leading Catholic
    intellectual.

1529   Yzermans, Vincent A., ed. AMERICAN PARTICIPATION IN THE SEC-
        OND VATICAN COUNCIL. New York: Sheed and Ward, 1967. xvi,
        684 p.

    Extensive collection of documents illustrating the role of
    American Catholics in the Second Vatican Council, 1962-65.
    Chiefly consisted of interventions by American bishops re-
    garding the Council's declarations.

PACIFISM

General

1530   Bainton, Roland H.   CHRISTIAN ATTITUDES TOWARD WAR AND
        PEACE.   New York: Abingdon Press, 1960.   299 p.

        A historical survey from antiquity to 1945, analyzing such
        topics as the "just war," war and crusading in the Old Tes-
        tament, the rise of peace churches, and problems confronting
        Christian pacifists today.

1531   Brock, Peter.   PACIFISM IN THE UNITED STATES FROM THE COLO-
        NIAL ERA TO THE FIRST WORLD WAR.   Princeton, N.J.:   Princeton
        University Press, 1968.   1,005 p.

        Describes much religion-related pacifism, including extensive
        discussion of the pacifism of the Quakers, Church of the
        Brethren, Mennonites, Jehovah's Witnesses, and Aventists.

1532   Curti, Merle E.   THE AMERICAN PEACE CRUSADE, 1815-1861.   Dur-
        ham, N.C.:   Duke University Press, 1929.   250 p.

        A scholarly study of early nineteenth-century organized paci-
        fism, which began with local societies and culminated in the
        creation of the League of Universal Brotherhood and a group
        of international peace congresses.

1533   _____.   PEACE OR WAR: THE AMERICAN STRUGGLE, 1636-1936.
        New York: W.W. Norton and Co., 1936.   374 p.

        A history of the peace movement in the United States by a
        historian sympathetic to pacifism.

1534   Ellsworth, C.S.   "The American Churches and the Mexican War."
        AMERICAN HISTORICAL REVIEW   45 (1940): 301-26.

        Survey of attitudes toward the war shows that the churches
        were divided, with those with a stake in the Southwest favor-
        ing it.

1535   Gribbin, William.   THE CHURCHES MILITANT: THE WAR OF 1812
        AND AMERICAN RELIGION.   New Haven, Conn.:   Yale University
        Press, 1973.   210 p.

        Analyzes the split among Christians that the war caused.
        Especially concerned with examining the New England Con-
        gregationalists, who opposed the war.

1536   Lieberman, Mark. THE PACIFISTS: SOLDIERS WITHOUT GUNS.
        New York: Praeger Publishers, 1972. 127 p.

>   Brief sketches of seven American pacifists and war resisters,
>   including William Penn, William Lloyd Garrison, Jane
>   Addams, John Haynes Holmes, A.J. Muste, and Daniel
>   and Philip Berrigan.

1537   Long, Edward LeRoy. WAR AND CONSCIENCE IN AMERICA.
        Philadelphia: Westminster Press, 1968. xiv, 130 p.

>   Concise description of the issues involved in Christian
>   participation in and opposition to war.

1538   Mayer, Peter, ed. THE PACIFIST CONSCIENCE. Chicago: Henry
        Regnery Co., 1966. 478 p. Bibliog.

>   An anthology of writings by pacifists and non-pacifists from
>   Lao-Tzu to Martin Luther King, including selections from
>   the works of such twentieth-century Americans as A.J.
>   Muste, William James, Randolph Bourne, Reinhold Niebuhr,
>   Dorothy Day, Henry Cadbury, and Albert Einstein.

1539   Ramsey, Paul. WAR AND THE CHRISTIAN CONSCIENCE. Durham:
        Duke University Press, 1961. xxiv, 331 p.

>   An analysis of Augustine's concept of the "just war" in
>   the modern world, including a chapter on this issue in
>   contemporary American Protestant thought.

1540   Wright, Edward Needles. CONSCIENTIOUS OBJECTORS IN THE
        CIVIL WAR. Philadelphia: University of Pennsylvania Press, 1931.
        274 p.

>   A well-researched study of conscientious objectors and
>   noncombatant objectors in the military, stressing such
>   groups as the Mennonites and Quakers. Bibliography of
>   primary and secondary works.

Twentieth Century

1541   Abrams, Ray H. "The Churches and the Clergy in World War II."
        ANNALS OF THE AMERICAN ACADEMY OF POLITICAL AND SOCIAL
        SCIENCE (MARCH 1948): 110-19.

>   A brief analysis of the generally anti-interventionist stance
>   of the American clergy from 1939 to 1941 and its reluctant
>   willingness to support the war effort after the attack on
>   Pearl Harbor.

1542 _____. PREACHERS PRESENT ARMS. New York: Round Table Press, 1933. xix, 297 p. Bibliog.

> An analysis of the relationships between Christian preach-
> ing and American nationalism during World War I, and of
> the role of the churches as distributors of pro-war propa-
> ganda. Argues that many clergymen supported the war
> effort because the symbols of nationalism parallelled those
> of Christianity.

1543 Batchelder, Robert C. THE IRREVERSIBLE DECISION, 1939-1950. Boston, Mass.: Houghton Mifflin Co., 1962. 306 p.

> An analysis of the ethical issues surrounding the American
> manufacture and use of the atomic bomb in World War II
> and its aftermath, also stating the data used in critiques
> of American policy.

1544 Chatfield, Charles. FOR PEACE AND JUSTICE: PACIFISM IN AMERICA, 1914-1941. Knoxville: University of Tennessee Press, 1971. xiv, 447 p. Bibliog.

> Focuses primarily upon pacifist groups from the social
> gospel wing of the church (especially the Fellowship of
> Reconciliation) and pays less attention to the historic peace
> churches (such as the Mennonites) and their role in the
> interwar period. A well-researched study.

1545 _____, ed. PEACE MOVEMENTS IN AMERICA. New York: Schocken Books, 1973. xxxii, 191 p.

> A well-edited and useful collection of scholarly articles
> on aspects of pacifism and anti-war movements during the
> first half of the twentieth century. Essays, for example,
> on Ernest Howard Crosby, A.J. Muste, Kenneth Boulding,
> and the United World Federalists.

1546 Chatfield, Charles, and DeBeneditti, Charles, eds. KIRBY PAGE AND THE SOCIAL GOSPEL: PACIFIST AND SOCIALIST ASPECTS. New York: Garland Publishing Co., 1977.

> An anthology of the writing of Kirby Page, a leading paci-
> fist during the interwar period. Introduced with an exten-
> sive biographical essay.

1547 Finn, James, ed. A CONFLICT OF LOYALTIES: THE CASE FOR SELECTIVE CONSCIENTIOUS OBJECTION. New York: Pegasus Books, 1968. 287 p.

> A collection of essays on the philosophy and religious basis
> of conscientious objection.

1548   Hentoff, Nat, ed. THE ESSAYS OF A.J. MUSTE. Indianapolis:
        Bobbs-Merrill Co., 1967. xvii, 515 p. Bibliog.

> Autobiography of A.J. Muste (1885-1967), a Netherlandic-
> American clergyman and pacifist who was active in the
> Fellowship of Reconciliation, the War Resisters' League,
> and the Church Peace Mission. Covers the years from
> 1905 to 1966. Abridged bibliography of Muste's published
> works.

1549   Jack, Homer A., ed. RELIGION AND PEACE PAPERS FROM THE
        NATIONAL INTER-RELIGIOUS CONFERENCE ON PEACE. Indianap-
        olis, Ind.: Bobbs-Merrill Co., 1966. xvi, 137 p.

> Speeches and reports by Christians and Jews on the role of
> religion in the formation of national policy and the moral-
> ity of military intervention.

1550   Marchand, C. Roland. THE AMERICAN PEACE MOVEMENT AND
        SOCIAL REFORM, 1898-1918. Princeton, N.J.: Princeton University
        Press, 1973. xix, 441 p.

> Contains an important chapter putting church-oriented
> peace activity into the context of the professionalization
> of social reform in the Progressive era.

1551   Peterson, H.C., and Fite, Gilbert C. OPPONENTS OF THE WAR,
        1917-1918. Madison: University of Wisconsin Press, 1957. xiii,
        399 p. Bibliog.

> A well-documented study of the persecution of pacifists and
> other anti-war groups in the United States during World
> War I. Considerable attention paid to clergy, Quakers,
> Mennonites, and other religious groups.

1552   Van Kirk, Walter W. RELIGION RENOUNCES WAR. New York:
        Willett, Clark, and Co., 1934. 262 p.

> Documents the shift from flag-waving involvement, des-
> cribed by Abrams (1541), to post-1918 opposition to war.

1553   Wentz, F[rederick].K. "American Catholic Periodicals React to
        Nazism." CHURCH HISTORY 31 (1962): 400-420.

> A concise analysis of the Roman Catholic press in the
> United States from 1933 to 1937, illuminating the difficul-
> ties it had in commenting on National Socialism after the
> Reichskonkordat was concluded in July 1933, and the
> tendency of some Catholics to regard Hitler, ostensibly a
> fellow believer and an avowed foe of Communism, as less
> dangerous than Stalin.

1554 _____. "American Protestant Journals and the Nazi Religious Assault." CHURCH HISTORY 23 (1954): 321–38.

> Poses the question "How did American Protestants . . . conceive the role of Christian Society?" By examining seventeen pertinent journals representing a wide range of theological and political stances, illuminates several answers to this question and diverse reactions to the emergence of National Socialism as a major threat to Christianity.

1555 Wilson, E. Raymond. UPHILL FOR PEACE. Richmond, Ind.: Friends United Press, 1975. xx, 432 p.

> History of the activities of an early Protestant legislative lobby, the Friends Committee on National Legislation, written by the man who ran the committee.

1556 Wittner, Lawrence S. REBELS AGAINST WAR: THE AMERICAN PEACE MOVEMENT, 1941-1960. New York: Columbia University Press, 1969. 339 p.

> Traces the collapse and rebuilding of the peace movement in the United States, focusing on such individuals as Linus Pauling and A.J. Muste, and such organizations as the Fellowship of Reconciliation and the National Committee for a Sane Temperance Movement and Prohibition.

THE TEMPERANCE MOVEMENT AND PROHIBITION

1557 Asbury, Herbert. THE GRAND ILLUSION: AN INFORMAL HISTORY OF PROHIBITION. New York: Doubleday and Co., 1950. 344 p.

> One-volume general social history made up of two parts, a chronological survey of the temperance movement and a history of the Prohibition period from 1920 to 1934. Written by a descendant of a temperance leader. Recommended for high school students.

1558 Byrne, Frank L. PROPHET OF PROHIBITION: NEAL DOW AND HIS CRUSADE. Madison: State Historical Society of Wisconsin, 1961. 184 p.

> Well-documented but poorly edited biography of this nineteenth-century leader of the temperance movement in Maine. Some attention paid to churches, especially Congregational, in the movement.

1559　Chalfant, Harry Malcom. THESE AGITATORS AND THEIR IDEA.
Nashville: Cokesbury Press, 1931. 363 p. Bibliog.

> Loosely-written account of Benjamin Rush, Lyman Beecher,
> Neal Dow, Frances Willard and eleven other temperance
> advocates. Antiquated bibliography.

1560　Cherrington, E.H. THE EVOLUTION OF PROHIBITION IN THE
UNITED STATES OF AMERICA. Westerville, Ohio: American Issue
Press, 1920. 384 p.

> A partisan chronicle of the temperance movement by one
> of its leaders. Considerable emphasis on the role of
> Christian denominations and other religious groups. No
> footnotes or bibliography.

1561　Clark, Norman H. DELIVER US FROM EVIL: AN INTERPRETATION
OF AMERICAN PROHIBITION. New York: W.W. Norton and Co.,
1976. 246 p. Bibliog.

> A derivative synthesis of earlier literature pertaining to
> the temperance movement and prohibition, interpreting the
> movement as an expression of bourgeois Protestants, but
> ignoring contributions of Catholics, immigrants, and others.

1562　Coffey, Thomas M. THE LONG THIRST. PROHIBITION IN AMERICA,
1920-1933. New York: W.W. Norton and Co., 1975. 346 p.
Bibliog.

> A readable but weakly documented popular history of pro-
> hibition. Role of religious groups given some attention.
> Short bibliography listing mainly secondary works.

1563　Dabney, Virginius. DRY MESSIAH: THE LIFE OF BISHOP CANNON.
New York: Alfred A. Knopf, 1949. 353 p. Bibliog.

> A critical biography of James Cannon (1864-1944), a
> Methodist bishop who fought for temperance for decades in
> the Anti-Saloon League and founded the World League
> Against Alcohol. Detailed but weakly documented.

1564　Dobyns, Fletcher. THE AMAZING STORY OF REPEAL; AN EXPOSE
OF THE POWER OF PROPAGANDA. Chicago: Willett, Clark and
Co., 1940. 457 p.

> A detailed but confused account of the temperance move-
> ment, the prohibition era, and the role of interest groups
> in terminating prohibition in 1933. Brief discussion of
> religious groups' part in the temperance movement.

1565 Gusfield, Joseph R. SYMBOLIC CRUSADE: STATUS POLITICS AND THE AMERICAN TEMPERANCE MOVEMENT. Urbana: University of Illinois Press, 1963. 198 p.

> A social history of the temperance movement utilizing Richard Hofstadter's theory of the "status revolution" to explain motivations of its adherents. Protestant churches interpreted as chief vehicles of the movement.

1566 Kobler, John. ARDENT SPIRITS; THE RISE AND FALL OF PROHIBITION. New York: G.P. Putnam's Sons, 1973. 386 p. Bibliog.

> A light-hearted, flippant treatment of the history of temperance and prohibition.

1567 Krout, John Allen. THE ORIGINS OF PROHIBITION. New York: Alfred A. Knopf, 1925. 339 p.

> Up to the passage of the Maine liquor law, in 1851, the Eighteenth Amendment seen as the culmination of a fundamental change over one hundred years rather than the result of temporary conditions.

1568 Merz, Charles. THE DRY DECADE. Garden City, N.Y.: Doubleday, Doran, and Co., 1931. 343 p.

> A well-documented legislative history of the enactment of the Eighteenth Amendment, efforts in the 1920s to end prohibition, and the difficulties of enforcement. Illuminating as a study written two years before repeal.

1569 Sinclair, Andrew. PROHIBITION: THE ERA OF EXCESS. Boston: Little, Brown, and Co., 1962. 480 p.

> A detailed history of the temperance movement and the prohibition era, analyzing the ultimate failure of prohibition. Views the temperance movement as "an assertion of the rural Protestant mind against the urban and polyglot culture that had emerged at the end of the nineteenth century," an interpretation that ignores the role played by city dwellers and immigrants.

1570 Timberlake, James H. PROHIBITION AND THE PROGRESSIVE MOVEMENT, 1900-1920. Cambridge, Mass.: Harvard University Press, 1963. 238 p.

> Contains a summary description of the forces that converged in the successful prohibition campaign of 1918, with chapters devoted to the religious, scientific, social, economic, and political arguments for prohibition. However, fails to do justice to the significance of religious factors,

and neglects the positive role played by immigrants in the movement.

FUNDAMENTALISM

1571 Bass, Clarence B. BACKGROUNDS TO DISPENSATIONALISM: ITS HISTORICAL GENESIS AND ECCLESIASTICAL IMPLICATIONS. Grand Rapids, Mich.: William B. Eerdmans Co., 1960. 184 p.

A dispassionate analysis of the theological system called dispensationalism and a discussion of John Nelson Darby, the founder of this school of interpretation. Although author does not make the point, dispensationalism important in understanding Fundamentalism.

1572 Carter, Paul A. "The Fundamentalist Defense of the Faith." In CHANGE AND CONTINUITY IN TWENTIETH CENTURY AMERICA: THE 1920s, edited by John Braeman, p. 179-214. Columbus: Ohio State University Press, 1968.

A useful short introduction to the main themes of the 1920s which cites, as well, a great deal of contemporary literature.

1573 Cole, Stewart Grant. THE HISTORY OF FUNDAMENTALISM. New York: R.R. Smith, 1931. xiv, 360 p. Bibliog.

An early, accurate, and still useful attempt to place the Fundamentalist controversy in historical perspective. Emphasis on Baptists, Presbyterians, Episcopalians, Methodists, and Disciples of Christ.

1574 Furniss, Norman K. THE FUNDAMENTALIST CONTROVERSY, 1918-1931. New Haven, Conn.: Yale University Press, 1954. 199 p. Bibliog.

An error-filled description of the Fundamentalist controversy in certain American Protestant denominations and an effort to understand the psyche of the so-called Fundamentalists.

1575 Kraus, C. Norman. DISPENSATIONALISM IN AMERICA: ITS RISE AND DEVELOPMENT. Richmond, Va.: John Knox Press, 1958. 156 p. Bibliog.

A concise and illuminating analysis of this millenarian theology, tracing its origins in nineteenth-century England and its reception in the United States.

1576   Machen, J. Gresham. CHRISTIANITY AND LIBERALISM. New York: Macmillan Co., 1923. 189 p.

> A classic statement by this conservative Presbyterian juxtaposing in black and white terms his interpretation of Christianity and a simplistic view of some of the liberalizing trends in Protestant theology and the moral decay of modern culture.

1577   Moore, LeRoy, Jr. "Another Look at Fundamentalism: A Response to Ernest R. Sandeen." CHURCH HISTORY 37 (1968): 195-202.

> A mild disagreement with Sandeen (1581) for his emphasis on millenarianism and Biblical literalism as the roots of Fundamentalism and his alleged neglect of the 1920s. Instead, would have two categories: a "doctrinaire Fundamentalism," which Sandeen analyzed, and "Fundamentalism as a party movement" within denominations troubled by the Fundamentalist-Modernist controversy.

1578   Rudnick, Milton L. FUNDAMENTALISM AND THE MISSOURI SYNOD. St. Louis, Mo.: Concordia Publishing House, 1966. 152 p. Bibliog.

> A brief attempt to analyze the influence of Fundamentalism on the Lutheran Church--Missouri Synod, arguing that the Synod derived its doctrine of Biblical inerrancy from Lutheran orthodoxy, not from modern American sources, and explaining why the Synod did not cooperate closely with other conservative Protestant bodies in the United States.

1579   Russell, C. Allyn. VOICES OF AMERICAN FUNDAMENTALISM: SEVEN BIOGRAPHICAL STUDIES. Philadelphia: Westminster Press, 1976. 304 p.

> Sketches of J. Frank Norris, John Roach Straton, William Bell Riley, J.C. Massee, J. Gresham Machen, William Jennings Bryan, and Clarence E. Macartney. Clear presentation of data, but sometimes weak in interpretation, especially for Bryan, for whom Szasz (1584) is recommended.

1580   Sandeen, Ernest R. THE ORIGINS OF FUNDAMENTALISM: TOWARD A HISTORICAL INTERPRETATION. Philadelphia: Fortress Press, 1968. 27 p.

> A summary of Sandeen's longer work (1581), originally published in CHURCH HISTORY 36 (1967): 66-83.

1581 _____. THE ROOTS OF FUNDAMENTALISM: BRITISH AND
AMERICAN MILLENARIANISM, 1800-1930. Chicago: University of
Chicago Press, 1970. 347 p.

> Dismisses the controversies of the 1920s as a red herring
> and argues that Fundamentalism was a self-conscious,
> structured, long-lived entity that had its origin in nine-
> teenth-century Anglo-American millenarianism (especially
> dispensational millenarianism) and found its leadership in
> northern urban areas among the Presbyterian and Baptist
> denominations.

1582 Singleton, Gregory. "Fundamentalism and Urbanization: Quantitative
Critique of Impressionistic Interpretations." In THE NEW URBAN
HISTORY: QUANTITATIVE EXPLORATIONS BY AMERICAN HISTORI-
ANS, edited by Leo F. Schnore, p. 205-27. Princeton, N.J.:
Princeton University Press, 1975.

> Like so many quantitative historians, finds it necessary to
> reiterate criticism of "impressionistic" historians, in this
> case because they tell us so little about Fundamentalism
> as a social movement. But author's opening paragraphs
> wildly impressionistic, creating categories such as "defi-
> nitely Fundamentalist" into which whole denominations are
> placed on the basis of quite flimsy justification. Analysis
> of Los Angeles does not rate much better marks.

1583 Stonehouse, Ned B. J. GRESHAM MACHEN, A BIOGRAPHICAL
MEMOIR. Grand Rapids, Mich.: William B. Eerdmans Publishing
Co., 1955. 520 p.

> Detailed, sympathetic biography of John Gresham Machen
> (1881-1937), the conservative New Testament scholar who
> resigned his professorship at Princeton Theological Seminary
> and founded Westminster Theological Seminary in Philadel-
> phia in the 1920s.

1584 Szasz, Ferenc M. "William Jennings Bryan, Evolution, and the Fundamentalist Controversy." NEBRASKA HISTORY 56 (1975): 259-78.

> The best treatment of Bryan's post-1915 career, making
> clear that Bryan was a late convert to anti-evolution and
> only marginally associated with the Fundamentalist move-
> ment.

NEO-EVANGELICALISM

1585 Bloesch, Donald G. THE EVANGELICAL RENAISSANCE. Grand
Rapids, Mich.: William B. Eerdmans Publishing Co., 1973. 165 p.

A sympathetic analysis of the resurgence of conservative Protestantism and a warning against allowing this movement to isolate itself from other forms of Christianity or harden into a rigid dogmatism.

1586   Casper, Louis. THE FUNDAMENTALIST MOVEMENT. The Hague, Netherlands: Mouton and Co., 1963. 181 p.

Broad but superficial history of Fundamentalist organizations such as the National Association of Evangelicals, and their attacks on more liberal Christians since the 1920s.

1587   Coleman, Richard J. ISSUES OF THEOLOGICAL WARFARE: EVANGELICALS AND LIBERALS. Grand Rapids, Mich.: William B. Eerdmans Publishing Co., 1972. 206 p.

Discusses the positions of the "liberal" and "evangelical" camps on the nature of Christ, the authority of the Bible, social action, and other theological topics.

1588   Henry, Carl F.H., ed. CONTEMPORARY EVANGELICAL THOUGHT. New York: Harper and Brothers, 1957. 320 p. Bibliog.

Excerpts from the works of Carl F.H. Henry, Frank E. Gaebelein, Edward J. Young, and several other evangelicals illustrating this wing of American Protestantism during the 1950s.

1589   Jorstad, Erling. "Two on the Right: Comparative Look at Fundamentalism and New Evangelicalism." LUTHERAN QUARTERLY 23 (1971): 107-17.

An analysis of the separation of self-styled evangelicals from the Fundamentalism of the 1920s, and a sketch of the theological position of such neo-evangelicals as Carl Henry.

1590   Kelley, Dean M. WHY CONSERVATIVE CHURCHES ARE GROWING: A STUDY IN THE SOCIOLOGY OF RELIGION. New York: Harper and Row, 1972. xiii, 184 p.

Argues that the "evangelical" and Pentecostal denominations are more effectively interpreting the meaning of experience for Christians than the more liberal communions, whose energies are being sapped by ecumenism, dialogue, and attempts at renewal. Provocative study, but many untenable generalizations.

1591   Lindsell, Harold. THE BATTLE FOR THE BIBLE. Grand Rapids, Mich.: Zondervan Publishing House, 1976. 218 p.

A study of the doctrine of Biblical infallibility and challenges to it in the twentieth century, especially among Southern Baptists and Missouri Synod Lutherans.

1592   Murch, James D. COOPERATION WITHOUT COMPROMISE: A HISTORY OF THE NATIONAL ASSOCIATION OF EVANGELICALS. Grand Rapids, Mich.: William B. Eerdmans Co., 1956. 220 p.

A tendentious chronicle of this association, which was created in the 1940s to unite certain groups of conservative Protestants and counter the inroads of liberalism in American religion.

1593   Nash, Ronald H. THE NEW EVANGELICALISM. Grand Rapids, Mich.: Zondervan Publishing House, 1963. 188 p. Bibliog.

A sympathetic analysis of one wing of conservative Protestantism since World War II and its reaction against the Fundamentalism of the 1920s and 1930s. Emphasis on neo-evangelicalism as represented by E.J. Carnell, Carl Henry, Bernard Romm, Gordon Clark, and Harold Ockenga.

1594   Quebedeaux, Richard. THE YOUNG EVANGELICALS: REVOLUTION IN ORTHODOXY. New York: Harper and Row, 1974. xii, 157 p.

A quite personal, journalistic account of the intramural politics of Fundamental-Evangelicalism in the mid-1970s. Written by a campus minister at the University of California at Santa Barbara.

1595   Sandeen, Ernest R. "Fundamentalism and American Identity." ANNALS OF AMERICAN ACADEMY OF POLITICAL AND SOCIAL SCIENCES 387 (January 1970): 56-65.

Argues that Fundamentalism lives in symbiotic relationship with other forms of religion and with cultural trends, leading the Fundamentalist believer, paradoxically, to affirm both his despair over the world and his identification with much of the world's culture. Notes that the Fundamentalist has resolved this tension through the creation of innumerable parallel institutions that affirm essentially worldly values.

1596   Towns, Elmer L. IS THE DAY OF THE DENOMINATION DEAD? Nashville: Thomas Nelson, 1973. 160 p.

Argues that the large "mainline" Protestant denominations are declining in power and influence, while many smaller, aggressive communions are replacing them as the cutting edge of Christianity in the United States.

1597   Wells, David F., and Woodbridge, John D., eds. THE EVANGELICALS: WHAT THEY BELIEVE, WHO THEY ARE, WHERE THEY ARE CHANGING. Nashville: Abingdon Press, 1975. 304 p.

In twelve essays, "evangelicals" and other Christians seek to answer the three questions posed in the subtitle and thereby draw tenable generalizations about this variegated movement in contemporary Protestantism.

RADICAL RIGHT AND THE CHURCHES

1598   Clabaugh, Gary K. THUNDER ON THE RIGHT: THE PROTESTANT FUNDAMENTALISTS. Chicago: Nelson-Hall Co., 1974. 281 p. xx, 261 p.

A study of a few leaders of the radical right during the 1960s, including Carl McIntire, Billy James Hargis, Fred C. Schwarz, and Edgar C. Bundy. Concentrates on the controversy over sex education in the schools in the opening chapters, and the last three chapters deal with the ideology of these leaders.

1599   Clouse, Robert G., et al. THE CROSS AND THE FLAG. Carol Stream, Ill.: Creation House, 1972. 261 p.

The limits of the common belief that conservative Protestants are politically conservative examined by eleven writers.

1600   Hopkins, Joseph Martin. THE ARMSTRONG EMPIRE: A LOOK AT THE WORLDWIDE CHURCH OF GOD. Grand Rapids, Mich.: William B. Eerdmans Publishing Co., 1974. 304 p. Bibliog.

A critical analysis of the "World Tomorrow" broadcast, PLAIN TRUTH magazine, Ambassador College, and the other domains of the empire built by Herbert W. and Garner Ted Armstrong, and an analysis of the doctrines of the Worldwide Church of God.

1601   Jorstad, Erling. THE POLITICS OF DOOMSDAY: FUNDAMENT-ALISTS OF THE FAR RIGHT. Nashville: Abingdon Press, 1970. 190 p.

An analysis of the political involvement of such militant

conservative Protestants as Carl McIntire and Billy James Hargis since World War II, and an attempt to link their politics to millenarianism and biblicism.

1602 Pierard, Richard V. THE UNEQUAL YOKE: EVANGELICAL CHRISTIANITY AND POLITICAL CONSERVATISM. Philadelphia: J.B. Lippincott Co., 1970. 191 p. Bibliog.

Acknowledgment by conservative Protestant that political conservative politics is rampant in his branch of the faith, and his regret that "if the trend toward political, economic, and social conservatism is not reversed, evangelical Christianity will soon be facing a crisis of disastrous proportions." Helpful for understanding the state of conservative Protestantism just before the evangelical resurgence of the 1970s.

1603 Redekop, John Harold. THE AMERICAN FAR RIGHT: A CASE STUDY OF BILLY JAMES HARGIS AND CHRISTIAN CRUSADE. Grand Rapids, Mich.: William B. Eerdmans Publishing Co., 1968. 232 p. Bibliog.

Good description of one of the leading anti-Communist movements of the 1950s and 1960s, but the analytical sections are less successful. Bibliography of Hargis's works and other published materials pertaining to Christian involvement in politics since World War II.

1604 Roy, Ralph Lord. APOSTLES OF DISCORD; A STUDY OF ORGANIZED BIGOTRY AND DISRUPTION ON THE FRINGES OF PROTESTANTISM. Boston: Beacon Press, 1953. 437 p.

Not designed as an impartial examination as the title shows, may be viewed as an example of the irritated and angry response of one liberal to what he judged to be the "bigotry" of the 1950s. Included in the survey are anti-Semitic racist, anti-Catholic, anti-Communist, and anti-liberal groups of many degrees of extremism.

1605 Smith, Geoffrey S. TO SAVE A NATION: AMERICAN COUNTER-SUBVERSIVES, THE NEW DEAL, AND THE COMING OF WORLD WAR II. New York: Basic Books, 1973. 256 p.

Well-written analysis of Father Charles E. Coughlin and his Christian Front, William Pelley and his Silver Shirts, and Fritz Kuhn and his German-American Bund. Argues that these groups were "inverted nativists," persons defending American values and beliefs with imported symbolic apparatus.

1606   Streiker, Lowell D., and Strober, Gerald S. RELIGION AND THE
        NEW MAJORITY: BILLY GRAHAM, MIDDLE AMERICA, AND THE
        POLITICS OF THE 70s. New York: Association Press, 1972. 202 p.

> Argues that conservative, revivalistic Protestantism of the
> sort identified with Graham continues to be a strong force
> in the United States and that it exists in a powerful, sym-
> biotic relationship with conservative politics.

1607   Tull, Charles J. FATHER COUGHLIN AND THE NEW DEAL. Syracuse
        N.Y.: Syracuse University Press, 1965. 292 p.

> A well-documented study of Charles E. Coughlin, the
> Irish-American radio priest who initially supported Franklin
> Delano Roosevelt and the New Deal, but became a power-
> ful opponent in the middle-1930s.

MID-CENTURY ASSESSMENTS OF RELIGION

1608   Berger, Peter L. THE NOISE OF SOLEMN ASSEMBLIES: CHRISTIAN
        COMMITMENT AND THE RELIGIOUS ESTABLISHMENT IN AMERICA.
        Garden City, N.Y.: Doubleday and Co., 1961. 189 p.

> A descriptive analysis of American Protestants' undefined
> commitment to religiosity in the 1950s, and the problems
> that churches face in the decline of this commitment.

1609   Eckardt, A. Roy. THE SURGE OF PIETY IN AMERICA: AN APPRAISAL.
        New York: Association Press, 1958. 192 p.

> An impressionistic and critical interpretation of the religi-
> osity of Americans since the end of World War II.

1610   Gustafson, James M., ed. THE SIXTIES: RADICAL CHANGE IN
        AMERICAN RELIGION. ANNALS OF THE AMERICAN ACADEMY OF
        POLITICAL AND SOCIAL SCIENCE 387 (January 1970).

> Fourteen articles collected for what has come to be the
> Academy's decennial survey of American religion. Includes
> surveys of morality, war, and contraception, and essays
> devoted to Protestant, Catholic, Jewish, Orthodox, and
> Fundamentalist denominations.

1611   Lambert, Richard D., ed. RELIGION IN AMERICAN SOCIETY.
        ANNALS OF THE AMERICAN ACADEMY OF POLITICAL AND SOCIAL
        SCIENCE 332 (November 1960). 220 p.

> A compendium of fourteen articles by leading scholars who
> analyze such topics as the role of the laity, the prolifera-

tion of cults and sects, ecumenism, and the impact of religion on American education and politics. Helps illuminate the popular religiosity of the 1950s.

1612   Marty, Martin E.; Rosenberg, Stuart E.; and Greeley, Andrew M. WHAT DO WE BELIEVE: THE STANCE OF RELIGION IN AMERICA. New York: Meredith Press, 1968. 346 p.

Written by three religious leaders--a Protestant, a Jew, and a Roman Catholic--who discuss various dimensions of continuity and change in their respective faiths today. Emphasis on interaction of religion and society. Complete with 180 pages of statistical data taken largely from opinion polls.

1613   Stark, Rodney, and Glock, Charles Y. AMERICAN PIETY: THE NATURE OF RELIGIOUS COMMITMENT. Berkeley and Los Angeles: University of California Press, 1968. 230 p.

A detailed statistical analysis of the religiosity of Americans in the 1960s. Explores such topics as frequency of attendance at worship, extent of religious knowledge, denominational conversions, and personal morality.

1614   Tapp, Robert B. RELIGION AMONG THE UNITARIAN UNIVERSALISTS: CONVERTS IN THE STEPFATHERS' HOUSE. New York: Seminar Press, 1973. 280 p.

Analyzes members of the Unitarian Universalist Association on the basis of their responses to a questionnaire survey conducted in 1968. On assumption that this denomination may be a portent of things to come (a religious deconversion), examines the questionnaire results to see if some estimate can be made of the character of religion in post-traditional society. The usefulness of this aspect of the study invalidated by the dubious assumption that the members of the UUA may be typical of future religious Americans.

THE IMPACT OF EASTERN RELIGIONS

1615   Bridges, Hal. AMERICAN MYSTICISM FROM WILLIAM JAMES TO ZEN. New York: Harper and Row, 1970. 208 p. Bibliog.

Examines the works of several twentieth-century American mystics, such as Thomas Merton, Rufus Jones, and Thomas Kelly, and the reception of Zen in the United States.

1616   Ellwood, Robert S. THE EAGLE AND THE RISING SUN: AMERI-
        CANS AND THE NEW RELIGIONS OF JAPAN. Philadelphia: West-
        minster Press, 1974. 224 p.

> An introduction to five new, monotheistic cults of Japa-
> nese origin which are practiced in the United States.
> Included are Tenrikyo, the Religion of Heavenly Wisdom;
> Nichiren Shoshu of America; the Church of World Mes-
> sianity; Seicho-no-Ie, the House of Growth; and Perfect
> Liberty.

1617   Judah, J. Stillson. HARE KRISHNA AND THE COUNTERCULTURE.
        New York: John Wiley and Sons, 1974. xv, 301 p.

> Not a description of the group but an analysis of the
> traditions of Hindu thought on which the Hare Krishna is
> based and their relevance to modern America. Argues
> that this Eastern religious tradition is bringing an ethical
> stance, a sense of religious mystery, and a feeling of
> community to believers.

1618   Merton, Thomas. MYSTICS AND ZEN MASTERS. New York: Dell
        Publishing Co., 1961. 303 p.

> Sixteen essays by the renowned Trappist monk, illumi-
> nating parallels between Catholic mysticism and Zen
> Buddhism.

1619   Needleman, Jacob. THE NEW RELIGIONS. New York: Doubleday
        and Co., 1970. xii, 245 p.

> Discusses six faiths--Zen Buddhism, Transcendental Medi-
> tation, Meher Baba, Subud, Krishnamurti, and Tibetan
> Buddhism. Explains their growing popularity in twentieth-
> century America, and looks at California as the nucleus
> of this interest.

1620   Nordstrom, Louis, ed. NAMU DAI BOSA: A TRANSMISSION OF
        ZEN BUDDHISM TO AMERICA. New York: Theatre Arts Books, 1976.
        xxix, 262 p. 26 illus.

> A collection of writings from three persons important in
> the transmission of Zen Buddhism to America--Nyogen
> Senzaki (1876-1958), Nakagawa Soen Roshi (B. 1907),
> and Shimano Eido Roshi (b. 1932).

1621   Riepe, Dale. THE PHILOSOPHY OF INDIA AND ITS IMPACT ON
        AMERICAN THOUGHT. Springfield, Ill.: Charles C. Thomas, 1970.
        xvii, 339 p. Bibliog.

> A comprehensive study of the reception of Indian Hinduism

and Buddhism in the United States from Transcendentalism to the early nineteenth century.

ALTERNATIVE RELIGIOUS EXPRESSION IN THE 1960S

1622   Braden, William. THE PRIVATE SEA: LSD AND THE SEARCH FOR GOD. Chicago: Quadrangle Books, 1967. 255 p.

Hypothesizes that the growth of pantheism and a revived interest in metaphysics in Western religion are a result of increased Eastern influence and revolt against scientific rationalism in the twentieth century. Sees evidence of links between LSD and the "New Theology" as part of this movement. No bibliography; study is based on interviews and personal observations of the author, a journalist.

1623   Clark, Walter Houston. CHEMICAL ECSTASY: PSYCHEDELIC DRUGS AND RELIGION. New York: Sheed and Ward, 1969. 179 p. Bibliog.

Argues that psychedelic drugs can stimulate genuine religious experiences, and that churches should not neglect their potential value any more than rituals and incense should be ignored.

1624   Cohen, Daniel. THE NEW BELIEVERS: YOUNG RELIGION IN AMERICA. New York: M. Evans and Co., 1975. 192 p. Bibliog.

Sketches of such contemporary movements as the Unification Church, Satanism, witchcraft, and Hare Krishna.

1625   Ellwood, Robert S., Jr. RELIGIOUS AND SPIRITUAL GROUPS IN MODERN AMERICA. Englewood Cliffs, N.J.: Prentice-Hall, 1973. 334 p.

A tour of the variety of non-traditional religions flourishing in Los Angeles in the early 1970s, including Theosophical and Rosicrucian groups, Spiritualism, UFO cults, initiatory groups, Neo-Paganism, and Hindu movements. Weak opening methodological chapter.

1626   Gish, Arthur G. THE NEW LEFT AND CHRISTIAN RADICALISM. Grand Rapids, Mich.: William B. Eerdmans Publishing Co., 1970. 158 p. Bibliog.

A brief analysis of parallels between the Anabaptist movement of the sixteenth century and the New Left of the 1960s, and an attempt to state a nonviolent Christian theory of social change based on biblical faith.

1627   Glock, Charles Y., and Bellah, Robert, eds. THE NEW RELIGIOUS
        CONSCIOUSNESS. Berkeley and Los Angeles: University of Cali-
        fornia Press, 1976. xviii, 391 p.

        A collection of fifteen essays, all related to the religious
        culture of young people in the San Francisco area during
        the early 1970s. Very much a miscellany and the editors
        themselves offer contrasting assessments of the data pre-
        sented.

1628   Roberts, Ron E. THE NEW COMMUNES: COMING TOGETHER IN
        AMERICA. Englewood Cliffs, N.J.: Prentice-Hall, 1971. xiv, 144 p.

        So abbreviated in treating individual groups that its use-
        fulness is impaired. Attempts to cover all communal ac-
        tivity in the nineteenth and twentieth centuries. The gen-
        eral analytical chapters a bit better.

1629   Roszak, Theodore. THE MAKING OF A COUNTER CULTURE. Garden
        City, N.Y.: Doubleday and Co., 1969. xiv, 303 p.

        A critical look at the development of modern, technolog-
        ical society, and a qualified affirmation of alternate life
        styles advanced by young people dissatisfied with the de-
        personalizing tendencies of modernity.

1630   Sobel, B.Z. HEBREW CHRISTIANITY: THE THIRTEENTH TRIBE. New
        York: John Wiley and Sons, 1974. xiv, 413 p.

        Divided into two main parts: The first sociological, and
        based upon a study of one congregation of converts in
        Newark, New Jersey, and some acquaintance with Jews
        for Jesus in Israel; the second, historical, and based upon
        secondary literature and a few primary sources.

1631   Veysey, Laurence R. THE COMMUNAL EXPERIENCE: ANARCHIST
        AND MYSTICAL COUNTER-CULTURES IN AMERICA. New York:
        Harper and Row, 1973. 495 p.

        A well-written, scholarly analysis of the communal move-
        ment of the 1960s, which discusses the Vedanta movement
        in a long chapter.

THE JESUS MOVEMENT

1632   Ellwood, Robert S., Jr. ONE WAY: THE JESUS MOVEMENT AND

ITS MEANING. Englewood Cliffs, N.J.: Prentice-Hall, 1973.
150 p.

> Description of over a dozen groups associated with the
> Jesus movement of the 1970s and an attempt to relate
> these groups to American culture and the Western tradition.

1633 Enroth, Ronald M.; Ericson, Edward E., Jr.; and Peters, C. Brecken-
ridge. THE JESUS PEOPLE: OLD-TIME RELIGION IN THE AGE OF
AQUARIUS. Grand Rapids, Mich.: Wm. B. Eerdmans Publishing Co.,
1972. 249 p.

> Provides, in the first part of the book, descriptions
> of a number of California-based groups, including
> the Children of God, Christian World Liberation
> Front, Hollywood Free Paper, and Arthur Blessitt.
> The theology of these groups from a neo-evangeli-
> cal perspective (the authors are connected with
> Westmont College) analyzed in the second part.

1634 Jorstad, Erling. THAT NEW-TIME RELIGION: THE JESUS REVIVAL
IN AMERICA. Minneapolis, Minn.: Augsburg Publishing House, 1972.
143 p. Bibliog.

> A superficial and loosely organized book, in which the
> Jesus movement among American youth is linked to modern
> revivalism and the surge of popular religiosity in the
> United States since World War II.

1635 Vachon, Brian. A TIME TO BE BORN. Englewood Cliffs, N.J.:
Prentice-Hall, 1972. 139 p.

> A loosely-written account of the Jesus movement among
> young Americans in the 1970s.

MEXICAN-AMERICAN CHURCHES

1636 Brackenridge, R. Douglas, and Garcia-Treto, Francisco O. IGLESIA
PRESBITERIANA: A HISTORY OF PRESBYTERIANS AND MEXICAN
AMERICANS IN THE SOUTHWEST. San Antonio, Tex.: Trinity Uni-
versity Press, 1974. xiv, 262 p.

> A good history of one denomination's interaction with
> Mexican-Americans, based upon archival materials,
> periodicals, and personal interviews.

1637 Grebler, Leo, et al. THE MEXICAN AMERICAN PEOPLE: THE NA-
TION'S SECOND LARGEST MINORITY. New York: Free Press, 1970.
xviii, 777 p. Bibliog.

A comprehensive portrait of Mexican-Americans, past and present. Emphasis on their social and economic situation, but some attention is paid to their Roman Catholic and Protestant churches, especially in terms of social work performed by the churches.

1638 Holland, Clifton L. THE RELIGIOUS DIMENSION IN HISPANIC LOS ANGELES: A PROTESTANT CASE STUDY. S. Pasadena, Calif.: William Carey Library, 1974. xxxii, 541 p.

Surveys the Mexican-American community in Los Angeles historically, sociologically, and demographically. Discusses the impact of Protestantism upon that community on a denomination-by-denomination basis.

1639 Stoddard, Ellwyn R. MEXICAN AMERICANS. New York: Random House, 1973. xvii, 269 p. Bibliog.

A concise, general survey of Mexican-American society, with brief sections on the religiosity and "folk Catholicism" of this ethnic group and the inroads made by Protestantism.

AUTHOR INDEX

This index consists of authors, editors, compilers, and others who have contributed to works cited in the text. Alphabetization is letter by letter and numbers refer to entry numbers.

A

Abell, Aaron I.   136, 604, 1096
Abrahamson, Harold J.   1486
Abrams, Ray H.   '1541, 1542
Adams, James Luther   1454
Adams, William C.   544
Agonito, Joseph   143
Agrimson, J. Elmo   1258
Ahern, Patrick H.   568
Ahlstrom, Sydney E.   9, 17, 35, 112, 1434, 1441, 1467
Ahmann, Mathew   1048
Aiken, John R.   1203
Akers, Charles W.   197
Albanese, Catherine L.   520
Albright, Raymond W.   346, 748, 1086
Alcott, A. Bronson   898, 899
Aldridge, Alfred Owen   308, 498, 499
Allen, Gay Wilson   1369
Allen, James B.   781
Altizer, Thomas J.J.   1468, 1469, 1470, 1471
Ames, William   182
Anderson, C.A.   431
Anderson, Courtney   1273
Anderson, Hugh George   1113
Anderson, Nels   771
Anderson, Richard   772

Anderson, Rufus   1274
Andrew, John A. III   1275
Andrews, Edward Deming   924, 925, 926, 927, 928
Andrews, Faith   927, 928
Arden, G. Everett   1142
Armstrong, Maurice W.   431
Arndt, Karl J.R.   934, 935
Arnett, Willard E.   1403
Arrington, Leonard J.   773
Asbury, Francis   387
Asbury, Herbert   1557
Ashmore, Jerome   1404
Atkins, Gaius Glenn   1078
Averill, Lloyd J.   1146
Ayer, A.J.   1333

B

Bach, Marcus   1213, 1214
Bachman, Calvin George   467
Backus, Isaac   366
Baepler, Walter A.   1129
Bailey, Kenneth K.   1065, 1066
Bailyn, Bernard   521, 522
Bainton, Roland H.   1530
Baird, Robert   721
Baker, Frank   388
Baker, Gordon Pratt   389
Baker, Robert A.   373
Banner, Lois W.   817

Author Index

Author Index

K

L

Author Index

Tolles, Frederick B. 420, 421, 422
Tomasi, Silvano M. 623
Torbet, Robert G. 384
Towns, Elmer L. 1596
Townsend, Leah 385
Tracy, Joseph 277
Trelease, Allen W. 991
Trinterud, Leonard J. 442, 443
Trisco, Robert F. 601
Trueblood, G. Elton 403
Tucker, Louis Leonard 354, 518
Tucker, William E. 745, 1109
Tull, Charles J. 1607
Tussman, Joseph 542
Tuveson, Ernest Lee 34
Twomby, Robert C. 992
Tyler, Alice F. 826

U

Ulrich, Laurel Thatcher 837
Underhill, Ruth M. 99
Upham, Charles W. 239
Urofsky, Melvin I. 668

V

Vachon, Brian 1635
Vahanian, Gabriel 1478
VanAllen, Rodger 1515
Vander Velde, Lewis G. 1063
Van de Wetering, John E. 269, 294, 519
Van Dusen, Henry P. 1480
Van Dyken, Seymour 216
Van Kirk, Walter W. 1552
Varg, Paul A. 1296, 1297
Vaughan, Alden T. 114, 170, 171
Veysey, Laurence R. 1631
Visser't Hooft, Willem A. 1187
Vollmar, Edward 133
Vorspan, Max 686

W

Wall, Robert 201
Wallace, Anthony F.C. 115, 116
Wallace, Paul, A.W. 496
Walls, William J. 1011
Walsh, James 295
Walter, Ronald G. 977, 1095

Walton, Hanes, Jr. 1042
Wangler, Thomas E. 631, 632, 633
Warch, Richard 296
Ward, Hiley H. 1036
Wardin, Albert W. 1110
Washburn, Wilcomb E. 92
Washington, Joseph R., Jr. 1012, 1013
Watters, Leon L. 687
Weatherford, Willis D. 1076
Webber, Everett 923
Weber, Francis J. 134, 164, 602
Weber, Ralph E. 603
Weigel, Gustave 1306
Weinlick, John Rudolf 466
Weisberger, Bernard A. 700
Weisenburger, Francis P. 1084, 1085
Weisser, Celestin D. 1463
Welch, Claude 815
Wells, David F. 1597
Wells, Ronald Vale 912
Welter, Barbara 838
Wenger, John C. 490, 491, 492
Wentz, Frederick K. 1123, 1553, 1554
Werkmeister, W.H. 57
Wernecke, Herbert H. 453
West, Jessamyn 404
West, Ray B. 741
West, Robert F. 746
West, William G. 747
Whalen, William J. 8
Whicher, Stephen E. 879, 884
White, Andrew Dickson 1173
White, Edward A. 1174
White, Elizabeth W. 260
White, Eugene E. 297
White, Morton G. 50, 58, 64, 1328, 1340, 1341
White, Timothy 1245
Whitehead, Alfred North 1410
Wieman, Henry Nelson 1160, 1440
Wiener, Philip P. 1342, 1355
Wilbur, Earl M. 850
Wilbur, Sibyl 1240
Willging, Eugene P. 135
Williams, Daniel Day 29, 1161
Williams, George Huntston 202, 857
Williams, Melvin D. 1053
Williams, Roger 230
Wills, Garry 1528

TITLE INDEX

In this index titles of articles are in quotation marks. Titles of books are capitalized. Numbers refer to entry numbers; alphabetization is letter by letter.

A

"Abolitionism and Theological Education at Andover" 975

"Abraham Lincoln and American Civil Religion" 564

ADDRESSES AND PAPERS 1293

"Adin Ballou's Hopedale Community and the Theology of Antislavery" 970

ADVENTURE IN FREEDOM: THREE HUNDRED YEARS OF JEWISH LIFE IN AMERICA 646

AFRICAN COLONIZATION MOVEMENT, 1816-1865, THE 972

AFRICAN METHODIST EPISCOPAL ZION CHURCH, THE 1011

AGE OF ANALYSIS, THE: TWENTIETH CENTURY PHILOSOPHERS 1340

ALEXANDER CAMPBELL AND NATURAL RELIGION 746

"Alexander Garden and George Whitefield: The Significance of Revivalism in South Carolina, 1738-1741" 286

ALFRED NORTH WHITEHEAD; AN ANTHOLOGY 1410

ALFRED NORTH WHITEHEAD; A PRIMER OF HIS PHILOSOPHY 1416

"Alienation in America: the Immigrant Catholic and Public Education in Pre-Civil War America" 613

ALL LOVES EXCELLING: AMERICAN PROTESTANT WOMEN IN WORLD MISSION 827

ALL THINGS ARE POSSIBLE: THE HEALING AND CHARISMATIC REVIVALS IN MODERN AMERICA 1263

ALMOST CHOSEN PEOPLE, THE: A STUDY OF THE RELIGION OF ABRAHAM LINCOLN 1064

AMANA THAT WAS AND AMANA THAT IS 957

AMAZING STORY OF REPEAL, THE; AN EXPOSE OF THE POWER OF PROPAGANDA 1564

AMERICA: A SKETCH OF ITS POLITICAL, SOCIAL, AND RELIGIOUS CHARACTER 800

AMERICAN ABBOT, AN: BONIFACE WIMMER, O.S.B., 1809-1887 591

AMERICAN AS REFORMER, THE 1101

AMERICAN CATHOLIC CROSSROADS 1511

AMERICAN CATHOLIC DILEMMA: AN INQUIRY INTO THE INTELLECTUAL LIFE 1510

AMERICAN CATHOLIC EXODUS 1526

"American Catholic Historical Societies" 134

D

I

Title Index

U

V

VALLEY OF DISCORD: CHURCH AND SOCIETY ALONG THE CONNECTICUT RIVER, 1636-1725 188

VATICAN AND THE AMERICANIST CRISIS, THE: DENIS J. O'CONNELL, AMERICAN AGENT IN ROME, 1885-1903 625

"Vertuous Women Found: New England Ministerial Literature, 1668-1735" 837

"View of Man Inherent in New Measures Revivalism, The" 709

VIRGIL MICHEL AND THE LITURGICAL MOVEMENT 1503

"Virgin Land and Savage People" 106

VISIBLE SAINTS: THE HISTORY OF A PURITAN IDEA 194

VISIONS OF THE HEAVENLY SPHERE; A STUDY IN SHAKER RELIGIOUS ART 928

VOICES OF AMERICAN FUNDAMENTALISM: SEVEN BIOGRAPHICAL STUDIES 1579

W

WALL AND THE GARDEN, THE: SELECTED MASSACHUSETTS ELECTION SERMONS, 1670-1775 210

WALTER RAUSCHENBUSCH 1206

"Walter Rauschenbusch and Education for Reform" 1203

WAR AND CONSCIENCE IN AMERICA 1537

WAR AND THE CHRISTIAN CONSCIENCE 1539

WASHINGTON GLADDEN: PROPHET OF THE SOCIAL GOSPEL 1188

WAYWARD PURITANS: A STUDY IN THE SOCIOLOGY OF DEVIANCE 219

WAYWARD SHEPHERDS: PREJUDICE AND THE PROTESTANT CLERGY 693

"Wealth, War and Religion: The Perfecting of Quaker Asceticism, 1740-1783" 414

"'We Are Well As We Are': An Indian Critique of Seventeenth-Century Christian Missions" 109

WE HOLD THESE TRUTHS: CATHOLIC REFLECTIONS ON THE AMERICAN PROPOSITION 556

WEST VIRGINIA JEWRY: ORIGINS AND HISTORY, 1850-1958 681

WHAT DO WE BELIEVE: THE STANCE OF RELIGION IN AMERICA 1612

WHAT MANNER OF MAN: A BIOGRAPHY OF MARTIN LUTHER KING, JR. 1037

WHAT MUST I DO TO BE SAVED? THE GREAT AWAKENING IN COLONIAL AMERICA 269

WHITEHEAD'S METAPHYSICS, AN INTRODUCTORY EXPOSITION 1418

WHITEHEAD'S ONTOLOGY 1415

WHITEHEAD'S PHILOSOPHICAL DEVELOPMENT; A CRITICAL HISTORY OF THE BACKGROUND OF PROCESS AND REALITY 1417

WHITEHEAD'S PHILOSOPHY; SELECTED ESSAYS, 1935-1970 1413

WHITEHEAD'S PHILOSOPHY OF ORGANISM 1412

WHITEHEAD'S THEORY OF REALITY 1414

WHITE OVER BLACK: AMERICAN ATTITUDES TOWARD THE NEGRO, 1550-1812 985

WHITE PROTESTANTISM AND THE NEGRO 989

WHITE SECTS AND BLACK MEN IN THE RECENT SOUTH 1071

WHITE TERROR: THE KU KLUX KLAN CONSPIRACY AND SOUTHERN RECONSTRUCTION 991

WHY CONSERVATIVE CHURCHES ARE GROWING: A STUDY IN THE SOCIOLOGY OF RELIGION 1590

WILDERNESS CHRISTIANS: THE MORAVIAN MISSION TO THE DELAWARE INDIANS 103

WILL AND THE WORDS, THE: THE POETRY OF EDWARD TAYLOR 267

WILLIAM AND MARY QUARTERLY 87

WILLIAM AUGUSTUS MUHLENBERG:

SUBJECT INDEX

This index is alphabetized letter by letter. Numbers refer to entry numbers.

A

Abbott, Lyman 1164. See also Congregationalists and Evolution

Abolitionism 214, 408, 416, 423, 755, 961, 962, 963, 964, 965, 966, 967, 968, 969, 970, 971, 972, 973, 974, 975, 976, 977, 978, 979, 987, 996

Adventism, Seventh-day 732, 733, 734, 735, 736

Afro-Americans 622, 690, 962, 963, 967, 981, 983, 985, 986, 987, 989, 990, 991, 992, 996, 1004, 1005, 1006, 1007, 1008, 1009, 1010, 1011, 1012, 1013, 1014, 1015, 1016, 1017, 1018, 1019, 1020, 1021, 1022, 1023, 1024, 1025, 1026, 1027, 1028, 1029, 1030, 1031, 1032, 1033, 1034, 1035, 1036, 1037, 1038, 1039, 1040, 1041, 1042, 1043, 1044, 1045, 1046, 1047, 1048, 1049, 1050, 1051, 1052, 1053, 1054, 1071. See also Abolitionism; Black Muslims; King, Martin Luther, Jr.; Malcolm X; and South, religion in the

Agassiz, Louis 1171. See also Evolution

Alcott, A. Bronson 898, 899, 911. See also Transcendentalism

Alemany, Joseph Sadoc 585. See also Catholic clergy

Allen, Richard 1017. See also Afro-Americans and Methodists

Altizer, Thomas J.J. 1472. See also "Death of God" theology

Amana 957, 958. See also Utopianism

Amat, Thaddeus 602. See also Catholic clergy

Americanist heresy 599, 624, 625, 627, 628, 631, 633, 1501. See also Catholic clergy and Catholicism, Roman

American Protective Association 637. See also Nativism; Prejudice

American Revolution. See Revolution, American

Ames, William 182, 199. See also Puritanism

Amish 467, 468, 469, 470. See also Mennonites

Anderson, Rufus 1274. See also Missions

Antinomian controversy 218, 220, 222. See also Hutchinson, Anne

Asbury, Francis 387, 388, 397. See also Methodists

Assemblies of God 1248, 1252. See also Pentecostalism

B

Backus, Isaac 366, 370. See also

Subject Index

Baptists; Church-state relations
Ballou, Adin 970
Ballou, Hosea 854. See also Universalism
Baptists 72, 273, 366, 367, 368, 369, 370, 371, 372, 373, 374, 375, 376, 377, 378, 379, 380, 381, 382, 383, 384, 385, 386, 502, 724, 728, 993, 998, 1030, 1067, 1070, 1072, 1075, 1110, 1205, 1317
Beecher, Catharine 834. See also Women
Beecher, Edward 969. See also Abolitionism; Congregationalists
Beecher, Henry Ward 1089. See also Congregationalists
Beecher, Lyman 755, 976. See also Abolitionism; Presbyterians
Berrigan, Daniel and Philip 1516. See also Catholic clergy; Catholicism, contemporary state of
Bible 545, 808
Black Muslims 1044, 1045, 1046, 1047, 1049. See also Afro-Americans
Blair, James 363. See also Episcopalians
Bojnowski, Lucyan 1488. See also Catholic clergy
Bradstreet, Anne 253, 260. See also Puritanism
Bray, Thomas 359, 365. See also Episcopalians; Missions
Brethren, Church of the 456, 457, 458, 461, 462
Brook Farm 943, 944, 948. See also Transcendentalism; Utopianism
Brooks, Phillips 1086
Brownson, Orestes A. 907, 908, 910. See also Catholicism, Roman; Transcendentalism
Bruderhof 960. See also Utopianism
Bryan, William Jennings 1180, 1584. See also Fundamentalism
Burke, John J. 1513. See also Catholicism, Roman; Press, Religious
Bushnell, Horace 802, 803, 804. See also Congregationalists

C

Campbell, Alexander 743, 746. See also Disciples of Christ
Campbell, Thomas 744. See also Disciples of Christ
Cannon, James 1563. See also Methodists; Prohibition
Carroll, John 143, 144, 146, 147, 149. See also Catholic clergy; Catholicism, Roman
Cartwright, Peter 752. See also Methodists; Revivalism
Catholic clergy 138, 144, 147, 149, 163, 568, 569, 570, 571, 573, 578, 579, 580, 581, 582, 583, 585, 587, 588, 589, 590, 591, 592, 594, 595, 597, 600, 602, 616, 633, 1487, 1488, 1490, 1492, 1495, 1504, 1516, 1519, 1522, 1607. See also Catholicism, contemporary state of; Catholicism, Roman
Catholicism, contemporary state of 1486, 1516, 1517, 1518, 1520, 1521, 1524, 1526, 1527, 1528. See also Vatican Council, Second
Catholicism, Roman 8, 37, 69, 101, 102, 108, 119, 128, 129, 130, 131, 132, 133, 134, 135, 136, 137, 140, 141, 142, 145, 146, 148, 150, 151, 152, 153, 154, 156, 157, 160, 161, 162, 164, 530, 556, 572, 577, 584, 586, 596, 598, 601, 603, 604, 605, 606, 608, 609, 611, 613, 615, 617, 619, 620, 621, 622, 623, 625, 626, 628, 629, 630, 632, 636, 907, 908, 910, 1048, 1055, 1116, 1269, 1308, 1312, 1489, 1491, 1493, 1494, 1496, 1497, 1498, 1499, 1500, 1501, 1502, 1503, 1507, 1508, 1509, 1510, 1511, 1512, 1513, 1514, 1515, 1523, 1525, 1529, 1553. See also Catholic clergy; Catholicism, contemporary state of; Ecumenical movement; Missions; Monasticism
Channing, William Ellery 839, 840,

Subject Index

Ely, Richard T. 1183, 1190. See also Social Gospel

Emerson, Ralph Waldo 10, 865, 868, 869, 870, 871, 872, 873, 874, 875, 876, 877, 878, 879, 880, 881, 882, 883, 884, 896. See also Transcendentalism; Unitarians

Emerton, Ephraim 38

England, John 578

Enlightenment 274, 275, 337, 339, 342, 498, 499, 500, 501, 507, 508, 512, 515, 516.

Ephrata 460

Episcopalians 73, 346, 347, 349, 350, 351, 352, 353, 354, 355, 356, 357, 358, 359, 360, 361, 362, 363, 364, 763, 764, 766, 1019, 1056

Eschatology 34, 191, 271, 303, 526, 732, 734, 736, 937, 1241, 1246, 1571, 1575, 1580, 1581. See also Adventism, Seventh-Day; Jehovah's Witnesses

Ethical Societies 1158

Evangelical and Reformed Church 453

Evangelical Church 748

Evangelical Covenant Church 1106

Evolution 603, 1163, 1164, 1165, 1167, 1168, 1170, 1171, 1172, 1174, 1175, 1176, 1177, 1178, 1179, 1180, 1181, 1342, 1584

F

Fahs, Sophia Lyon 846. See also Unitarians

Faith healing 1219. See also Pentecostalism

Federal Council of Churches 1303. See also Ecumenical movement

Felicians 594. See also Catholic clergy

Finney, Charles Grandison 706, 707, 708, See also Revivalism

Flaget, Joseph 597. See also Catholic clergy

Fosdick, Harry Emerson 1149. See also Liberalism

Fourier, Charles 942, 945, 946, 947. See also Utopianism

Fox, Margaret 1222. See also Spiritualism

Francke, August Hermann 444. See also Pietism

Franklin, Benjamin 424, 498, 503. See also Enlightenment

Franks family 658. See also Jews

Free Religious Association 1157. See also Unitarians

Freethought 511, 769

Frelinghuysen, Theodorus Jacobus 452, 455. See also Great Awakening

Fuller, Margaret 905

Fundamentalism 430, 717, 1069, 1105, 1132, 1176, 1177, 1571, 1572, 1573, 1574, 1575, 1576, 1577, 1578, 1579, 1580, 1581, 1582, 1583, 1584, 1585, 1586, 1587, 1588, 1589, 1590, 1591, 1592, 1593, 1594, 1595, 1596, 1597, 1598, 1599, 1600, 1601, 1602, 1603, 1604, 1605, 1606

G

Garrison, J.H. 1109. See also Disciples of Christ

Garrison, William Lloyd 974. See also Abolitionism

Garvey, Marcus 1026. See also Afro-Americans

Gibbons, James 571. See also Catholic clergy

Gladden, Washington 1183, 1188, 1196. See also Social Gospel

Godfrey, John 234. See also Witchcraft

Gordon, Alexander 286

Gordon, Samuel 201. See also Puritanism

Graham, Billy 714, 715, 719, 1606. See also Revivalism

Gray, Asa 1165. See also Evolution

Great Awakening 269, 272, 277, 278, 279, 280, 281, 282, 283, 284, 285, 286, 287, 288, 289, 290, 291, 292, 293, 294, 295, 302, 310, 349, 361, 367, 368, 369, 370, 371, 372, 378, 380, 452, 455